DEEPENING DEMOCRACY?

Deepening Democracy?

The Modern Left and Social
Movements in Chile and Peru

KENNETH M. ROBERTS

STANFORD UNIVERSITY PRESS

STANFORD, CALIFORNIA

Stanford University Press
Stanford, California
© 1998 by the Board of Trustees of the
Leland Stanford Junior University

Printed in the United States of America

CIP data appear at the end of the book

To my parents, Morgan and Jean Roberts

To Angela, Natalia, Alejandra, and Tristan

*And to all those who retain the hope
and the courage to struggle—against great
odds—to make popular sovereignty a
reality in Chile and Peru*

Acknowledgments

IT is with mixed emotions that I submit this book to its readers. I wish that the stories it tells and the analysis it presents were more optimistic regarding the prospects for social reform and the deepening of democracy in contemporary Latin America. It is not my intention to dismiss the personal struggles and sacrifices—from the mundane to the heroic—that have been devoted to the causes of resisting authoritarianism, constructing democracy, and promoting social justice in modern Latin America. Neither do I wish to denigrate the tangible gains that have been made in the region; I started research for this book early enough to experience the Pinochet regime in Chile, and am convinced that even the most limited of democracies is a vast improvement over the horrors of military dictatorship. I am also convinced, however, that progressive causes in Latin America are not furthered by inflating expectations unrealistically, romanticizing ephemeral expressions of social mobilization, and ignoring the profound structural constraints on the exercise of popular sovereignty. The experience of recent decades should disabuse the Latin American Left and its North American sympathizers of the illusion that each new form of social organization is part of a groundswell that leads ineluctably to popular empowerment.

I firmly believe that the first step toward a deepening of democracy in Latin America must be an assessment of the impediments that have repeatedly blocked it. It is with this spirit that I have undertaken the critical, and often sobering, analysis contained in this book. I offer no magical solutions or bold prescriptions to resolve the dilemmas of the partisan Left and social movements in Latin America. My more modest hope is that this book might contribute to a clearer understanding of the nature of these dilemmas so that they may one day be tackled more effectively.

Any project that has been this long in the making necessarily incurs debts of gratitude too numerous to mention, and certainly that is the case with this book. Nevertheless, I would like to acknowledge the special contributions of some individuals who have made indelible impressions on this study, either by opening doors for my research or by providing me with new insights and angles from which to approach my topic. They have improved this work immeasurably, and although they bear no responsibility for the flaws in my analysis, they deserve much of the credit for that which proves useful.

I am especially grateful to Richard Fagen, Terry Lynn Karl, and Philippe Schmitter, who served as my advisers at Stanford University and guided my research when this project was still in gestation. They were inspiring teachers, sage advisers, and incisive yet constructive critics. Always supportive, they made invaluable contributions to my professional and intellectual development. I am also deeply indebted to Karen Remmer, whose mentoring and collegiality have greatly enriched my early career in academia. Her creative insights have inspired new directions in my research, from which I have benefited greatly. I doubt that many junior faculty members have the luxury of a senior colleague who is willing to take three theoretical chapters in the morning and return written comments before lunchtime; I know I'm the better for it.

I would also like to thank colleagues and friends who assisted my field research in Latin America. I am grateful to Norbert Lechner and the faculty and staff at FLACSO-Chile for providing me with resources and facilities to aid my research and for offering a supportive environment in which to work. Tomás Moulian, Mañuel Antonio Garretón, Hernan Gutiérrez, Enrique Hermosillo, and Robert Barros offered intellectual support and helpful insights into the complex Chilean political reality. In Peru, Fernando Tuesta and Aldo Panfichi provided friendship, logistical support, and a wealth of new contacts and resources. To the numerous other Chileans and Peruvians who offered or arranged interviews, helped locate documentation, invited me to special events, welcomed me into their homes, or shared their personal histories with me, I express my heartfelt appreciation.

My field research could not have been undertaken without the generous financial support of the Mellon Foundation, the Mac-Arthur Foundation, and the U.S.–Chile Fulbright Commission. Additional financial assistance was provided by the Institute for the Study of World Politics, the Center for Latin American Studies and the Center for International Security and Arms Control at Stanford University, and the Research Allocation Committee and the Gene Gallegos Lectureship at the University of New Mexico. The Helen Kellogg Institute for International Studies at the University of Notre Dame also provided me with financial support and a collegial environment in which to write and study during an earlier phase of this research.

Excerpts from Chapter 5 of this book first appeared in Kenneth M. Roberts, "From the Barricades to the Ballot Box: Redemocratization and Political Realignment in the Chilean Left," *Politics and Society*, vol. 23, no. 4, pp. 495–519, © 1995 by Sage Publications, Inc.; reprinted by permission of Sage Publications, Inc. Excerpts from Chapter 7 and Chapter 8 first appeared in Kenneth M. Roberts, "Economic Crisis and the Demise of the Legal Left in Peru," *Comparative Politics* 29 (October 1996); reprinted with permission.

Many colleagues have provided helpful input or read portions of this research at its various stages of development. In particular, I thank Neil Mitchell, William Stanley, Philip Oxhorn, Susan Stokes, Scott Mainwaring, Katherine Hite, Cynthia Sanborn, and Paul Sigmund for their encouragement, suggestions, and criticisms. I am grateful to Eric Wibbels, Moises Arce, Judy Palier, Darryl Dieter, Ernestina Cruz, Elizabeth Putnam, and Jessica Bartholow for their capable research assistance. My intellectual development has also been deeply influenced by my friendships with Dan Abbasi, Steve Fish, Alfonso Lara, Mark Peceny, and Kurt Weyland, several of whom have challenged just about every point I ever made in our endless political debates. For forcing me to think and to question my presumptions, I am eternally grateful.

I would also like to thank Muriel Bell and Stacey Lynn for shepherding this book through the publication process at Stanford University Press. Trudie Calvert's editorial assistance did much to make the manuscript more readable.

Finally, I thank my parents, Morgan and Jean Roberts, for the boundless support and encouragement they have given me through the years as I pursued my educational and professional goals. Without the sacrifices they made, I would never be where I am today. I am also deeply indebted to Angela for her patient assistance, confidence, and devotion during the decade she has lived with this research project. She has seen this book through from beginning to end; as a committed companion in the field, she aided my research in innumerable ways, and she subsequently picked up the slack far too often when research and writing kept a husband and father away from home. Ultimately, this book is a testament to our common labor and our shared commitments, and I dedicate it to her and to my parents. It is dedicated as well to Natalia, Alejandra, and Tristan; without them this book might have been completed much sooner, but it would have much less sense of purpose.

K.M.R.

Contents

Figures and Tables

DEEPENING DEMOCRACY?

CHAPTER 1

Introduction: The Paradox of Latin American Democracy

THE recent wave of democratization in Latin America poses a striking paradox. On one hand, it has spawned the most durable period of democratic governance in the region's turbulent political history, encompassing more nations than any previous wave of democratization. It has also extended voting rights to traditionally excluded social categories, making near-universal adult suffrage a general democratic norm for the first time in Latin American history.[1] On the other hand, numerous scholars have decried the limitations and shallowness of democratic practices in the region, spawning a veritable cottage industry of efforts to qualify democracy with diminutive adjectives.[2] The proliferation of concepts such as "low-intensity democracy,"[3] "schizophrenic democracy,"[4] "protected democracy,"[5] "exclusionary democracy,"[6] and "delegative democracy"[7] suggests that the initial euphoria surrounding the demise of military dictatorships has yielded to a growing malaise regarding the ambiguous character and quality of new civilian regimes. The shallowness of these regimes can be seen in democratic procedures as well as substantive outcomes, including the weakness of representative institutions, military tutelage of the political process, technocratic patterns of decision making that marginalize citizen input and are unaccountable to electoral mandates, and the accentuation of socioeconomic inequalities that mock the formal political equality of democratic citizenship.[8]

The recent attention that has been focused on these limitations suggests that scholars have entered a third phase in the study of democratization in Latin America. The first phase was primarily concerned with transitions from authoritarian rule and the establishment of democratic regimes.[9] The second phase emphasized issues of democratic consolidation and stability.[10] The third phase, by contrast, explores more systematically the character and quality of democratic practices in the region. As Latin America approaches the end of the millennium, the dominant issue on the political agenda is no longer whether democracy can survive but whether it can become a meaningful way for diverse sectors of the populace to exercise collective control over the public decisions that affect their lives. This collective control, or popular sovereignty, is the essence of the democratic conception of governance and its most distinctive (and attractive) feature in comparison to various forms of authoritarianism. Nevertheless, it has been notably lacking in the recent Latin American experience. As Susan Stokes demonstrates, elections have been ineffective instruments for translating citizens' preferences into policymaking alternatives, and other forms of popular input have been sporadic and tenuous.[11] In much of the region, democratic form survives in the absence of democratic substance.[12] What, then, prevents popular majorities in Latin America from exercising political influence through democratic institutions and procedures? And why do institutions that are supposed to embody popular sovereignty produce elitist and exclusive outcomes when subaltern sectors constitute a large majority of the population?

These questions are especially troubling for social movements and the political Left in Latin America since they struggled against military dictatorships and worked to establish new democratic regimes under the assumption that democracy represented a popular conquest.[13] These actors saw military regimes as both politically repressive and economically exclusive—that is, as forms of governance that represented the narrow interests of privileged minorities who relied on coercion to maintain social and political domination.[14] Democracy, therefore, was seen as much more than a set of formal procedures for the selection of rulers; it was understood as an arena for the empowerment of Latin America's "popular sectors," the lower- and middle-class majorities that were typically excluded from participation, and often violently repressed, under authoritarian regimes. Democracy provided a framework of legal rights that facilitated the organization of popular political subjects, along with channels of expression and representation that should—in theory—hold state institutions accountable to their interests.

Indeed, many actors from the political Left and social movements entered the formal democratic arena under the assumption that grass-roots activism would popularize the state and engender social and economic reforms.[15] Widespread appeals to "deepen," "extend,"[16] or "democratize"[17] democracy reflected faith in the elasticity of democratic institutions, and particularly in their capacity to expand participation in the making of collective decisions and enhance governmental responsiveness to popular concerns. In common parlance, the concept of deepening democracy, or *profundizando la democracia*, became the leitmotiv of the social and political Left, a "master frame" that guided the collective praxis of a multitude of popular subjects.[18] This master frame was imbued with both procedural and substantive connotations, ranging from popular participation in the policymaking process to redistributive socioeconomic reforms. Above all, it aimed to inject greater social content into the democratization process, a content that was inextricably associated with popular sovereignty or empowerment.

This open-ended vision of deepening democracy was tailor-made for a Left that had lost faith in the revolutionary teleology of classical socialism. Likewise, it gave political meaning to the collective endeavors of diverse new social movements, identifying them as the seeds of a new social order at a time when the working class was too weak and fragmented to play the central role in the process of social emancipation assigned to it by Marxist theory. Consequently, the idea of deepening democracy provided a rationale for the construction of new alliances between parties of the Left that were in search of social subjects and popular organizations that needed institutional representation in formal policymaking arenas. Among the most prominent of these alliances were those formed by the Workers' Party (PT) in Brazil, the Party of the Democratic Revolution (PRD) in Mexico, the United Left coalition in Peru, the Broad Front in Uruguay, the Radical Cause party in Venezuela, and the Farabundo Martí Front for National Liberation (FMLN) in El Salvador.

The grass-roots organizing efforts contained within these alliances have played a vital role in democratizing civil society, and they have often produced significant changes in individual lives and local social, economic, or political relationships. Nevertheless, all of these alliances have been frustrated in their efforts to translate diverse forms of popular organization into a national-level political and economic alternative, and none has effectively challenged the structural foundations of social and political domination in Latin America. In response, the early, optimistic prognoses for the transformative potential of popular collective actors have yielded to more sober assessments as Latin America's wave of democratization traverses its second decade.[19] But if the limited gains of these efforts to deepen democracy have become more evident, the impediments they confront have yet to be systematically evaluated. In this book I suggest that such an evaluation must start with an analysis of the structural conditions that shape and constrain the aggregation and articulation of lower-class interests by the partisan Left and social movements in an effort to understand the process by which societal demands are channeled and processed (or dispersed and suppressed) within the institutional arenas of democratic politics.

In particular, I argue here that strategies for the deepening of democracy have been obstructed by problems of collective action and political coordination that arise in the process of translating Latin America's popular social majorities into political majorities with the organizational strength required for the exercise of popular sovereignty. The success of deepening strategies does not rest primarily on the force of numbers—that is, the weight of individual voters aggregated periodically in the electoral arena. Rather, it is heavily contingent on the power of organization and the continuous participation of collective political subjects from subaltern sectors of society. As Evelyne Huber, Dietrich Rueschemeyer, and John D. Stephens argue, only the organization of subaltern sectors can create a societal power balance that is favorable for a shift from purely "formal" democratic practices to more "participatory" or "social" forms of democracy.[20] Groups that seek to organize the lower classes, however, must operate in terrain that is structured by political and economic institutions—the electoral process and the marketplace—that systematically fragment civil society and privilege individual over collective actors. The marketplace is driven more by the myriad individual decisions to produce, consume, invest, or exchange than by the collective behavior of social classes or communities; indeed, the increasingly global scope and logic of the marketplace reduce its accountability to such collective actors. Likewise, the act of voting is ultimately solitary, even if it is shaped by social networks and identities, and the mass of unorganized individual voters typically outweighs those who are organized collectively. As a result, the constitution of collective popular subjects has lagged behind the atomizing effects of market competition and electoral choice, thus weakening the prospects for radical democratic projects and facilitating the marriage between neoliberal or free market economies and low-intensity democratic practices.

In short, there is a basic incongruence between the forms of political agency required for a project of deepening democracy and the structural and institutional environment of contemporary Latin America. In a context of social fragmentation engendered by the collapse of state-led development models and the subsequent spread of free market reforms, heterogeneous and decentralized forms of collective action have not been able to generate a stable electoral majority or a compelling programmatic alternative to undergird a radical democratic project. These forms of collective action remain too segmented and localized to develop a critical mass for a national political alternative, much less to challenge increasingly transnationalized concentrations of political and economic power.[21] In such a context, electoral support is likely to flow toward populist figures or amorphous catch-all parties that appeal to the mass of unattached individual voters but provide little impetus for a deepening of popular sovereignty.

In contrast to much of the existing literature, which emphasizes the ideological challenges and changes confronted by the contemporary Left in Latin America,[22] this book gives greater attention to the structural and sociological factors that have shaped and constrained the Left's political project. As such, it tries to avoid the voluntaristic bias that pervades the literature on democratic transitions. Guillermo O'Donnell and Philippe Schmitter were probably justified in arguing that periods of regime transition are relatively exempt from structural determination, thus magnifying the importance of the choices and behavior of political actors.[23] Efforts to *deepen* democracy, however, are more heavily conditioned by structural forces; the maneuvering space of political actors is typically narrowed, the risks of a political backlash are accentuated, and political outcomes become far less autonomous of the underlying balance of class and economic power as they begin to impinge on substantive relationships rather than procedural arrangements.

Nevertheless, the limited gains of the Left's deepening strategies cannot be attributed entirely to exogenous structural and institutional factors. Impediments have also existed in the conflicting approaches to democracy within the Left itself, which suggests that an integrative analytical approach is needed to join together both structural and ideational or agency factors. Many sectors of the Left have come to value democracy as an institutional framework for the management of social and political pluralism—that is, as a set of conflict-regulating mechanisms that construct order out of diversity and allow for the peaceful coexistence of competing projects for society. This perspective has been heavily influenced by the trauma of authoritarian repression and the search for more consensual formulas of governance. It is thus more inclined to put radical change on hold and to try to accommodate competing demands in the broader interests of democratic stability.

Therefore, although there is a broad new consensus within the Latin American Left on the value of political democracy, there remain fundamentally divergent conceptions of what democracy entails and why it is intrinsic to the project of the Left.[24] These different conceptions of democracy have been a consistent source of tension and conflict within the Left because they create a series of difficult choices and painful trade-offs. Should the Left try to mobilize its social constituencies to create political pressure for radical change, recognizing that such a strategy is likely to produce social polarization and political conflicts that carry an inherent risk of an authoritarian backlash? Or should it try to contain popular demands and compromise with competing interests to ensure democratic stability, even if the result is an elitist form of democracy that discourages popular participation and solidifies the social hierarchy? To what extent can the objectives of social reform and democratic consolidation be balanced or harmonized?

These questions strike at the heart of what Jorge Castañeda identifies as the democratic dilemma in Latin America: either democracy has engendered instability and authoritarian reactions by empowering popular majorities and threatening elite interests, or it has been rendered devoid of substantive content in the pursuit of political stability.[25] This dilemma suggests that the unprecedented durability of Latin America's new democratic regimes may not be attributable to the strength of representative institutions and procedures, but rather to their weakness at transmitting popular demands for change into the decision-making arena and thus to the timidity of their challenge to traditional structures of social and political domination. In short, democracy may survive because popular sectors are too weak or restrained to use its levers to mobilize threats to elite interests or place substantive alternatives on the policy agenda.[26] The fundamental challenge for the Left, then, is to make democracy a meaningful exercise in popular sovereignty without undermining the contingent bases of consent upon which democratic regimes rest.

This challenge is the central focus of this book, which has two basic purposes. First, it explores the different ways in which the Left has managed (or failed to manage) this dilemma in contemporary Latin American democracies, while trying to explain the factors that have led to the predominance of one strategy over another in different national contexts. Second, it analyzes the impact of the Left's choices on broader political dynamics. In particular, this book tries to explain how the orientation of the Left affects democratic stability and why the Left and its affiliated social actors have found it so difficult to empower subaltern sectors under new democratic regimes.

To understand the logic of different strategies followed by the Left and their broader political implications, I employ a comparative analysis of contrasting cases in Chile and Peru. These two nations share in common a recent democratic transition that was preceded by an upsurge of social mobilization, and in both nations the political Left became a major actor in the newly established democratic regime. Likewise, in both nations the strategic vision of deepening democracy helped to incorporate the Left into the institutional framework of electoral democracy, although cleavages emerged between leftist parties that prioritized regime consolidation and those that emphasized popular mobilization for deeper reforms.

The two nations differed significantly, however, in the competitive dynamic and the balance of forces that existed between these contending positions, with profound implications for their respective democratic regimes. In Chile, a massive protest movement with insurrectionary tendencies broke out against the military dictatorship of General Augusto Pinochet in 1983, but social mobilization tapered off in the late 1980s and shifted largely to the terrain of electoral contestation as the democratic transition proceeded. Concomitantly, the center of gravity in the political Left shifted from the Communist Party, which emphasized radical forms of social mobilization, to the most moderate wing of the Socialist Party, which favored a broad-based political accommodation to smooth the process of regime transition. Whereas the Communists were left on the margins of Chile's new democratic regime, the Socialists and their offspring, the Party for Democracy, became the principal partners of the centrist Christian Democrats in a new, multiparty governing coalition.

No other party with roots in the Marxist tradition has assumed such important national-level, executive-branch governmental responsibilities as the Chilean Socialist Party in Latin America's current wave of democratization. By all accounts, its prudence and moderation have played a vital role in the construction of a relatively stable, majoritarian political alliance to anchor the transition process in Chile. But although the comparative success of the Chilean Socialists is notable, it has also been qualified. The notion of deepening democracy was a conceptual centerpiece of the party's shift from a revolutionary Marxist stance to a European-type social democratic position under the Pinochet dictatorship. Nevertheless, in office the party has had to govern within a relatively rigid set of political and economic constraints bequeathed by the authoritarian regime. These include institutional impediments that were designed to skew political representation, safeguard military prerogatives, and circumscribe the political authority of democratic majorities. The Socialist Party and its centrist allies have also been reticent to challenge the neoliberal economic model implanted by the military regime, and they have adopted only modest reforms that can be accommodated within the core logic of the inherited model. Popular organizations that upheld the banner of democracy under the dictatorship have been widely demobilized, and grassroots participation has been largely supplanted by party professionalism and technocratic decision making. Therefore, while the new regime can justifiably boast of democratic stability, economic growth, and a reduction of poverty, it remains far removed from the logic of deepening democracy that exercised intellectual hegemony in the reformulation of the Socialist project in Chile.

If the Chilean case highlights the ambiguous nature of success for the Left in contemporary democracies, that of Peru provides Latin America's most striking and unmitigated failure of the democratic Left in recent times. Having experienced a more mild form of authoritarianism from 1968 to 1980, Peru inaugurated a democratic regime in 1980 which contained a powerful electoral Left backed by a dense network of labor, peasant, and urban popular organizations. For most of the decade, Peru's United Left (IU) coalition was the most formidable electoral force on the Left in all of South America, and by the middle of the 1980s it had become a serious contender for political power at the national level, making Peru one of the more likely scenarios for a deepening of democracy. As Peru's democratic regime teetered on the brink of collapse in the late 1980s because of an economic crisis and the spreading insurgency of the Shining Path guerrilla movement, however, the contradictions within the IU rose to the surface. IU moderates led by Alfonso Barrantes gave priority to electoral success and sought a "national accord" to defend and stabilize the democratic regime. In contrast, the coalition's more radical party organizations perceived the national crisis as an opportunity for social mobilization in support of more profound political and economic changes, while the Shining Path escalated its insurrectionary campaign to sweep aside the established order.

As recession and hyperinflation emasculated the organized social constituencies of the IU, the coalition's inability to craft a coherent response to the Peruvian crisis led to its division and subsequent collapse as an electoral force. This collapse, in turn, set the stage for the emergence of an independent political outsider, Alberto Fujimori, who captured the atomized electoral constituency of the Left, only to harness it to an authoritarian neoliberal project. In the end, the Left neither consolidated nor deepened Peru's fragile democratic institutions, and it all but vanished as an independent political force by the mid-1990s.

Together, these contrasting cases are indicative of the range of experiences that the Latin American Left has traversed in recent decades, and they clarify the structural, institutional, and organizational dilemmas associated with efforts to deepen democracy. The divergent outcomes of democratic regimes in Chile and Peru reflect numerous social, political, and economic differences, and they clearly cannot be attributed solely to political dynamics on the Left. Nevertheless, the social and political Left has been a major actor in both countries, and its strategic choices have heavily influenced broader regime dynamics. The hegemonic position of moderate Socialists within the Chilean Left allowed the Christian Democratic–led coalition to govern Chile with a majoritarian social and political base and limited forms of competition. It also helped to incorporate popular sectors into the democratic process as individual citizens and voters, rather than as mobilized collective actors. This form of incorporation posed few threats to business or military interests, and it enabled the new democratic regime to establish a broad constituency and a centrist orientation, both highly favorable for democratic consolidation, though not for a clean break with Pinochet's authoritarian legacy. In contrast, the fractious IU in Peru was never able to determine whether it wanted to mobilize popular sectors within or against the established democratic regime. Indeed, the IU solidified neither the normative nor the institutional foundations of the regime, and its internecine battles created a political vacuum that was ultimately filled by an autocratic personalist leader who had little interest in democratic checks and balances.

The Chilean and Peruvian cases suggest, then, that the Left may play a significant role in either consolidating or destabilizing a democratic regime. Neither case, however, provides a compelling formula for deepening democracy, despite the prevalence of that discourse in diverse sectors of the Left in both countries. Instead, the two cases manifest a significant gap between the intentions that lie behind the Left's democratic participation—or at least the stated rationale for it—and the empirical realities of contemporary democracies. As such, the capacity of the Left to inject substantive content into the formal procedures of electoral democracy remains an open question in Latin America.

These cases ultimately help to explain why democratization has not taken place in the continuous, integral manner associated with the vision of deepening democracy. The deepening notion relies on a conception of democracy as a principle of social organization, one that is applicable to any social domain where power relations exist or collective decisions are made. It sees democratization, therefore, as a seamless web of popular empowerment that extends logically from political to social and economic relationships. Under Latin American conditions, however, the process of democratization has been segmented rather than integral; that is, the expansion of democratic norms and practices within civil society has had a limited effect on elitist practices at the level of political regimes and even less in the domain of economic relations, where hierarchical forms of domination have been retained or accentuated. This logic of segmentation insulates the effects of democratic practices in self-contained spheres of social interaction and thus short-circuits potential linkages that would deepen or extend the social domain subject to popular democratic control. As Rueschemeyer, Stephens, and Stephens argue, democracy "inevitably stands in tension with the system of social inequality," and it is possible only "if there exists a fairly strong institutional separation . . . of the realm of politics from the overall system of inequality in society."[27] Under contemporary conditions in Latin America, this institutional separation has been carried almost to the point of a complete divorce, which allows formal democratic regimes to exist despite acute socioeconomic inequalities by circumscribing the domain of democratic practices and draining them of substantive content. Even in the narrowly defined political-legal arena, O'Donnell has noted the partial and segmented character of citizenship rights in areas where the state is incapable of enforcing equality before the law, allowing private concentrations of power that operate undemocratically to exercise de facto political authority.[28] Likewise, these cases help to explain how formal democratic procedures can be made compatible with neoliberal economic restructuring, and they illustrate the difficulties the Latin American Left has had in crafting a viable economic alternative to neoliberalism. The two cases focus on opposite sides of Latin America's market-oriented neoliberal revolution:[29] for Peru, the analysis looks at the failure of a powerful Left to take political advantage of an economic crisis and provide a compelling alternative *before* a neoliberal adjustment has been implemented, whereas the Chilean case highlights the difficulties of modifying a neoliberal order that previously was imposed by force. Together, the two cases help to explain several phenomena that have perplexed observers of the Latin American political scene. The first is the capacity of neoliberalism to thrive in democratic contexts,[30] thus confounding earlier assumptions that authoritarian coercion was a functional correlate of neoliberalism's need to contain consumption demands, promote capital accumulation, and suppress political opposition and rent-seeking activities.[31] The second is the weakness of popular sector political resistance to economic reforms that have typically reduced wages, employment, and social spending while exacerbating income inequalities.[32] This study suggests that neoliberalism is both a cause and a consequence of the fragmentation and weakening of popular collective actors who are integral to any radical democratic alternative.

The inability of the Left to mobilize social and political opposition to neoliberalism has been a poignant symbol of its failure to deepen democracy—that is, to energize grass-roots participation as an antidote to technocracy—and to promote collective self-determination as an alternative to market individualism. To explain this failure, it is first necessary to have a theoretical understanding of the political logic that undergirds the concept of deepening democracy. Chapter 2 explores this political logic and explains why it has been an attractive response to the multidimensional crisis of the Left in Latin America. From that point of departure, it should be possible to analyze the structural, institutional, and organizational impediments to deepening strategies, a task that is undertaken in Chapter 3. Chapters 4 and 5 analyze the transformation of the Chilean social and political Left and their role in the process of redemocratization, while Chapter 6 provides a bottom-up perspective toward political change through interviews with base-level party militants in Chile. Chapter 7 explores the social and political conditions that facilitated the strengthening of the Peruvian Left in the 1970s and early 1980s. Chapter 8 explains the collapse of the Peruvian Left and the rise of new forms of autocratic populism at the end of the 1980s. The conclusion compares the Chilean and Peruvian experiences to draw theoretical insights regarding the prospects for the deepening of democracy in Latin America's neoliberal era.

PART I

Theoretical Considerations

CHAPTER 2

Deepening Democracy and the Transformation of the Left in Latin America

THE post–Cold War era is a time of unprecedented uncertainty and redefinition for the Latin American Left. A generation ago, the Left was swept by a wave of revolutionary optimism, drawing political inspiration from the Cuban Revolution and intellectual justification from variants of dependency theory that dismissed the possibility of democratic reform and capitalist development. In the 1990s—when Cuba adopted market reforms in a desperate struggle to survive, the Central American revolutionary vanguards evolved into electoral opposition parties, the Soviet Union was a discredited entry in the historical archives, and neoliberalism was on the ideological ascendance—the Latin American Left has faced the daunting task of critically reevaluating and redefining its political project.

The centerpiece of the Left's attempt at renewal—or, as it is called in Latin America, its *renovación*—has been the idea of democracy.[1] As a series of regime transitions swept military rulers from power in the 1980s, parties of the Left and even former guerrilla movements rushed to integrate themselves into new democratic regimes by participating in electoral contests and seeking representation in national legislatures and municipal governments. The breadth of this integration and the enthusiasm with which it was pursued left little doubt that an intellectual sea change had occurred in the thinking of the Left vis-à-vis political democracy. A profound reassessment of the value of democratic norms and procedures was under way, which challenged the Left's traditional conceptions of political power and social transformation.

Although parties of the Left had long participated—when allowed to—in electoral processes in Latin America, the nature of their integration into new democratic regimes in the 1980s was qualitatively different from that of the past. Historically, two responses to formal democratic institutions predominated in the Latin American Left.[2] The first response was one of outright rejection, based on the assumption that electoral democracy was an instrument of, and a facade for, bourgeois class domination. This response viewed any participation in formal democratic institutions as a diversion from revolutionary objectives that would compromise socialist principles and brake the development of a revolutionary consciousness among the masses. The second approach rationalized participation on instrumental grounds, on the assumption that democratic institutions could be used to "accumulate forces" for an eventual revolutionary confrontation. The Left could thus participate in democratic institutions as a form of political proselytization, aiming not so much to gain access to government office as to spread its message, expand its organizational networks, and develop a critical consciousness among popular sectors to hasten the dawning of a revolutionary situation.

Either way, electoral democracy was not considered integral to the socialist and revolutionary projects that were embraced by most of the Latin American Left.[3] This disparagement of liberal democracy was not attributable to an avowedly antidemocratic stance on the part of the Left, but rather to the belief that liberal democracy was fraudulent or illusory and thus disassociated from the struggle for popular empowerment and socioeconomic transformation. The tendency, then, was to distinguish "formal" or "bourgeois" democracy, which provided formal rights of citizenship in the political domain but safeguarded domination in the social and economic spheres, from "advanced" forms of democracy that empowered popular sectors and promoted social equity by means of a socialist transformation. Elections and legislatures were widely dismissed as procedural formalities that were devoid of substance and thus alien to the project of the Left. As terrain that belonged to other political forces, such institutions had to be either rejected by the Left or cautiously exploited for the tactical purposes of an alternative socialist project.[4]

The integration of the Left into democratic regimes in the 1980s was qualitatively different, however, because it was accompanied by a newfound emphasis on the intrinsic value of formal democratic institutions and procedures. The view of democracy as an illusion or an instrument for the pursuit of other objectives yielded gradually to an insistence on the integral character of democracy for the transformative project of the Left. As stated by the Chilean intellectual and Socialist leader Mañuel Antonio Garretón, democracy became, in many countries, "a central element of the socialist project, a part of its identity which is as essential as the social and economic proposals for overcoming capitalism."[5] This shift from an instrumental to an integral conception of democracy has been widely hailed for its contribution to a new intellectual climate in which authoritarianism in any form is delegitimized and democratic norms are more widely diffused.[6]

Nevertheless, if there is broad consensus within the Latin American Left on the need to "revalue" political democracy, there is no unanimity on precisely what it is that is being revalued. Although the minimum procedural attributes of democratic regimes are more widely recognized and respected than ever before,[7] two very different conceptions of democracy continue to circulate within the Latin American Left. The first conception values democracy primarily as a process of popular empowerment—that is, as an arena for the self-constitution of popular political subjects and the exercise of popular sovereignty over collective decision making. The logic of this conception leads inexorably to an emphasis on the progressive "deepening" or extension of democratic norms and practices to encompass more direct, participatory mechanisms of self-government, along with new institutional domains or social relationships. In contrast, the second conception emphasizes the value of democracy as an institutional framework for the management of social and political pluralism. That is, it conceives democracy as a more narrowly defined political regime that contains a set of conflict-regulating mechanisms that construct order out of diversity and allow for the peaceful coexistence of competing projects for society. Whereas this second conception has been heavily influenced by the trauma of authoritarian repression and the consequent search for more consensual formulas of governance, the first has been shaped more directly by the demise of revolutionary socialist models and the effort to reformulate a program of radical change that returns to the democratic roots of the socialist tradition.

The concept of democracy as popular empowerment has dominated the contemporary discourse of the Latin American Left, as it expresses greater continuity with traditional ideals and identities. But the second conception has been very influential in practice, and the differences between these two perspectives have undergirded many of the contemporary debates in the Left because they reflect distinct priorities and different notions of the virtues, potentialities, and limits of political democracy. To understand these competing conceptions of democracy and how they shape the role of the Left in new democratic regimes, it is necessary to identify their roots in the paradigmatic crisis of the Left. This chapter briefly explores these roots, then dissects the theoretical underpinnings of the competing conceptions of democracy. It concludes with an analysis of the factors that encourage or inhibit change within the modern Left.

Crisis and Renovation in the Latin American Left

Both regional and global events over the past quarter of a century have wreaked havoc with the classical paradigm of the Latin American Left. This paradigm was based on three pillars: a Marxist-Leninist theoretical foundation, the political ideal of revolution, and faith in socialism as the solution to problems of underdevelopment.[8] The early twentieth-century schism in the European Left that produced the alternative trajectories of social democracy and revolutionary Marxism-Leninism had relatively little impact on the Latin American Left; as José Aricó has argued, the Marxism that became popular in Latin America was predominantly Leninist in character,[9] whereas the political space for social democracy was largely foreclosed by populist competitors, unstable democratic institutions, and the paucity of resources in underdeveloped economies. Although the pro-Moscow communist parties in the region generally sought integration into democratic regimes after the mid-1930s and upheld the possibility of a "peaceful road" to socialism during the turbulent 1960s, their servile attachment to Soviet ideological orthodoxy prevented them from developing a theoretical framework for a democratic version of socialism. The New Left of the 1960s, dazzled by the Cuban Revolution, was even less ambiguous, openly dismissing electoral democracy as a means of popular empowerment and opting for revolutionary guerrilla warfare as the exclusive road to power. In general, the fierce debates in the Latin American Left in the 1960s between advocates of the peaceful road and proponents of guerrilla warfare reflected a conflict between different variants of Leninism rather than a cleavage between social democrats and revolutionaries.

Although the definitive collapse of the Leninist paradigm occurred at the end of the 1980s, its erosion was under way long before that. First, a series of political and military defeats in the 1960s and 1970s forced a reassessment of both reformist and revolutionary strategies for building socialism in the region. The deaths of Che Guevara and Salvador Allende were poignant symbols of the defeat of both the *vía armada* and the *vía pacífica*, while the spread of military dictatorships that repressed the Left in the name of "national security" provided graphic evidence of the costs of failure. Second, the brewing crisis in the Soviet bloc spread disenchantment with the Soviet model of socialism, both for its authoritarian and bureaucratic political structure and for its overly centralized, inefficient command economy. Although important sectors of the Latin American Left had long rejected elements of Soviet domestic or foreign policies, the Soviet bloc had still been an important reference point for virtually all of the Latin American Left, especially in the economic sphere, making it inevitable that the crisis of communism in Eastern Europe would reverberate throughout Latin America. Finally, the debt crisis of the early 1980s and the neoliberal revolution in Latin America undermined state-led models of economic development while weakening the organized labor movements that were identified as central protagonists of the socialist project in the classical paradigm.

These events challenged basic conceptions of politics, economics, and social change in the Left and subjected the classical paradigm to an unprecedented reassessment and withering self-criticism. As Angel Flisfisch has argued, the classical paradigm was so tightly interwoven that the erosion of one of its pillars threatened the entire edifice with collapse.[10] The crisis of this paradigm thus developed simultaneously along three distinct but interrelated dimensions: a teleological dimension, as seen in the diminished attractiveness of socialism as an alternative mode of social organization and the fading vision of the ultimate content of socialist political and economic models; a strategic dimension, which involved the failure of both violent and pacific means for the construction of a socialist alternative, as manifested by the series of defeats suffered by guerrilla movements and political parties of the Left in the 1960s and 1970s; and a dimension of political agency, which was rooted in the inability of the proletariat to fulfill the revolutionary mission prescribed for it by Marxist theory, along with the spreading disillusionment with political leadership vested in partisan or guerrilla vanguards.

Although orthodox and fundamentalist positions survive in the Latin American Left, as seen, for example, in Peru's Shining Path, varied patterns of change and renewal have been the predominant response to this paradigmatic crisis. As Robert Barros has persuasively demonstrated, one response was to embrace democracy as a framework for social and political coexistence, while effectively abandoning socialism's historic transformative project. More typical, however, has been the effort to salvage this transformative project by reconceptualizing it as a process of deepening democracy.[11] This reconceptualization was not a cure-all; in particular, it did not resolve the teleological crisis associated with the collapse of socialism as an alternative mode of social organization. Nevertheless, it allowed the Left to enter the procedural and institutional terrain of liberal democracy, while distinguishing its substantive agenda from that of other democratic actors. Most important, it provided a strategy, a direction, and a new set of agents for social and political change, even if the denouement of the process was unknown.

In the best tradition of German social democratic theorist Edward Bernstein, socialism no longer constituted a predetermined model of society, an alternative mode of production with a corresponding form of political organization.[12] Instead, socialism was conceived as a creative, open-ended process of social transformation, achieved through the progressive empowerment of popular sectors and the deepening of democratic practices. Under this new perspective, socialist transformation does not follow a script; it is guided by an emancipatory ethic but does not follow a universal, authoritative source of doctrinal inspiration. Metaphorically, it is akin to a voyager who carries a compass to chart a course but does not possess a road map to locate an ultimate destination. Revolution, likewise, is not a singular conquest of state power or the founding moment of a new social order but a continuous process of change aimed at the progressive elimination of various forms of exploitation and domination.[13] An influential statement of this new vision by one of its architects merits quotation at some length:

Given that there is no "seizure of power," given that there is a permanent struggle, within the democratic system, in all areas where there is power and domination . . . the socialist project now defines itself much more as a *process* than as a *society*. This means that socialism cannot be defined as a model for society that is established once and for all . . . in this view there is no "socialist society" as such, because socialism is a principle of social transformation, of the elimination of various kinds of alienation, oppression, and exploitation. It is based on the ideas of social emancipation and popular empowerment, with the workers and the dominated as the chief protagonists, but socialism is not a mechanistic order, a predetermined social system. In this sense the concept of the "transition to socialism" loses all meaning. There is no transition from one society to another, but rather a permanent transformation. There is no socialist model, only a socialist process; the latter is reversible and malleable, unlike models for a society. The idea of a model for society is, to a certain extent, contradictory to the principles of a democratic regime.[14]

This reconceptualization allowed the Left to build on the creative political energy of grass-roots social organizations such as neighborhood associations, Christian base communities, and women's groups. These organizations had proliferated under military dictatorships when political parties and labor unions were repressed, and they were widely viewed by the Left as organs of popular power, the breeding grounds for a new cultural and political hegemony with a more radically democratic ethos based on equality, direct participation, and community solidarity.[15] As autonomous political protagonists in their own right, rather than instruments of a partisan vanguard, popular organizations were primary agents for social change and the propellant force for the deepening of democracy.[16] This new perspective borrowed heavily from Antonio Gramsci's emphasis on the struggle for hegemony in civil society, thus shifting the locus of revolutionary activity away from a frontal assault on state power.[17] It also heralded new, more heterogeneous popular subjects for the socialist project at a time when the political weight of organized labor had been diminished by a combination of political repression, economic crisis, and neoliberal reforms. Socialism, therefore, was not seen as a class project but as a national project that rested on the secure foundation of a diverse and pluralistic social bloc.[18]

This vision of a deeper, more profound process of democratization became a rallying cry for leftist groups that retained a strong commitment to radical change but no longer possessed a predefined model for either socialism or revolution. It drew force from its capacity to weld together two values that were previously disjoined in the collective imagination of the Latin American Left—the idea of political democracy on one side and the notion of popular empowerment leading to socioeconomic transformation on the other. Rather than provide a facade for class domination, democracy could be conceived as infinitely elastic, allowing popular empowerment and social transformation to develop cumulatively as the logic of political majorities gradually suppressed class privileges and social hierarchies. To deepen democracy was therefore the political equivalent of having your cake and eating it too: it offered a vision of social revolution within the institutional confines of electoral democracy, without the polarizing dynamics and violent reactions that had distorted or demolished revolutionary struggles in the past.

This vision, however, rests on an expansive conception of democracy that is at odds with most contemporary theorizing. It conceives of democracy as a guiding principle of social organization, not a mere ensemble of institutional arrangements that constitute a particular type of political regime, which is how democracy is generally treated in the contemporary literature on transitions. This guiding principle gives the idea of deepening democracy its radical and integral thrust because it poses a direct challenge to the segmented characteristics of democratic regimes in contemporary Latin America. An understanding of this challenge requires a more thorough analysis of the theoretical distinctions that undergird different conceptions of democracy.

Democratic Theory and the Deepening of Democracy

The different approaches to democracy that can be found in the Latin American Left have deep theoretical roots, reflecting fundamental cleavages in modern democratic theory. Etymologically, the concept of democracy combines two basic ideas: *demos*, meaning the people, and *kratos*, meaning rule or power. The democratic ideal clearly suggests that the people are sovereign and that they engage in collective self-government. But the core concept of popular sovereignty is less straightforward than it seems because it leaves unanswered questions.[19] Two are of particular interest here because they relate directly to the problem of deepening democracy as it is conventionally understood in the Latin American Left. The first question concerns the form in which popular sovereignty is to be exercised—that is, whether it is a direct or indirect method of governance. The second concerns the scope or operative domain of its exercise;[20] in particular, it asks whether democracy is best conceived as a specific type of political regime or a broader principle of social organization that can potentially be extended to other spheres of social and economic relations.

As for the first question, the idea of deepening democracy is generally associated with a preference for direct as opposed to indirect forms of exercising popular sovereignty. This does not mean that it rejects the practice of representation; it is well known that classical models of direct democracy were formulated in political communities (the Greek city-states) with limited territory, population, and citizenship, where participation in decision making was made possible by the ease of gathering the citizenry in popular assemblies that deliberated and voted directly on the issues.[21] The constraints of territory, population, information, and expertise make some form of representation inevitable in large-scale democratic communities in complex modern societies. Nevertheless, the logic of deepening democracy calls for the maximization of popular control by expanding opportunities for direct citizen input, oversight, and participation in the policymaking process and by enhancing the accountability of elected representatives to their constituents.[22] This process necessarily entails diminished autonomy for public officials and a decentralization of decision making to make it more accessible to grass-roots participation and oversight.[23]

The second question concerning the scope of democratic practices is more complex, and it requires a more systematic analysis. This question reflects a long-standing cleavage between reductionist and holistic conceptions of democracy. The deepening logic is often embedded in a holistic, integral conception of democracy that extends from the political regime to the social order. It thus clashes with the general thrust of most contemporary scholarship on democratization, which reduces the domain of democracy to formal regime institutions that are separate and distinct from their social environs. Indeed, much of the literature on democratization is doubly reductionist. It begins with a narrow conception of democracy as a set of political institutions and procedures, usually reduced to the "procedural minimum" required to ensure associational rights, universal adult suffrage, and open competition for electoral office.[24] It then treats these institutional arrangements as nominal or discrete variables that yield categorical distinctions but do not differentiate between degrees of democracy. That is, this approach provides dichotomous, either-or distinctions between democratic and nondemocratic regimes and may help identify different subtypes of the democratic genus, but it does not recognize different levels or degrees of democracy.[25] Samuel P. Huntington, for example, begins with a Schumpeterian conception of democracy as a political system based on electoral contestation, then uses this criterion as the benchmark for a dichotomous analysis of the transition from nondemocratic to democratic regimes.[26] Philippe C. Schmitter and Terry Lynn Karl adopt a more demanding set of criteria but still treat democracy as a discrete variable in which subtypes are identified by categorical or qualitative distinctions rather than gradations. In their words: "Since no single set of actual institutions, practices, or values embodies democracy, polities moving away from authoritarian rule can mix different components to produce different democracies. It is important to recognize that these do not define points along a single continuum of improving performance, but a matrix of potential combinations that are *differently* democratic."[27]

The treatment of democracy as a discrete variable is useful as a descriptive, typological exercise, but it poses significant theoretical and analytical problems for comparative purposes. The idea of a procedural minimum logically presumes the existence of a procedural maximum; however, the discrete conception of democracy not only fails to specify the criteria or empirical indicators for such a maximum but denies its very existence. It thus provides evaluative criteria or benchmarks by which to judge regimes that fall short of democracy's procedural minimum but offers only descriptive, categorical terms for regimes that lie above the democratic threshold. It compares and differentiates democratic regimes according to their varying ensembles of discrete institutional attributes but does not establish a common set of analytical dimensions along which to evaluate or measure democratic practices. The variety of democratic institutional arrangements may be intrinsically interesting, but they are also significant for their impact on competition, participation, and accountability. These latter concepts, all integral to democratic governance, are continuous by nature, and they cannot be adequately assessed with discrete indicators alone. In short, democracy is not only an either-or but also a more-or-less, and the evaluation of its gradations remains as essential to comparative analysis as the identification of its types.[28]

The conceptualization of democracy as a discrete variable does not follow inevitably from its reductionist definition as a political regime. Were such a definition to be anchored in a central analytical dimension (or dimensions) rather than discrete empirical indicators, it might well yield a continuous measure of democratic practices. Robert Dahl's influential conception of polyarchy, for example, evaluated democratic practices along two central analytical dimensions, participation and contestation, which provided continuous estimations of the degree of polyarchy.[29] More recently, Kenneth A. Bollen has argued for a continuous conception of political democracy based on the relative balance of political power between elite and nonelite sectors of society.[30] Consequently, a continuous conception of democracy does not require that it be extended beyond the political domain—what O'Donnell and Schmitter call "socialization"[31]—by incorporating "substantive" socioeconomic outcomes.[32] Continuous measures are logically compatible with political and procedural definitions of democracy as well as holistic or substantive ones.

Under the reductionist approach, however, democratic criteria are narrowly confined to formal political institutions. A democratic regime carries no connotation that social interaction beyond the formal political arena will be organized democratically, since the political sphere is seen as an institutionally separate domain of activity, and diverse forms of social hierarchies and inequalities are compatible with the procedural minimum of democracy within that institutional domain. The logical correlate of the contraction of the public sphere of democratic decision making is an expansive notion of the private sphere of social and economic relationships that lies beyond the proper domain of democratic citizenship. In any given society, the sharper the distinction between public and private domains and the more narrowly circumscribed the public domain, the more segmented democratic practices are likely to be; that is, the more likely they are to be contained within discrete institutional arenas that have limited spillover effects on broader forms of social interaction. A segmented democracy is prone to limit the exercise of citizenship rights to narrowly defined political and legal circles, most prominently to the act of voting, while erecting impediments to the extension of citizenship rights to social and economic relationships. The logical progression from political to social and economic citizenship that T. H. Marshall traced in Western Europe has confronted innumerable detours in the Latin American context;[33] not surprisingly, critics have been quick to contend that the reductionist conceptions of democracy enshrined in the transitions literature have been reflected in the segmented character of emergent democratic regimes in Latin America.[34]

In contrast, the holistic perspective associated with the deepening logic conceives democracy as a property of the social order and not merely that of a political regime. As the term *deepening* implies, this conception of democracy is inherently continuous rather than discrete; it revolves around the central analytical dimension of popular sovereignty or empowerment, which makes democracy a matter of degrees, of more-or-less rather than an either-or distinction between regime categories or subtypes. This approach treats democracy as an elastic and dynamic phenomenon that contracts or expands over time in accordance with the extent of popular control over collective decision making. This is very different from the conception of democracy as a discrete variable, which deals with institutional attributes that are essentially static and thus more amenable to the logic of democratic consolidation. The logic of consolidation presumes that core institutions and procedures have been locked into place and can be modified only according to internally prescribed procedures.

The holistic conception of democracy also lends itself easily to an expansion of the public domain.[35] Indeed, it makes the democratic norms of equality and popular sovereignty potentially applicable to virtually any social unit that contains a system of power relations and has a significant impact on its constituents' lives, whether it be a political regime, a business enterprise, a civic organization, or a neighborhood community.[36] Under this perspective, democracy is not merely a political regime but a broader set of social relations.[37] This conception of democracy has deep roots in the socialist tradition, which posits two principal reasons for the extension of democratic norms and practices to the sphere of socioeconomic relationships. First, to the extent that business enterprises are collective social systems with authority structures that have an important impact on the lives of workers and communities, they should be democratically accountable to those they affect. To treat them as a purely private sphere of activity that is insulated from public accountability is to create reserve domains for authoritarian practices. Second, social and economic inequalities can easily be translated into concentrations of power in the political sphere that skew the articulation of popular interests and block the exercise of popular sovereignty.[38] According to this perspective, social equity is not a substantive outcome that is external to the functioning of democratic procedures but a prerequisite for equal access and unbiased democratic contestation and thus a vital indicator of procedural fairness.[39]

The possibility of expanding the scope or domain for the application of democratic norms makes clear that there are really two dimensions to the core principle of popular sovereignty. These two dimensions, although analytically distinct, are frequently conflated in popular discourse about the deepening of democracy in the Latin American Left. Properly speaking, the logic of *deepening* democracy is one of intensifying popular sovereignty in the political sphere, that is, moving from hierarchical forms of elitist or bureaucratic control to forms of popular self-determination by means of more direct participation in the decision-making process or more effective mechanisms for holding elected representatives and public officials accountable to their constituents. Alternatively, the logic of *extending* democracy pertains to the scope or domain of the social units and collective issues to which democratic norms are applied; that is, it refers to efforts to extend the democratic norms and procedures of collective self-determination from the formal sphere of state institutions to new spheres of social and economic relationships.[40] These analytical distinctions are depicted in Figure 2.1, in which the vertical axis represents the dimension of democratic deepening and the horizontal axis the dimension of democratic extension.

The four cells in Figure 2.1 represent the space in which democratic expansion or contraction occurs in both political and socioeconomic domains. The Western model of liberal capitalism combined with representative democratic institutions would be located in the first cell. In comparative terms, democratic practices in this cell would be narrow (i.e., restricted to formal state institutions) and shallow owing to a series of constraints on the exercise of popular sovereignty, especially indirect and sporadic participation in decision making, the limited accountability of party and bureaucratic elites, and concentrations of economic power that lead to differential access to policymaking arenas.

European social democracy could be located in the second cell, indicating efforts to extend democratic controls over economic activities that the liberal democratic model reserves for the private domain of the marketplace. The social democratic model extends

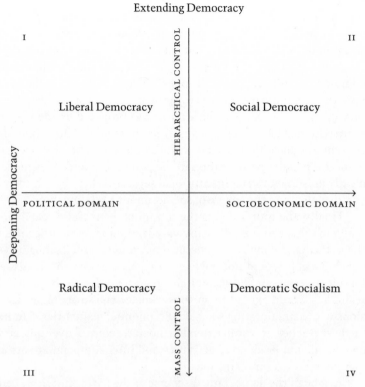

FIG. 2.1   A model for deepening and extending democracy.

citizenship rights to socioeconomic claims and reduces inequalities through such means as an interventionist welfare state, tripartite corporatist bargaining, and coparticipation in the workplace. Traditional social democracy, however, has long been plagued by stifling bureaucratic hierarchies in the welfare state, labor unions, and political parties, generating demands for greater accountability and responsiveness, along with "left-libertarian" challenges that emphasize decentralization and community-based participatory democracy.[41] Therefore, although social democracy is likely to be deeper as well as more extensive than liberal democracy, it remains above the horizontal axis in Figure 2.1.

The third cell would include radical democratic alternatives that enhance popular sovereignty through greater participation in the decision-making process or more effective mechanisms to hold representative officials and public agencies accountable to their constituencies.[42] Although the effect of radical democratic initiatives would be limited if they did not extend to social and economic relationships, there is no necessary reason why they could not be contained within the political sphere. Indeed, with the collapse of socialist economic models and the growing strains of social democracy in a global economy, the alternatives proposed by the Left in Latin America have been progressively drained of their economic content and have thus become focused on more effective mechanisms for popular participation in the political sphere. This model clearly presumes a strict institutional separation between the democratic polity and the sphere of socioeconomic relationships.

Finally, the fourth cell is the terrain of democratic socialism. Although this cell is empirically vacant, it remains significant for theoretical and conceptual purposes as an ideal-type comparative benchmark. It would not only include participatory mechanisms for self-government and accountable representation in the political realm but would extend them to workplace and investment decisions while ameliorating social and economic inequalities.[43] In its furthest reaches, it would extend democratic control over property ownership and productive activities and intensify popular participation in their administration.

Although the democratic discourse of the Latin American Left has incorporated the logics of both extension and deepening, the vertical dimension has tended to predominate. In part, this is attributable to the withering of the socialist utopia and to the growing difficulty of envisioning an alternative to capitalism as a mode of production. It also reflects the impediments to the extension of national democratic controls over economic activities in an increasingly global economy. In general, then, the debate over "renovation" in the Latin American Left has revolved much more around political, ideological, and organizational issues than economic ones.[44] Although attention has been directed to the need for markets to ensure economic efficiency,[45] there has been strikingly little discussion of schemes that would combine market efficiency with public or cooperative control of productive enterprises.[46]

The greater attention directed to the political dimension of deepening democracy is also attributable to the growing importance of grass-roots popular organizations in the project of the Left. These organizations are well situated to strengthen popular participation in municipal governments or other local decision-making arenas; however, they rarely pose a direct challenge to the existing structure of economic power or provide mechanisms to extend collective democratic control over the primary spheres of economic activity, even where they collectivize consumption activities as a shield against market insecurities. They are thus more directly relevant as subjects for the deepening of democracy than for its extension to the economic domain.

Even without a full extension of democratic norms to the socioeconomic sphere, however, the logic of deepening democracy has radical implications in a region with concentrated political power and profound structural inequalities. Indeed, the further the process of deepening goes politically, the fewer barriers would exist to its extension to other domains. Nevertheless, the proponents of deepening strategies have said little about how they would make popular empowerment palatable to conservative and elite sectors that have steadfastly, and often violently, resisted it in the past.[47] This concern has been paramount, however, in the other major tendency that has emerged within the Latin American Left. This second tendency conceives democracy less as a process of popular empowerment than as a framework for the mutual accommodation and coexistence of competing projects for society. This framework is explicitly understood to be a political regime rather than a social order, and its consolidation is upheld as a primary political objective. This perspective places the tension between social transformation and democratic stability at the center of its calculations and develops a very different project for the Left than that associated with the deepening of democracy.

Democracy as a Framework for Accommodation and Coexistence

Whereas the Latin American Left could find inspiration in the socialist tradition for the idea of deepening democracy, the conception of democracy as a mode of conflict resolution was more novel and controversial. This perspective draws heavily from liberal and pluralist interpretations of democracy and thus represents a sharp break with the Marxian theoretical tradition of the Latin American Left. The strength of this perspective in the Latin American Left is also very recent because it is predominantly a response to the polarized conflicts and traumatic political violence of recent decades.

Traditionally, the Latin American Left paid little theoretical attention to the issues of political pluralism and accommodation. It viewed itself as the local bearer of a universal historical project whose eventual success had been scientifically presaged by Karl Marx. Competing forces and alternative projects were to be vanquished or superseded during the forward march of history to communism; once established, communism would be a classless, stateless society free from social contradictions and the factions or competing interests they generate. This conception of politics was essentially Manichean, and in its purest forms it approached the political realm with a logic akin to warfare, as a struggle between the forces of good and evil, between those who had history on their side and those who did not.[48] This logic could tolerate a temporary truce but not a genuine accommodation of interests because it was founded on notions of victory and defeat, parallel outcomes that were considered to be definitive and irreversible in the Left's revolutionary teleology.

This conception of politics was put to the test in the 1960s and 1970s, when intense conflicts developed between alternative projects for society, and the Left found itself repeatedly on the wrong side of the divide between victory and defeat. The heady optimism of the Left was crushed as its attempts to mobilize popular sectors for socialism provoked the counterimposition of authoritarian forms of capitalism.[49] The result was an unprecedented wave of repression that was directed not only at the organized political Left but also at the labor unions and other social constituencies affiliated with the Left. The suppression of formal channels of political representation drove left-wing politics underground, and linkages to groups in civil society were often ruptured or attenuated.

The trauma of military repression had several important effects on the Left, which saw a generation of activists imprisoned, tortured, murdered, "disappeared," or driven into exile or clandestinity. It placed human rights on the agenda of the Left in a most immediate and personal way, enhancing appreciation for individual rights and liberties that the Left had traditionally dismissed as "bourgeois" concerns or subordinated to collective social and economic rights. This, in turn, produced a new appreciation for the protective measures afforded to individuals by formal democratic institutions. Much like David Held's model of "protective democracy," sectors of the Left came to value democratic restrictions on state power when they were confronted with predatory, repressive state institutions.[50] Only democratic procedures could carve out a domain of private activities where state intervention was prohibited and establish individual rights that were irrevocable by state action. Indeed, formal democracy was seen as a prerequisite for the existence of citizenship rights, without which the very practice of politics was called into question. For this reason, as Barros points out, democracy was transformed into a unifying banner for a "multitude of proscribed aspirations," ranging from drinking water in the local shantytown to basic human rights or socialist transformation, none of which had access to the formal political arena under conditions of military autocracy.[51]

Perhaps even more fundamentally, the trauma of military repression encouraged sectors of the Left to view democracy not only as a guarantor of individual rights and liberties but as an institutional framework that made possible the coexistence and accommodation of different projects for society. Ultimately, military repression was less a problem of individual human rights than a manifestation of the violent suppression of one political-economic project and the imposition of another. Therefore, in a context in which the revolutionary defeat of authoritarian capitalism was increasingly remote, many on the Left concluded that a mutual accommodation was the only alternative to a state of perpetual warfare in which their opponents enjoyed a virtual monopoly of armed force.

In theory, formal democratic institutions provide the best political arrangement for the coexistence of mutually antagonistic projects for society, primarily because they preclude definitive victories or defeats.[52] Democratic politics are transparently iterative, making all outcomes contingent and potentially reversible, or at least subject to future modification. Civil and political rights not only protect minority interests but, more important, ensure that minorities will be allowed to continue to participate in the political process and work to transform themselves into the majority during future iterations of the competitive process. Political majorities and the policies they implement are thus temporal and subject to permanent contestation within the prescribed procedural norms.[53] As Schmitter and Karl argue, the adherence of contending actors to the rules of the game does not necessarily require a normative commitment to democratic principles; they may adhere through a form of "contingent consent" so long as other actors abide by the rules and keep channels of contestation open.[54] Democracy can thus emerge as a strategic equilibrium between self-interested political actors, none of which is capable of imposing its preferred political model on the others.[55]

Clearly, this view of democracy presumes the inevitability and legitimacy of a plurality of interests. Democracy, in fact, becomes a process of managing pluralism and regulating conflict by establishing formal guidelines and boundaries for political competition. Competing projects are made compatible through procedural mechanisms which ensure that losers will not be deprived of their basic rights or their capacity to challenge winners in the future. Although the outcomes of democratic competition remain uncertain, the institutional framework provides a competitive structure that places boundaries on uncertainty and thus reduces the risk associated with loss or defeat.[56]

Nevertheless, the principal actors in democratic transitions may offer additional guarantees to protect the interests of adversaries so as to induce their cooperation in the democratization process. That is, they often do not rely entirely on the contingent consent produced by procedural rules for the management of conflict, fearing that the levels of uncertainty and risk may still be inordinately high for actors who feel threatened by democratic majorities. It is this drive for greater security and reduced uncertainty that produces democratic pacts, the negotiated agreements that underpin many contemporary regime transitions.[57] The logic of pacts is to limit the potential weight and leverage of democratic majorities through preemptive accords among elites. These accords are designed to protect vested interests and narrow the range of potential democratic outcomes, typically by sharing power, limiting competition, removing controversial issues from the political agenda, or inducing commitments to contain popular mobilization.[58] As such, they have been characterized as "undemocratic means" for the construction of democratic regimes.[59]

As indicated by Adam Przeworski's depiction of pacts as "cartels of incumbents," pacts are generally conservative instruments because they may be crafted to "restrict competition, bar access, and distribute the benefits of political power among the insiders."[60] That is, precisely, what enables them to convince conservative elites that authoritarian rule is dispensable and that the risks posed by potential democratic majorities can be contained. But if pacts help stabilize democratic transitions by broadening their base, or at least neutralizing their opponents, they pose significant dilemmas for the Left in Latin America because they clearly contradict the logic of deepening democracy. Pacts adhere to a logic of mutual accommodation and institutional consolidation, and they invariably require that the Left postpone or moderate objectives for political and socioeconomic transformation. Contentious issues such as property rights or military accountability for human rights violations may be removed from the political agenda by negotiated pacts, and the Left may be required to underuse its capacity for popular mobilization so as not to threaten democracy's more contingent supporters. In the words of O'Donnell and Schmitter, "The only realistic alternative for the Left seems to be to accept . . . restrictions and to hope that somehow in the future more attractive opportunities will open up."[61]

Even if they do not completely "freeze" limited democratic outcomes in place, pacts clearly put objectives for the deepening or extension of democracy on hold. Nevertheless, even a narrow form of democracy may be attractive to sectors of the Left if it provides a framework for political coexistence, especially if the alternative is a continuation of authoritarian rule or the abyss of unfettered confrontation in a context where the Left is militarily inferior. The strategic dilemma of the Left is clear: it can contribute to the consolidation of new democratic regimes by demonstrating a willingness to accommodate other political actors, but this is likely to entail a more limited form of democratic governance and a trade-off in transformative objectives. Conversely, the Left can push to deepen or radicalize democratic practices, but this strategy is likely to engender political polarization that destabilizes the regime by encouraging conservative elites to abandon the democratic arena. Over the long term, the tensions and trade-offs between democratic depth and democratic stability may be attenuated; indeed, these dual objectives may prove to be mutually reinforcing, as "shallow," pacted democracies are likely to be fragile if they are unable to incorporate new actors and respond to new challenges, whereas deeper forms of democracy may establish a broader and more secure base of support.[62] Nevertheless, in the highly contingent, short-term context of emerging democratic regimes, the logic of consolidation is likely to conflict with the logic of deepening, forcing the Left to choose between mutually incompatible values and objectives.

Where the Left is a political actor capable of mobilizing a broad base of popular support, its choice between the alternative logics of deepening or consolidating democracy can have a major impact on broader regime dynamics. Two principal variables interact to determine the impact and role of the Left in processes of democratization. The first is the Left's capacity to mobilize political support; the second is the choice between alternative strategic orientations. These two variables are depicted in Figure 2.2, which identifies four possible political roles that the Left can play in a process of democratization. In the two cells in the top row, the Left has little capacity to mobilize popular support and thus has a limited impact on broader regime dynamics. In such a context, where the Left pursues an accommodative strategy in the interest of democratic consolidation, its role can best be described as one of co-optation. Parties of the Left would seek incorporation within the democratic regime and perhaps support negotiated social or political accords in exchange for modest political payoffs. Their incorporation, however, would be from a position of weakness, as subordinate actors who play on terrain that is largely defined by others. Alternatively, the Left may press more radical demands to deepen the democratiza-

Strategic Orientation Toward Democracy

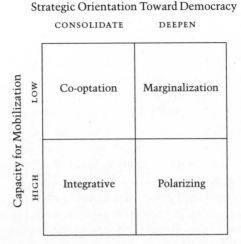

FIG. 2.2 Political roles of the left in emerging democracies.

tion process, but in the absence of significant mobilizing capabil- · ities, this is a recipe for sectarian marginalization that has little effect on the character of the regime.

The cells in the bottom row are more important because they contain cases in which the Left is capable of mobilizing broad support and exerting a major impact on the democratization process. In the third cell, the major actors of the Left prioritize political accommodation and democratic consolidation; when combined with a significant base of support, the outcome is an integrative role, whereby the Left helps to draw popular sectors into the democratic process in a nonconfrontational manner. This integration broadens the base of the democratic regime and solidifies its institutional foundations and conflict-regulating capabilities by ensuring that popular demands are processed through prescribed channels. It also exerts a centripetal effect that moderates competition by diminishing the gap between alternative projects and marginalizing more radical or antisystemic actors, which are deprived of a mass constituency.[63] This integrative role, therefore, is ideal for democratic consolidation and stability; it is unlikely, however, to produce the radical changes associated with deepening strategies because it is premised on a logic of social and political accommodation, and it tends to dampen autonomous political mobilization in civil society.

The final cell combines broad support with a more radical strategy for deepening and extending democracy, whereby the Left consciously tries to mobilize and empower popular sectors. Clearly, this combination holds the greatest potential for the radical transformation of power relations in social, economic, and political spheres. It also poses the greatest threat to entrenched elites and is likely to generate the most virulent resistance. For this reason, the role of the Left could be characterized as polarizing because it creates a centrifugal effect that directs political energy toward two competing poles, one representing radical change and the other a conservative retrenchment.[64] So long as the dynamic of polarization prevails, political accommodation is precluded; indeed, polarization logically culminates in either decisive victory or defeat, depending on the relative balance of power resources, making political outcomes in this cell the most uncertain and the most prone to high-stakes drama.

These four roles are ideal-type configurations, and there clearly can exist intermediate categories and variations on the ideal types. In particular, the variables that constitute accommodative and deepening strategies are continuous in nature, meaning that different gradations are possible. Nevertheless, these ideal types provide a frame of reference that should assist in the comparative analysis of the role of the Left in processes of democratization. The democratic transition in Chile, much like that in Spain before it, was solidified by the accommodative strategy and the integrative role of the Socialist Party, which surpassed the Communist Party in popular support during the regime transition and subsequently marginalized its more radical competitor.[65] In contrast, accommodative forces failed to establish a hegemonic position in Peru's United Left coalition during the 1980s, and the overall impact of the Left was more polarizing than integrative. Indeed, the internecine battles between proponents of accommodative and deepening strategies helped destroy Peru's legal Left; the collapse of the

Left, in turn, was a prime factor in the breakdown of institutional representation that ultimately led to the emergence of an autocratic ruler and the dissolution of Peru's democratic regime in the early 1990s.

Why was it, then, that accommodative strategies came to predominate in the Chilean Left by the late 1980s but never achieved hegemony in the Peruvian Left? More fundamentally, why did the bulk of the Chilean Left firmly embrace electoral democracy in the late 1980s, whereas the Peruvian Left remained profoundly ambivalent about the role of electoral democracy in its broader transformative project? These questions suggest that the process of political change has been very uneven across different cases, and they direct attention to the factors that shape and constrain the strategic choices of party leaders. The final section of this chapter thus explores the interactions among contextual, experiential, and organizational variables that influence the strategic orientation of Leftist parties in different national settings.

Party Leadership and Political Change: Learning, Context, and Organization

Party elites are clearly major actors in the changing role of the political Left in Latin America. Nevertheless, elites cannot change parties at their will because the more developed political parties are complex organizations with embedded constituencies, entrenched collective beliefs and identities, routinized procedures, and interdependent social networks. To change their trajectories requires more than a mere act of political volition by strategically placed elites with shifting preferences or calculations. It also requires a political environment that allows party elites to commit their organizations and social constituencies to the changes being initiated. Such an environment is a function of both experiential and contextual factors that shape and constrain party options, as well as organizational structures that facilitate political innovation.

Experiential factors are particularly important for the patterns of political learning they engender. Political learning can be either affirmative or disconfirming. Strategic success—whether it is in attracting electoral support, mobilizing new social constituencies, or achieving programmatic goals—typically leads to affirmative learning patterns because it validates the tactics and beliefs that elicited partisan gains. In contrast, strategic failure tends to be disconfirming because it indicates that established beliefs or tactics were somehow erroneous or poorly adapted to political realities. For this reason, strategic failure is also divisive, spawning an intra-party reassessment or self-criticism of norms and practices that may be at the core of collective identities. A common outcome of strategic failure is thus a confrontation between the defenders of tradition and party reformers, since traditionalists and reformers typically interpret strategic failures in different ways and extract divergent lessons from shared experiences.

The Chilean Left provides an unusually compelling example of such disconfirming experiential learning. This learning was a product of the traumatic events of the early 1970s, when the Left gained political power for the first time, lost it in a military coup, and suffered severe repression as a result of its strategic miscalculations. As Chapter 4 shows, this crushing defeat provoked intense debate within the Left-wing political and intellectual elite: different tendencies maneuvered to interpret the causes and assess responsibilities for the destruction of the "Chilean road to socialism," and in the process they extracted lessons from the experience that would shape patterns of resistance to the military dictatorship that followed. Within five years of Allende's overthrow, a complex realignment was under way, and crucial sectors of both the Socialist and Communist Party leaderships rejected their respective pre-coup positions and developed new strategic orientations. By the early 1980s the two parties had reversed positions in the Chilean political system: the previously moderate Communist Party shifted to an insurrectionary stance, while the previously militant Socialist Party embraced a reformist vision of democratic rule and cultivated a strategic alliance with the centrist Christian Democrats.

In short, "catastrophic" learning precipitated important changes in both political parties, but since the leaders of the two parties extracted opposite lessons from their shared experience, the parties "crisscrossed" and evolved in opposite directions.[66] The authoritarian experience encouraged a "revaluation" of democracy and a more moderate stance in the Socialist Party, whose reformist sectors engaged in a self-criticism of their party's revolutionary pretensions, blamed it for polarizing the political system under Allende, and envisioned a new democratic order founded on an accommodation between the Center and the Left.[67] This was not a uniform response to the dictatorship in the Chilean Left, however.[68] Indeed, this response was on the defensive over the first half of the 1980s, when the strategic environment created by a massive protest movement breathed life into the insurrectionary stance of the Communist Party, which had roots in that party's self-critical assessment of its failure to develop a "military policy" to defend Allende's experiment in democratic socialism. As seen in Chapter 5, the hegemony of the moderate Socialist stance in the Chilean Left was secured only over the latter half of the 1980s, when a fundamental shift in the strategic environment occurred. As the protest movement waned, the military regime ill-advisedly sought to institutionalize authoritarian rule through a plebiscite campaign that encouraged opposition forces to converge on electoral forms of resistance, which ultimately favored the strategic orientation and political ressources of the Socialist Party's moderate tendency.

In contrast, the leftist coalition that rose to political prominence in Peru in the 1980s had not experienced comparable prodemocratic learning experiences. Historically, the Peruvian Left had fared poorly in electoral competition; its surge in influence occurred under the watch of an authoritarian regime which, in contrast to Chile, was not designed to repress militarily the partisan Left and social movements. Indeed, as shown in Chapter 7, the Velasco military regime in Peru implemented much of the Left's social agenda, inadvertently facilitated its political mobilization, and strengthened a multitude of lower-class social organizations. This radically different historical experience with both democracy and authoritarianism made the leaders of the Peruvian Left less inclined to value democracy as a guarantor of human rights and civil liberties. Likewise, they did not conceive it as a popular conquest over elitist and hierarchical political forces. To the contrary, they viewed redemocratization as a "step backward to the pre-1968 status quo," with a "return to traditional political institutions and rules that . . . had favored conservative groups."[69] Since their acceptance of Peruvian democracy was more instrumental than normative, their longing for revolutionary alternatives remained intact, and their willingness to accommodate other political forces in the interest of democratic stability was far less than in Chile.

These experiential factors were reinforced by strategic considerations that were rooted in the parties' respective social, economic, and political contexts. Simply put, it is difficult for a moderate program of democratic reform to achieve hegemony in the Left so long as socialist or revolutionary alternatives remain plausible. This was the challenge faced by Chile's moderate Socialist leaders in the first half of the 1980s, when a profound economic crisis made the military dictatorship vulnerable to mass protests, thus sustaining popular sentiments for a radical break with both the military regime and its neoliberal economic model. After 1986, however, the plausibility of such a radical break seemed increasingly remote, as the protests waned, the economy entered a prolonged expansive phase, and the overwhelming military advantage of the regime was reaffirmed. The new strategic context definitively foreclosed insurrectionary options while offering new opportunities and incentives for pragmatic and accommodative orientations. The strategic choices adopted by Socialist leaders were thus not merely a voluntaristic reflection of political learning and changing ideological preferences but also a rational adaptation to political opportunities and constraints as they were structured by an evolving external environment.

The strategic environment of the electoral Left in Peru could hardly have been more different. Whereas the dynamism of Chilean capitalism after 1986 encouraged Socialist leaders to opt for moderate reform over a revolutionary rupture, the profound crisis of Peruvian capitalism in the 1980s helped sustain ideological commitments to radical alternatives, however ill-defined they may have been in practice. Likewise, the relentless advance of the Shining Path insurgency—which began the decade as a fringe movement in a remote corner of the Andean hinterland and ended it with half the nation under a state of emergency—seemed to suggest that revolutionary strategies were viable in the Peruvian context, even if the legal leftist parties were repulsed by the Shining Path's sectarian dogmatism and brutal militarism. As shown in Chapter 8, the Shining Path contributed to the polarization of the electoral Left by driving moderate elites to embrace accommodative strategies to salvage the democratic regime, while simultaneously creating competitive pressures at the grass-roots level that encouraged more radical leaders to maintain their traditional revolutionary discourse.

Given these contextual and experiential differences, the Left in Chile and Peru shared precious little in common by the end of the 1980s. Sixteen years of harsh dictatorship had caused the bulk of the Chilean Left to associate democracy with a wide variety of values, ranging from individual security and socioeconomic justice to collective political and organizational rights. Although the Left recognized that democracy would not guarantee the complete fulfillment of its socioeconomic and political objectives, it increasingly saw democracy as a precondition for their pursuit and thus as an intrinsic value in its own right. Conversely, after a decade in which Peruvian democracy was plagued by an ever-deepening economic crisis, an ascendant guerrilla insurgency, and widespread human rights violations, the major parties of the Left continued to search for an alternative mode of governance, convinced that the democratic regime was divorced from the substantive political and economic outcomes embedded in their conception of popular sovereignty.

If patterns of strategic and ideological change in political parties are driven by this interaction between contextual factors and experiential learning, it must also be recognized that innovative beliefs and practices have to be filtered through internal party organizational structures. As Herbert Kitschelt argues, a party's organizational structure is an intervening variable between its external environment and its strategic choices.[70] Parties do not respond mechanically to a changing external environment, nor do they necessarily learn in a cohesive manner from their experiences. The process of change is inherently political and conflictual, and it is inevitably conditioned by internal organizational characteristics. Organizational structures can determine how external influences are filtered, screened out, or absorbed in an individual party; they can open or close different response options; they shape the internal norms and procedures for debate, dissent, decision making, and policy implementation; they condition the process by which competing positions or factions can mobilize resources or interpret political experiences; and they frame internal cleavages and power relationships. Even a cursory glance at the Chilean Socialist and Communist Parties suggests that organizational dynamics may lead to radically different learning patterns and highly divergent responses to shared experiences or environmental pressures.

Previous studies have suggested that some types of party organization are more adaptable than others, that is, they are more likely to modify political beliefs or practices in response to historical experiences or changes in their external environment. According to Angelo Panebianco, parties that are highly structured and institutionalized—that is, those with a strict vertical chain of command, centralized authority, well-developed bureaucracies, highly defined operational rules and disciplinary norms, and homogeneous local and regional subunits—are better able to resist environmental pressures or perturbations.[71] These parties tend to be more insulated from their environment and more homogeneous in nature because subunits are under the direct control of hierarchical authority. Internal pluralism and factions are not allowed, giving the party organization a monolithic character. Highly structured parties are less permeable to external influences and are slower to change in response to exogenous factors; subunits or factions cannot autonomously initiate change or interact with the environment, making innovation contingent on the initiative of entrenched authorities or a leadership succession.[72]

High levels of institutionalization thus facilitate organizational stability and continuity by creating orderly rules, routines, and internal relationships.[73] In the process, however, such bureaucratic organizations typically undercut the strategic flexibility that is needed to respond to a changing external environment because they "give little weight to innovative new participants."[74] Communist and other vanguardist parties organized according to Leninist norms of democratic centralism share many of these cumbersome organizational features: they possess powerful central authorities that exercise hierarchical control over an extensive party appara-

tus, along with a highly developed cellular structure with disciplined party cadres operating in workplaces, shantytown communities, and cultural or professional circles. These organizational
features suppress innovative tendencies from below and make it
difficult for reformers to take control of the party apparatus from
above.

In contrast, parties that are less highly structured or institutionalized have more fluid and decentralized leadership arrangements, more flexible decision- making and operational norms, and
more subunit autonomy and heterogeneity. These parties are more
highly differentiated and pluralistic internally; they are prone to
factionalism because they have lax disciplinary norms, a weaker
vertical chain of command, and more autonomy for subunits to
compete with one another and interact directly with the environment. According to Panebianco, these parties provide multiple
points of entry to external influences and multiple loci for the initiation of change.[75] They are less insular, more permeable to environmental perturbations, and less resistant to exogenous pressures for change. The loose coupling of internal party units and lack
of bureaucratic constraints also provide a significant measure of
political autonomy for party leaders to initiate changes in strategic
directions.[76]

In short, a highly structured and institutionalized party organization can inhibit change in three basic ways: by closing political
space internally for the autonomous generation of innovative practices; by erecting barriers to the penetration of external influences;
and by limiting interaction with the external environment and its
political actors. The opposite is true of less highly structured or
institutionalized party organizations: they can facilitate change by
opening political space for internal pluralism, debate, and innovation; they tend to be easily penetrated by external influences; and
they allow multiple levels and forms of contact with the external
environment.

Both types of parties will be found in this book. The Chilean
Communist Party is highly structured and institutionalized, with
centralized authority relations, a well-developed bureaucracy, and
vertical disciplinary norms that historically limited factionalism
and internal dissent, at least until the collapse of the Soviet bloc

and strategic miscalculations during Chile's democratic transition plunged the party into an internal crisis in 1990. These factors have not completely inhibited change in the party; the Communist Party altered its strategic orientation under the military regime in response to its pattern of experiential learning. But this change was narrowly limited to tactical and strategic issues, leaving the party's ideological objectives and identities intact. This corresponds to Karl Deutsch's characterization of "simple" learning, which produces changes in tactics or means to the attainment of specified ends without altering the ends themselves.[77] The party's narrow, monolithic ideological discourse combined with its rigid organizational structure to foreclose debate over ultimate political objectives and limit the range of strategic options.[78] Strategic innovation was thus contingent on the exclusive and encapsulated initiative of party authorities, who imposed a new strategic line on an unsuspecting party apparatus that had not had an opportunity to debate alternative courses of action. This hierarchical and restrictive pattern of political innovation was also characteristic of the dominant parties in the Peruvian Left, which combined ideological and organizational rigidity with highly personalistic authority relations.

In contrast, the Chilean Socialist Party is a prime example of a loosely structured party organization. The party's congenital factionalism, ideological pluralism, and lax disciplinary norms ensured that the strategic defeat of 1973 would be subject to competing interpretations and thus yield a range of political "lessons" with very different implications for the party's evolutionary trajectory. Dissent and debate occurred at multiple locations within the party and quickly transcended narrow strategic concerns to focus on fundamental ideological principles that struck at the core of the party's collective identity. This more "complex" pattern of experiential learning caused both means and ends to be contested within the party and ultimately to be thoroughly reconceptualized as part of the "Socialist Renovation."[79]

The open, fluid character of the Socialist Party's organizational structure allowed renovation to occur through three principal mechanisms of change. The first, endogenous innovation, involved the internal generation and transmission of new ideas or practices. Given high levels of internal pluralism and subunit autonomy, there existed multiple loci and ample opportunities for debate, dissent, and innovation following the 1973 military coup. Initiatives for change originated at various points in the party and were given the space to develop and compete for acceptance without being suppressed by organizational hierarchies or ideological litmus tests, as the party leadership was unable to establish any coherent control over a highly fragmented party apparatus. Party leaders and sectional committees in exile operated with a high degree of autonomy, borrowing freely from ideas and experiences encountered in their new environments and actively promoting the fundamental changes associated with the process of renovation. Socialist intellectuals and other activists were afforded considerable latitude for political debate and self-criticism and were free to organize a series of conferences in exile that diffused the principal ideas of the renovation process and established new personal networks with representatives of Chile's Christian Left.[80] In the absence of hierarchical authority to suppress dissent and discipline minorities, the impetus for renovation developed in decentralized locations, from both lower and higher levels of the party apparatus, then diffused horizontally through unofficial publications, informal intellectual networks, organized conferences, and active proselytization. What emerged as an intellectual dissent developed into an amorphous and decentralized political tendency, which gradually congealed organizationally and established hegemony in Chilean socialism as the strategic context shifted in the late 1980s.

The second mechanism of change, organizational absorption, refers to the openness of the Socialist Party to new social and political forces and its capacity to incorporate them in its ranks. As Kitschelt has argued, the recruitment of new party activists can be an important source of innovation, while also enabling a party to diversify its appeal.[81] As shown in Chapter 4, much of the early impetus for renovation came from intellectuals associated with Chile's Christian Left parties, who influenced—then eventually joined—the Socialist Party. This absorption was heavily dependent on the flexible organizational structure and internal pluralism of the Socialist Party, which made it more adept at attracting new blood and fresh ideas than the more closed, insular, and homogeneous Communist Party.

The final mechanism of change, ideological penetration, was also attributable to the open and pluralistic character of the Socialist Party's organizational structure. Parties that are not highly structured and institutionalized tend to be permeable to exogenous influences and ideas because they have fluid boundaries and limited autonomy from their environment. With weak central authority and lax discipline, there are few screening devices to block out external influences or impose doctrinal orthodoxy. Likewise, internal pluralism and subunit autonomy enhance interaction with other political forces because they provide multiple points of contact to the external environment and multiple points of entry to external ideas. The fragmentation and dispersion of the Socialist Party under authoritarian rule and exile after 1973 facilitated this ideological penetration; it not only exposed the party to diverse European perspectives on socialism and democracy but ensured that there was no unified central authority to enforce ideological orthodoxy or otherwise block the importation of "heretical" ideas. Indeed, there existed competing authority centers both inside and outside of Chile which established their own external contacts and served as vehicles for the importation of novel ideas into the party.

This fragmentation gave the competing party tendencies considerable latitude to introduce innovative beliefs and practices, borrowing explicitly from European perspectives and experiences.[82] In contrast, the Communist Party leadership was able to maintain a much tighter rein on the political activities of party members in exile and limited their contact with non–Soviet bloc actors. The party's cohesive leadership and hierarchical structure were generally effective at blocking the penetration of non-Leninist ideological influences, while reserving strategic initiative for the party directorate.

These very different degrees of openness to external influences were especially important in the international context of the 1970s and 1980s, a period of extraordinary ferment in Socialist thinking and practice. As Castañeda suggests, the collapse of communism at the end of the 1980s posed a severe challenge to the Left internationally, whether or not a particular leftist group in another country was politically identified with the Soviet bloc.[83] Analysis of the Peruvian and Chilean cases, however, suggests that the impact of communism's collapse varied widely, depending on the characteristics of the Left in different national contexts. For leftist parties in Latin America that had never seriously questioned the core ideological and strategic tenets of Leninism, the crisis in the Soviet bloc was devastating because it shredded their collective identities, shrouded their teleological visions, and undermined their external legitimacy in society. This was not only the case of the Chilean Communist Party, which had thoroughly identified with the Soviet bloc, but also of the dominant parties in Peru's legal Left, which had Leninist orientations but different international referents. These parties all suffered a precipitous political decline that coincided with the crisis in the Soviet bloc.

The Chilean Socialist Party, however, had been deeply influenced by the international debates over the "crisis of Marxism" in the 1970s and 1980s and had already subjected Leninist orthodoxy to a withering internal critique before Mikhail Gorbachev's reforms shook the international Left in the latter half of the 1980s. By the time of communism's collapse, Leninism had been marginalized in the party and had virtually disappeared as a source of collective identity. Consequently, the collapse of communism ratified and reinforced the process of ideological and strategic redefinition that had already taken place in the party: it buttressed the position of reformists in the party leadership, weakened their more orthodox competitors both inside and outside the party, and enhanced their strategic flexibility in building new political alliances and recasting the party's electoral appeal to attract new social constituencies.

These various influences on the process of political change can be depicted in a simplified model, as seen in Figure 2.3. In the model, the domestic and international political environments influence party change by altering the strategic context in which par-

FIG. 2.3 Model of party change.

ties must operate. Likewise, political experiences engender learning processes that can alter a party's core beliefs or practices. These independent variables are filtered through the mediating influence of an intervening variable, a party's organizational structure, which determines the relative flexibility and openness of different parties to strategic and ideological innovation.

This model helps to explain why the Left in Chile and Peru embarked on such radically different political trajectories in the 1980s and why the Socialist rather than the Communist Party emerged from the Chilean dictatorship in a hegemonic position at the end of the decade. But despite these important differences in strategic orientations and political practices, the discourse of deepening democracy was prevalent in a Left in both countries that had broad popular support. The objective of deepening democracy, however, proved to be an elusive vision in both countries. Why, then, has it been so difficult to translate this popular support into more profound democratic reforms? Chapter 3 outlines the theoretical groundwork for the analysis of the Chilean and Peruvian cases, identifying the structural and institutional constraints that shape patterns of collective action in Latin America and the problems of political agency that result. As the case studies indicate, these problems have made it difficult to aggregate popular interests and identities into a cohesive political alternative with the requisite weight to deepen the process of democratization.

CHAPTER 3

Social Structures, Collective Action, and the Deepening of Democracy

IF the idea of deepening democracy in the Latin American Left was in part a response to the collapse of the traditional revolutionary teleology, it was also inspired by the rise of new social movements under the military dictatorships of the 1960s and 1970s.[1] Neighborhood associations, women's groups, human rights organizations, peasant federations, Christian base communities, and myriad other forms of collective action lifted the spirits of the political Left and restored its faith in progressive political change during the darkest days of military repression and political retreat. These were not groups with which the Left could launch a revolutionary assault on state power; they were, however, integral to the survival and recomposition of a democratic civil society under authoritarian rule, and they raised hopes for more meaningful forms of democratic participation in the aftermath of regime transitions. Indeed, the Left pinned its hopes for the socialization of political and economic power on the democratic struggle of the popular movement "to be a subject of history, to constitute itself as a social force capable of constructing its social and political order."[2]

The optimism of the early period of democratic transitions has clearly abated, and more sober assessments of the transformative potential of new social movements have come into vogue.[3] The Left's vision of deepening democracy presumed that diverse and often discrete forms of collective action could have an additive or cumulative effect and ultimately influence power relations at the national level. Fernando Calderón and Elizabeth Jelin, for example, saw new social movements as potential bearers "of a new social order that demands a 'new model' of economic development and a certain political vision of the totality of society."[4] But the realities of segmented democracy attest to the difficulties the Left has had in harnessing the political energies of new popular subjects: either diverse forms of popular collective action have not proven to be aggregative and cumulative in the political arena, or new democratic institutions have not been responsive to their articulated needs, or both.

In this chapter I argue that the failure of efforts to deepen democracy is attributable primarily to problems of collective action and political coordination that arise in the process of translating popular social majorities into political majorities with the requisite weight to carry through democratic reforms. These problems can be traced, in part, to political and economic structures that privilege individual actors and fragment popular sectors. To explain these collective action and coordination problems, an integrative approach is adopted which identifies obstacles to collective empowerment at three levels of analysis. The structural level is associated with the social fragmentation and political constraints of an era of economic crisis and neoliberal reform. The institutional level poses problems of democratic accountability and institutional access. Finally, the level of political agency poses the challenge of integrating fragmented social constituencies within a common political project. Taken together, these three levels of analysis explain the prevalence of either political and economic individualism or forms of "segmented collectivism" that do not add up to an alternative political project.[5]

Collective Action and the Political Project of the Left

Many social movements, along with the scholars who study them, are wary of the partisan Left. Social organizations in Latin America have a lengthy and troubled history of political manipulation and instrumentalization, not only by parties of the Left but by the state and nonleftist parties as well.[6] For many of the new social actors who emerged in recent decades, the right to autonomous cultural and political expression has been a central demand and a basic source of collective identity.[7] Consequently, there exists a broad range of relationships between social movements and parties of the Left in Latin America. Some social movements have insisted on strict political independence or are more concerned with sociocultural expression than organization for political change.[8] Others have entered tactical alliances with the Left to gain access to formal representative institutions and policymaking arenas, while still others exist in an organic symbiosis with parties of the Left.

In contrast to this wariness, parties of the Left have generally been enthusiastic in embracing new social movements, assigning them an integral role as political protagonists in "renovated" socialist projects. In part, this stance is attributable to perceptions of political and ideological affinity. Since many new social movements developed in opposition to authoritarian rule, they often represent new forms of democratic collective identity within subaltern sectors, and they seemingly embody an alternative ethos or political culture that challenges the values of capitalism. According to many observers, this new ethos emphasizes community solidarity over individualism, equality over hierarchy, and participation over technocracy and bureaucratic decision making.[9]

The Left's embrace of new social movements also corresponds to a functional logic, namely, the Left's political dependence on collective action in the social sphere. The project of deepening democracy is heavily contingent on extraelectoral forms of social organization; that is, the mere aggregation of individual voters in the electoral arena is not an adequate political foundation for a radical project of deepening democracy. Electoral support for a program of radical change is usually premised on the existence of extensive social networks, and the implementation of such programs requires organized support beyond the transitory mobilization of an electoral constituency.

There are three principal reasons for this dependence on collective action outside the electoral arena. First, electoral mobilization alone leaves the Left and its constituencies at a serious disadvantage in power relationships in socioeconomic and political spheres outside the electoral arena, given the structural advantages enjoyed by capital over labor and other subaltern groups. Since a government's popularity is heavily contingent on overall economic performance, states are highly dependent on the willingness of property owners to perform their function as capitalists, that is, to produce and invest.[10] The structural weight of capital is reinforced by the fact that capitalists do not have to rely on collective action to defend their interests; that is, the uncoordinated decisions of individual capitalists to withhold investment or exit from an unfavorable domestic environment can, in the aggregate, exert enormous pressure on national policymakers.[11] In contrast, popular sectors are not placed in a strategic location of economic importance, and their individual actions have negligible leverage because the withholding of labor by individual workers is meaningless in labor-surplus economies. Lower classes are thus more reliant on collective action to advance or defend their interests, which is why organization has long been the weapon of the weak, the political tool that can help neutralize structural imbalances by mobilizing the weight of numbers.

Second, the logic of deepening democracy goes far beyond the election of a progressive government to implement a reformist agenda. Electoral cycles produce episodic forms of political mobilization, with prolonged periods of inertia punctuated by brief moments of hyperactivity. This cycle of mobilization and demobilization is prone to populist appeals during electoral conjunctures followed by unaccountable forms of technocratic governance in the interim. In contrast, the deepening logic requires that citizens do more than exercise their right to vote because it rests on a continuous and participatory notion of collective self-government that demands sustained levels of popular mobilization. Social organizations are integral to this vision because they are forms of popular expression, vehicles for direct participation, and collective instruments for the exercise of political oversight and the maintenance of democratic accountability. Without such forms of collective action, there is unlikely to be the sustained political protagonism needed to expand the boundaries of democratic governance.

Finally, collective action in the social sphere is integral to the development of a critical political consciousness among popular sectors, without which the Left is unlikely to mobilize electoral support for a program of radical change. The political strength of the Left clearly cannot be inferred from the objective existence of social inequalities or large working and lower classes; it must be socially and culturally constructed through collective experiences and historical struggles that bond individuals around common interests and identities, while distinguishing them from groups with antagonistic interests or identities.[12] Social organization can thus be an intervening variable between the existence of popular grievances and their process of politicization because there is nothing automatic about the politicization of class cleavages or socioeconomic discontent, nor do common interests automatically engender class or social solidarity. As Przeworski argues, particular interests invariably dominate in the absence of collective organization, meaning that unorganized workers will compete with each other, fail to act in accordance with their collective interests, and be more subject to the hegemonic appeal of capital.[13] Therefore, a counterhegemonic project is invariably a social construct, an organic political expression that transcends the mere aggregation of individual voters in the electoral arena. Such a project is the manifestation of a new ethic or political consciousness,[14] a collective transformation that is the product not of individual conversions but of processes of social conflict and cooperation that engender new collective identities and novel forms of organization.[15]

The deepening of democracy thus emerges first and foremost as a problem of collective action, a problem of inducing individuals with common interests to act collectively in pursuit of collective goods. Mancur Olson's classic formulation of the collective action problem demonstrates that political organization cannot be inferred from common interests or goals.[16] His formulation is poorly suited, however, to explain the challenges confronted by popular sectors and the political Left in contemporary Latin America. Olson's argument is premised on the assumption that individuals are rational utility maximizers who have perfect information. These individuals are able to perceive that they share interests in common and that organization could provide a collective good that is unattainable through individual action alone. The collective good goes unprovided, however, because it cannot be withheld from those who do not contribute to its provision, and each individual would prefer to "free ride" (enjoy the collective good without contributing to its provision) rather than bear the costs of organization. The most important collective action problems confronted by the Left and popular sectors in Latin America are different, and the rational choice approach popularized by Olson cannot explain them because it strips individuals of their social environs. The individual utilitarians of rational choice theory are universal actors who appear to be without personal histories or social positions, actors who have been removed from the structural locations that shape their interests and the social networks that give meaning to their existence.[17] They are actors who have interests and calculations but no identities, commitments, or social relationships. Consequently, they will participate in collective action only if they are coerced into doing so or induced by the provision of "selective incentives" that offer private gains.

Even within the rational choice perspective, however, it has been recognized that individuals will join organizations for political motives or group goals if they have less than perfect information about the costs and benefits of collective action. Likewise, the perspective acknowledges that in small group settings with face-to-face interaction the possibilities for communication and coordination allow for the emergence of cooperation through bargaining.[18] What the rational choice perspective fails to explain is how these settings, and in some cases even larger ones, can yield forms of collective identification and group solidarity that transcend narrow calculations of self-interest and help generate new forms of organization. Utilitarian calculations are thus not the only foundation for the formation and maintenance of social organizations, as collective action may also be rooted in a group logic or a conception of "shared fate" that reflects a particular construction of social meaning.[19]

Therefore, the rational choice approach is useful only to explain the subset of human behavior that is instrumental and adheres to an individualist logic;[20] to the extent that social movements are expressive or follow a collectivist logic, rational choice theory cannot account for their origins, behavior, or dynamics. It follows, then, that collective action problems may not be attributable solely to the interest calculations that engender the free rider phenomenon; they may also reflect social contexts in which networks of interaction are ruptured, identities are fragmented, and a sense of "shared fate" is inhibited from emerging. Indeed, where interest calculations *do* underlie collective action problems among popular sectors in Latin America, the free rider phenomenon is not at the heart of the problem. The free rider problem assumes that individuals are able to recognize the existence of common interests or collective goods, along with the instrumental value of organization, but are prohibited from acting collectively because of individual calculations of costs and benefits. The more pervasive problem in Latin America, however, is that the social fabric is so fragmented that common interests among popular sectors are not perceived or are too narrowly defined to serve as the foundation for an alternative political and economic project. Collective action, therefore, either does not occur or is too isolated and "segmented" to empower popular sectors. The problem is less one of overcoming individual free riders than overcoming social atomization, that is, constructing a recognition of common interests and a conception of shared fate that can undergird more expansive collective identities and broader forms of collective action.

This points to an alternative conceptualization of collective action problems, one that starts with an analysis of the structural conditions that shape and constrain popular interests, then explores the problems of social coordination and political agency that inhere in the effort to overcome the "transaction costs" attendant to organization. Following the work of Sidney Tarrow, this approach will treat collective action as an inherently social and political process rather than a mere aggregation of individual decisions.[21]

Social Networks and Structural
Change in Latin America

As Tarrow persuasively demonstrates, the origins of social movements are to be found in networks of personal and social interaction. His work is valuable for understanding the political contexts, or "political opportunity structures," that cyclically activate and deactivate these social networks around diverse forms of collective action. But while this approach helps identify political and institutional factors that constrain or facilitate collective action, it says little about the ways that socioeconomic structures configure social networks and thus condition the forms of collective action that are able to emerge.[22] In Latin America, the Left has had to adapt its political project to dramatic changes in the social landscape and to the different potentialities for collective action that they entail. Accordingly, the challenges faced by the Left are best understood through an analysis of the interrelationships among three sets of variables: the social structure, the organizational density and forms of collective action in civil society, and agents of political representation.

Structural conditions are most important for the ways they aggregate and differentiate social forces. The aggregation of individuals in similar structural locations can lead to close personal interaction, a recognition of shared interests, and the emergence of a collective identity, which transforms a group from a mere aggregation of individuals into an organic entity. Perhaps more important for collective action, however, is the process of differentiation, which separates groups according to their structural locations and competing interests. The conflicts that arise from this process of differentiation help define common interests within each contending side, and they are integral to the development of collective identities and solidarities.[23] As Marx stated, "The separate individuals form a class only insofar as they have to carry on a common battle against another class; otherwise they are on hostile terms with each other as competitors."[24] Conflict, therefore, simultaneously separates and binds social groups, thus generating the basic cleavages that undergird competition and mobilization in the political system.[25]

Different structural contexts, however, separate and bind social forces in very different ways, and the distinct cleavage structures that they generate have important implications for collective action. The structural conditions for collective action by popular sectors vary along four principal dimensions:

(1) Centrality vs. Diffuseness of Cleavage Structure Some social contexts provide a dominant, central cleavage such as class, ethnicity, region, or religion, which structures social mobilization and political conflict. Other cleavages may exist in such societies, but they tend to be subordinate to the dominant cleavage and revolve around it. Political conflict, therefore, tends to be polarized and "totalizing," with sharp distinctions between alternative macrosocietal projects. In contrast, other social contexts provide for a multiplicity of cleavages in distinct issue spheres, none of which is dominant across the full range of issues. The latter structural context would be expected to give rise to more heterogeneous forms of collective action; while these partial, pluralist expressions of group interest could jointly target a broad range of issues, each of them would likely be limited to a particular issue domain, and none would provide a foundation for wholesale transformation of the social order.

(2) Concentration vs. Dispersion of Popular Sectors Whereas some social structures concentrate a large number of individuals together in close interaction, others isolate or disperse them more widely. This variable has both territorial and functional dimensions; that is, it can apply to work activities as well as residential patterns. A smallholding peasantry, for example, is likely to be dispersed both geographically and in productive relations, which inhibits class solidarity and collective action. This can be seen in Marx's famous description of the French peasantry as "a vast mass, the members of which live in similar conditions but without entering into manifold relations with one another. Their mode of production isolates them from one another instead of bringing them into mutual intercourse."[26] In contrast, workers in a large factory are concentrated in their work environment and interact closely in productive activities. Residents of a shantytown community are territorially concentrated but may engage in highly diverse economic activities. The legendary militancy of miners and other workers in isolated enclaves is generally attributed to their unusual combination of territorial and functional concentration, that is, their dense concentration in remote working communities that are conducive to the development of class solidarity and an autonomous political culture.[27]

(3) Homogeneity vs. Heterogeneity of Popular Sector Interests Whereas some structural conditions unify popular sectors around relatively homogeneous interests, others tend to fragment them along competing or heterogeneous interests. For example, social formations with a large, stable industrial labor force generate a relative commonality of interests among workers based on their shared structural location in the division of labor. Such conditions are more favorable to union organization and class-based collective action than a social formation with a highly segmented and differentiated labor market, as discussed below. In the political realm, authoritarian rule can provide a "negative referent" or common target against which diverse strands of opposition can unify and mobilize, whereas democracy removes this least common denominator and may divide popular sectors along competing partisan or group loyalties.[28]

(4) Clarity vs. Ambiguity of Interest Conflicts Many relationships of domination and exploitation can be obfuscated by paternalism or forms of hegemonic control, and social contexts differ significantly in the extent to which basic cleavages or conflicts of interest are readily identifiable by subaltern sectors. An independent indigenous community that lost its land to the encroachment of a hacienda is likely to have a clear target against which to mobilize, if the political environment is tolerant of such forms of mobilization. Likewise, a large factory environment or mining camp is likely to pose relatively clear and stable distinctions between the interests of labor and capital, which are conducive to class solidarity and collective action. In contrast, individuals who scrape out a living in the informal sector of the economy typically occupy an ambiguous class position because many do not participate in a steady wage labor relationship with an employer, and they may engage in small-scale entrepreneurial activities of their own. Such individuals are unlikely to identify fully as either workers or capitalists, and their economic activities do not necessarily bring them into continuous conflict with other class actors. Similarly, residents of an urban shantytown may develop an adversarial relationship to the state or government agencies in the process of articulating various claims, but they are just as likely to cultivate cooperative and clientelistic relationships to extract resources or benefits.[29] The structural location of shantytown communities

does not establish a homogenizing conflict of interest with outsiders, and the diversity of interests that they contain are conducive to heterogeneous political expressions.

Historically, the Left has assumed that social mobilization and
popular empowerment would be facilitated where there is a central
class cleavage between capital and labor, dense concentrations of
workers, a homogenization of working-class interests, and a sharp
differentiation of interests leading to class conflict. These assumptions flowed from Marx's analysis of the course of capitalist development. Marx assumed that capitalism would engender the proletarianization of the peasantry and the petite bourgeoisie, creating
a bipolar social formation with a central cleavage between workers
and capitalists. Industrialization was expected to concentrate an
ever larger number of workers in factory environments that would
homogenize conditions, engender class solidarity, and sharply differentiate class interests, eventually leading to social revolution.
The economic determinism of Marx's original formulation led to
the relative neglect of nonmaterial interests and social cleavages
other than those of class.

As Przeworski and others have demonstrated, capitalist development did not follow the course envisioned by Marx. Even in
Western Europe the industrial proletariat rarely constituted a nu-
merical majority, and industrialization created more complex and
differentiated social formations rather than dichotomous ones.[30]
The working class alone was an inadequate foundation for a socialist project, and European social democracy was most successful
where it articulated an agenda with multiclass appeal.[31] In Latin
American societies, where the industrial proletariat was much
smaller and politically weaker, the logical tendency was to create
multiclass, catch-all or populist parties rather than parties that appealed to narrow class interests or identities.[32]

Nevertheless, where the Left has been most successful historically in expanding the boundaries of political democracy—in the
northern European social democracies—it relied heavily on organic
ties to large, centrally organized labor movements. The industrial
workforce provided a stable and relatively cohesive constituency
for social democracy, one that was concentrated in large industrial establishments, shared basic interests in common (i.e., wages,

hours, legal rights, social benefits) as a result of comparable structural locations in the division of labor, and had easily identifiable common adversaries in the capital-owning classes. Although electoral success required a multiclass base of support, the organized working class was still at the core of social democratic political coalitions.

Likewise, in Latin America, where the Left has risen to electoral prominence—in Chile before 1973, in Peru in the late 1970s and early 1980s, in contemporary Brazil—strong, militant labor movements have been bastions of political support. Organized labor, in fact, has been at the core of the broad social and political networks built by the Left in these countries. These networks have incorporated diverse social actors, but they have often been radical in character and not merely additive. A radial network has a core actor in the center around which others tend to gravitate;[33] in Peru, for example, labor unions were a driving force in the creation of regional civic fronts that coordinated diverse social actors in the struggle against the military regime in the late 1970s,[34] and they were a primary source for the diffusion of a class-conscious, adversarial political culture to shantytown communities.[35] Labor movements have thus provided a sizable core political constituency, a national organizational structure, social activists with political experience and organizing skills, and a capacity for social outreach that diffuses organizational models and methods of collective action to other sectors of civil society. A strong, centralized labor movement is hardly a sufficient condition for a powerful political Left, as the Argentine case demonstrates, and the Latin American experience provides ample evidence of labor unions whose pursuit of narrow, particularistic interests leaves them isolated from broader forms of social organization. Nevertheless, a strong labor movement may well be a necessary condition because the region does not provide an example of sustained leftist strength in the absence of organic ties to powerful unions.

If this is the case, recent structural changes in Latin American societies pose a serious challenge to the Left rivaling that posed by the collapse of the traditional socialist teleology.[36] The import-substitution industrialization model of development that dominated the region from the Great Depression of the 1930s until the onset of the debt crisis in the 1980s encouraged the growth of significant concentrations of workers in large, protected industries. Unionization was promoted by leftist and populist parties and, at times, by states that were willing to extend organizational rights and social benefits in exchange for political support and corporatist controls. Although organized labor remained weaker than in Europe, it was nevertheless a significant political force and the fulcrum of popular sector organizing strategies.[37]

This situation changed dramatically, however, with the onset of the debt crisis in the early 1980s and the neoliberal structural adjustments that followed. Hyperinflation, economic stabilization, recession, and free market reforms have had a devastating effect on labor movements in Latin America. In much of the region, deindustrialization and government spending cuts led to massive layoffs of workers in heavily unionized sectors of the economy such as basic industries and public services. Labor movements were further undermined by neoliberal reforms that were designed to enhance business competitiveness and create more "flexible" labor markets by reducing job security guarantees, scaling back government regulations, and facilitating the use of temporary contract labor.

Whereas Marx expected capitalist development to lead to proletarianization and a homogenization of working-class interests, Latin America has experienced a process of deproletarianization and structural differentiation of the workforce. Indeed, even in the European bastions of social democracy, industrial reorganization has led to a dispersion and differentiation of the workforce, in the process eroding the mobilizational capacities and policy leverage of labor unions and leftist parties.[38] The new structural conditions erect serious impediments to class-based collective action. These impediments have little to do with the free rider problem, however, as they are rooted in the severing of social networks that undergird the construction of collective identities and the recognition of common interests. This severing can be seen in several different areas.

The first is the segmentation or structural heterogeneity of the workforce and the fragmentation of interests that follows. As the number of permanent workers in the formal sector has declined, more and more individuals have turned to temporary contract labor or the informal sector of the economy to survive. The interests of these distinct sectors are diffuse and often incongruent: the issues of employment security, wage indexation, and public benefits that galvanize unions in the formal sector may have little salience to temporary or informal workers who do not receive legal protections or entitlements.[39] Indeed, unions and their affiliated parties may be relegated to the defense of the particularistic interests of a relatively privileged sector of the workforce, a role that makes it exceedingly difficult for them to serve as the axis of a broader, popular project for the deepening of democracy. The heterogeneity of interests makes it increasingly difficult to craft a common agenda, much less construct a collective identity on the basis of a conception of shared fate.

Second, as the process of informalization proceeds—it surpassed 50 percent of the economically active population in Peru during the crisis of the late 1980s and early 1990s—there is an increasing dispersion of the workforce.[40] Fewer workers are concentrated in stable wage labor positions in large productive establishments, where there is close interaction and a relative commonality of interests based on the division of labor. Increasingly, productive activities are subcontracted out to smaller enterprises that rely on fewer workers and precarious forms of employment.[41] In the informal sector, work is typically done independently or in small groups that revolve around personal or familial entrepreneurial networks.[42] Economic activities in the informal sector are diverse, fragmented, and small in scale; they thus produce a range of interests that are poorly connected to each other, and they do not provide the forms of social interaction or interdependence that engender large-scale collective action.

Third, informal economic activities are far less conducive to the construction of collective identities than traditional wage labor. Informal workers tend to rely on individual initiative and personal contacts to advance, rather than collective action. Indeed, given their conditions of labor and ambiguous class positions, those in informal sectors may not identify as workers at all. Consequently, in a society with an informalized, deproletarianized workforce, the centrality of the capital-labor cleavage invariably diminishes, and it no longer serves as the axis of popular mobilization. There may be acute socioeconomic inequalities and a large percentage of the population living in poverty, but class cleavages are likely to be obfuscated so that they no longer provide a foundation for collective action among subaltern sectors.

In such a context, the dilemma is not merely one of the shrinkage of organized labor or the diminution of its political weight. It is, more fundamentally, the loss of its centrality, or the erosion of its radial potential as the fulcrum of popular sector organizing strategies. The new social structure in Latin America transforms organized labor into yet another special interest group, one that is looking out for the particular interests of a narrow constituency. Under such conditions, labor can make no claim to a universal mission, nor can it anchor a counterhegemonic project. As O'Donnell argues, economic crisis and social dislocation have eviscerated collective social projects, as individuals adopt a survival mentality that has a short time horizon and an orientation toward self-protection that produces a "generalized de-solidarization" and disaggregation of social life.[43]

If there is no dominant cleavage, no axial conflict to structure social mobilization, there can be no universal social or political subject, as in the classical Marxist view of the proletariat. It is at least partly in response to this structural constraint that the Latin American Left has turned to new social movements in an effort to renew its political project. But is it possible for new forms of local, community-based organizations to compensate for the weakness of large-scale secondary associations? And can a multitude of partial or discrete collective subjects, none serving as the linchpin to an alternative social order, energize a broader process of social transformation that challenges entrenched structures of hierarchy and domination? It is on these questions that the potentiality for deepening democracy rests.

Decentralized Collective Action and the Challenge of Political Coordination

Whereas Marx expected social transformation to erupt from the homogenization of popular interests that results from bipolar class conflict, most contemporary scholarship has located it in the cumulative, syncretic articulation of heterogeneous and decentralized collective subjects, each manifesting a unique cultural or political identity and pressing a distinct set of claims in the public arena.[44] Identity approaches to the study of social movements assume that modern capitalism has diminished the centrality of class cleavages and put a plethora of new issues and conflicts on the political agenda, with new collective identities emerging out of the struggle to give meaning to novel forms of cultural and political contestation.[45] This emphasis on heterogeneity is an important advance, as it recognizes the significance of collective action that is grounded in gender, ethnicity, community, and other nonclass identities, and it breaks with the stifling economic determinism of classical Marxism. Nevertheless, this approach has not adequately addressed the challenge of creating horizontal linkages to articulate diverse collective subjects; indeed, to the extent that it emphasizes the autonomous expression of discrete movements, it is often wary of political linkages that skew or mediate such expressions. Consequently, it has yet to clarify, in theory much less in practice, the forms of political praxis that can lead to cumulative changes in the power relationships and structural inequalities of Latin American societies. Although many scholars have warned against judging new social movements against such exacting standards, the project of the Left clearly links these movements to macro-level societal changes, and it needs to be evaluated according to its established objectives.[46]

Following the theoretical insights of Gramsci and Michel Foucault, the Left's new conception of transformative politics sees power relations as broadly diffused through a multitude of social interactions and not narrowly concentrated at the level of state institutions.[47] The struggle for social transformation, therefore, occurs at multiple points in civil society and is driven by the political protagonism of diverse social actors, from labor unions to neighborhood associations, ecclesial base communities, women's groups, human rights organizations, and other forms of grass-roots collective action. For this new conception of political agency, social transformation is not directed from above following the conquest of state power by a party or guerrilla vanguard. Instead, it occurs in a decentralized manner through a multiplicity of grass-roots initiatives and eventually percolates upward through the cumulative modification of power relations.

However compelling in theory, this logic of social transformation is subject to problems of both collective action and social coordination. The collective action problem is rooted in the widespread tendency of the poor to opt for individual measures to address their problems rather than some form of horizontal organization. Patron-client relationships are a time-honored example of this strategy, whereby individuals cultivate a personal relationship with a patron of higher social status who can offer employment or some other material benefit in exchange for political support or personal services.[48] These reciprocal exchanges are inherently asymmetrical and exploitative, but they remain attractive in a context where economic opportunities are limited and the benefits from collective political action are seen as remote. Patron-clientelism creates vertical linkages that are contrary to the horizontal ties of class or community that undergird collective action. Alternatively, many individuals have opted for independent entrepreneurial activities in the informal economy, trying to carve out a market niche that will allow for economic survival in a context of limited employment options. Although this strategy does not necessarily entail vertical linkages to a patron and occasionally generates forms of sectoral organization within market niches, it represents a very different logic for advancement than that of collective action. For all the attention directed to grass-roots organizations in Latin America, the fact remains that their members are a small minority among popular sectors;[49] the heart of the collective action problem resides in the proclivity of the atomized majority to pursue individualist solutions to their problems.

Moreover, the political expressions of this atomized majority are hardly conducive to a strategy of deepening democracy. If fluid and precarious socioeconomic relationships erode the social networks required to sustain collective action, they also inhibit the development of stable political loyalties and representative institutions. Castañeda is right when he asserts that the demise of the working class and the spread of the urban poor have undermined the social foundations for a reformist democratic project and created a potential constituency for extremist movements like the

Shining Path in Peru.[50] But the most common political response of the urban poor to their plight is not revolution but some variant of populism, that is, a direct, unmediated attachment to a personalist leader who symbolizes strong authority, embodies the yearning for political and economic change, and induces support through the manipulation of patronage or clientelist ties.[51] As the social and economic crisis of the 1980s weakened such representative institutions as political parties and labor unions, new forms of populism emerged to fill the political void, often binding popular sectors to autocratic political projects that culminated in neoliberal reforms.[52] In many nations, autonomous forms of collective action lost ground to the populist temptation, as the poor put their faith in a popular *caudillo* rather than their own organizing efforts.

Even where individuals opt for collective action over individual initiatives or political autocracy, there remains the challenge of social and political coordination, or the horizontal linkage of decentralized forms of organization. For the Left's project of deepening democracy to be successful, means have to be found to translate diverse forms of micro-level collective action into a cumulative process of change that modifies macro-level structures of domination expressed in state institutions and productive relations. As Barros points out, the discrete and often particularistic discontents expressed by grass-roots actors do not translate automatically into a unified project for social and political transformation.[53] Indeed, according to Tarrow, these forms of collective action may suffer from "the defects of their virtues" because by "encouraging base autonomy and allowing activists free spaces of democracy and participation, they permit—and indeed encourage—a lack of coordination and discontinuity."[54]

Several problems stand out when assessing the transformative potential of these organizations: they are generally local in scale, with limited projection onto the national political scene;[55] they are often isolated and disconnected from each other, in part because of their insistence on political autonomy; and they generally focus on immediate, particularistic needs or partial demands that do not have generalized appeal, do not project a comprehensive ideological vision, and do not challenge macro-level structures of political or economic power.[56] Therefore, the political praxis of grass-roots actors may enhance personal autonomy or collective self-determination in local spheres of interaction, but such changes, however laudable in their own right, may remain too fragmented or isolated to impinge on the reproduction of macro-level power structures. A community soup kitchen, for example, can empower local actors by extending collective controls over the procurement and distribution of scarce food resources. Frequently, however, such forms of collective action are crisis-induced survival strategies that remain on the margins of the dominant economic order, more of a refuge from market inequalities than a force to transform them. Likewise, women's groups have played a vital role in raising consciousness of patriarchal domination in private spheres as well as public institutions. But if the personal is political, making household relations a valid sphere for democratization, it nevertheless remains distant from the public realm of state institutions, as well as the economic realm of inequality based on property ownership. To have an impact on these realms, the struggle against gender-based inequalities requires effective articulation with forms of collective action that are directed against other spheres of social and political domination.

The logic of segmented democracy is to separate and fragment such forms of collective action into discrete, particularistic struggles that can be selectively accommodated or neutralized. In short, the social corollary to segmented democracy is a form of segmented collectivism that keeps popular actors self-contained in their democratizing potential so as to preclude a cumulative process of popular empowerment. Segmented collectivism does little to overcome the structural fragmentation of popular interests in Latin America; indeed, it is a reflection of it, showing the importance of structural factors in shaping the form and content of collective action. In a striking twist, structural changes in Latin America have partially reversed the cumulative historical process identified by Tarrow in which collective action evolves from local, immediate, and particularistic claims to more integrated and overarching national movements.[57] If the development of industrial capitalism spawned the first shift analyzed by Tarrow, the crisis and subsequent restructuring of capitalism in contemporary Latin America have driven its reversal.

The process of articulation and integration—of building horizontal linkages that overcome self-containment—thus emerges as the crux of the dilemma for deepening and extending forms of democratic self-determination. Such a process, however, is fraught with difficulties. As Debra Friedman and Doug McAdam argue, social movement organizations may broaden the scope of their mission in an effort to appeal to new groups, but in the process they may actually narrow their "field of potential participants." Goal or issue expansion can engender new internal conflicts, obfuscate basic objectives, and dilute collective identities. As such, "social movement organizations that attempt to construct all-purpose collective identities may . . . appeal to a narrower audience than those that stand fast to a more limited conception."[58] Not surprisingly, in contexts where interests are fragmented and encompassing collective identities are absent, it is often easier to integrate diffuse popular sectors around a charismatic figure—the populist or "delegative" solution—rather than through large-scale representative institutions.

Furthermore, to build horizontal linkages presumes some form of coordination and thus the creation of intermediary organizational forms. This necessarily implies, however, some sacrifice of organizational autonomy on the part of grass-roots collective actors, something that many groups are loath to accept, given the negative historical memories of corporatist state control or instrumentalization by political parties. Autonomy emerged as a primary value for many of the popular organizations that developed under authoritarian rule because it was a logical correlate of their self-constitution and a necessary condition for the creation of political space for independent self-expression. The problem they confront is that absolute autonomy is incompatible with the desire to overcome political self-containment because it is a recipe for isolation and marginalization. As Ernesto Laclau suggests, autonomy and articulation correspond to competing logics.[59] To have sustained impact on the broader political arena, that arena has to be engaged institutionally, a process that is virtually inconceivable without horizontal organizational linkages.

Horizontal coordination does not necessarily imply that popular organizations have to work through party intermediaries. Numerous efforts have been made to link diverse social organizations at local, regional, and even national levels while bypassing formal party institutions. As Orlando Fals Borda demonstrates, these linkages can help fill the void left by the failure of political parties to channel popular demands adequately into the political arena.[60] Nevertheless, social organizations generally do not have representation or direct access to decision-making levers in parliamentary bodies or other state institutions. While corporatist arrangements may facilitate representation by centralized peak associations, they do not incorporate the multitude of discrete, decentralized social organizations operating at grass-roots levels. Typically, then, social movements are left on the margins of the decision-making process under formal democratic institutions: they may lobby government agencies, put pressure on political parties, or protest in the streets, but they are located outside the mainsprings of decision-making power, and their institutional access is generally mediated by other actors.[61]

Therefore, despite efforts to construct new forms of direct participation by social movements in the political process, there remains a strong proclivity for some form of party mediation as a response to the problems of political coordination and institutional access.[62] Parties are the privileged agents of representation in liberal democracy, given their aggregative function in the electoral process, and social movements have yet to spawn institutional alternatives to fulfill parties' basic functions. The relationship between parties and social movements is invariably problematic, as the process of mediation is bound to compromise the autonomy of social movements, and it can never fully translate social concerns into political action. Nevertheless, this intersection between social movements and political parties lies at the heart of the Left's democratic project because it provides a political organization to serve as a potential agent of social integration. As explained below, the party-movement nexus offers several alternative models for this process of social integration, each with important implications for the project of deepening democracy.

The Challenge of Political Agency:
Parties as an Integrative Force

It is widely recognized that the strength of political parties is not necessarily associated with the vitality of social movements; indeed, the two may be inversely related. The emergence of new social movements may reflect the repression of traditional political parties or their exhaustion and delegitimation as agents of representation.[63] Likewise, the resurgence of parties during democratic transitions may precipitate the demobilization of social movements, as parties often inject competing loyalties into popular organizations, channel grass-roots activists and energies out of social work and into electoral activities, or try to dampen social mobilization in the interests of political stability.[64]

Nevertheless, there are several ways that parties can strengthen social movements or enhance their transformative potential. Parties are a primary source of political entrepreneurs, the activists who undertake the basic tasks of organization and recruitment at the grass-roots level.[65] Especially under conditions of military dictatorship, when openly partisan tasks are prohibited, underground party activists may play a vital role in the reconstruction of social networks and popular organizations.[66] Parties or party activists may also provide a broader ideological vision that can "frame" social problems in ways that manifest their structural dimensions and encourage collective rather than individualist solutions.[67] Parties may be able to provide organizational resources such as skilled cadres, material resources, and means of communication that can help overcome the social transaction costs of collective action. Finally, they provide broader, often national-scale organizational networks that can facilitate horizontal linkages between base-level groups, and they are a major channel of access to the formal institutions of representation and governance.

There is no necessary reason, then, why parties and social movements cannot complement each other. But there is no consensual formula on how to do this, and parties have entered into a variety of relationships with social movements. Three basic models of party-movement articulation can be identified in the Latin

American Left. The first might be called the vanguard model because it has deep roots in the Leninist tradition. This model is
associated with hierarchically organized parties that have cellular
structures and highly disciplined cadres or militants. These cadres
are deeply inserted in organizational work in the social terrain,
whether it be with labor unions, peasant associations, student
groups, urban popular organizations, or others. In this nexus, however, the party is paramount; social work is seen as an extension of
party organizing, as an effort to build social bases for the party's
political project. There is a tendency, then, for the party to try to
establish political control over diverse forms of social organization
and to shape collective action in conformance with the party's political objectives.

The second model might be called the organic model because it
is associated with parties, such as the Workers' Party in Brazil, that
emerge as the political expression of organized groups in civil society. In the organic model, distinctions between the party and its
constituent social organizations are deliberately blurred; indeed,
the party may appear to be more of a movement than an apparatus
for electoral contestation, as it is directly engaged in social struggles outside the sphere of institutional politics, and party members
and leaders are drawn directly from social movements rather than
from the ranks of a separate, professional political caste. Although
tensions inevitably arise between the social and electoral spheres
of activity, organic parties try to avoid subordinating their social
work to the logic of political power, in contrast to vanguard parties.[68] Likewise, given their genesis in diverse forms of popular
organization, organic parties tend to be more open, inclusive, and
pluralistic in their organizational structure, with less hierarchical
control and more political space for democratic participation at the
grass roots.

Finally, the electoralist model is associated with parties that
give priority to the mobilization of an electoral constituency, as
opposed to the construction of popular collective subjects in civil
society. These parties are likely to respect the autonomy of social
organizations, in part because their political project is less contingent on the support of collective actors. Instead, it is focused on
garnering the broadest possible base of electoral support, which

means reaching beyond organized social constituencies to attract the mass of unorganized and often independent voters. One variant of the electoralist model emphasizes the construction of a catch-all political party that can appeal to an amorphous, multiclass electoral constituency.[69] A second variant is more populist in character, using the personalist appeal of a charismatic leader to aggregate diverse constituencies in the electoral arena.

As Panebianco states, "There is a strict connection between parties' activities and their internal organization."[70] It is not surprising, then, that these different modes of articulation are closely related to specific types of political programs and organizational characteristics in leftist parties. Vanguard parties tend to be more ideologically rigid, given their disciplinary norms and sectarian organizational structure. In contrast, organic parties need to be ideologically pluralistic, while electoralist parties invariably dilute ideological objectives and adopt a moderate, pragmatic political style to avoid alienating potential voters. Vanguard parties are hierarchical and centralized, but they have highly developed base-level structures and devoted core constituencies organized into exclusive cadres. Organic parties try to mobilize a mass base, and they are likely to be factionalized, decentralized, inclusive, and participatory. Finally, electoralist parties tend to be top-heavy, with prominent leaders who remain in the public eye and base-level structures that are activated only during electoral campaigns. As such, they are inclined toward a combination of technocracy and clientelism when given access to governmental office.

Given their organizational discipline and cellular structure, vanguard parties often thrive under authoritarian rule because they have ideologically committed cadres with an unparallelled capacity to do underground political work in diverse social networks. These cadres supply many of the "early risers" who are at the forefront of the protest waves that often emerge with the first visible cracks in authoritarian regimes.[71] These same characteristics, however, make vanguard parties too narrow and sectarian to achieve electoral success in a competitive democratic environment. Electoralist parties are the opposite: they may enter into remission under authoritarian rule because they do not have the base-level structures required for effective work in the social terrain, especially if repression mandates clandestine operation. Yet they can explode on the political scene when public space for electoral contestation opens, given their capacity to mobilize periodic electoral support among sectors of the populace that are not permanently active. Organic parties are more flexible because they are capable of operating effectively in both authoritarian and democratic contexts, but they are likely to have difficulty expanding their electoral support much beyond their organized social constituencies since their demanding, participatory logic limits their natural appeal to activist circles. The exception is when these organized social constituencies become linked to charismatic leaders with broad appeal, creating a hybrid between the organic model and the populist electoral model, as can be seen at one point or another with Luís Ignacio "Lula" da Silva in Brazil, Cuauhtémoc Cárdenas in Mexico, Alfonso Barrantes in Peru, and Tabaré Vázquez in Uruguay.[72] The challenge, then, is to find formulas to aggregate diverse and often atomized popular interests without slipping into populist forms of mobilization that engender hierarchical control or displace the autonomous protagonism of organized popular subjects.[73]

These different models of party organization and party-movement articulation will take concrete form in the case studies that follow. The Communist Party in Chile and the Unified Mariateguista Party (PUM) in Peru are classic embodiments of the vanguard mode. Catch-all electoralist parties will be represented by the Chilean Socialist Party and its offspring, the Party for Democracy (PPD). The populist variant of the electoralist model will find expression in the personalist project of Alfonso Barrantes in Peru. The organic model will be ubiquitous in the discourse of virtually all of these actors, demonstrating the impact of Lula and the PT on the collective imagination of the Latin American Left; the failure of all these actors to develop institutions and political practices that conform to their discourse is indicative of the sui generis character of the Brazilian phenomenon.

These case studies provide evidence of a double paradox that afflicts efforts to deepen democracy in Latin America, one that is rooted in the character of political agency under the structural constraints of a fragmented social order. The first paradox is that the strength of a leftist party in civil society is no guarantee of success

in the electoral realm; in fact, in contrast to the historical experience in Western Europe, it may not even be a good indicator of
electoral strength.[74] It follows, then, that electoral success is not
contingent on a party's organizational strength in civil society. The
second paradox is that the electoral success of the partisan Left does
not necessarily contribute to the deepening of democracy. Indeed,
the requisites for electoral success are frequently in tension with
such a deepening because a context of social fragmentation encourages populist or catch-all electoralist strategies that bypass autonomous organizational expressions in civil society. It is only by
unlocking these paradoxes that it is possible to understand the
obstacles to the deepening of democracy in Latin America.

PART II

Dictatorship, Democracy, and the Left in Chile

CHAPTER 4

Authoritarian Rule and the
Transformation of the Chilean Left

ON March 11, 1990, Patricio Aylwin assumed the presidency of Chile as the country's first elected head of state after nearly seventeen years of harsh military dictatorship. Aylwin's candidacy was sponsored by a multiparty, Center-Left coalition that was anchored by his own Christian Democratic Party and the Chilean Socialist Party. The coalition government maneuvered cautiously within the institutional constraints bequeathed by the military regime of General Augusto Pinochet, and it negotiated modest political and economic reforms with conservative opposition parties that had only recently been supporters of authoritarian rule. In marked contrast to the ideological polarization and political conflicts of the recent past, the new democratic regime demonstrated a penchant for consensus building that attracted the appellation of *la democracia de los acuerdos*, or "the democracy of agreements."[1] After four years of political stability, low inflation, and sustained economic growth, Aylwin stepped down as the most popular president in Chile's modern history, and the governing coalition won a landslide reelection under the leadership of the Christian Democrat Eduardo Frei.

A country that for nearly two decades was synonymous with the worst abuses of authoritarianism has thus been restored to its historic position as a showcase of Latin American democracy. Although Chile was a latecomer to the most recent wave of regime transitions in the region, it became quickly and widely recognized as a paradigmatic case of successful redemocratization. O'Donnell has favorably noted the comparative strength of Chile's representative institutions,[2] while Gerardo Munck has hailed its rapid progress toward democratic consolidation, claiming that Chile "has undoubtedly made greater strides toward democratic consolidation than any other country in Latin America."[3] The reelection of Chile's Center-Left coalition was a political landmark in a region where voters have routinely turned out incumbents who have been buffeted by economic crises and political corruption.[4]

Since the pressure for a democratic transition began to build in the mid-1980s, it has become commonplace to speak of the moderation and ideological "secularization" of Chile's new, and putatively more democratic, political culture.[5] This secularization is, at least in part, a myth; the Chilean Right has historically been able to recognize and defend its interests, but never before have these interests been embedded in such a distinctive and all-encompassing ideological vision as they are today under neoliberalism. A process of secularization on the Left, however, has fundamentally altered the political role and strategic orientation of the Chilean Socialist Party. The consensus-building proclivities of Chile's democratic regime have been supported by the new disposition of the centrist Christian Democrats to broker agreements and anchor a broad governing coalition,[6] a reflection, perhaps, of the political lessons drawn from their earlier role in the polarization and breakdown of Chilean democracy in the 1960s and 1970s.[7] But the moderation of political conflict under the new democratic regime is more than anything attributable to the basic shift from a polarizing to an integrative role on the part of the Socialist Party, along with the attendant marginalization of the more radical Communist Party. These changes in the Left made the Christian Democrats more receptive to an alliance, and they dampened the fears of conservative forces that redemocratization would precipitate a renewal of ideological conflict or grass-roots pressure for radical change.

Indeed, the transformation of the Left has produced a fundamental modification of the Chilean party system. The party system in Chile before the 1973 breakdown of democracy was noted for the depth of its ideological polarization, which produced high levels of political conflict and a centrifugal pattern of competition.[8] In contrast, the new party system is marked by an integrative character and centripetal competitive dynamics. These new systemic dynamics can be understood only in the context of the highly contentious patterns of change that occurred in the Chilean Left under the military dictatorship.

Two basic paradoxes underlie the political transformation of the Chilean Left. The first is the "crisscrossing" of the Socialist and Communist Parties under authoritarian rule. The two parties had been the pillars of Salvador Allende's proposed "peaceful road to socialism" between 1970 and 1973, but in that era the Socialists represented the more radical, "revolutionary" position in Allende's Popular Unity coalition, whereas the Communists adopted a more cautious, moderate approach to political and socioeconomic change. As an architect of the *vía pacífica*, or peaceful road, the Communist Party favored multiclass political alliances, pragmatic changes in property relations, strict adherence to constitutional legality, and negotiated compromise with opposition forces. In contrast, the Socialist Party advocated a more narrow, class-based "Workers' Front" alliance and rapid economic socialization. Believing that revolutionary armed confrontation was inevitable on the road to socialism, the Socialists resisted Allende's efforts to negotiate a compromise with the opposition, and they sought to create grass-roots organs of "popular power" as an alternative to "bourgeois" democracy.

The two parties extracted very different lessons from the failure of Allende's experiment in democratic socialism, however, and they reversed positions under the Pinochet dictatorship.[9] Political defeat and military repression engendered a process of radicalization in the Communist Party, which eventually took up arms against Pinochet, only to be left standing on the sidelines as moderates negotiated a return to democratic rule under military tutelage. In contrast, the Socialist Party underwent a self-critical and highly divisive process of ideological renovation that centered on the "revaluation" of democracy. After a painful internal schism, the moderate Socialist faction broke with the party's long-standing Communist allies and initiated a new partnership with the Christian Democrats and other centrist forces in an effort to extricate Pinochet from power. This new alliance made the Socialists a central actor in Chile's democratic transition and the first party with Marxist roots to assume major national-level governmental responsibilities during Latin America's contemporary wave of democratization.

The second paradox results from a shift in the relative strength of the Socialist and Communist Parties during the final years of the dictatorship and the period of democratic transition. The Socialist and Communist Parties were roughly equal partners during their alliance in the 1960s and early 1970s, and both were severely repressed in the aftermath of the 1973 military coup that overthrew Allende. The Communist Party was considerably stronger in the clandestine struggle against the Pinochet regime through the mid-1980s, however, and it was a more vital force in the wave of mass protests that rocked the regime between 1983 and 1986. Its previous clandestine experience, along with its hierarchical authority and disciplined cellular structure, enabled the Communist Party to maintain its institutional coherence and organizational presence in civil society more effectively under military repression. The party and its militants were thus able to play an integral role in the survival and recomposition of collective democratic subjects in the labor, student, and urban popular movements. In contrast, the Socialist Party splintered under the pressures of authoritarian rule, and its various factions were secondary actors to the more powerful Communist and Christian Democratic Parties in defining the strategic alternatives and shaping the dynamics of Chile's democratic resistance. The Socialist Party was so preoccupied with its internal conflicts and emasculated by organizational dispersion that it had a limited capacity to project itself in civil society or to activate the associational networks that eventually laid the foundation for Chile's democratic transition.

The irony, then, is that the Socialist Party emerged as the dominant force on the Left during the democratic transition, enabling it to reap electoral rewards that belied its earlier organizational weakness and dispersion. What makes this irony even more perplexing is that the faction of the Socialist Party with the most tenuous links to social movements eventually asserted its hegemony over the ideological discourse and strategic practice of the Chilean Left. This paradox—the gap between what parties sow in the resistance to authoritarianism and what they reap in the process of democratic transition—is indicative of the competitive advantages and disadvantages held by vanguardist and electoralist parties in different political contexts. Equally important, it provides important insights as to why social mobilization so often accelerates as authoritarian regimes enter into crisis, only to wane as the process of democratization comes to be structured by electoral competition and elite-level compromises. It is widely believed that the deactivation of social movements can be attributed, in part, to their displacement by reemerging political parties.[10] The Chilean case suggests that social movements may decline not only because they are displaced by parties but because they are linked to parties that themselves enter into decline during the process of democratization. Both phenomena, in turn, are associated with the emergence of democratic regimes that are prone to elitist patterns of decision making and a cautious pragmatism toward the modification of the political and economic legacies of authoritarianism.

As will be shown, the institutional constraints and social dislocations left behind by the military regime have erected serious obstacles to the deepening of democracy in Chile. Other obstacles exist, however, that are related to the realignment of the partisan Left, particularly the shift in the balance of power from a movement-oriented Left to an electoralist Left that gives priority to democratic consolidation. This shift has enhanced the integrative role of the Left under the new democratic regime and buttressed the conflict-regulating capacity of democratic institutions. It has not, however, encouraged the popular participation for the deepening of democracy that was an integral component of the Socialist Party's ideological redefinition under authoritarian rule. Neither has this participation emerged spontaneously from the highly fragmented civil society that is a defining feature of the neoliberal revolution initiated under Pinochet and sustained by his democratic successors. Chile thus provides an unusually clear example of the tensions the Left may face between the deepening and consolidation of political democracy.

Prelude to Crisis: The Development of the
Left and the Chilean Road to Socialism

The Chilean Left has had more extensive experience with efforts to deepen democracy than any other in Latin America, and perhaps no other Left has been so thoroughly shaped by the successes and failures of such efforts. For most of the 40 years before the 1973 coup, Chile boasted both the strongest socialist party and the strongest communist party electorally in the entire region. The development of a powerful Left with a solid base of working-class support helped to create a party system that was more similar to those in Europe than the rest of Latin America, with a "three-thirds" division among distinct leftist, centrist, and rightist tendencies, each supported by close to a third of the electorate.

Historically, the Left's "third" was deeply embedded in the strength and militancy of the Chilean labor movement.[11] The Communist Party traces its roots back to the founding of the Workers' Socialist Party (POS) by a small group of miners and shoemakers in the northern port of Iquique in 1912. Under the guidance of the legendary printer, journalist, and labor organizer Luís Emilio Recabarren, the POS quickly developed a small but vibrant national organization, establishing branches in working-class sectors of Santiago and southern cities to complement its core base of support in the nitrate mining regions of Chile's northern desert. In contrast to the anarcho-syndicalists who also wielded influence in Chile's growing labor movement, Recabarren believed it was essential for the working class to organize itself into a political party and take advantage of legal democratic channels to advance its interests.[12]

Following the Russian Revolution, Recabarren established ties with the Comintern, and the POS changed its name to the Communist Party in 1922.[13] The party adapted its organizational structure to the Leninist norms of democratic centralism in the late 1920s under the authoritarian regime of Carlos Ibáñez, when the party experienced its first period of clandestinity. Although the Communist Party did not fully adhere to the Comintern's sectarian "class against class" line of this period, it declined to support the small socialist and military factions led by Marmaduke Grove that founded Chile's short-lived "Socialist Republic" following a coup in June 1932. In the mid-1930s, however, as the Comintern shifted to an antifascist "popular front" line, the party became an advocate of broad, multiclass social and political alliances for democratic reform.[14] In one form or another, the party maintained this stance for nearly half a century, until it finally took up arms against the Pinochet dictatorship in 1980. The party's line under the democratic regime that lasted from 1933 until 1973 presumed that socialist revolution was not on the immediate political agenda. Consequently, socialism would have to be preceded by a stage of democratic and capitalist development led by a broad alliance of anti-imperialist and antioligarchic forces, including the middle class and the national bourgeoisie in addition to workers and peasants.

This strategic orientation created a disposition for alliance building that began to bear fruit after the founding of the Socialist Party in 1933. Following the collapse of the Socialist Republic after only twelve days, four small groups converged to create the Socialist Party, adopting a relatively open and pluralistic conception of Marxism along with a nationalistic, Latin Americanist stance. From the outset, the Socialist Party served as a pole of attraction for diverse leftist groups seeking a viable alternative to the ideological orthodoxy, organizational rigidity, and international loyalties of the Communist Party. Thus the Socialist Party was born—and remained—an open, inclusive, and heterogeneous organization that rather awkwardly aggregated left-wing freemasons, populists, and democratic socialists under the same flag as revolutionary Marxists, Trotskyists, and anarcho-syndicalists.[15]

The Socialist Party quickly developed a base of support among workers and the middle class. The party helped organize a new labor confederation shortly after its birth, which joined with Communist and Radical Party–backed unions to found the Confederation of Chilean Workers in 1936. In contrast to the Communists, the Socialists advocated a more restrictive "United Workers' Front" alliance between manual and intellectual labor, eschewing political ties with business groups. Nevertheless, they joined the Communist Party and the centrist Radical Party in a Popular Front coalition in 1938. The Popular Front elected three successive Radi-

TABLE 4.1. *Percentage of the Vote Received by Major Chilean Parties in Congressional Elections, 1937–73*

Party	1937	1941	1945	1949	1953	1957	1961	1965	1969	1973
Right										
Conservative	21.3	17.2	23.6	22.7	14.4	17.6	14.3	5.2	–	–
Liberal	20.7	14.0	20.1	19.3	10.9	15.4	16.1	7.3	–	–
National	–	–	–	–	–	–	–	–	20.0	21.3
Center										
Radical	18.7	23.0	19.9	27.7	15.6	22.1	21.4	13.3	13.0	3.7
Christian	–	3.4	2.6	3.9	2.9	9.4	15.4	42.3	29.8	29.1
Democratic										
Left										
Socialist	11.2	22.1	12.8	9.4	14.2	10.7	10.7	10.3	12.2	18.7
Communist	4.2	11.8	10.3	–	–	–	11.4	12.4	15.9	16.2
Others	23.9	8.5	10.7	17.0	42.0	24.8	10.7	9.2	9.1	11.0

SOURCE: Adapted from Arturo Valenzuela, *The Breakdown of Democratic Regimes: Chile* (Baltimore: Johns Hopkins University Press, 1978), p. 35.

cal presidents between 1938 and 1946, and the Socialist Party accepted several cabinet positions. The electoral strength of the Left increased rapidly during the early period of the Popular Front, as the Socialists obtained 22.1 percent of the vote and the Communists another 11.8 percent in the 1941 congressional elections (see Table 4.1).

The limited scope of reforms, however, made participation in a coalition government led by a centrist party highly divisive for the Socialists. The Socialist Party formally withdrew from the Popular Front in 1941, although it temporarily retained its cabinet positions. A series of divisions in 1940, 1943, 1948, and 1952 left the Socialist Party substantially weakened and eroded its willingness to enter into alliances with centrist forces. Support for the various Socialist factions fell to 9.4 percent of the vote in the congressional elections of 1949. The Communist Party, in contrast, saw its support rise to 17 percent of the vote in the 1947 municipal elections, and the party briefly accepted three cabinet positions in the third Popular Front government led by President Gabriel González Videla. In 1948, however, Cold War tensions, an increase in labor unrest, and fear of the Communists' growth led González Videla to betray his allies. The Communist Party was outlawed and repressed, reducing its membership from 30,000 in 1946 to only 5,000 to 10,000 in 1950.[16] The party thus began its second period of clandestinity, which lasted, in modified form, until it was relegalized in 1958.[17]

A faction of the Socialist Party made a final effort to build broad coalitions by briefly supporting the populist government of former military dictator Carlos Ibáñez, who was elected to the presidency in 1952. A second faction led by Senator Salvador Allende, however, worked to rebuild an alliance with the underground Communist Party, thus launching the basic coalition that would be the axis of the Left's electoral strategy for the next twenty years. The Socialist Party was reunited in 1957 behind a strict "Workers' Front" line that eschewed multiclass coalitions, and it joined the Communist Party and two smaller Left parties in an electoral alliance that narrowly missed electing Allende to the presidency in 1958. Allende received 28.6 percent of the vote, compared to 31.2 percent for the rightist candidate Jorge Alessandri[18] (see Table 4.2). Although the Communist Party continued to advocate a broader alliance, the 1958 election demonstrated that the Left could aspire to executive office on its own with a mere plurality among Chile's three-thirds.

Furthermore, changes in the social and political landscape were favorable to the strengthening of the Left. The import-substitution industrialization policies of the Popular Front era expanded the social base for labor union organizing, and urban union membership more than quintupled between 1932 and 1952.[19] Union member-

TABLE 4.2. *Results of the 1958, 1964, and 1970 Presidential Elections*

1958		1964		1970	
Candidate	Percent	Candidate	Percent	Candidate	Percent
Alessandri	31.2	Frei	55.7	Allende	36.2
Allende	28.6	Allende	38.6	Alessandri	34.9
Frei	20.5	Durán	4.9	Tómic	27.8
Bossay	15.2				
Zamorano	3.3				

SOURCE: Adapted from Timothy R. Scully, *Rethinking the Center: Party Politics in Nineteenth- and Twentieth-Century Chile* (Stanford: Stanford University Press, 1992), p. 164.

TABLE 4.3. *The Growth of Unions in the Urban and Rural Sectors,*
1932–73

	Urban Sector			Rural Sector		
Year	Number of unions	Union members	Percent unionized	Number of unions	Union members	Percent unionized
1932	421	54,801	.07	–	–	–
1940	629	91,940	18.7	–	–	–
1952	1,982	282,383	19.3	15	1,035	.04
1960	1,892	272,141	14.3	23	1,825	0.6
1970	4,001	436,974	19.4	510	114,112	20.7
1973	5,632	704,499	30.5	870	229,836	37.6

SOURCES: Calculated from Timothy R. Scully, *Rethinking the Center: Party Politics in Nineteenth- and Twentieth-Century Chile* (Stanford: Stanford University Press, 1992), p. 156; Arturo Valenzuela, *The Breakdown of Democratic Regimes: Chile* (Baltimore: Johns Hopkins University Press, 1978), p. 28; and Esteban Jadresic, "Evolución del empleo y desempleo en Chile, 1970–1985. Series anuales y trimestrales," *Colección Estudios CIEPLAN* 20 (December 1986): 151–52.

ship stagnated in the 1950s and actually declined under the conservative administration of Alessandri between 1958 and 1964. Membership growth picked up again, however, under the more supportive administration of the Christian Democrat Eduardo Frei in the mid-1960s, and it surged under Allende in the early 1970s to reach a peak of 32 percent of the economically active population in 1973, an exceptionally high figure in the Latin American context[20] (see Table 4.3).

New social and political constituencies also became available to the Left in the 1960s. Historically, the peasantry had not been a significant base of support for the Left because many peasants remained under the political control of landlords, and the Socialist and Communist Parties had made concessions during the Popular Front era to abandon organizational efforts in the countryside in exchange for cabinet posts and greater access to urban labor. Electoral reforms in 1958, however, guaranteed a secret ballot and blocked the traditional practice of vote buying in the countryside, thus loosening landlords' political controls and opening access to the peasantry for new political parties. The land reforms of the Frei government in the 1960s further undermined oligarchic controls and patron-client relationships in the countryside, and they were accompanied by extensive Christian Democratic efforts to organize the peasantry. Although the Christian Democrats got a head start in mobilizing landed peasants, the Left concentrated new energy on the landless and made rapid strides in the late 1960s and early 1970s. From less than 2,000 members in 1964, peasant associations grew to encompass 114,112 members in 1970 and 229,836 in 1973, with membership evenly split between Christian Democratic and leftist federations.[21]

Likewise, the Frei government made efforts to organize the urban poor, and this competition encouraged the Left to direct new attention to potential political constituencies in the rapidly growing urban popular districts or *poblaciones*. Large-scale mobilizations among the urban poor for land and housing provided fertile terrain for the organizing strategies of the Left, and the Socialist and Communist Parties were active participants in the land invasions that led to the establishment of new poblaciones in the 1960s and early 1970s. Meanwhile, a series of electoral reforms extended the suffrage to women and illiterates and made voter registration mandatory; the result was a surge in electoral participation and intense partisan competition for the loyalties of new constituencies, as the percentage of the population registered to vote rose from 9.9 percent in 1949 to 44.1 percent in 1973.[22]

Ironically, although these changes opened new organizational space and electoral opportunities for the Left, the Socialist Party became more critical of Chile's "bourgeois" democratic institutions. The party had always incorporated both revolutionary and democratic socialist currents in its ranks,[23] but political dynamics in the 1960s shifted the party's center of gravity toward the revolutionary pole.[24] The Cuban Revolution had a profound impact on the Socialist Party, and it fueled the imagination of many university students who were frustrated with the limited gains of democratic participation. The Socialist Party lost an important sector of its youth organization in 1964 when student leaders from Concepción and Santiago abandoned the party to found the Movement of the Revolutionary Left (MIR), which raised the banner of armed struggle in Chile. Disillusionment with electoralism spread within the Socialist Party after Allende was soundly defeated by Frei in the 1964 presidential race by a vote of 55.7 to 38.6 percent; the Left had held high hopes of winning the presidency in a three-way race, but the Christian Democrats won easily when the Right declined to sponsor a candidate of its own and threw its support to Frei to block the advance of the Left. In its 1965 party congress, the Socialist Party proclaimed itself to be a Leninist organization for the first time and disavowed the electoral road to socialism. In a subsequent congress in 1967, the party reiterated that "peaceful or legal forms of struggle . . . do not lead by themselves to power. The Socialist Party considers them to be limited instruments of action, incorporated into the political process that carries us to armed struggle."[25]

The Socialist Party thus continued its participation in Chile's established democratic regime, while openly declaring that this participation was merely a prelude to an eventual institutional rupture that would culminate in armed confrontation. This deepened the contradictions within the left-wing alliance because the Communist Party had formalized its longtime, de facto commitment to the "peaceful road" in response to Nikita Khrushchev's destalinization campaign and his foreign policy embrace of peaceful coexistence. Despite these strategic differences, the Left rallied behind Allende's 1970 presidential campaign and obtained a narrow, surprise victory when the Right, infuriated by Frei's reforms, abandoned the Christian Democrats and gambled on another candidacy by Allessandri. Allende won a plurality with 36.2 percent of the vote, followed by Alessandri with 34.9 percent and the Christian Democrat Radomiro Tómic with 27.8 percent.

Chile thus embarked upon an experiment in democratic socialism that was unprecedented in the depth and scope of its reforms, in Latin America or elsewhere. Within the framework of a constitutional democracy, Allende sought to bring the commanding heights of the Chilean economy under state control by nationalizing the foreign-owned copper industry, the banking system, and the largest industrial establishments. He also pledged to accelerate the land reform program begun under Frei, redistribute income by increasing wages and social benefits, and introduce participatory forms of self-management in the workplace.[26] The impediments confronted by Allende were enormous: his fractious coalition controlled the executive branch of government, but it lacked a legislative majority and faced judicial and military establishments that were skeptical, if not hostile, to his intentions. The hostility of the United States and domestic economic elites was a foregone conclusion.

Allende's government was seriously plagued, moreover, by the contradictions within the Left. Although Allende was a member of the Socialist Party, his strategic vision of a peaceful road to socialism was much closer to that of the Communist Party, and he received lukewarm support from the leadership of his own party. The Socialists anchored the more radical wing of Allende's Popular Unity coalition, which sought to accelerate and expand the expropriation of factories and landed estates and often joined the MIR in promoting land or factory occupations to force the government's hand.[27] In contrast, the Communist Party and its allies preached caution and prudence: they favored strict adherence to constitutional legality and urged Allende to move slowly so as to consolidate gains and minimize opposition. The contrasting approaches of the two parties were perhaps best summarized in their respective slogans: whereas the Socialists pledged to "advance without compromise," the Communists preferred to "compromise in order to advance."[28]

Allende's reforms and the process of lower-class mobilization which they engendered provoked intense opposition from economic elites, small business owners, and the political Right.[29] After a year of rapid, demand-driven growth, the economy stagnated and inflationary pressures accumulated as consumption surged, investment and productivity plummeted, international credits dried up, and goods were hoarded. Political conflict and economic dislocations drove the Christian Democrats and much of the middle class into an alliance with the Right, which increasingly looked to the military to protect its interests. Allende and the Popular Unity moderates tried in vain to negotiate a compromise with the Christian Democrats to isolate the Right and prevent a democratic breakdown, but an agreement was blocked by Christian Democratic conservatives and Socialist hard-liners.[30] As the Right openly promoted a military coup, the radical Left tried to mobilize grassroots organs of popular power in the factories and urban shantytowns, and the government was paralyzed as political conflict transcended the boundaries of formal democratic institutions.

The military coup of September 11, 1973, was one of the most violent in Latin American history, demonstrating the depth of the political polarization and class conflict in Chilean society. Far more than an overthrow of the government, it constituted a military occupation of society that was designed to crush the political institutions and social networks that had nourished the growth of the Chilean Left. Although the Left was able to survive this effort at extermination, it was fundamentally transformed by the bitter experience of political defeat and military repression. The Left that reemerged on the national political scene in the 1980s would be very different from that which governed under Allende, and it would compete in a social and political environment that bore little resemblance to that which undergirded its development before 1973.

After the Deluge: Military Repression and Clandestine Organization

The military coup marked the end of an era in Chilean politics. The coup swept aside a democratic regime that had operated without interruption since 1933, and it buried a democratic tradition that was among the oldest and strongest in Latin America. Allende, who had rejected military offers to be flown into exile, refused to abandon the presidential palace, and he committed suicide when the palace was stormed by army troops after aerial bombardments. The military proceeded to crush the representative institutions that had allowed Chile to become the first nation in the world to elect a Marxist head of state. Congress was closed, the constitution was abrogated, the electoral registry was burned, and parties, labor federations, and peasant associations were dissolved. Factories, universities, and shantytowns were occupied by security forces, who killed thousands of left-wing activists who resisted the coup or were detained in custody.[31] Within six months they had arrested 80,000 persons, and 160,000 suffered politically motivated job dismissals.[32] An estimated 200,000 persons, including political refugees and their family members, went into exile in the global diaspora of the Chilean Left.[33]

The military takeover was an unmitigated disaster for the Left, which had grown accustomed to electoral participation and open trade union activism. The MIR, which tried to resist the coup militarily, was decimated by the end of 1974. The Socialist and Communist Parties both had very small contingents with military preparation, but they were inoperative against the overwhelming military force arrayed against them.[34] Both parties had their leadership decapitated three times during the first three years of the military dictatorship, and their ranks were decimated by repression, exile, and political withdrawal. In the Socialist Party, 7 of the 47 members of the Central Committee were killed or "disappeared" following the coup, and a dozen others were imprisoned.[35] Secretary General Carlos Altamirano and other leaders slipped into exile from clandestinity, while many others were captured and relegated to harsh concentration camps before being sent into forced exile.[36] Local and regional party officials were also targets of repression; seven regional secretaries had been killed and 20 imprisoned by early 1974.[37] In some cases entire regional directorates were assassinated.[38]

The Socialist Party established a dual directorate following the coup, with Altamirano leading the External Secretariat in Berlin and a group of clandestine Central Committee members and youth leaders running the Internal Directorate inside Chile. The principal leaders of the Internal Directorate were detained and disappeared on June 25, 1975, however, and most of their replacements met the same fate in December 1975, thoroughly disarticulating the party organization inside Chile. A third group of youthful leaders recomposed the Internal Directorate and began the long process of party reconstruction in January 1976.[39]

Political repression, however, was not the only problem to plague Socialist efforts to construct a coherent clandestine organization inside Chile. The party's congenital factionalism led to the emergence of competing centers of authority in clandestinity, as a group known as the National Coordinator of Regions (CNR) and other splinter groups contested the legitimacy of the Internal Directorate's leadership. Given the severe constraints on communication and the existence of internal conflict, many party militants

recognized the authority of the CNR rather than that of the Internal
Directorate, and the party's exiled leadership compounded the confusion by funneling assistance to both groups.[40] This led to serious
conflicts between the Internal Directorate and the exiled leadership and contributed to the eventual division of the party in 1979.

Although the Communist Party was subjected to equally severe repression, its centralized structure and hierarchical discipline
made it far more successful at maintaining leadership cohesion and
organizational coherence under authoritarian rule. Six members of
the Central Committee were killed in the immediate aftermath of
the coup, and eleven others "disappeared" in May 1976, including
Sub-Secretary General Victor Díaz, who directed the party's clandestine apparatus following the arrest of Secretary General Luís
Corvalán in October 1973.[41] The clandestine directorate which
succeeded that of Díaz, under the leadership of Fernando Ortiz, was
also captured and disappeared in December 1976, and 20 regional
committees were destroyed that same year in a paroxysm of terror.
The party thus temporarily transferred authority to the exiled directorate in Moscow, which was led by Corvalán following his 1976
release in a prisoner exchange involving the Soviet Union. The
recomposition of the internal hierarchy began in earnest in late
1978 when Gladys Marín, the former leader of the party youth
organization, was transferred back to Chile along with other party
leaders to oversee the clandestine apparatus.[42]

Clearly, organizational survival and reconstruction were the
first orders of business for both parties. In the Communist Party,
this process meant streamlining an apparatus that had grown to
195,000 members before the coup, with another 87,000 in the youth
organization, and resurrecting the clandestine structures that the
party had used during previous periods of repression. Despite its
experience with persecution and clandestinity, the party had been
unprepared for a sudden shift to violent forms of political confrontation, as it eventually acknowledged in a frank admission of error:
"The Party had not foreseen the magnitude of the coup. Illusions
weighed over us about the irreversible character of the democratic
process. In these conditions we committed the error of showing all
the body. There was also a loss of historical experience on how to
conduct ourselves in periods of illegality, a fact made even more

grave when it is taken into account that this has been the most bloodthirsty repression ever against the Party and the people."[43] In response to military repression, the party reduced the size of its cells and restricted horizontal contacts to lessen the risks of detec-·tion.[44] Lines of succession for leadership positions were predesignated so that fallen leaders could be quickly replaced. Political activities were conducted clandestinely, and party militants assumed pseudonyms. The party benefited from its long-standing organizational centralization and its well-defined hierarchy because strict vertical lines of authority linked the different levels of the party apparatus inside and outside of Chile: the Political Commission controlled the Central Committee, which directed the regional committees, which oversaw the work of local committees, which themselves directed the activities of base-level cells. These linkages were sometimes severed by repression, especially between 1976 and 1978, and the difficulties of party organization often forced base-level militants to focus their energies on work in the less risky, nonpartisan social terrain.[45] Nevertheless, the Communist Party's organizational discipline made it possible to avoid serious manifestations of the twin dangers that plagued the Socialist Party under Pinochet: the existence of a sharp cleavage between internal and external directorates and the competition for leadership between distinct political and ideological factions.

The Socialist Party, in fact, was virtually paralyzed by the combination of repression and factionalization. The party had never fully developed a cellular structure before 1973, as base-level units, or *nucleos*, often organized around electoral campaigns or party congresses only to dissolve in their aftermath.[46] The Socialists had relied heavily on open local assemblies rather than cells in workplaces and other grass-roots organizing sites, but these assemblies clearly could not function under conditions of military repression. Furthermore, the party's decentralized structure and lax disciplinary norms had allowed local and regional subunits to operate with high levels of autonomy, often revolving around prominent personalities or caudillos. These characteristics made the party prone to factionalism, and they left individual militants isolated under the dictatorship in the mid-1970s, as repression and infighting severed their ties to intermediate and national levels of the party hierarchy.

The party was so fragmented that it was not even clear which self-proclaimed faction of the hierarchy should be recognized as authoritative. Therefore, while Socialist militants were very active in grass-roots social resistance, their work was relatively decentralized and autonomous and often lacked political coordination.

Pre-1973 organizational characteristics thus shaped and constrained the manner in which these two parties exercised clandestine resistance to the dictatorship. Perhaps more important, these organizational characteristics also influenced the nature of the political debate and self-criticism that inevitably erupted in both parties in response to their catastrophic defeat. The collapse of the Allende experiment and the trauma of military repression created a dynamic of political learning in both parties; however, the two parties ultimately extracted very different lessons from their defeat, and their efforts to rectify their errors created divergent evolutionary trajectories that would eventually bifurcate the Left and profoundly influence the character of Chile's democratic transition.

The Lessons of Defeat: Self-Criticism and
Political Learning in the Chilean Left

If the military coup put the organizational survival of the Socialist and Communist Parties at stake, it also wreaked havoc with the political strategies and the conceptions of politics that had guided these parties over the course of a generation. For Communists, the coup shattered illusions about the uniquely democratic character of the Chilean polity, and it challenged the long-standing faith that socialism could be developed within the strictures of liberal democratic institutions. For Socialists, the coup demonstrated the utter failure of the Left to prepare for the institutional rupture and military conflicts anticipated by their party doctrine. It also posed troubling questions about the role of their party in the polarization of Chilean society and its tepid support for Chile's democratic institutions.

The process of self-critical reassessment precipitated by the coup planted the seeds of political learning and political change in both parties. What is ironic is that their respective patterns of political learning eventually led each party to reject much of its own pre-coup positions and grant at least partial legitimacy to the political line that was previously adopted by the other party in the heated debates that plagued the Allende government. These divergent patterns of political learning set the stage for the parties' reversal of positions under the military regime and for their contrasting roles in Chile's process of redemocratization.

This reversal, however, was not the parties' immediate response to the coup. In the Communist Party the initial reaction was one of continuity, as the leadership affirmed the party's faith in the *vía pacífica*, along with the validity of its pragmatic strategies. The party attributed Allende's defeat to the political isolation of his government and the treachery of its foreign and domestic opponents, while blaming "ultra-Left" sectors for exacerbating conflict and driving the middle class into the arms of the Right.[47] This interpretation stressed the political factors that led to Allende's downfall, particularly the failure of the Popular Unity to reach some sort of accommodation with the Christian Democrats. As the party's first serious critical reflection on the Popular Unity experience in early 1974 asserted, "Our defeat was the expression of the isolation of the working class. This indicates that more than a military defeat, we were conquered politically."[48]

In keeping with this moderate stance and political emphasis, the Communist Party made the construction of a broad, multiclass "antifascist front" the centerpiece of its strategy to isolate and defeat the military dictatorship.[49] The party thus gave top priority to an alliance between the Left and the Christian Democratic Party— the largest party in Chile—despite the latter's opposition to Allende and its initial support for the coup. The Communist Party was confident that the repressive character of the military regime and its regressive socioeconomic policies would drive the Christian Democrats into opposition and eventually into an alliance with the Left. In reality, however, this strategic line was highly unrealistic because the Christian Democrats were inalterably opposed to any alliance with the Communist Party, even after the Christian Democratic Party shifted into opposition to the dictatorship.[50]

Furthermore, the Communist Party grossly underestimated the fortitude of the dictatorship, assuming that it was a transitory phenomenon wracked by illegitimacy and internal divisions. The party believed that the military regime was fragile and thus vulnerable to the political pressure of a broad democratic alliance.[51] Consequently, the Communist Party opposed "terrorist" attacks against the dictatorship, arguing that they were incompatible with the objective of opposition unity, and it advocated forms of mass political struggle, particularly a general strike, as weapons to be used against Pinochet. The party also eschewed socialism as an immediate objective and called for the reconstruction of democracy behind a government of national unity. Pinochet was kept in office less by the force of arms, it asserted, than by the dispersion and disunity of Chile's democratic forces.[52]

The antifascist front line remained at the heart of the Communist Party's resistance strategy until 1980. But as early as the mid-1970s a new twist was added to the party's interpretation of Allende's defeat: it began to emphasize military factors and the inability of the Allende government to defend itself from antidemocratic forces.[53] This retrospective reassessment entailed a more self-critical analysis of the party's own failures and limitations, and not merely those of its coalition partners and the "ultra-Left." The centerpiece of this self-criticism was recognition of the party's vacío histórico, or its historic failure to design a "military policy" to influence the Chilean armed forces and develop the party's own military capabilities.[54] This partial reinterpretation was not necessarily a renunciation of the vía pacífica but an effort to incorporate the reality of military force into the party's strategic calculations, something that had been previously neglected. In particular, the party said it had erred by "absolutizing" the vía pacífica, which limited its ability to adapt forms of struggle in accordance with changes in the political environment and prevented it from operating in the military terrain chosen by counterrevolutionary forces.[55] This strategic reassessment reflected common themes of debate within the party's exiled leadership and its intellectual advisers, as well as Soviet and Cuban criticisms of the Allende experience.[56] It also echoed the pre-coup concerns of the MIR and the radical wing of the Socialist Party, which had anticipated that the vía pacífica would culminate in an institutional rupture and violent confrontation.

This early process of reassessment and political learning in the Communist Party had several notable characteristics. First, the self-critical element appeared only after several years of reflection on a traumatic political defeat, as the initial reaction was to reaffirm the party's historic line. Second, self-critical debate focused on relatively narrow tactical and strategic issues related to the means of struggle; it did not touch the ideological foundations of the party's political identities or its teleological vision of socialism.[57] Third, these strategic debates mirrored the party's organizational characteristics. That is, debate was centralized, hierarchical, and largely encapsulated within the party's political commission and the "official" intelligentsia that was linked to the leadership.[58] These characteristics enabled the party leadership to control the terms of debate and modify the party line in a manner that was highly insulated and autonomous from lower levels of the party apparatus. Accordingly, the strategic debate did not become a source of serious factional divisions within the ranks of the party.

The process of debate and political learning could hardly have been more different in the Socialist Party. Debate among Socialists was immediately self-critical, becoming a vehicle by which the party's contending factions could settle scores and assess blame for the disaster that had befallen the Left. Political debate, therefore, was decentralized and broadly dispersed, as the absence of a coherent hierarchy prevented the imposition of an official history and encouraged a proliferation of competing interpretations. Likewise, debate in the Socialist Party was intensely ideological, touching not only on tactical and strategic issues but on the very character of the socialist project itself. It thus represented a more complex process of political learning than that which occurred within the Communist Party.[59] Ironically, although the factionalism and institutional weaknesses of the Socialist Party undermined its capacity for effective clandestine organization, they also created political space for debate and innovation that ultimately helped the party adapt to its changing social and political environment.

The factionalism of the Socialist Party meant that both "political" and "military" interpretations of Allende's defeat were articulated from the outset. Initially, the major proponent of the political interpretation was the clandestine Internal Directorate. Much like the Communist Party, the Internal Directorate represented a combination of strategic moderation and Leninist ideological orthodoxy. It joined the Communist Party in denouncing "ultra-Left" forces both inside and outside the Popular Unity coalition, including the radical wing of the Socialist Party itself. Indeed, the Internal Directorate criticized the narrowness of the Socialist Party's alliance strategy and its unwillingness to make tactical compromises or find common ground with the Christian Democrats. It thus blamed the radicalism of the Socialist Party for "the political dispersion which impeded the consolidation of the hegemony of the working class."[60] As stated in the directorate's primary analysis of Allende's defeat,

The defeat of the people and the triumph of the counterrevolutionary alternative cannot be explained as the simple military defeat of the direct resistance to the coup. The political defeat of the popular movement was sealed before September 11, being determined by the degree of isolation of the working class and the absence of a real leading force capable of making use, with possibilities of triumph, of the latent revolutionary potential in the forces of the masses and in the instruments of institutional power within reach of the government.[61]

In keeping with this political emphasis, the Internal Directorate joined the Communist Party in advocating a broad, multiclass alliance against Pinochet, a stance that represented a controversial departure from the party's long-standing Workers' Front line. It also insisted that the Socialist Party should implement Leninist norms of democratic centralism in its organizational life, something that was called for in the party's formal doctrine but never observed in practice. The directorate diverged from the Communist Party by insisting that military force would eventually be required to sweep away the dictatorship. Taken together, the strategic orientation and alliance posture of the Internal Directorate alienated the party's radical wing, at the same time that its Leninist organizational orthodoxy alienated those who valued the party's independence from Soviet-bloc political models.[62]

The more radical wing of the Socialist Party tended to emphasize the military factors in Allende's defeat. Initially, this wing found partial expression in the External Secretariat led by Secretary General Altamirano, who had been a symbol of the party's "revolutionary pole" since the 1960s. Altamirano argued that a peaceful transition to socialism had not been possible in Chile, and he claimed that the Allende government allowed itself to get trapped and paralyzed by Chile's democratic institutions because the Popular Unity had failed to build alternative organs of popular power or develop an adequate military strategy to defend against the inevitable threat of counterrevolution.[63] Inside Chile, the party's revolutionary pole was represented by the National Coordinator of Regions, a faction with Trotskyist tendencies which had organized informally under Allende to support the "popular power" strategies of the MIR. The CNR rejected the vía pacífica and interpreted the coup as the defeat of "reformism" in Chile. It denounced the party leadership for fleeing into exile and denied the authority of the Internal Directorate, which it belittled as a reformist organization that would subordinate the Socialist Party to Communist control. The CNR rejected multiclass alliances and advocated the creation of workers' councils as organs of popular power and potential centers of armed resistance to the military dictatorship.[64]

Despite these political conflicts and the different interpretations of the Allende experience, there was a general consensus in these early years between the Internal Directorate, the External Secretariat, and the CNR that armed resistance would eventually be required to overthrow the dictatorship. Likewise, these factions agreed on Marxism-Leninism as the doctrinal foundation for the party and subscribed to the Leninist conception of revolution as the conquest of state power. Political debate within the Socialist Party changed dramatically, however, under the influence of disparate intellectuals who became the main protagonists of the so-called Socialist renovation in Chile.[65] The most prominent of these intellectuals were affiliated initially with the small parties that had broken off from the Christian Democratic Party to support the Popular Unity government—the Movimiento de Acción Popular (MAPU), MAPU-Obrero Campesino, and the Izquierda Cristiana. Operating in exile centers such as Rome and Paris and in Chilean think tanks with international support like FLACSO, these intellectuals diffused the main themes of ideological renovation to leaders of the Socialist Party in exile and were eventually incorporated into the party in the 1980s.

These intellectuals' analysis of Allende's defeat shared important points in common with the "political interpretation" of the Communist Party and the Internal Directorate of the Socialist Party. They blamed the coup on Allende's political isolation and on the failure of his coalition to accommodate the Christian Democrats and earn middle-class support.[66] The primary lesson they extracted from the Allende experience was that a socialist project "must be capable of convoking and incorporating a broad national majority as the only way to impede the violent reaction of those forces which are unleashed against it."[67]

In contrast to the Communist Party and the Internal Directorate, however, which blended strategic moderation with strict Marxist-Leninist ideological orthodoxy, the intellectuals integrated their strategic analysis with a profound critique of Leninism. Drawing initially from Gramsci, the intellectuals claimed that the popularized Marxism-Leninism of the Chilean Left was too sectarian, dogmatic, and exclusive to found an alternative hegemonic project because it segregated the Left and the working class and blocked the construction of a multiclass sociopolitical bloc.[68] Moreover, the emphasis on the conquest of state power created a logic of warfare that was intolerant of pluralism and prone to political polarization. By rationalizing an elite revolutionary vanguard with exclusive claims to doctrinal legitimacy, Leninism engendered hierarchical forms of political authority that clashed with socialist ideals for mass democratic participation.[69] These theoretical reassessments led inexorably to a rejection of state-centric, bureaucratic models of socialism, and they made the "revaluation" of democracy and civil society the centerpiece of ideological change. For proponents of renovation, democracy was conceived not as an instrument for the attainment of other ends but as an intrinsic value of the socialist project. Socialism, in fact, was not a preconceived model of society but an open-ended process of transformation achieved through the progressive extension and deepening of democratic norms to new spheres of political and socioeconomic relations.[70]

These ideas were not entirely new in the Chilean Left. They had clear roots in Allende's own conception of democratic socialism, as well as that of the early Socialist theoretician and political leader Eugenio González.[71] Nevertheless, these ideas had been very much on the defensive in the Socialist Party during the 1960s and early 1970s, when the party disavowed formal democratic institutions and denied the possibility of a democratic road to socialism. Their resurrection in the mid-1970s was an explicit response to political defeat and to the perception of many intellectuals that this defeat was at least partially attributable to the radicalization of the Socialist Party. Likewise, it reflected the new appreciation for democratic rights and liberties that was generated by the trauma of authoritarian repression.[72]

Although this critical perspective was initially concentrated within small groups of intellectuals inside Chile and in exile, it diffused rapidly outside the country, as intellectuals were afforded considerable latitude for critical expression in the open and fragmented political culture of the Socialist and Christian Left. In the late 1970s their critical themes were circulated at conferences of Chilean exiles in Italy and France, and they began to penetrate the exiled leadership of the Socialist Party in Europe. They thus set the stage for the crisscrossing of the Socialist and Communist Parties at the beginning of the 1980s.

Renovation and Rebellion: The Dynamics of Political Change

These divergent patterns of political debate and political learning led inexorably to profound changes in both the Socialist and Communist Parties. The most dramatic transformation occurred in the exiled leadership of the Socialist Party. After setting up exile headquarters in Berlin, Altamirano became disillusioned with socialism in Eastern Europe; in his words, "It wasn't paradise. . . . I was enormously affected by the absence of liberty. It was a coercive society, in which the decisions were made from above and orders passed down, limiting liberty enormously."[73] Altamirano eventually relocated to Paris, and in Western Europe he was influenced by the experiences of Eurocommunism and social democracy, as well as the debates over renovation generated by socialist and Left Christian intellectuals from Chile. Long a symbol of the Socialist Party's radical wing, Altamirano was transformed into an ardent promoter of renovation within its ranks, assisted by his closest collaborators from the exiled leadership, Jorge Arrate and Ricardo Núñez.

Altamirano's political rebirth, however, deepened the contradictions in the Socialist Party. Inside Chile, the rigors of clandestine struggle had reinforced Leninist organizational principles and limited the circulation of "renovated" perspectives within the party apparatus.[74] Likewise, clandestine leaders had little exposure to the political solidarity of European social democrats and limited access to the financial support provided by social democratic parties and foundations. The struggle to recompose the party organization in clandestinity had eventually led the Internal Directorate to assert its authority over the CNR during the late 1970s, when the latter was undermined by repression, factionalism, and less effective grass-roots organizational work in the social sphere. But this struggle did little to weaken the ideological orthodoxy of the Internal Directorate, especially when its principal internal competitor represented the party's revolutionary pole. Consequently, Altamirano's transformation only exacerbated the already strained relations between the internal directorate and the exiled leadership. The Internal Directorate fought with Altamirano over his management of financial resources, his support for different clandestine leaderships, and the ultimate locus of political authority.[75] Altamirano's supporters, meanwhile, criticized the Internal Directorate for its hierarchical practices, for trying to transform the party into an orthodox replica of the Communist Party, and for sending party cadres for political training in the Soviet bloc.[76]

The conflict came to a head in April 1979, when a definitive rupture of the Socialist Party occurred. Charging that Altamirano had "opened . . . a breach for the penetration of the social democratic project in the interior of the Party,"[77] the Internal Directorate and its supporters on the External Secretariat removed Altamirano from his post as secretary general and replaced him with Clodomiro Almeyda, the former foreign minister of Allende who was in exile in Berlin and a member of the External Secretariat. This decision was not accepted by Altamirano and his supporters on the External Secretariat, who produced a schism by continuing to recognize Altamirano as the party secretary general. The external party organization thus split into two principal factions: a pro-Altamirano sector, which was based in Western Europe and advocated a process of ideological and strategic renovation that brought it close to European social democracy, and a pro-Almeyda sector, which kept its base in Berlin and retained a more orthodox Marxist-Leninist orientation, as well as the party's traditional alliance with the Chilean Communists.

The division, however, had no immediate impact on the Socialist Party inside Chile, other than to provoke disorientation among clandestine militants who were insulated from the ideological changes that were swirling in the exterior and largely ignorant of the political evolution of Altamirano's faction.[78] The exiled leadership of Almeyda had the unanimous support of the Internal Directorate and the loyalty of the bulk of the party's dispersed militants inside Chile. The Altamirano sector, in contrast, had no organizational presence inside Chile at the time of the rupture, despite the tenuous control of the Internal Directorate over an atomized membership. Consequently, the Altamirano sector—still claiming to be the true Socialist Party of Chile—was forced to begin the work of building a party organization from scratch in the interior. This process began in earnest in 1980, when Ricardo Núñez replaced Altamirano as secretary general and returned to Chile in clandestinity.[79] Ironically, by the time Chile entered a democratic transition in the late 1980s, this sector would be the hegemonic force on the Chilean Left, despite the shallowness of its organizational roots and the weakness of its ties to grass-roots social actors at the beginning of the decade.

If the dynamics of political learning and political change led to the emergence of a new moderate tendency in the external apparatus of the Socialist Party, the dynamics could hardly have been more different in the Communist Party, where a process of radicalization occurred. The party's shift in strategic emphasis from political to military factors in the mid-1970s was the first step in this process and a precursor to the party's 1980 advocacy of "mass popular rebellion" in the struggle against the dictatorship. This strategic shift displaced the earlier advocacy of an antifascist political front and entailed a commitment to employ "all forms of struggle," including revolutionary violence, against the military regime.[80]

A confluence of domestic and international factors played a role in this strategic shift. The Nicaraguan Revolution was an important external influence, along with the Soviet Union's reassessment of revolutionary prospects in Latin America. The Communist Party interpreted the Nicaraguan Revolution as evidence that personal dictators could be overthrown through a combination of mass political mobilization and guerrilla warfare. Like Cuba before it, Nicaragua showed that a Communist Party wedded exclusively to nonviolent forms of struggle ran the danger of being marginalized in an insurrectionary process led by other political forces. The Nicaraguan experience also suggested that diverse social and political forces, including bourgeois and middle-class sectors, would lend support to a revolutionary political-military vanguard if it exhibited the power to confront a dictatorship.[81] Alliance formation, therefore, was contingent not on political will or a spirit of compromise but on political and military strength and audacity, as an assertion of power could help aggregate new forces behind a revolutionary project.

Political developments inside Chile, however, were even more important than these international factors in explaining the Communist Party's strategic shift. The failure of the antifascist front line was patent, as the Christian Democrats resolutely rejected an alliance with the Communists, even though their opposition to the dictatorship grew over the course of the late 1970s. With the Christian Democrats following a path of independent opposition and the Socialist Party paralyzed by repression and internal disputes, "the policy of the anti-Fascist front clashed with reality," and popular resistance to the dictatorship was desultory.[82] The new strategy of "popular rebellion," therefore, was an effort to jump-start the nearly moribund opposition movement and to overcome the aura of invincibility that surrounded the regime and led to apathy and resignation among the opposition. The purpose of the strategy was to breathe life into sporadic, isolated, and uncoordinated opposition efforts by taking the political offensive.

The other critical domestic factor in the Communist Party's

strategic shift was Pinochet's effort to create a constitutional framework for the institutionalization of authoritarian rule. The constitution was ratified by a plebiscite in September 1980, the same month that the Communist Party declared its commitment to "all forms of struggle." The constitution was designed to lend permanence and legitimacy to the socioeconomic and political transformations imposed by the dictatorship. The successful imposition of a new constitution demonstrated the continuing vitality of the authoritarian project, and it belied the overly optimistic—and even triumphalist—early pronouncements of the Communist Party regarding the regime's isolation and vulnerability. This institutionalization process caused Communist Party leaders to conclude that Pinochet could not be forced to surrender power by political pressure alone;[83] the only viable option, they believed, was to mobilize a popular insurrection to confront the regime on the military terrain that sustained it. With party militants operating clandestinely under constant danger and persecution, temptations were strong to answer violence with violence and to develop a capacity for armed self-defense. The popular rebellion strategy thus represented an attempt to rectify the strategic imbalance by meeting force with force, under the belief that violent repression could not be countered—politically or militarily—with nonviolent forms of resistance.

Although Communist parties in Colombia, El Salvador, and Guatemala have also taken up arms in recent decades, the Chilean case was perhaps the most surprising. The Chilean Communist Party had experienced singular success in the electoral arena, and it was a prominent advocate of peaceful democratic reform in the 1960s and 1970s, a position that separated the Moscow-line parties from guerrilla movements throughout Latin America. But if this strategic shift challenged the party's traditional political praxis, it did not require major changes in ideological principles. Indeed, the strategic shift was portrayed as a recuperation of a basic Leninist tenet which the party had long neglected: the need to adapt tactics and forms of struggle in accordance with changes in the political context.[84] The new orientation was not a disavowal of traditional practices but a supplement required for a more flexible and integral revolutionary strategy.

Given the Communist Party's ideological continuity and hierarchical discipline, the adoption of an insurrectionary line did not precipitate a major schism within the ranks of the party, although dissent existed among individual party militants. The decision was made by a handful of leaders on the party's Political Commission, most of whom were in exile in Eastern Europe. The new line received its theoretical elaboration from a group of young party intellectuals based in East Germany, commonly known as the "Leipzig Group."[85] When the new line was announced in a radio address by exiled Secretary General Corvalán in September 1980, it took party militants completely by surprise because it had not been debated within the ranks of the party, and even some Central Committee members had no inkling of the impending change.[86] Nevertheless, the new strategy was sufficiently broad and ambiguous to encompass a wide range of both violent and nonviolent methods of resistance, and its immediate practical implications were unclear, since the party did not unveil a military force of its own until 1983. Consequently, the vast majority of party militants accepted the new line as a continuation of their underground social work and a means to revitalize popular mobilization.[87] Party discipline and the rigors of clandestine struggle ensured that most of those who were skeptical kept their dissent to themselves.[88]

In short, patterns of political debate and innovation in the Communist Party were confined to tactical and strategic issues, and they were almost hermetically sealed within the party leadership and select intellectual circles. Whereas the process of ideological renovation in the Socialist Party exacerbated internal conflicts and contributed to the fragmentation of the organization, the strategic shift in the Communist Party was directed from above and implemented without serious internal resistance. But if the strategy of popular rebellion could be implemented within the party's traditional ideological frame of reference, it eventually produced a militarization of party cadres that represented a dramatic break with the political practices that were ingrained in the partisan subculture of Chilean Communists. For generations, this subculture had revolved around electoral contestation and trade union organization; neither of these, however, would be central to the strategy of popular rebellion. The insurrectionary line of the Communist Party cultivated a new style of political participation, and it mobilized new political subjects, primarily among the urban poor, who had been molded by the socioeconomic transformations wrought by the military dictatorship. The explosion of popular protests in the 1980s would be heavily conditioned by the linkages between these social changes and new forms of political agency within the Left.

The Neoliberal Revolution and Structural Change in Chilean Society

The military regime that crushed the Popular Unity's experiment in democratic socialism did not rely merely on physical repression to eliminate the Left as a contender for political power in Chilean society. After two years of economic stabilization, the regime implemented Latin America's first full-scale neoliberal structural adjustment, one that transformed the social landscape and modified relationships between the state and society. The structural changes associated with this neoliberal revolution fundamentally altered the social matrix in which the Left had historically cultivated its political support.[89]

One important structural change was the drastic curtailment of the state's role in economic affairs, which had important implications for the politicization of social and economic demands. Historically, the Chilean state had played an exceptionally strong role in the process of economic development. Even before import-substitution industrialization began in earnest in the 1930s, the state's role was magnified by its control over nitrate export revenues. The election of the Popular Front in 1938 brought the expansion of the state's role in social welfare activities, as well as the establishment of a public agency, CORFO, which planned and financed much of the industrialization process in mid-twentieth-century Chile. By the time of Allende's election, the state already accounted for nearly half the GNP and 75 percent of gross domestic investment.[90] Chile's chronic postwar inflation problems required the state to mediate the distributive effects of price and wage increases, as different social sectors expressed demands for wage indexation, price controls or adjustments, or other measures to protect their income shares. The annual inflation-induced wage adjustment became a perennial political battleground in Chile, with business associations and labor unions pressuring the state to defend their conflicting interests and channeling demands through political parties to maximize their leverage.

The Chicago-school technocrats who managed the economy under Pinochet were determined to dismantle the developmentalist state in Chile.[91] Public enterprises were privatized, diminishing the role of the state and enhancing that of the private sector in the spheres of investment, production, and capital accumulation. Social programs were also cut and decentralized to the municipal level, while markets were left free to determine wages and prices, curtailing the state's role as the arbiter of distributive outcomes. The new model of development thus restricted the levers by which the state had traditionally influenced economic activity. It also sought to extricate the state from sectoral conflicts and thus insulate it from the social and economic demands that historically undergirded the mobilizing strategies of the partisan Left.

Perhaps more important, the neoliberal model combined with political repression to weaken dramatically the large-scale secondary associations that popular sectors had traditionally relied on to articulate their demands and protect their interests. National confederations of workers had been bastions of political support for the Left since the 1930s, while national peasant confederations helped the Left extend its influence into the countryside after the late 1960s. But the military regime's war on the Left extended to the social organizations that were affiliated with it. Organized labor was hit especially hard because of its historic linkages to the Socialist and Communist Parties. As stated by Mañuel Barrera and J. Samuel Valenzuela, "It is not possible to determine the number of leaders who were killed, imprisoned, exiled, or just simply fired, but the result undoubtedly was that the union movement lost many if not a majority of its most experienced cadre."[92] The central labor confederation, the CUT, was declared illegal following the 1973 coup, along with the two peasant confederations affiliated with the Left. Meanwhile, a series of executive decrees implemented by the military junta led to the suspension of collective bargaining and the emasculation of surviving unions. Among other measures, these decrees made it easier for employers to fire workers, particularly those who had led strikes in the past.[93]

TABLE 4.4. *Evolution of Employment and Unemployment in Chile,*
1973–83 (thousands)

Year	Agriculture	Mining	Industry	Construction	Services	Unemployed
						(%)
1973	611.1	94.0	554.9	148.0	604.3	4.8
1974	621.2	90.3	540.9	163.3	584.3	9.1
1975	578.2	88.7	492.7	125.9	556.5	17.6
1976	586.2	87.6	477.9	105.8	564.9	21.9
1977	614.0	84.5	483.3	113.7	626.5	18.9
1978	635.2	83.5	492.5	129.4	673.6	18.0
1979	625.1	79.3	489.6	142.7	732.1	17.3
1980	638.4	78.1	492.6	161.7	765.6	17.0
1981	640.6	77.9	484.3	205.9	840.9	15.1
1982	591.2	67.3	394.0	126.6	766.6	26.1
1983	595.5	72.6	377.6	102.7	743.1	31.3

SOURCE: Esteban Jadresic, "Evolución del empleo y desempleo en Chile, 1970–1985: Series Anuales y Trimestrales," *Colección estudios CIEPLAN* 20 (December 1986): 152.

Politically motivated job dismissals were compounded by the effects of a stabilization-induced recession in 1974–75 and the tariff cuts that accompanied trade liberalization. The result was widespread deindustrialization and massive layoffs in highly unionized sectors of the economy, along with sharp cuts in public sector employment. During the first ten years of the dictatorship, employment in industry fell 32 percent, in construction 30.6 percent, and in mining 22.8 percent.[94] Unemployment, which had averaged 5 to 7 percent during the 1960s, averaged 18.1 percent during the latter half of the 1970s and surged to 31.3 percent during the second severe recession in 1982–83[95] (see Table 4.4). As the ranks of the unemployed and underemployed swelled, a growing number of workers took refuge in the informal sector of the economy, which accounted for over a quarter of the urban workforce by the early 1980s.[96]

These social and economic changes in the urban industrial sector seriously eroded the structural foundations for class-based collective action in Chile. Structural changes in the countryside were equally unfavorable. In the immediate aftermath of the coup, military repression and landlord retaliation decimated the leadership of left-wing peasant unions, and the military regime began to parcel out the more than 5,800 large agrarian estates that had been expropriated under Frei and Allende.[97] The objective of the military was not to return to the prereform agrarian structure, where large, often inefficient haciendas monopolized the best farmland and generated resentment among resident peasants and landless rural workers. Rather, the intention was to break up the cooperative and state-owned estates created by the land reform so as to disperse land ownership more widely among individual farmers. This parcelization discouraged collective action in three principal ways. First, it created thousands of new small and medium-sized producers who had gained title to their land, thus removing the principal motivation for radical forms of mobilization. Second, the structural locations and individualized productive activities of these farmers left them relatively isolated and dispersed, inhibiting organization on the basis of collective interests or solidarities. Third, in place of a class cleavage between landlords and peasants, it created new conflicts between individual farmers who had to compete with each other to gain access to a limited supply of land grants. In a serious blow to peasant union activists, a military decree passed in December 1973 prevented peasants who had led land seizures in the past from receiving these land grants. The military government also withdrew state financial and technical assistance that was vital to the functioning of peasant unions, especially at a time when political repression had severely diminished external support from political parties.[98]

In addition to these structural changes, the neoliberal model entailed the elaboration of a new legal framework that was designed to ensure that the labor movement remained weakened and fragmented. The new labor code adopted in 1979 ended compulsory union membership, placed a sixty-day time limit and other constraints on the right to strike, allowed employers to hire strikebreakers, facilitated job dismissals, and encouraged multiple unions in the same workplace. It also effectively restricted collective bargaining to wage issues and mandated that collective bargaining take place at the level of the individual plant or agrarian estate, thus eliminating the role of labor and peasant confederations in the process of bargaining.[99] The legislation was crafted to create a more "flexible" labor market with fewer political and organizational impediments to individual market exchanges between capitalists and workers. With the weakening of collective actors and the diminution of their political weight, workers would be subjected more directly to the discipline of the labor market, and capitalists would be free to contract labor at the lowest available cost. According to Barrera and Valenzuela, "In no area of economic life is the association between the attempt to produce a fully free market . . . and the authoritarian imposition of norms and regulations by the state . . . more apparent than here."[100]

Taken together, political repression, economic restructuring, and legal emasculation cut union membership in the urban sector from over 32 percent of the workforce under Allende to less than 10 percent by 1983, and the absolute number fell from 704,499 union members in 1973 to 320,903 in 1983.[101] In the rural sector, the decline of peasant unions was even more dramatic, falling from 229,836 members in 1972 to only 30,000 in 1980, or a decline of nearly 87 percent.[102]

The secondary associations that were the backbone of popular organizing strategies for the Left before 1973 were thus decimated during the first decade of military dictatorship. The resulting fragmentation of civil society and the atomization of social relationships had three complementary functions for the military regime: they undermined the bases of collective resistance to the dictatorship, they eroded the social and organizational networks that could provide a foundation for the political resurrection of the partisan Left, and they weakened the collective actors that articulated an alternative to the market individualism of neoliberalism. Consequently, the powerful, centralized social organizations that helped cultivate democratic support for the Left were not available to buttress the parties' resistance to authoritarianism. The social resistance that did exist during Pinochet's first decade—from human rights groups, student organizations, community groups, and the like—was sporadic, decentralized, and uncoordinated. It generally was not conducted under the aegis of political parties but under the relative forms of protection afforded by local parishes or universities. Linkages to party organizations were indirect and largely attributable to the activist roles of individual party militants in social networks rather than organic relationships between collective actors in the social and political spheres.

Conclusion

If the political growth of the Chilean Left after 1933 coincided with the development of organized lower-class social constituencies, the violent repression of the Left after 1973 coincided with the dramatic weakening of peasant and labor associations. In this new, more atomized social landscape, the partisan Left could hardly be reconstituted in its traditional role as the political representative of densely organized, class-based collective subjects. Following the alternative trajectories of their post-coup patterns of political learning and self-criticism, however, both the Socialist and Communist Parties found ways to adapt to the constraints of this new social environment. The Communist Party, under the new clandestine leadership of Gladys Marín, retained a firm commitment to a vanguard role in the organization of collective subjects. But it shifted its emphasis from the labor movement and the productive sphere to the territorial domain of Chile's burgeoning urban shantytowns, where impoverishment and marginalization created a tinderbox of political resentment and a potential social constituency for the party's new strategy of popular rebellion. The Socialist Party, by contrast, led by the Altamirano-Núñez branch, gradually deemphasized collective action in favor of elite-level political pacts and an electoralist strategy that could appeal to the mass of individual voters.

These respective modes of adaptation heavily conditioned the roles these parties would play in Chile's democratic transition, as well as the character of the transition process itself. The Communist Party thrived during the three-year period of social protest and mass mobilization that began in May 1983, following the crash of Pinochet's highly touted neoliberal economic "miracle." The social networks built by the party were vital to the resurrection of civil society and to the emergence of a resistance movement with insurrectionary characteristics. As the protest movement waned and the democratic opposition shifted toward electoral forms of contestation in the late 1980s, however, the Communist Party began to decline, whereas the influence of the moderate Socialists increased dramatically. This realignment enabled the Left to play an integrative role that helped to stabilize Chile's democratic transition; however, as shown in Chapter 5, it also placed constraints on the depth of the democratization process and encouraged a demobilization of the popular sectors that had been at the forefront of resistance to the military dictatorship.

CHAPTER **5**

Transition, Realignment, and the
Struggle to Deepen Democracy

ONE of the central issues in the study of democratization concerns
the impact of different types of regime transition on the character
of the democratic regime that emerges.[1] Terry Lynn Karl has argued
that there is a close relationship between the two and that the
prospects for democratic consolidation are conditioned by the nature of the transition process. In particular, she suggests that democratic stability is more likely, at least in the short term, when elites
rather than masses are ascendant during the process of transition
and when they define the parameters of political and economic
change through negotiated political pacts rather than the forceful
imposition of any single actor's political project.[2] Pacted, elite-led
transitions are most likely to culminate in relatively stable but
conservative democratic regimes that ameliorate elite opposition
by containing lower-class challenges to the social hierarchy.

The process of democratization in Chile presents an unusually
propitious test case of these propositions.[3] Alternative models of
regime transition were clearly articulated in Chile, and they were
backed by powerful and well-organized social and political forces.
Indeed, the process of transition in Chile passed through two distinct stages that were marked by highly divergent models of political change. The first stage lasted from May 1983, when an explosion of popular protests broke out against the Pinochet regime,
through the middle of 1986, when protest activity sharply declined.

This stage was marked by the ascendance of mass social and political actors, the failure of attempts to negotiate a framework for regime transition, and the prominence of insurrectionary strategies that sought a definitive break with the political and economic project of the military regime. The second stage began in late 1986 and was marked by the efforts of opposition elites to remove Pinochet within the institutional constraints established by his 1980 constitution and to negotiate a process of transition with supporters of the military regime. This latter mode of transition ultimately prevailed, and it set the tone for political dynamics under the new democratic regime in the early 1990s. This new regime, to date, seems unusually solid and stable by Latin American standards, but it has made only modest adjustments to the political and economic legacies of the Pinochet regime.

The victory of an elite-ascendant, negotiated mode of transition over a mass-ascendant insurrectionary mode was reflected in the realignment of forces within the Left. The Communist Party thrived during the first stage of the transition process, when the waves of social protest gave new purpose to its grass-roots networks and breathed life into its insurrectionary line. The party resisted the 1986–87 shift in the strategic context from social protest to electoral contestation, but it lacked the social and political strength to block it and entered into decline when it could not adapt to the new political environment. In contrast, the moderate Núñez branch of the Socialist Party was among the first to recognize the character and constraints of the second stage of the democratization process, and its astute strategic adaptation enabled this party to become the hegemonic force within the Chilean Left, despite the shallowness of its organizational roots in civil society.

In short, the Communist Party excelled when political struggle escaped the formal boundaries of governing institutions and became a form of social expression and confrontation. The party was structured as a vanguard organization whose design enabled it to operate in a social and political environment dominated by force. It thrived when politics was played out in the streets, when political struggle incorporated the mass of common citizens organized in their neighborhoods, schools, and workplaces, and when politics became a test of wills rather than a striving for consensus. The party entered its demise when politics became the art of compromise, when it revolved around bargaining and pacts among professional politicians, and when electoral competition provided political dividends not to the parties with the strongest grass-roots organization but to those that claimed the most prominent personalities and were the most adept at building consensus. The Núñez Socialists were the opposite: ill-suited for the politics of confrontation as a result of their grass-roots weakness and organizational deficiencies, their party was a collection of relatively autonomous personalities who had the strategic flexibility needed to serve as political brokers and appeal to diverse electoral constituencies.

The Núñez Socialists (along with their offspring, the Party for Democracy, or PPD) thus proved to be adept at the two political skills that were at a premium during Chile's democratic transition: electoral mobilization and the art of negotiation and consensus building. These skills were crucial to their party's integrative role in the democratization process because they enabled supporters of the Left to be incorporated procedurally into the new democratic regime without threatening the contingent consent of conservative elites to the democratization process. But these were skills that reflected the top-heavy character of the Socialist Party, and they did not lead automatically to grass-roots organization or empowerment. Indeed, in many respects they were at odds with them, posing serious dilemmas for the deepening of democracy.

The Socialist Party ultimately hoped to deepen democracy by negotiating reforms with the Christian Democrats and the Right. As a governing partner in the new democratic regime after March 1990, it very consciously eschewed the path of grass-roots mobilization to create social and political pressure for more far-reaching reforms. Meanwhile, the dramatic weakening of labor and peasant associations as a result of Pinochet's neoliberal revolution ensured that autonomous demands from civil society could be kept in check. The problem is not merely that this served to limit the scope and depth of reforms; given the political and institutional constraints, there may not have been any other viable course of action for the Left that could have produced more profound change without an inordinate risk of an authoritarian backlash, and Socialist leaders could undoubtedly argue that their moderate, gradualist course provides the most secure foundation for a secular process of deepening democracy. The more serious problem is that the process of political and economic reform has been elite-initiated and highly divorced from grass-roots collective action, which was integral to the Socialists' renovated vision of an expansive, participatory democratic order. The enduring irony of the Chilean Left is that those who most persuasively articulated a theoretical vision for the deepening of democracy through the political protagonism of collective popular subjects have been the least connected to such subjects in practice. This gap between theory and practice, between the social base and the political leadership, emerged as a vital contradiction at the heart of the Left's project for deepening democracy, and it largely accounts for the ambiguous character of the Left's contemporary political success in Chile.

Social Mobilization and Political Confrontation: The First Stage of Redemocratization

The 1980s began with the Pinochet regime in a seemingly impregnable position. The imposition of a new constitution formalized the regime, while the neoliberal economic model of the "Chicago Boys" allowed Pinochet to bask in a period of rapid growth and tout Chile's "economic miracle." After the severe repression of the regime's first five years, visible opposition was kept in check through an efficacious combination of selective repression and a consumer binge made possible by cheap foreign credit, liberalized imports, and an overvalued exchange rate. Chile's once formidable political parties were formally banned and largely invisible, the labor movement was a shadow of its former self, and popular resistance was fragmented and politically isolated.

The scenario changed dramatically, however, when a financial crisis plunged Chile into the worst recession in its modern history, causing the economy to shrink by nearly 13 percent in 1982–83. The economic crisis created fissures in the authoritarian coalition and made the military regime appear vulnerable for the first time.

It thus breathed new life into opposition groups and led to an outbreak of massive political protests in May 1983.[4] The first day of national protest was declared by the Confederation of Copper Workers, but it was heeded by a multitude of newly activated popular organizations across the country, as demonstrators stayed home from work or school, participated in marches, banged pots and pans, and built barricades in the lower-class districts or *poblaciones*. The outpouring of mass discontent led to a series of monthly protest days in 1983, along with escalating political and military repression.

The economic crisis and the resurrection of popular resistance helped to reactivate all of Chile's opposition parties, which lent political support to the protest movement. No party, however, was more intimately involved in the groundswell of popular mobilization than the Communist Party, which had a strategic orientation in favor of insurrectionary forms of resistance, along with organizational advantages in a context of direct, grass-roots confrontation with a repressive dictatorship.[5] In the face of repression, the Communists had been more effective than the Socialists in maintaining their internal coherence and organizational presence in civil society. Its previous experience with clandestine operation, as well as its hierarchical discipline and cellular structure, enabled the Communist Party to maintain a cohesive authority structure and functioning base and intermediate-level organizations that helped guide the activities of party militants in diverse social networks.

These networks, in fact, had never disappeared, even at the height of the repression in the mid-1970s. The extreme dangers of partisan political work had caused many base-level militants to retreat to the somewhat less risky social terrain, working patiently to rebuild labor, student, and *poblador* organizations. These organizations often operated under the protective umbrella of the Catholic Church and included Socialist, Christian Democratic, and other party militants in addition to Communists. Other members of grass-roots organizations were nonpartisan, and base-level groups often articulated new collective identities that emphasized political pluralism and autonomy from party control or manipulation.[6] Nevertheless, grass-roots organizations provided fertile ground for partisan political work and allowed the Communist

Party to develop a network of activists who were strategically located to catalyze popular mobilization in the years to come.

A major challenge faced by the Communist Party was that organized labor, the traditional bastion of the party, had been seriously weakened by the political and economic transformations wrought by the dictatorship. The Communist Party tried to compensate for the weakening of the labor movement by directing new organizational energies toward the sprawling urban poblaciones. When union members were laid off from their jobs or faced the threat of economic retaliation, they often transferred their political activities to their residential communities, contributing to a proliferation of territorially based popular organizations.[7] The growing network of soup kitchens, youth and women's groups, economic workshops, neighborhood associations, and human rights organizations helped to reconstitute Chilean civil society, and many became politicized as their demands clashed with a repressive and exclusive authoritarian state.

Consequently, poblador associations provided space for the resumption of grass-roots political participation, and they became primary building blocks of popular resistance to the dictatorship. Indeed, pobladores, and especially poblador youth, became the backbone of the Communist Party's popular rebellion strategy in the 1980s. Party militants in the labor movement found it difficult to embrace highly confrontational tactics because they were easily identifiable for political repression or economic retaliation, and they were reluctant to jeopardize the increasingly public organizational space conquered by unions. Insurrectionary tactics thus clashed with the labor movement's tradition of articulating public demands for economic gains and organizational rights.[8] In contrast, pobladores had a degree of cover, as the relative obscurity and anonymity of urban popular communities facilitated clandestine operation, and their activities entailed less risk of economic loss. Therefore, the most consistent and radical forms of protest during the three-year cycle of mass mobilization occurred in the poblaciones.

In its initial stages, the popular rebellion strategy focused on the construction of social networks for popular resistance. For most party members, this was a logical extension of the organizational efforts of the 1970s, rather than a strategic rupture. Indeed, there was considerable uncertainty as to what had really changed in the party's strategic posture. The precise content of the new strategy did not congeal until 1983, when the mass protests transformed Chile's political landscape and the Communist Party unveiled the "military policy" that was at the heart of popular rebellion. This military policy entailed the creation of an armed revolutionary force, the Mañuel Rodríguez Patriotic Front (FPMR), along with popular militia units known as the *milicias Rodriguistas*.[9] While the FPMR practiced bombings and urban guerrilla activities, the militias provided recruits and a form of rear-guard defense, activating students and shantytown youth to erect barricades to seal off poblaciones and block the encroachments of security forces.[10] Some party cadres were withdrawn from social work to help compose the FPMR, where they joined other cadres that had received military training in Cuba and participated in revolutionary struggles in Central America. The FPMR was set up as a separate, parallel clandestine structure with links to the internal party leadership, but it was not formally considered to be the armed wing of the party.[11] This partial institutional separation was designed both to shield party cadres from repression and to broaden the scope of the FPMR by incorporating leftist militants from outside the ranks of the Communist Party.[12]

The Communist Party saw these forms of violent resistance as part of a multifaceted arsenal of weapons to be employed against the dictatorship, ranging from such nonviolent means as labor strikes, protest marches, and boycotts to mass insurrection and guerrilla warfare. The Communists were not alone in this endeavor; although the FPMR was essentially a Communist initiative, the Almeyda Socialists and other smaller leftist groups tried to propel the protest movement in an insurrectionary direction as well.[13] The Almeyda Socialists, in fact, had welcomed the Communist Party's shift toward popular rebellion as a ratification of the strategic orientation followed by the Socialist Party since the 1973 coup and as a sign of growing strategic unity on the Left.[14] The role of the Almeyda Socialists in popular rebellion, however, was clearly subordinate because they did not have the organizational strength or coherence required to develop a military capability. Even within the Almeyda branch, which agreed on the moral right to rebellion and the legitimacy of quasi-insurrectionary forms of mass mobilization, there was no consensus on the desirability of creating an armed apparatus.[15] The party, in fact, suffered several new divisions after 1982: moderate leaders broke off to collaborate with the Núñez Socialists, while a radical faction known as the "Comandantes" exited to pursue a more revolutionary strategy.[16] Lacking strategic consensus inside the party, the Almeyda Socialists devoted their energies not to armed struggle but to grass-roots organization, relying on the social networks the party had inherited as the direct descendant of the post-coup Internal Directorate.[17]

While the Communist Party and the Almeyda Socialists worked to develop the social bases for a popular insurrection, the Núñez branch of the Socialist Party began a gradual process of organization building inside Chile. The centerpiece of this process was an organizational "convergence" in the early 1980s between scattered fragments of the Socialist Party, MAPU, MAPU-OC, the Izquierda Cristiana, and independent left-wing intellectuals in exile and inside Chile. Inspired by the ideals of the socialist renovation, a group known as the Socialist Convergence was formed in 1980, followed by the establishment of a multilateral coordinating committee in 1981 and the founding of the Socialist Bloc in 1983.[18] The Socialist Bloc was undermined by tactical disputes and different alliance strategies, but it nevertheless created momentum for the composition of a more broad-based party apparatus inside Chile under the leadership of Núñez and his collaborators.

The Núñez sector broke with the long-standing tradition of a united Left coalition between the Socialist and Communist Parties to promote a broad, Center-Left alliance with the Christian Democrats that would provide a viable governing alternative to the military regime. The Núñez Socialists and the Christian Democrats supported nonviolent forms of resistance, and they were heartened by the outbreak of protests in 1983. But these two parties rejected the more violent forms of protest, particularly the guerrilla activities of the FPMR, fearing that they would unify the military regime, provoke generalized repression, and narrow the social bases of the protest movement.[19]

Although the Christian Democrats rejected an alliance with the Communist Party, they cooperated with this new, more moderate manifestation of the Socialist Party. The Christian Democrats had followed an independent course of opposition to the dictatorship after the mid-1970s, in keeping with their historic opposition to alliances with the Left. The party became more receptive to a strategy of alliance building in the early 1980s, however. In part, this was a response to the institutionalization of the military regime and its constitutional project, which made clear that Pinochet intended to remain in power indefinitely and created new incentives for collaborative opposition efforts. It was also a response to the emergence of a new current within Chilean socialism that had broken with the Communist Party and proclaimed a firm commitment to representative democracy. The process of socialist renovation narrowed the ideological and strategic gap between the Christian Democrats and the Núñez Socialists, and it paved the way for a political accommodation.[20] Informal contacts between party leaders led to a series of meetings to craft a joint opposition strategy as the protest movement blossomed in 1983. In September 1983, the Christian Democrats and Núñez Socialists helped found the Democratic Alliance, the first in a series of multiparty pacts that eventually culminated in the fourteen-party Concertación alliance that defeated Pinochet in the 1988 plebiscite.

This alliance made the Núñez party more visible, but it remained a minority faction among Socialists inside Chile until late in the decade. Its primary strength lay among exiles and middle-class and professional circles, with some scattered support in the labor movement. Although Núñez temporarily remained behind the scenes, other political and intellectual leaders of the Socialist Bloc became prominent figures in the opposition movement as the protests opened political space for public challenges to the regime.

In short, the eruption of monthly mass protests in 1983 opened the first serious fissures in Pinochet's edifice, forcing Chile's opposition parties to define their respective strategies for regime transition. In so doing, the opposition quickly split into competing camps. The two strongest parties of the Left, the Communist Party and the Almeyda Socialists, were the main actors in a broad leftist coalition known as the Popular Democratic Movement (MDP) that was formed in September 1983. The strategic orientation of the

MDP was driven by the popular rebellion line of the Communist Party, which aimed at a complete rupture with the military regime and the creation of a new, more "advanced" form of democracy under the hegemony of the Left. In contrast, the Núñez party was a secondary partner to the Christian Democrats in the Democratic Alliance, which supported nonviolent popular mobilization to create pressure for a negotiated transition to democracy led by a Center-Left coalition. The Democratic Alliance entered into a dialogue with the military regime's interior minister, Sergio Jarpa, in late 1983, but the negotiations proved fruitless when Pinochet refused to step down or consider a return to democratic rule.

This basic alignment, and the balance of forces that it represented, remained intact so long as the political dynamic was dominated by social protests against the military regime. In a political context dominated by force, the Communist Party had numerous advantages over its Socialist counterparts. These advantages included a highly disciplined cellular structure that enabled base-level militants to operate effectively under clandestinity; an extensive network of party militants in grass-roots social organizations; a cohesive authority structure, which prevented factionalism and schisms; hierarchical control of party subunits, which provided coordination and direction for base and intermediate-level operatives; and, especially after 1980, a strategic orientation that prioritized grass-roots organization and diverse forms of popular resistance.

These features, then, made the Communist Party the predominant force within the Chilean Left through the mid-1980s and a central actor in the protest movement that rocked the dictatorship. A fundamental change in the political context occurred, however, as the second, decisive stage of Chile's democratic transition began in 1986. The gradual shift from violent confrontation to electoral contestation placed a premium on new organizational features, political resources, and strategic orientations. Whereas the Communist Party was slow to adapt to this new context—in fact, it furiously resisted it—the Núñez Socialists were among the first to discern it and the most adroit in exploiting it. These different responses to an evolving strategic environment set the stage for the eclipse of the Communist Party and the relative ascendance of the Núñez Socialists during Chile's regime transition.

Demobilization and the Realignment of the
Left in the Second Stage of Transition

The dynamics of Chile's democratic transition and the changing balance of opposition forces were heavily influenced by the
efforts of the Pinochet regime to institutionalize authoritarian rule.
The explosion of mass protests in the mid-1980s suggested that the
balance of forces was turning in favor of democratization. Nevertheless, Pinochet refused to acknowledge this new correlation of
forces, and as the tide of protests ebbed after July 1986, it became
clear that social mobilization alone was insufficient to topple a
dictatorship that retained its internal cohesiveness and coercive
capabilities.[21] But if Pinochet could not be forced from power, neither could he rely indefinitely on purely coercive forms of rule, as
the protest movement demonstrated that long-term stability required at least the partial restoration of representative institutions.
The 1980 constitution offered a solution because it established a
framework for a "transition" to an authoritarian regime that would
tolerate limited forms of electoral representation under strict military tutelage.[22] The demise of the protest movement after 1986
provided a favorable context for the implementation of this regime
transition, which called for a national plebiscite on a presidential
candidate chosen by the military junta, followed by restricted elections for a subordinate congress. Such a process could buttress the
regime's legitimacy among wavering supporters, while driving a
wedge between moderate and radical opponents.

The grand achievement of the Núñez Socialists and the Christian Democrats was to recognize that Pinochet could be trapped in
his own institutionality—that is, that democratic forces could subvert a process originally designed to legitimate and extend authoritarian rule. The turning point came in late 1986, which the Communist Party had correctly dubbed the "decisive year," albeit for
the wrong reasons. After months of partisan bickering in the opposition movement, a diverse Civic Assembly convoked a mass
mobilization for early July, little knowing that it would be the
last major protest against the dictatorship. Two subsequent events
drove a deep wedge between the moderate and insurrectionary ten-

dencies in the opposition movement. In August, the military regime discovered a large cache of weapons in Chile's northern desert that the FPMR had imported with Cuban assistance, and in early September a daring attack on Pinochet's motorcade by the FPMR wounded but failed to assassinate the dictator. The regime responded with a new wave of repression, and the armed forces rallied behind Pinochet, who began a thinly veiled campaign for nomination as the sole candidate in the plebiscite scheduled for 1988.[23]

The Christian Democrats and Núñez Socialists denounced the Communists' violent tactics, claiming that they exacerbated repression and provoked fear of a generalized militarization of society. More important, the Socialists and Christian Democrats retreated from their support of the protest movement, which had become less pluralistic as political moderates and middle-class sectors stayed home out of fear of violence, leaving the pobladores and students increasingly isolated in their militant tactics.[24] Prominent Socialist intellectuals from the Núñez party quietly postulated the failure of the protest movement, arguing that it was impossible to defeat the dictatorship on the terrain where it was strongest, that of naked confrontation and force. The only option, they argued, was to contest the regime where it was most vulnerable, at the ballot box, even if that meant operating within the institutional constraints established by the 1980 constitution.[25]

In 1987 both the Christian Democratic Party and the Núñez Socialists adopted this electoral course. They began with a civic campaign to try to force the dictatorship to hold open, competitive elections rather than a plebiscite with a single candidate. It became clear, however, that the regime would not budge from its prescribed formula and that Pinochet was preparing his own candidacy for a plebsiscite that could lock him in the presidential palace for eight more years. In response, the two parties took the decisive step of initiating a full-scale electoral mobilization to vote against the dictator. This entailed the February 1988 construction of a broad fourteen-party coalition known as the Concertación de Partidos por el "No" to direct the opposition campaign.

Knowing that a large turnout would be essential to defeat Pinochet, the Concertación sponsored a massive voter registration drive and tried to convince the population that electoral fraud could be controlled through the training of poll watchers, mock balloting exercises, and a parallel, computerized system of vote counting run by the opposition itself.[26] The largest opposition parties also began to register members to achieve legal recognition under a new political parties law. In a move that would yield enormous political dividends, the Núñez Socialists circumvented a constitutional ban on parties of Marxist inspiration by legalizing a new, nonideological "instrumental" party known as the Party for Democracy (PPD). Under the direction of Socialist leader Ricardo Lagos, the PPD incorporated independent figures as well as Socialists and began to fill the political void between the centrist Christian Democrats and the traditional partisan Left. The PPD provided a protective umbrella for Socialist leaders during the critical transition period and enabled them to be politically active without granting Socialist Party recognition to Pinochet's constitutional framework.

The principal locus of political contestation thus shifted in 1987–88 from street protests and shantytown barricades to electoral mobilization. The Christian Democrats and Núñez Socialists effectively exploited this new terrain, even though it was structured by the timetable and procedural framework established by the military regime. The Communist Party, however, staunchly resisted this electoral strategy, arguing that the regime would never sponsor a clean electoral contest or recognize the outcome if it were defeated. The Communists feared that participation would legitimize Pinochet's institutionalization project, and they insisted that popular rebellion remained the only viable strategy to drive the dictator from power.[27]

The Communist Party's refusal to acknowledge a change in the strategic environment left it isolated politically, as the Almeyda Socialists joined the moderate opposition in opting to challenge Pinochet in the electoral arena. Although the Almeyda Socialists did not formally dissolve their ties to the Communist Party, they moved into a tactical alliance with the Christian Democrats and the Núñez Socialists and joined the Concertación when it was formed in 1988. This strategic shift reflected the penetration of the main themes of the Socialist renovation within the party leadership, as well as the impact of Gorbachev's reforms in the Soviet

Union, which challenged the party's orthodox tendencies. As the descendants of the Internal Directorate of the 1970s, the most important young leaders of the Almeyda Socialists inside Chile had never represented the more radical tendencies in Chilean socialism; with the exodus and marginalization of the Comandantes in the mid-1980s, remaining leaders came to advocate a vision of democratic socialism that was highly compatible with that of the Núñez sector.[28]

Most important, this shift also reflected changes in the strategic environment that forced the Almeyda Socialists to reconsider the prospects for toppling Pinochet. The party's earlier radical stance had been reinforced by the quasi-insurrectionary character of the protest movement, which made the regime look vulnerable. By the middle of 1985, however, moderate leaders of the Almeyda Socialists were concerned that the protest movement had ceased to accumulate forces, and they believed it was imperative to unify the opposition movement along a common line of action. These leaders gradually began to distance the Almeyda branch from the Communist Party while cultivating relationships with the Christian Democrats and Núñez Socialists, a process that accelerated after the FPMR's failed assassination attempt in September 1986.[29] By late 1986 the regime appeared more formidable as economic growth resumed, the protests waned, and Pinochet began to campaign for an eight-year extension of his presidency. Since the dictatorship retained an overwhelming advantage in military force and had proven its ability to withstand economic crisis and mass popular resistance, the Almeyda Socialists concluded that Pinochet could be defeated only in the political and electoral terrain, where his popularity was highly suspect.

Chile's democratic transition ultimately followed the script of the Christian Democrats and the Socialists, as even the Communist Party made a belated entry into the plebiscite campaign to avoid complete isolation and placate the desires of many party loyalists. The parties that wrote the script were rewarded at the ballot box; the Communist Party, which entered the electoral arena with ambivalence while retaining its line of popular rebellion, suffered electorally. Pinochet was defeated in the plebiscite by a vote of 54.7 percent to 43 percent and grudgingly accepted the reality of a regime transition while working to solidify institutional checks against the exercise of popular sovereignty by Chile's democratic majority. After the Concertación negotiated a package of constitutional reforms with Pinochet's interior minister and conservative political leaders, presidential and congressional elections were held in December 1990. The Concertación elected the Christian Democrat Patricio Aylwin to the presidency, while the two main branches of the Socialist Party placed three members each in his cabinet and another seven subsecretaries between them. The Núñez Socialists in conjunction with the PPD elected 18 deputies to the 120-seat national congress and 4 senators out of 38 seats at stake, while the Almeyda Socialists elected 6 deputies and 1 senator.[30]

Shortly after the election, the Socialist Party was reunified along the ideological and strategic principles advocated by the Núñez sector and the moderate leadership of the Almeyda sector, and the bulk of MAPU, MAPU-OC, and the Izquierda Cristiana were incorporated within the ranks of the party.[31] The party leadership was evenly divided between the Núñez and Almeyda branches, while the more orthodox wing of the Almeyda sector created an internal party faction under the leadership of congressional deputy Camilo Escalona.[32] Over the course of the early 1990s the party's congenital factionalism gradually lost its ideological coloring and came to revolve around the competing interests of personalistic networks more than programmatic distinctions. Escalona moved quickly toward the party mainstream and accepted the basic tenets of the renovation process. By 1994 he was chosen consensually as the party president, then in 1995 he defeated Senator Núñez and two other rivals in internal elections for the party presidency. The ascendance of the Escalona faction demonstrated the continuing influence of traditional identities within the party rank and file, although it was increasingly difficult to discern meaningful strategic or ideological positions that distinguished his faction.[33] In a sense, the advocates of renovation won the battle to determine the party's ideological and strategic trajectory, but the leaders of the renovation process shared control over the party apparatus with more traditional sectors.

Despite the continued factionalism, both the Socialist Party and the PPD gained in electoral strength during the early 1990s, and

TABLE 5.1. *Congressional and Municipal Election Results in Chile,*
1989–96 (% of valid votes)

Party or coalition	1989 congressional	1992 municipal	1993 congressional	1996 municipal
Concertación	51.5	53.5	55.4	56.0
Christian Democratic	26.1	28.9	27.1	26.0
Socialist	–	8.5	12.0	11.2
PPD	–	9.3	11.8	11.8
Rightist Opposition	43.2	37.4	36.6	34.4
RN	18.2	18.0	16.2	18.5
UDI	9.2	11.4	12.1	13.1
UCC	–	8.0	3.2	2.8
Leftist Opposition	5.3	6.6	7.9	5.9
MIDA/PC	–	6.6	6.5	5.9

ACRONYMS: MIDA—Movement of the Democratic Allendista Left (Communist Party–led alliance); PC—Communist Party; PPD—Party for Democracy; RN—National Renovation; UCC—Center-Center Union; UDI—Independent Democratic Union.
SOURCES: For 1989–93, Gerardo L. Munck, "Democratic Stability and Its Limits: An Analysis of Chile's 1993 Elections," *Journal of Interamerican Studies and World Affairs* 36 (Summer 1994): 18. For 1996, *El Mercurio,* October 28, 1996, p. A1.

by the 1993 congressional elections their combined vote of 23.8 percent was approaching parity with that of the Christian Democratic Party (see Table 5.1). The congressional delegation of the two parties increased from 5 to 7 senators and from 24 to 31 deputies.

While the Socialist Party basked in its return to governmental responsibilities, there was no disguising the fact that the course of Chile's democratic transition represented a major strategic defeat for the Communist Party. The party had gambled on an insurrectionary rupture with the military regime and an uninterrupted process of revolutionary transformation; instead, Pinochet was eased out of office within the constraints of his own constitutional framework, which continued to structure the process of regime transition. Although the Communist Party threw its support to the Aylwin campaign, it remained outside the Concertación and was not considered for cabinet positions. The Communists participated in the congressional elections as part of a coalition with four minor leftist parties, but none of the Communist candidates were elected.[34] The party initially declared a position of "constructive independence" toward the new government, but it moved quickly into opposition, claiming that the Concertación was merely administering the political and economic legacy of the dictatorship. Completely locked out of Chile's formal representative institutions, the Communist Party gave priority to grass-roots organization in the social domain to mobilize the sectoral demands of workers, pobladores, and human rights groups for more radical political and economic reforms.[35]

The Communist Party's strategic defeat, its political marginalization, and its ambivalent posture toward the transition process combined with the impact of events in Eastern Europe to plunge the party into the worst crisis in its modern history. Indeed, the party's legendary discipline began to unravel as the leadership tried to steer a middle course through the swirling winds of unfavorable domestic and international changes. The party had awkwardly welcomed Gorbachev's perestroika as a democratic "renovation" in Soviet socialism,[36] while denying its relevance for the Chilean context and embracing the revolutionary orthodoxy of Cuba.[37] Likewise, the leadership had tried to keep one foot in the insurrectionary camp while inserting the other in the democratization process in the late 1980s; this ambiguity contributed to the division of the FPMR into "autonomous" and pro-party factions in 1987, and it produced a quiet exodus of young pobladores who had been attracted to the "heroic" struggle of popular rebellion but were disillusioned with the mundane politics of a pacted electoral transition. By 1990, as Aylwin prepared to take office, this ambiguity had produced widespread dissent within the party's more moderate professional and middle-class sectors, who wanted the party to overcome its political isolation by fully embracing the democratization process, renouncing popular rebellion, and supporting the government of the Concertación. These sectors represented a new, "renovated" tendency within the ranks of the party which denounced its historic fealty to the Soviet Union, rejected Leninist organizational models, and advocated a socialist project centered on the logic of deepening democracy.[38]

When the party leadership moved to censure prominent political and intellectual figures in 1990 for making their dissent public, an explosion of protest erupted within the party's moderate wing. Ironically, the very organizational features that helped ensure the party's coherence and survival under the dictatorship—its hier-

archical structure, disciplinary norms, and monolithic authority—
became obstacles to a flexible response to the shifting strategic
context of Chile's democratic transition. When serious differences
over strategic and ideological questions emerged, the party's organizational structure became a major point of contention, blocking
the flow of information and the expression of dissenting views.[39]
Dissidents decried the suppression of debate within the party and
the absence of channels for internal democratic expression.[40] The
party eventually suffered its first major schism since the 1920s in
November 1990, with the exodus of hundreds of intellectuals, professionals, and students. While some of these dissidents opted to
join the Socialist Party or the PPD, the largest faction created a
new organization known as Democratic Left Participation (PDI).[41]
Therefore, having lost its most radicalized young pobladores and
much of its moderate, middle-class wing, the Communist Party
was left with a reduced core of party loyalists drawn primarily from
union and poblador circles. These sectors adhered loyally to the
ideological and strategic guidance of the party hierarchy, which
was now dominated by Gladys Marín and her closest collaborators
who managed the party's clandestine apparatus during the era of
popular rebellion.

Redemocratization and the Changing Balance of Forces

As Chile returned to democratic rule in 1990, it was clear that a
dual shift in political power had occurred within the Chilean Left
during the second stage of the democratic transition: from the
Communist Party to the Socialist Party and from the more radical
to the more moderate tendencies in the Socialist camp. These
changes ratified the demise of vanguardist party models and the
ascendance of an electoral model, along with a shift from a polarizing to an integrative role in Chile's transition process. This dual
shift had important implications for a strategy of deepening democracy in Chile, but it was not exempt from contradictions. Indeed, it
was characterized by a major paradox: while the new hegemonic
force on the Left, the Núñez faction of the Socialist Party, had the
most clearly elaborated theoretical vision of socialism as the deep-

ening of democracy, it was also the furthest removed from the popular collective actors who could make that vision a reality, and its strategic calculations of what was possible during Chile's democratic transition led the party to retreat from the radical implications of a deepening strategy. Consequently, the hegemony of the Núñez Socialists represented the ascendance of a professional political class and its electoral project within the Chilean Left and the relative demise of the collective popular subjects who were preeminent during the protest period.

This dual shift reflected the dynamics of a new strategic environment, as well as the differential capabilities of the parties in adapting to (and capitalizing on) new opportunities and constraints. Several features of this new strategic environment warrant closer scrutiny. First, the transition process in Chile, and in particular the institutional constraints established by the Pinochet regime, gave powerful advantages to the party of the Left that was most adept in establishing an alliance with the Center. The historic division of the Chilean polity between Left, Center, and Right "thirds," along with the status of the centrist Christian Democrats as the largest party in Chile, made it exceedingly unlikely that the Left alone could have toppled a regime as formidable as that of Pinochet— something that even the Communists recognized. But while the insurrectionary line of the Communist Party widened the gulf that separated it from the Christian Democrats, the Núñez Socialists implemented strategic and ideological changes that were consciously designed for a rapprochement with the Center. This was not only necessary to create a political majority to confront Pinochet in the plebiscite but was also essential for electoral success in the unusual, highly disproportional binomial system designed by Pinochet's advisers to augment the congressional representation of the Right and diminish that of the Left.[42] Therefore, whereas Socialist candidates could be elected to Congress with Christian Democratic and other centrist votes, the narrow electoral alliance of the Communist Party excluded it from national representative institutions.

Second, the shift in the late 1980s from grass-roots protest to electoral contestation was clearly unfavorable to a vanguard organization like the Communist Party but had natural advantages for open, multiclass, catch-all parties like the Núñez Socialist Party and the PPD. The rigors of clandestine resistance during the earlier period had placed a premium on the organizational attributes possessed by the Communist Party: its cellular structure provided a measure of protection, its hierarchical discipline ensured the maintenance of political authority and direction, and its cadres had deeply rooted identities and ideological commitments that sustained activism in the face of repression. In contrast to electoral mobilization, clandestine resistance was not a mass activity; it was organized by selective, disciplined, and highly motivated political minorities, precisely the type of cadres found within the Communist Party. The rigid demands associated with militancy in a vanguard party limit membership to the most committed activists, those for whom politics is an all-consuming way of life. It is these individuals who are most likely to be on the front lines of a resistance movement against authoritarianism. Communist Party cadres were thus crucial to the survival and reconstruction of a democratic civil society under the dictatorship, and they were vital catalysts for the broader forms of popular mobilization that erupted during the protest movement.

But even at their height, the protests never involved more than an activist minority within the democratic opposition to Pinochet.[43] During the second stage of transition, those who were more fluid or tentative in their identities, more episodic in their political participation, less ideologically motivated, and more risk-averse in their political expressions counted for more in the electoral terrain than the activist networks and vanguard cadres that earlier had led the underground resistance. Opinion polls suggested that the bulk of the population was located in the moderate political center;[44] when these sectors mobilized to vote, they were far more likely to gravitate to electoralist parties like the Christian Democrats, the Núñez Socialists, or the PPD, with their social and ideological pluralism, pragmatic moderation, and lax membership requirements, rather than a vanguard party with disciplined ideological cadres and a segregative working-class/poblador identity like the Communist Party.[45]

Indeed, the PPD had remarkable success in capturing these voters. Initially seen as a short-term tactical instrument of the Núñez Socialists, the PPD quickly carved out an independent niche as a progressive but nonideological catch-all party that appealed to a broad range of unaffiliated moderate leftists and secular centrists who did not identify with the historical traditions of either the Socialists or the Christian Democrats. The PPD declared itself to be open to all social categories, and it eschewed ideological definition beyond a commitment to the reconquest of political democracy, preferring to promote pragmatic and concrete programmatic goals over abstract ideological principles.[46] Initially, many leaders and members of the PPD had dual membership in the Socialist Party, but as the PPD attracted support from political independents and demonstrated its ability to contest the Christian Democrats' control of the centrist terrain, the new party began to assert an autonomous political identity. The Socialist Party and the PPD separated ranks in 1992 but maintained an electoral federation or subpact within the broader Concertación alliance, with Ricardo Lagos serving as the titular electoral leader of both parties.[47]

Socialist leaders, for their part, consciously promoted a relaxation of criteria for party membership. Traditional conceptions of membership had stressed permanent activism and a selfless, near total commitment of an individual's energy and talent to the work of the party. These exacting standards were relaxed to cultivate support among individuals with varying levels of commitment and activism.[48] For many, identification and commitment did not extend beyond episodic support in the voting booth. This gained new acceptance, however, as it enabled the party to expand its electoral constituency well beyond the ranks of core party activists, and it also placed few base-level constraints on the political autonomy and strategic flexibility of the party leadership as it developed alliance policies and accepted governmental positions. This electoralist strategy of appealing to individual voters also fit well in the more atomized social structure that the parties confronted at the end of the Pinochet era. With rural peasant unions virtually eliminated, urban labor movements drastically weakened, and urban popular movements highly fragmented within and between different poblaciones, no large, organized social collectivities were available for electoral encapsulation by individual parties. Electoral success, in other words, was contingent on a party's ability to reach out to individuals in diverse social settings while articulating a political agenda with generalized rather than sectoral appeal.

The shift in the balance of power between vanguardist and electoralist parties also reflected the inherent elitism of Chile's democratic transition, with the preeminence of political pacts, negotiated compromises, and institutional engineering. Patterns of elite strategic interaction are often consciously insulated from base-level political pressures; this insulation can quickly lead to social demobilization and a weakening of parties with grass-roots orientations. In the Chilean case, Socialist and Christian Democratic leaders were wary that popular mobilization would frighten the military and the political Right and thus destabilize the democratic transition. Hence they sought to keep popular pressures in check and channel grass-roots participation into less threatening forms of electoral mobilization. This could be seen, for example, in the effort of the parties of the Concertación to replace autonomous leaders of the Unitary Congress of Pobladores (CUP) with more compliant party loyalists after the CUP sponsored a hunger march in June 1988 that the parties feared would be polarizing.[49]

The elitism inherent in a shift toward electoralism can also be seen in the emphasis on political personalities rather than grass-roots organization. Here again, the Núñez Socialists had a decisive advantage as the democratic transition progressed. Although the party was weak in its base-level organization, it was top-heavy in prominent figures, as its moderation, centrist alliances, and academic and international connections enabled party leaders to "go public" earlier and have access to media sources that were denied to the Communist Party and the Almeyda Socialists. The Communist Party had to hold its 1989 congress—the first since the coup—in semiclandestinity, and the party's most compelling leader, Gladys Marín, did not emerge from clandestinity until January 1990. As for the Almeyda Socialists, by the time Clodomiro Almeyda returned to Chile from Berlin in 1987, he was aging and in ill health; the young leader of the radical wing of the Almeyda party, Camilo

Escalona, was little known outside the party after years of exile and clandestinity. In contrast, the Núñez Socialists had an open congress in 1989 and a bevy of political and intellectual figures who had operated publicly for much of the decade, the most prominent being Ricardo Lagos, a leader of the Democratic Alliance and the driving force behind the creation of the PPD. Lagos became widely recognized as the most forceful and charismatic leader in the opposition movement; as the first leftist leader to gain access to television in 1988, he stunned the nation (and infuriated the military regime) by pointing his finger at the camera and personally challenging Pinochet. The weight of these personalities enabled the Socialist-PPD bloc to broaden its electoral appeal far beyond the scope of its base-level organization.

Finally, the Núñez Socialists continuously accumulated forces throughout the transition process as a result of their tactical successes. The strategic alliance with the Christian Democrats, the early decision to enter the electoral arena, the creation of the PPD, and the construction of the Concertación all yielded political dividends that reinforced the relative position of moderate Socialists.[50] In contrast, the Communist Party suffered cumulative losses as the transition traversed a path that was different from the one it had foreseen. Even if the party leadership had recognized and accepted the change in the strategic environment in 1986–87, it is doubtful that the party could have quickly reversed course and embraced the highly restricted regime transition that followed. The insurrectionary strategy of the 1980s had produced significant changes in the Communist Party: the revolutionary identity of new recruits (especially poblador youth), the militarization of cadres, and the ambitious strategic objectives created an inertial logic that could not be reversed abruptly. Indeed, the domestic and international context of the 1980s created parallel but conflicting pressures toward militarization and renovation within the ranks of the Communist Party, and the effort of the party leadership to split the difference only alienated both sides and contributed to the fragmentation of the party. Consequently, the demise of the Communist Party and the ascendance of the Núñez Socialists were two sides of the same process, just as the decline of the protest movement and the rise of electoral mobilization were inextricably linked.

The Tension Between Deepening and Consolidating
Democracy: The Left in the New Democratic Era

For the Socialist Party, returning to power in an alliance with the Christian Democrats was both a significant achievement and a formidable challenge. The process of renovation in the party had been designed to demonstrate that it was mature enough to assume governmental responsibilities, while sponsoring a strategic vision of a Center-Left alliance backed by a solid social and political majority as the foundation for any project of democratic reform. This sociopolitical bloc was seen as the driving force for efforts to deepen democracy by removing the authoritarian enclaves inherited from the Pinochet regime, encouraging popular participation in the political process, and alleviating the "social debt" accumulated during the period of authoritarian rule.

Several factors, however, worked against this vision of progressively deepening democracy. First, the authoritarian enclaves implanted by Pinochet's efforts to establish a "protected democracy" proved to be highly resistant to modification, and they erected serious impediments to the exercise of popular sovereignty by Chile's democratic majority.[51] Second, the Concertación alliance gave priority to the objective of democratic consolidation, and the Socialist Party opted to play an integrative role that downplayed mass mobilization in favor of elite-negotiated social and political pacts to mitigate the fears of conservative sectors.[52] Third, social movements entered the new democratic era in a weak and highly fragmented state that limited their capacity to generate political pressure for more far-reaching reforms. An analysis of these mutually reinforcing constraints should help explain why there has been a relatively high degree of social and economic continuity despite Chile's regime transition and why the vision of deepening democracy has proven to be so elusive in practice.

Like many military regimes, the Pinochet dictatorship tried to create "reserve domains" of authoritarian influence that were shielded from democratic contestation.[53] What made the Pinochet regime exceptional was its elaborate design for building multiple, interlocking institutional checks against the exercise of popular sovereignty and its relative success in structuring the regime transition to ensure that it proceeded within the boundaries of these institutional confines.[54] Indeed, Gerardo Munck and Carol Skalnik Leff assert that "incumbent elites may well have exerted more control over the transition" in Chile "than in any other recent case of regime change."[55] In contrast to the military regimes in Argentina, where the Falklands War seriously discredited the military and undermined its control of the transition process, and Brazil, where important sectors of the business community broke with the regime to support redemocratization,[56] the Chilean military regime remained remarkably cohesive, and it retained staunch support among economic elites who had become ardent defenders of the neoliberal model implemented by Pinochet's Chicago-school technocrats.[57] These factors contributed to the durability of the regime and prevented the democratic opposition from deposing Pinochet and dictating the terms of regime transition. Social mobilization and economic crisis were insufficient to force Pinochet from power; although he was defeated politically in the plebiscite, this defeat occurred within the regime's prescribed constitutional framework, and the transition adhered to the timetable and the core of the institutional blueprint elaborated by Pinochet's political advisers.

In short, Chile's regime transition was the product of a political deadlock or stalemate, rather than a definitive defeat of the dictatorship or an institutional rupture leading to the imposition of an alternative political order.[58] Pinochet was unable to achieve an electoral mandate to legitimize and extend his authoritarian project, but popular movements were likewise unable to topple his regime and impose an unfettered democracy. The transition to a limited democracy thus emerged as an intermediate or compromise solution to this political deadlock, a form of conflict resolution that relied on negotiated pacts to establish the terms of mutual accommodation. Given the lack of democratic vocation on the part of economic elites and the armed forces, this institutional compromise was fragile, and the threat of an authoritarian reversion limited the maneuvering space of the Concertación. Consequently, the Christian Democrats and the Socialists opted to avoid mass mobilization to pressure the military regime for radical changes in the constitutional framework following Pinochet's plebiscite defeat.

Instead, the Concertación entered into negotiations with the representatives of the political Right and the military regime to modify some of the more patently authoritarian features of the constitution, while acceding to many of the other restrictions that the regime placed on the process of democratization.

The result was a package of more than 50 constitutional reforms that were ratified in a plebiscite before the 1989 national elections. The most important of these reforms eliminated the constitutional proscription of Marxist parties; allowed union members to hold party affiliations; limited the emergency powers of the state; prevented the president from dissolving the lower house of congress; enhanced civilian representation on the National Security Council; increased the number of elected senators; and relaxed the requirements for future constitutional amendments.[59] The negotiated accord, however, left in place severe restrictions on civilian authority and democratic expression. In particular, the military regime retained the right to designate nine senators, equal to one-fifth of the upper house of congress, and the reforms did not empower the incoming elected president to remove the commanders in chief of the various branches of the armed forces. Additionally, the military regime imposed a disproportional binomial electoral system that ingeniously overrepresented the political Right in congress while excluding the Communist Party and other leftist forces outside the Concertación. It also took steps to pack the Supreme Court with new conservative supporters, insulate the Central Bank from democratic pressures, and block the democratic government from replacing civil servants. The institutional autonomy of the armed forces was buttressed by legal provisions that guaranteed them 10 percent of the export revenues from the state-owned copper industry, while a 1978 amnesty law ensured immunity from prosecution for the vast majority of human rights abuses committed under authoritarian rule.[60]

Consequently, the new civilian regime was established with highly skewed democratic representation, limited civilian authority, and a broad range of institutional "prerogatives" that maintained military tutelage of the political process.[61] The contradictions of Chile's pacted transition were perhaps best symbolized by Pinochet's delivery of the presidency to Aylwin while retaining his command of the army, a former dictator who remained a menacing force behind the formal facade of democratic institutions. Any strategy for the deepening of democracy under the new government was clearly predicated upon the removal of these institutional restrictions and authoritarian enclaves.

The Concertación, however, faced a basic strategic dilemma that exposed the inherent tensions between the deepening and consolidation of democracy. The trauma of the Allende experience had left Pinochet's civilian and military supporters inordinately wary of Chile's democratic majority, and they were fervent supporters of the neoliberal economic model. The tacit acceptance of a regime transition by the political and economic Right was thus highly contingent on the maintenance of the "protections" against the exercise of popular sovereignty that were built into Pinochet's institutional formula. The Concertación could try to mobilize social and political actors to put pressure on the Right to accept democratic reforms, but such a strategy entailed an inherent risk that the Right would abandon the democratic arena. Alternatively, the Concertación could try to build a consensus for reforms through negotiations with the Right, but the inherited institutional constraints provided very limited forms of democratic leverage to elicit concessions from Pinochet's erstwhile supporters.

In keeping with the political logic that had guided the Christian Democratic and Socialist Parties since late 1986, the Concertación chose the latter course once it came into office in March 1990. The alliance gave priority to democratic consolidation and macroeconomic stability, and it sought to avoid stimulating popular demands or forms of social mobilization that could endanger the Right's contingent acceptance of the democratization process. Socialist leader German Correa acknowledged that his party practiced forms of "self-limitation" and accepted continuity with the authoritarian period, arguing that "we were very clear that we could not introduce great changes in the country because of the fact that the fundamental objective was to consolidate democracy."[62] The objective of deepening democracy, therefore, was pursued in a piecemeal and nonconfrontational manner and was left contingent on the government's capacity to build a consensus and negotiate reforms with its conservative parliamentary opposition.

Despite the Concertación's solid electoral majority, it could not simply legislate reforms because the existence of Pinochet's designated senators gave the Right an unelected majority in the Senate and veto power over any impending legislation. The Concertación thus hoped to elicit the support of the conservative National Renovation party for new democratic reforms, under the assumption that it was more moderate and accommodating than the ardently pro-Pinochet Independent Democratic Union (UDI). National Renovation, however, resisted constitutional reforms and other legislation designed to modify the institutional constraints left in place by Pinochet. Although agreements were reached to hold elections for municipal councils and mayors in 1992, the Right blocked government efforts to eliminate the institution of designated senators, give the president authority to remove military commanders, and replace the binomial electoral system with a more proportional mode of representation. Likewise, the Right supported the military's efforts to uphold its legal immunity from prosecution for human rights violations. Although the Concertación had initially pledged to revoke the military regime's self-proclaimed amnesty law, in office it tacitly accepted the amnesty. The Aylwin government created a national commission to investigate human rights violations, but the commission was not authorized to identify the guilty parties, and its report was designed to pave the way for an ill-defined "national reconciliation" rather than to bring perpetrators to justice.[63] It was thus left to the family members of victims in a small number of cases that were not covered by the amnesty law to pursue judicial redress through a court system that had long upheld the military's veil of impunity.[64]

Similarly, the Concertación adopted a cautious approach to social and economic reform. For most of the authoritarian period, the parties of the Concertación had been ardent critics of Pinochet's neoliberal model, arguing that it had eroded Chile's industrial base, generated indebtedness and financial speculation, and enriched a privileged minority while expanding unemployment and poverty.[65] During the crisis of the early 1980s, Socialist leader Ricardo Lagos declared that the neoliberal model had "destroyed the economy" and "generated a profound abyss between two Chiles, between the Chile of the rich and powerful . . . and the Chile of the great majority."[66] Even after the economic rebound of the mid-1980s, the Chilean "miracle" left real wages more than 15 percent below their 1970 level in 1987 and the minimum wage 36 percent lower.[67] The percentage of Chileans living below the poverty line more than doubled between 1970 and 1987, from 20 percent to 44.4 percent.[68] Likewise, inequality worsened under the military regime, as the income share of every quintile of the population declined except for the upper quintile, which rose sharply during Pinochet's rule.[69]

As the democratic transition appeared on the horizon, however, the Concertación softened its opposition to the neoliberal model and backed away from any plan for a radical change in Chile's development trajectory. In part, this represented a political concession to economic elites and other supporters of Pinochet; the Concertación recognized that business sectors saw the military regime as the guarantor of the economic model, and it knew they would fervently oppose any regime transition that threatened to reverse Pinochet's free market revolution. Continuity in the economic model was the most viable way to alleviate the concerns of the business community and induce its political and economic cooperation with the new democratic government. In contrast, to challenge business interests by pushing for radical change would not only provoke intense political opposition but could also precipitate a capital strike that would destabilize the economy and undermine the new democratic regime.

Continuity in the economic model was not merely a tactical concession on the part of the Concertación, however; it also reflected the growing acceptance of a development strategy oriented toward private enterprise, market competition, and international economic integration. The crisis of Soviet-bloc command economies undermined ideological attachments to traditional conceptions of socialism within the Chilean Left,[70] while the debacle of heterodox economic experiments in postauthoritarian Brazil, Argentina, and Peru raised doubts about various statist alternatives to neoliberalism. Ultimately, however, the Concertación's acceptance of the core of neoliberalism was attributable to the recuperation and dynamism of the Chilean economy itself after the mid-1980s. Following the financial crisis of 1982–83, the economy began a period of sustained expansion in 1984, with growth rates

TABLE 5.2. *Main Economic Indicators for Chile, 1972–95*

Year	GDP growth	Growth in manufacturing	Real wages	Index of real wages (1970 = 100)
1972	1.4	3.5	1.0	126.6
1973	-3.6	-5.3	–	–
1974	4.3	-3.7	–	64.1
1975	-11.3	-28.5	-3.3	62.0
1976	4.5	6.7	5.5	65.4
1977	8.6	12.0	8.1	70.7
1978	7.8	10.1	6.2	75.1
1979	8.2	6.9	8.4	81.4
1980	7.5	5.0	8.7	88.5
1981	5.5	2.6	8.9	96.4
1982	-14.1	-20.9	-0.3	96.1
1983	-0.7	3.1	-10.7	85.8
1984	6.3	8.9	0.1	85.9
1985	2.4	2.7	-4.3	82.2
1986	5.7	7.6	1.9	83.8
1987	6.6	5.3	-0.2	83.6
1988	7.3	8.8	6.5	89.1
1989	9.9	10.9	1.9	90.8
1990	3.3	1.1	1.8	92.4
1991	7.3	6.6	4.8	96.9
1992	11.0	11.0	4.5	101.3
1993	6.3	5.1	–	–
1994	4.2	2.9	4.5	105.0
1995	8.5	6.5	4.1	108.7

SOURCES: For growth in GDP and manufacturing, InterAmerican Development Bank, *Economic and Social Progress in Latin America* (Washington, D.C., various issues); for wages, Programa de Economía y Trabajo, *Economía y trabajo en Chile: Informe anual* (Santiago, various issues).

averaging 6.4 percent annually during Pinochet's final six years in office and the four-year presidential term of Patricio Aylwin (see Table 5.2). In contrast to the highly speculative economic boom of the late 1970s, this new period of growth rested on a significant expansion of productive capacity in both agricultural and industrial spheres, with fruit, forestry, and fishing sectors leading an export boom that manifested the newfound competitiveness and diversity of the Chilean economy.

In a context of rapid economic growth, low inflation, and expanding employment, the Concertación had no intention of introducing radical changes in the development model. Since the mid-1980s, the Núñez Socialist Party had been trying to reassure Chilean capitalists that it had abandoned utopian projects and statist conceptions of socialism and that it recognized the "creative potential" of private enterprise as "the basic cell of the productive fabric."[71] When the party returned to power in alliance with the Christian Democrats—and placed one of its young technocrats, Carlos Ominami, as the minister of economy—it accepted the major structural changes associated with the neoliberal model as a fait accompli. Accordingly, the new government did not attempt to reverse the privatization of industries and the financial system, the parcelization of agricultural land, or the lowering of tariffs that symbolized the new outward orientation of the Chilean economy. Likewise, it largely accepted the shrinking of the state's entrepreneurial role, the privatization of such services as social security and health care, the centrality of market mechanisms, and the "flexibilization" of the labor market. Aylwin's team gave priority to the maintenance of macroeconomic stability and pledged to uphold investors' confidence and resist the "populist temptation" to increase social spending rapidly.[72]

The reforms promoted by the new government thus stayed within the bounds of neoliberalism's free market logic, aiming to harness the dynamism of neoliberalism to the requisites of a "growth with equity" strategy. Shortly after Aylwin took office, negotiations with the National Renovation party yielded an agreement for a temporary increase in the value-added tax from 16 to 18 percent, which combined with increases in personal and corporate income taxes to allow social spending to expand modestly beyond the growth rate of the economy.[73] A new Fund for Solidarity and Social Investment (FOSIS) was established to channel targeted financial resources to microenterprises and other grass-roots groups and encourage their participation in development projects. Although the new government accepted the privatization of health insurance and social security, it channeled new resources to the public health care and pension systems that catered to poorer individuals who could not afford the more expensive forms of private coverage.[74]

Chile's popular sectors clearly benefited from the expanding economy and increased social spending. More than 560,000 jobs were created between 1989 and 1993, driving the official unemployment rate down to 4.5 percent, although the informal sector continued to account for 17.6 percent of the workforce in Santiago.[75] Average real wages rose by 10.5 percent between 1989 and 1993 (see Table 5.2), and the real minimum wage increased more sharply by 33 percent.[76] The poverty rate, which stood at 44 percent of the population at the beginning of the democratic period, fell to 28.5 percent by the end of 1994.[77]

The problem of inequality proved to be more intractable, however, as the percentage of the national income earned by the lowest quintile of the population actually decreased from 5.5 percent in 1990 to 5.2 percent in 1995, compared to the 54.9 percent garnered by the wealthiest quintile.[78] Income distribution in Chile continued to be one of the most skewed in the world; according to a 1996 report from the World Bank, Chile's Gini index of income inequality ranked 59th out of 65 developing countries, ahead of only Panama, Kenya, Zimbabwe, Guatemala, South Africa, and Brazil.[79] Although government social spending increased sharply under Aylwin and Frei, it essentially followed the trend line of the national economy; during the first seven years of the democratic regime social spending only increased from 14 to 15 percent of the GDP, well below the 20 to 25 percent that it accounted for in the 1960s.[80]

These results indicated that in a context of rapid and sustained economic expansion, the neoliberal model could be adapted to allow more of its benefits to trickle down to popular sectors. But despite its achievements in the battle against poverty and unemployment, the new democratic government failed to devise a more equitable model of development, and the material gains of popular sectors were never allowed to challenge the core logic of neoliberalism. This generated considerable tension between the government of the Concertación and its most important organized popular constituency, the United Workers Central (CUT), which was under Christian Democratic and Socialist leadership until a 1996 realignment produced a new directorate controlled by an alliance of Socialist and Communist labor leaders. In the early period of democratic transition, the Concertación had high hopes that tripartite bargaining between the government, the CUT, and the peak business association, the Confederation of Production and Commerce

(CPC), would produce a "social pact" to establish a new framework of cooperative capital-labor relations.[81] Although a general accord was reached in April 1990 in which the CUT accepted the basic principles of Chile's market economy and obtained higher wages, the CPC rejected more specific agreements to reform the labor code inherited from Pinochet.[82] Later in the year, modest reforms were negotiated with National Renovation in congress to give legal recognition to labor confederations, pay indemnities to dismissed workers, permit voluntary collective bargaining beyond the enterprise level, and provide unions with more enterprise information.[83] The reforms fell far short of creating a level playing field between capital and labor, however, because the labor code still gave companies almost complete freedom to fire workers, maintained restrictions on union organization beyond the firm level, allowed the contracting of replacement workers during strikes, and made interenterprise collective bargaining contingent on an employer's consent. Moreover, some 85 percent of Chilean workers continued to be excluded from collective bargaining, including those in temporary agricultural work, construction, forestry, maritime, commerce, and public services, while others were denied the right to strike.[84] In particular, workers in the new strategic export sectors have yet to acquire the rights to strike or engage in collective bargaining.

Indeed, the government's early vision of social "concertation" proved to be an increasingly elusive target as Chilean democracy moved beyond the early transitional conjuncture. After a period of capital-labor dialogue in late 1989 and early 1990, the CPC chose a more hard-line leadership that had less interest in negotiations, resisted all reforms of the labor code, and dedicated itself to the defense of Pinochet's economic legacy.[85] A tripartite agreement was reached in April 1992 to adjust the minimum wage in accordance with inflation and increased worker productivity, and plans were made to establish tripartite commissions to study problems of labor education, health care, unemployment, and retraining. Four months later, however, the CUT temporarily "froze" relations with the Ministry of Labor, criticizing the government's technocratic style of decision making, its lack of consultation with the union movement, and its slow progress on labor reforms.[86] By 1994, the

CPC was not even participating in negotiations over the minimum wage, the CUT had suspended its participation in government-sponsored technical and study commissions, and the government had to adjust wages unilaterally after failing to reach an accord with the CUT. In July 1994 the CUT held its first protest march under the new democratic regime to demand the extension of collective bargaining rights beyond the firm level, encourage the expansion of social security coverage and worker indemnizations, and protest repeated firings of strike leaders and union organizers. Under government pressure, the CUT declared that the protest was directed against capital rather than the newly installed Frei administration, but there was no disguising organized labor's discontent with the meager fruits of a negotiating strategy that had produced few changes in economic policies or legal rights, while leaving labor in a clearly subordinate position relative to the interests of capital.[87] In response to the criticisms by organized labor, the Frei administration proposed new reforms to the labor code but was unable to get them passed by the conservative Senate majority.

In many respects, the democratic government was caught in a vicious circle. Since major changes in the legal framework of labor relations were precluded by the composition of the Senate and the structural dependence of the state on capital, the government saw the strengthening of the labor movement as a prerequisite for the creation of a political balance favoring deeper reforms. But the strengthening of the labor movement had a low ceiling in the context of the existing economic model and its corresponding labor legislation. Consequently, union membership grew rapidly during the early stages of Chile's democratic transition, but it leveled off quickly after the new regime was in place. Union membership increased from 446,194 in 1988, or 10.5 percent of the workforce, to 701,355 in 1991, representing 15.4 percent of the workforce. By 1993, however, union membership was declining once again, and by 1995 it had fallen back to 12.7 percent of the workforce, a far cry from the 32 percent registered before the 1973 coup (see Table 5.3).

Since the CUT represented about two-thirds of unionized workers, the organized labor movement manifested a relatively high degree of centralization, which was favorable for the government's scheme of tripartite bargaining and social concertation.[88]

TABLE 5.3. *Union Affiliation in Chile, 1973 and 1981–95*

Year	Labor force (000's)	Number of unions	Union members	% of workforce unionized
1973	2,923.8	6,502	934,335	32.0
1981	3,271.1	3,977	395,951	12.1
1982	2,943.9	4,048	347,741	11.8
1983	3,216.1	4,401	320,903	9.9
1984	3,268.1	4,714	343,329	10.5
1985	3,537.4	4,994	360,963	10.2
1986	3,895.7	5,391	386,987	9.9
1987	4,010.8	5,883	422,302	10.5
1988	4,265.8	6,446	446,194	10.5
1989	4,424.8	7,118	507,616	11.5
1990	4,459.6	8,861	606,812	13.6
1991	4,540.4	9,858	701,355	15.4
1992	4,773.3	10,756	724,065	15.2
1993	4,985.7	11,369	682,704	13.7
1994	4,988.3	12,109	661,966	13.3
1995	5,025.8	12,715	637,570	12.7

SOURCES: For 1973, calculated from Esteban Jadresic, "Evolución del empleo y desempleo en Chile, 1970–1985, Series anuales y trimestrales." *Colección Estudios CIEPLAN* 20 (December 1986), p. 151, and Timothy R. Scully, *Rethinking the Center: Party Politics in Nineteenth- and Twentieth-Century Chile* (Stanford: Stanford University Press, 1992), p. 156. For 1981–95, Programma de Economía y Trabajo, *Economía y trabajo en Chile: Informe anual, 1995–96* (Santiago), p. 286.

The labor "leg" of the tripartite arrangement, however, remained too weak to balance effectively the political and economic weight of capital, leaving Chile a far cry from the "organized" capitalism and corporatist arrangements of European social democracies, which counted on unionization rates as high as 70 to 80 percent in the Scandinavian countries and over 40 percent in much of the rest of the region.[89] The overall level of unionization in Chile is too low to make the CUT a genuinely effective and representative "encompassing association," leaving it with limited leverage to press for reforms and a questionable capacity to deliver the compliance of its social constituency to negotiated accords.[90] Indeed, the emphasis on elite-level bargaining and the political ties of the CUT leadership to the parties of the governing coalition created a notable gap between the union hierarchy and rank-and-file workers.[91] This gap opened political space for the more militant tactics of the Communist Party, which has consistently rejected social pacts in favor of a mobilizing strategy to press sectoral labor demands. By 1996, the Communist Party had maneuvered back into a position of influence within the CUT leadership, and the restoration of its alliance with Socialist labor leaders in the internal CUT elections had spawned serious tensions between the parties of the Concertación and their labor affiliates in the CUT. The mobilizing strategy of the Communist Party enabled it to claim the presidency of labor federations that represented half of the CUT's membership in 1996, including federations of the mining, construction, health care, metallurgical, transport, and textile workers.[92]

The structural conditions created by Chile's neoliberal revolution are not propitious for a significant modification of the basic correlation of social forces because the leverage of capital has been strongly reinforced by the cumulative changes of the past twenty years. Large-scale privatizations conducted at favorable prices provided new resources for private capital and concentrated greater wealth in the hands of a small number of diversified economic groups. They also gave the private sector thorough control over production and investment decisions; whereas the state accounted for 75 percent of investment in Chile in the early 1970s, the private sector now accounts for 75 percent.[93] The privatization of social services has also expanded the economic resources and political leverage of capital, and it helped reduce employment in the public sector from 270,000 (17 percent of the workforce) in the mid-1970s to 190,000 (only 7 percent of the workforce) in the early 1990s.[94] In Chile's open, internationally integrated economy, the government's policy options are constrained by its dependence on foreign investment and the opportunities for capital flight. Meanwhile, a domestic capitalist class that was historically dependent on state tutelage, subsidy, and protection has become more autonomous and assertive in locating dynamic international market niches. In principle, the new democratic government wants to craft policy incentives that will channel investment toward higher value-added products with greater levels of processing to make Chile's economic expansion more sustainable and less dependent on primary exports and cheap labor.[95] More than ever before, however, Chile's model of accumulation is contingent on the economic performance of private capital, and the Socialist Party's strategy for aiding popular sectors relies less on traditional welfare state programs than efforts to train and "capacitate" workers to take advantage of employment opportunities in new, internationally competitive market niches.[96]

Likewise, structural conditions militate against the efforts of popular sectors to counteract these basic trends through collective action. Although the first decade of neoliberalism produced widespread deindustrialization and dramatic cuts in industrial employment and wage labor, the post-1984 expansion brought a recuperation of industrial activity. Employment in manufacturing industries, which bottomed out at 374,000 during the crisis in 1982, surged to 835,000 by 1993.[97] This recuperation, however, hardly restored the pre-coup status quo ante, as it occurred in the context of a radically different labor market that had thoroughly transformed the Chilean working class in ways that inhibited collective action. As the new government took office, the informal sector continued to account for more than 20 percent of the workforce,[98] while various studies estimated that between 17 and 30 percent of wage workers were employed without a contract.[99] Many others worked with only temporary contracts that left them with few forms of legal protection and largely divorced from opportunities for collective bargaining. As a result, in 1992 13 percent of salaried workers earned less than the legal minimum wage, and 41 percent were estimated to earn less than the minimum required to meet basic needs.[100] The trend toward temporary employment was especially pronounced in the agricultural sector, where the proportion of temporary workers increased from 55 percent in 1975 to 75 percent at the end of the dictatorship,[101] half of whom worked without a contract.[102]

In short, although employment expanded rapidly after 1984, many of the new jobs were precarious, creating a fragmented, heterogeneous, and unstable workforce that confronted both structural and legal impediments to collective action. The neoliberal model thus had a paradoxical effect: while it concentrated capital in the hands of large, diversified business and financial conglomerates, it dispersed the workforce, as productive activities were increasingly subcontracted out to small and medium-sized enterprises that relied on "flexible" and precarious forms of employment.[103] In the urban sector, this dispersion and segmentation of the labor market reduced the centrality of permanent workers in large-scale industrial establishments, thus undermining the representativeness of the CUT and obstructing its organizational development as a counterweight to the power of capital. It also undermined the construction of collective identities, as workers were highly differentiated by legal status, employment conditions, and income levels, and many followed individualist strategies or turned to microenterprises to pursue economic mobility. It is not surprising, then, that labor militancy under the democratic regime has been concentrated not in the traditional industrial sectors but in white-collar public service sectors such as health and education, where unions can press economistic demands directly against the government rather than private capital.

Likewise, in the rural and agrarian sectors, the atomization of the workforce and the reliance on temporary and noncontract labor place significant constraints on lower-class collective action. The dictatorship all but eliminated popular collective subjects in the countryside by dissolving 80 percent of the 500 peasant cooperatives established through the land reform and cutting membership in agricultural unions from 229,836 salaried workers in 1973 to 30,000 in 1980.[104] By 1994, membership in agricultural unions had crept back up to 62,565,[105] representing well under 10 percent of the agricultural workforce, a mere shadow of the density of rural lower-class organization before the coup. In the absence of fundamental reforms of the labor code to facilitate collective bargaining by temporary workers, the agricultural sector continues to solidify elite dominance through lower-class atomization.

If the labor movement is no longer capable of adequately organizing and representing Chile's diffuse workforce, far less is it able to perform a "radial" function as the axis of diverse popular sector mobilizing strategies. As stated by Guillermo Campero, the labor movement historically served as the "standard bearer . . . of popular struggles for democratization and social justice."[106] Under the dictatorship, the copper workers' federation played a vital role in the initial convocation of the protest movement in 1983, but organized labor generally took a back seat to the poblador movement in the wave of protests that rocked the military regime. By the end of the decade, however, the poblador movement was a shell of its former self, and its always limited capacity for horizontal articulation had seriously eroded. Initiatives to construct a centralized coordinating mechanism for the poblador movement in the late 1980s were undermined by partisan competition and the deliberate effort of the Concertación to replace autonomous and militant leaders with party representatives who could channel popular energies into less threatening electoral arenas. Consequently, as the regime transition ensued, there was widespread demobilization in the poblaciones, and the collective action that did exist was highly fragmented, decentralized, and increasingly divorced from overarching political demands.

This fragmentation complemented the new government's strategy for addressing the needs of pobladores, which sought to respond to localized needs while avoiding the mobilization of strong collective pressures. The government's housing program, for example, provided subsidies in response to legally channeled petitions from individuals and small groups, in continuation of the military regime's effort to find "private" solutions to the housing deficit while avoiding the large-scale collective mobilizations that engendered land seizures in the 1960s and 1970s.[107] Likewise, the new government provided financial support for "popular economic organizations" (OEPs), which became increasingly oriented toward microenterprise productive activities in the 1990s, in contrast to the cooperative labor workshops and consumption-oriented communal kitchens of the 1980s. Over 3,200 OEP's existed in Santiago alone by the early 1990s, counting on more than 81,000 members.[108] Consequently, grass-roots organizations continued to be active in urban popular districts, but their character was different from those that predominated in the recent past.[109] The new groups are highly localized and particularistic, less inclined toward political mobilization, almost completely isolated from trade union activity or other horizontal ties, and more oriented toward finding private solutions within existing market niches and government programs than articulating broad-based sectoral demands. They are created more for the purpose of channeling resources from the government or nongovernmental organizations than for exerting pressure on the government to modify social and economic relationships.

Despite the growth of OEPs, Chile remains far removed from a reformed model of "popular capitalism," and the long-term economic viability of OEPs in the context of a highly concentrated capitalist economy is subject to doubt.[110] Although government-sponsored neighborhood councils and other territorially based grass-roots organizations have also grown under the new regime, levels of coordination and integration are low, and their capacity to engender popular participation has been very limited.[111] The dominant tendencies in Chile's social landscape, therefore, remain fragmentation, depoliticization, and diminished participation.[112]

The mass social mobilizations of the 1960s, early 1970s, and mid-1980s have been conspicuous by their absence during the early years of the new democratic regime, and there is little indication that they are looming on the horizon for the years to come, despite an increase in labor unrest in 1996.[113] There was a significant increase in strike activity during the early period of regime transition, but this was to be expected given the inauguration of a government that was sympathetic to labor after an extended period of severe labor restrictions and pent-up demands. Strike activity leveled off after 1991 and remained far below the levels reached during the pre-1973 period (see Table 5.4).

Demobilization has also occurred in the political sphere. Grass-roots participation in the local organs of the Socialist Party has shriveled between electoral campaigns, and the PPD remains a party of "notables" with only the most minimal forms of grass-roots organizational development. The declining importance of active, organized party militants with fixed ideological and political loyalties has paralleled these parties' pursuit of individual voters with diverse and fluid political identities. Likewise, given Chile's more diffuse and differentiated social structure, these parties do not specialize in the representation of specific social classes or sectors, aiming instead to appeal to the heterogenous interests of a national electorate, a shift that invariably requires a process of ideological dilution.[114] This strategy brought considerable electoral success in the 1990s: support for the Socialist Party increased from 8.5 percent of the vote in the 1992 municipal elections to 12 percent in the 1993 congressional elections and 11.2 percent in the 1996 municipal elections, while the PPD's vote increased from 9.2 percent in 1992 to 11.8 percent in both 1993 and 1996 (see Table

TABLE 5.4. *Strike Activity in Chile, Pre-1973 and 1983–93*

Year	Number of strikes	Workers involved	Work days lost
1966	1,073	195,435	2,015,253
1969	977	275,406	972,382
1971	2,709	302,397	1,414,313
1972	3,289	397,142	1,654,151
1983	36	3,571	46,243
1984	38	3,595	46,473
1985	42	8,532	67,603
1986	41	3,940	69,034
1987	81	9,913	104,213
1988	72	5,645	87,451
1989	101	17,857	298,561
1990	176	25,010	245,192
1991	224	46,215	733,794
1992	247	26,962	334,708
1993	225	25,153	314,246

SOURCES: For 1966–72, Henry A. Landesberger and Tim McDaniel, "Hypermobilization in Chile, 1970–1973," in Atul Kohli, ed., *The State and Development in the Third World* (Princeton: Princeton University Press, 1986), p. 187. For 1983–93, Patricio Frías, "Sindicatos en la transición: En la búsqueda de una nueva identidad," in Programma Economía y Trabajo, *Economía y trabajo en Chile: Informe anual, 1993–1994* (Santiago), p. 63.

5.1). The two parties also increased their share of municipal mayorships and counselors: jointly, they increased from 18.6 percent of the mayorships and 15.8 percent of counselors in 1992 to 21.7 percent of mayors and 20.9 percent of counselors in 1996.[115] These results brought the Socialist-PPD bloc to a position of virtual parity with the Christian Democrats within the Concertación, as only a 3 percentage point difference separated the Socialist-PPD vote from that of the Christian Democrats in both 1993 and 1996. In December 1997 congressional elections, the combined Socialist-PPD vote of 23.7 percent surpassed that of the Christian Democrats for the first time. This has given the PS-PPD bloc additional leverage to promote Ricardo Lagos as the next presidential candidate of the governing alliance; however, it has also led to new competition with the Christian Democrats, who lack a candidate of comparable appeal but have been loath to accept a norm of rotation in the leadership of the Concertación.

The position of the Communist Party in democratic Chile is starkly different. While the Socialist Party and the PPD have occupied the heights of state power, the Communist Party has remained deeply inserted in grass-roots organizing work in trade unions, poblaciones, and universities. The party has encouraged popular mobilization around sectoral demands to pressure the government for deeper political and economic reforms, and it made significant gains in the labor unions, the neighborhood councils, and the student movement in the mid-1990s. But if the Communist Party remains a force to be reckoned with in organized civil society, its electoral strength is minimal, and the binomial system of representation continues to exclude it from formal state institutions. In the early 1990s the Communist Party rebuilt a leftist coalition known as the Movement of the Democratic Allendista Left (MIDA) with radical splinters from the Socialist Party, the MIR, and other groups. But the electoral support of Communist-backed candidates, which stood at 6.6 percent in 1992, 6.5 percent in 1993, 5.9 percent in 1996, and 6.9 percent in 1997, remains too weak to overcome the political marginalization of the party, and the Christian Democrats have so far refused to admit the Communists into the Concertación, even though the governing alliance might benefit electorally from doing so.[116] Recognizing that the period of regime transition has been unfavorable to its interests, the Communist Party's strategy has been to "bunker down" within its core constituencies, banking on a long-term growth strategy that assumes the contradictions between democracy and neoliberalism will provide new opportunities for social mobilization. The party also anticipates a rupture in the Concertación as a result of the competition for leadership between the Christian Democrats and the Socialist-PPD bloc, thus paving the way for a reconstruction of a united Left coalition.[117]

Conclusion: Demobilization and the Deepening of Democracy

The Chilean Socialist Party has demonstrated that the Left is not necessarily doomed to political irrelevance in the post–Cold War, poststructural adjustment era in Latin America. Despite the social dislocations and the fragmentation of interests associated

with Chile's neoliberal revolution, the Socialist Party was able to
find a formula that enabled it to compete in the electoral arena,
along with an alliance strategy that provided it with access to
upper-level government positions. It has been less successful, however, at activating collective popular subjects to expand the narrow
boundaries of Chile's segmented democratic regime. Well into the
second government of the Concertación, the political arena in
Chile is thoroughly dominated by a caste of professional politicians
who control the policymaking process through bargaining relationships with economic elites and, secondarily, labor representatives.
Political input by other popular organizations is minimal, given
their fragmented state and a generalized withdrawal from nonelec-
toral forms of political participation.

In their more candid moments, leaders of the Left within the
Concertación profess not to be concerned with the demobilization
of collective popular subjects. Ricardo Lagos, for example, claims
that low levels of social mobilization are a reflection of "democratic normalcy," whereas the extensive mobilization of the mid-
1980s corresponded to the very different dynamics of an authoritarian conjuncture.[118] Nevertheless, the weakness and deactivation of
social movements in contemporary Chile make it exceedingly difficult for the Socialists to uphold their theoretical commitment to
the deepening of democracy. A low level of participation clearly
diminishes popular sovereignty: it limits input into the political
process, narrows the political agenda and the range of debate, un-
dermines the accountability of representatives to their constituents, and weakens the impetus for political and economic reform.
As Jonathan Fox has demonstrated, policy reforms arise out of the
interaction between state and society; government initiatives are
more likely to result in the implementation of significant reforms
when they count on organized support within civil society, which
can enhance the leverage of reformers, generate political pressure
for change, and provide allies against the resistance of conservative
opponents inside or outside the government.[119] Organization and
participation remain the primary weapons of the weak, the only
available means to mobilize the force of numbers as a counterweight to the de facto power that is derived from the ownership of
capital. In their absence, there has been little incentive for the Con-

certación to expand the inherited boundaries of a protected democracy and even less pressure on the Right to recognize a new balance of political forces. The institutional constraints on popular sovereignty in Chile have proven to be highly resilient. After nearly eight years of civilian rule, the Concertación has been unable to reach an accord with the Right to eliminate designated senators or introduce a more representative electoral system. Although Pinochet's term as army commander expired in March 1998, the former dictator assumed a new position as senator for life, buttressing the unelected rightist majority in the upper house of congress. These authoritarian enclaves are reinforced by structural constraints to the deepening of democracy that are securely rooted in the social transformations wrought by Chile's free market revolution. Demobilization in Chile is not a mere artifact of institutional design or the political cautiousness of a transitional conjuncture. It must be traced, instead, to the political defeat of the social protest movement of the mid-1980s, a defeat that determined the pacted character of Chile's regime transition, stamped the "genetic code" of the new civilian regime, and consolidated the socioeconomic revolution imposed by the dictatorship.[120] This defeat does not permanently foreclose the prospects for social mobilization, as the new sociopolitical matrix provides ample contradictions to spawn future cleavages and confrontations. The defeat does, however, ensure that there will no return to the status quo ante, meaning that any future wave of mobilization will have to be generated out of a social and cultural landscape that has been thoroughly reconfigured by an authoritarian experiment in market individualism. The social networks, organizational expressions, and generative mechanisms of such a future mobilization exist in only the most rudimentary form in contemporary Chile.

Although efforts to deepen democracy in the immediate future may be contingent on reformist initiatives and elite-level strategic interaction to eliminate the remaining authoritarian enclaves, over the long term negotiations from above are likely to have a limited democratizating effect unless they are buttressed by organized participation from below. Unfortunately, the pacted character of Chile's democratic transition has focused scholarly attention on the nation's professional political caste, to the general neglect of political dynamics at the level of party bases and social networks. Although the transformation of Chile's political class has been widely studied, virtually nothing is known about the dynamics of change from below. The following chapter tries to rectify this imbalance through an analysis of political change and continuity among left-wing party militants during the process of democratization in Chile.

CHAPTER 6

The View from the Base: Party Militants
and Political Change in Chile

IN many respects, the story of the Chilean Left over the past twenty years is one of bifurcation. The political alliance that anchored the Left for a generation broke apart in the 1980s, as the Socialist and Communist Parties chose different paths in the struggle against the dictatorship. The two parties followed distinct strategic trajectories, and the ideological breach between them widened dramatically as the Communist Party charted an insurrectionary course and the Socialist Party experienced an ideological renewal that centered on the reconceptualization of socialism as the deepening of democracy. On the surface, the divergence of the political leaderships and the political projects of the two parties seemed patently clear.

When viewed from below—from the level of grass-roots party militants—this bifurcation was less obvious. The Allende and Pinochet years spawned different interpretations within the Chilean Left, and their historical meaning was heavily contested. But these different interpretations did not divide the party memberships as neatly as they divided the party organizations and their leaderships. In fact, they often cut across partisan distinctions, as there continued to be considerable overlap in the core political beliefs of militants in the Socialist and Communist Parties, and considerable diversity existed within the ranks of both parties when Chile returned to democratic rule in the 1990s. When viewed from below, there was not a simple dichotomy between distinct party organizations but a fluid and complex array of contested meanings that circulated within and between the separate constituencies of the individual parties.

Indeed, as Chile returned to democratic rule and the teleological vision of socialism became increasingly opaque, a broad consensus existed within the ranks of the two parties on a political project of deepening democracy. Different perspectives on how to achieve such an ambitious goal cut across the separate party organizations. Despite the Socialist Party's new political alliance with the Christian Democrats, the traditional commitment to a united Left retained considerable appeal among militants of both the Socialist and Communist Parties. Clearly, the breach that separated the two parties at the leadership level was much less pronounced at the base.

The dynamics of change and continuity at the level of party militants may thus be very different from those at the level of party elites. Political and intellectual elites were major protagonists of change in both the Socialist and Communist Parties under the dictatorship, and they have had ample opportunities to speak and write for the public record to articulate their positions.[1] To date, however, virtually nothing is known about the process by which rank-and-file party militants have experienced these changes. This is especially unfortunate, given the integral role of grass-roots activists in any strategy for the deepening of democracy. Political parties in the Chilean Left have historically represented far more than voting affiliations; in reality, they have been social and political subcultures that claim the time, talent, and loyalties of party militants, while nourishing deeply rooted collective identities and self-images that are transmitted from one generation to the next and consciously socialized into newcomers. Traditional beliefs and practices are integral to these collective identities, and they are not easily modified, even when elites are committed to political change.

The more highly developed these subcultures are, the stronger the resistance to change is likely to be from within the ranks of the party itself. Consequently, the dynamics of political change cannot be understood merely through an analysis of elite-level political and intellectual discourse or through an examination of strategic interaction between party leaders. It is also necessary to take into account the perspectives of party bases and their interaction with political leaders. Only then is it possible to understand why strong partisan subcultures make it likely that change and continuity will coexist in permanent tension and in highly complex combinations. This chapter adopts a bottom-up perspective to analyze these tensions between change and continuity within the base-level militancy of the Socialist and Communist Parties. It explores the contested meanings of the Allende and Pinochet years for party activists, assesses their conformance to the "official" interpretations developed by party elites, and analyzes the logic of grass-roots support and opposition to elite-initiated political change in both parties. At a time when "renovation" has become a term of obligatory reference for virtually any political proposal in the Chilean Left, this chapter explores the varied meanings that have been attached to the term. In particular, it demonstrates the centrality of democratic norms in the redefinition of the Chilean Left, as well as the unifying force of the concept of deepening democracy.

Party Militants and Political Change

In this chapter party activists tell the history of the Allende and Pinochet years through their own words and articulate their own interpretations of the political triumphs and tragedies that have shaped their lives. They also express their opinions about the role of the Left in Chile's process of democratization. The analysis is based on personal interviews conducted by the author with 60 base-level party militants between January and August 1990. A total of 28 Communist militants were interviewed, along with 32 from the Socialist Party (16 from the Almeyda branch of the party and 16 from the Núñez branch, which led the party's process of renovation). Interviews were semistructured but open-ended to maximize the opportunities for interviewees to express their own ideas and interpretations. All interviews were conducted in Santiago, and militants were selected through personal references and networks of contacts in the parties and social organizations. Although a random sample was not taken, interviewees represented a cross section of Santiago militants according to age, gender, and social class. Thirty percent of the party militants interviewed were women, and the sample pool in each party was evenly divided between militants who lived in lower-class communities (poblaciones) and those from middle- or upper-class communities. The sample pool was also evenly divided in each party between militants who were politically active during the Allende years and younger militants who became active during the period of resistance to the military regime.

These interviews were conducted at a time of exceptional ferment and redefinition within the Chilean Left. It followed the December 1989 election of Patricio Aylwin to the presidency after nearly seventeen years of military dictatorship and the reunification of the Socialist Party the same month after a decade of fragmentation. During this period party militants were also struggling to comprehend glasnost and perestroika in the Soviet Union, the collapse of the East European Communist regimes in the fall of 1989, and the electoral defeat of the Nicaraguan Sandinistas in February 1990. In Chile, both the Socialist and Communist Parties were relegalized in 1990 after nearly seventeen years of repression and partial or total clandestinity; while Socialist militants reveled in their party's reunification and its return to governmental responsibilities through the Concertación alliance, the Communist Party was suffering through months of rare public dissent that led to the defection of most of the party intelligentsia, numerous prominent leaders, and hundreds of base-level militants. The period of interviewing was thus one of triumph for the Socialist Party and unprecedented crisis for the Communist Party, but it was, more fundamentally, a period of political and ideological redefinition for both.

The interviews provide evidence of the diversity of responses that have been adopted by Left party militants to these turbulent events. Some party militants embraced and reinforced the changes initiated by elite sectors, whereas others held fast to traditional beliefs or became disillusioned by the course of events and the fraying of historic ideological identities. For the purposes of comparative analysis, five basic syndromes or response patterns can be identified. The first is one of "disorientation," which refers to the social anomie that accompanies the breakdown of traditional partisan and ideological identities and the inability to construct (or accept) new belief systems, collective identities, and political roles. This syndrome is found among militants who have rejected or lost faith in previously held beliefs, often feeling that they had deceived themselves by embracing illusory political objectives or naively following the marching orders of misguided party organizations. For these militants, the collapse of the traditional belief system rooted in Marx and Lenin leads not to the articulation of a new one but to a distrust and rejection of all collective political projects. Typically, these militants lose their sense of political belonging or location. Many eventually withdraw from politics and retreat to the individual domain of their private lives.

A second syndrome is that of "fundamentalism." Fundamentalist militants typically blame external forces or circumstances for political defeats, while staunchly defending the validity of core principles and beliefs derived from the Marxist tradition. Once established, these core beliefs and identities are embedded in an enclosed conceptual universe that is largely impervious to external influences and highly resistant to change, even when it becomes seemingly incongruous with empirical realities. Core beliefs are treated as revealed truths and endowed with an aura of scientific certainty that does not tolerate questioning or dissent. The belief systems of fundamentalists are so thoroughly integrated and tightly woven that the coherence of the whole is contingent on the validity of the individual parts; consequently, they instinctually reject even modest efforts at reform or renovation as betrayals of a party's essential character.[2]

A third syndrome could be called "organizational loyalism." In contrast to fundamentalists, organizational loyalists owe their primary allegiance to a party organization rather than core ideological principles or beliefs. Political meaning is derived from membership and participation in the collectivity, and the sense of belonging to a political "family" is capable of generating powerful identities, particularly during periods of intense mobilization and conflict with outsiders. Since the collective identities of these loyalists are organizational rather than ideological, they are able to adapt to elite-initiated changes in beliefs or practices without experiencing politically debilitating cognitive dissonance or expressing active dissent. Indeed, loyalists are inclined to follow the lead of the party hierarchy on ideological and strategic issues, and the main challenges to their political identities are derived from intraparty elite divisions rather than ideological shifts or political defeats.

A fourth syndrome is that of the "renovationists." These militants represent a flexible and complex mixture of both change and continuity in political orientations. Renovationists are prone to reflect critically on traditional beliefs and practices and to modify them in accordance with changing circumstances or perceptions of efficacy. Nevertheless, they uphold the validity of core values from the socialist tradition and use them as building blocks for a new socialist project that is firmly grounded in democratic principles, both in the party and in the society at large. These militants are flexible and innovative agents of change, but their pragmatism is tempered by an idealism that embraces the goal of social transformation and resists abrupt or dramatic changes in traditional identities. Their basic response to social and political change is not to reject their party's traditional project but to try to adapt or modernize it for the exigencies of a new era.

The final syndrome, one of "pragmatism," reflects a loss of faith in traditional visions of radical socioeconomic and political transformation and a resulting retreat to more limited and pragmatic objectives related to electoral success and governmental participation. Unlike the "disoriented" militants, pragmatists remain politically active despite the loss of an ideological compass. While rejecting traditional beliefs and objectives, they try to construct a new project for the Left that is politically viable and focused on concrete programmatic issues rather than overarching teleological visions. The pragmatist syndrome thus represents a sharp break with traditional Marxist ideals and identities as it seeks to reconstruct the project of the Left on new cognitive and normative foundations. Pragmatists emphasize political realism over ultimate objectives and define success largely in terms of governmental access rather than social transformation.[3]

These syndromes are indicative of the complexity of change

and continuity in the Chilean Left, and they shed light on the divergent ways in which historical experiences are processed cognitively and transformed into political lessons. Although the pragmatist syndrome was largely absent among the Communist Party militants that were interviewed, it was present among Socialist militants, and the other four syndromes could be easily identified within both parties. This suggests that political cleavages in the Chilean Left cut across party lines and that they do not bifurcate partisan subcultures nearly to the extent that elite-level ideological changes and strategic choices have divorced the party organizations. The extracts from interviews presented below are designed to give concrete examples of the varying patterns of political learning and political change within these partisan subcultures and to show how they have shaped the reconceptualization of the socialist project as a process of deepening democracy.

Learning from Defeat: The Popular Unity
Experience and Resistance to Pinochet

The Chilean Left provides an example of "catastrophic" political learning that has few parallels in the modern world. The lessons derived from the experience of winning, losing, and trying to regain power profoundly influenced the evolution of political roles and strategies in the post-1973 period. These lessons also helped determine the respective positions of the Socialist and Communist Parties in Chile's subsequent democratic transition. The interpretations of the Allende experience articulated by party elites have clearly resonated within the ranks of their respective memberships; more than in any other issue area, the differences between Socialist and Communist militants are most distinct in the lessons they have drawn from the defeat of Chile's democratic socialist experiment.

In accordance with their party's self-criticism of its *vacío histórico*, or neglect of military force, Communist militants overwhelmingly emphasized military factors and the role of force when explaining the causes for Allende's defeat. Three elements of their "military" interpretation stand out: the need for leftist parties to have a capacity for military defense, the need to understand the character of the armed forces, and the permanent threat that elite sectors might resort to force and subvert democracy to defend their interests. As stated by one young poblador: "Any conquest must be defended. You have to know how to defend your gains with organization and consciousness of the masses, but you must also be able to defend yourself against repression, because the dominant sectors will never give up their repressive capacity. We can't stay weak before this danger. . . . So both the party and the people must have knowledge of the military art." The prevalence of these views was indicative of the thorough diffusion of the Communist Party's official reinterpretation of the Allende experience within the rank-and-file membership. Initially, this interpretation posed a serious challenge to the self-image of a party that had traditionally focused on electoral and trade union politics and had been wedded to the concept of a vía pacífica. Nevertheless, this interpretation was reinforced by the Communist Party's strategic shift in the 1980s and by the membership's practical experience with popular rebellion. By 1990 its lessons had been socialized and inculcated within the historical memory of both young and old party militants and had become an integral component of the core beliefs within the party subculture.

In contrast to their counterparts in the Communist Party, and in contrast to the early interpretations of their party's radical wing, Socialist militants placed very little emphasis on military issues. Very few argued that Allende's government fell because it was unable to defend itself or control the armed forces. Instead, most Socialist militants stressed the importance of political failings or errors, including the dangers of dogmatism and sectarianism within the Left, the failure of populist and clientelist methods of governance, and the counterproductive influence of Cuba or other "ultrarevolutionary" forces. Other common responses included the failure to maintain unity within the Left and the threat posed by political enemies who are willing to subvert democracy, both of which were also frequently mentioned by Communist militants. The following quote is representative of the most common responses within the Socialist Party: "There was a high level of ideology, and we did not understand that the role of the Christian Democrats would be so important. We made a mistake not to compromise with them, because everyone was too sectarian. You can't be sectarian and try to do everything by yourself; you have to combine forces in order to advance."

This "political" interpretation reflected patterns of self-criticism within the moderate wing of the party and the sectors that led the process of Socialist renovation. This self-criticism blamed the party's pre-1973 radicalism for alienating centrist and middle-class sectors and isolating the Allende government politically. In contrast to the Communist Party, however, there was less of a consensus among Socialist militants in the lessons extracted from the Allende experience, perhaps reflecting the political and ideological factionalism that plagued the party both before and after the 1973 coup. Since Socialist militants did not possess an "official" interpretation that could be offered reflexively as an explanation for the Left's defeat in 1973, they were prone to identify diverse political factors that played a role in the Popular Unity's demise.

Distinctions between "military" and "political" interpretations of Allende's defeat are significant not only for what they reveal about historical memories; more important, perhaps, is their correlation with subsequent patterns of political change in the two parties. Post-coup patterns of experiential learning shaped both parties' perspectives toward strategic alternatives in the long struggle against the Pinochet dictatorship, particularly regarding the use of force. Although all sectors of the Socialist and Communist Parties supported popular mobilization and protests against the dictatorship, there were significant disagreements about whether nonviolent forms of mobilization alone could produce a regime change or whether they had to be linked to forms of popular armed resistance.

These differences in party strategies were reflected in the base-level interviews. At the time of interviewing, there was a heated controversy within the Communist Party over the popular rebellion strategy. This controversy was caused in part by the defeat of the strategy during Chile's democratic transition, but it also was attributable to the party leaders' refusal to change the party's line during the transition process, to the chagrin of many party moderates. Nevertheless, only one Communist militant claimed to have opposed popular rebellion from the outset, and even she acknowledged faithful adherence to the party line when it was adopted. The other Communist militants argued that popular rebellion against the dictatorship was necessary and legitimate, at least until the shift in the political climate between 1986 and 1988. Indeed, they saw popular rebellion as the exercise of an inherent right in a context of political violence and repression. In the words of one older poblador, "We knew that to eliminate Pinochet it wasn't enough to paint walls and distribute pamphlets. It was necessary to have the force of arms too, along with a capacity for self-defense."

The interviews also gave evidence of the confusion that plagued the strategy of popular rebellion within the Communist Party, along with the varied interpretations to which it was subject. According to a young, middle-class militant who was active in party cultural groups,

When the party decided to adopt the strategy of popular rebellion, the response of intellectuals like myself was to write an article or act in a play, or to engage in some other type of intellectual or cultural activity. That was our idea of rebellion. What was I supposed to do, pick up a gun and become a guerrilla overnight? That would be totally alien to all my experience. But for the people in the *poblaciones*, popular rebellion was totally different. For them, it meant to go out into the streets and throw rocks at the police. So there were very different conceptions of popular rebellion within the party.

Other militants supported the strategy for its emphasis on mass organization, but they viewed popular rebellion as a process of social mobilization in the workplace or poblaciones more than a strategy for armed struggle. For these militants, popular rebellion was a logical extension of the grass-roots organizing work they were already doing, not a rupture in the party's strategic line. As stated by one elderly poblador activist: "Popular rebellion is a social rebellion, it doesn't have to mean that we take up arms. It is a process of social organization, like in the committees of those without homes, the committees of those with housing debts, and committees of the unemployed. To organize them to defend their rights is popular rebellion, along with the committees of vigilance which are necessary to defend us." And in the words of a longtime union leader who was troubled by his daughter's participation in the Frente Patriótico Mañuel Rodríguez:

It wasn't hard for me to accept popular rebellion—it was, is, and *always* will be legitimate. It is an eternal problem, and the workers always have the right to rebel. But the problem is, how do we understand rebellion? To take up a machine gun, or plant a bomb, or to kill a policeman? I was never for that type of rebellion, although I understood it. But my rebellion was with the workers. For the first time in our history the workers rebelled by saying "enough" and calling strikes and confronting the police in the streets. I will always be for that rebellion.

Finally, several Communist militants claimed that popular rebellion was legitimate in principle but acknowledged that its implementation was problematic if not unrealistic in the Chilean context. In particular, they argued that the strategy lacked mass support, that it scared and demobilized other sectors of the opposition to Pinochet, that it was prone to sectarianism and militaristic deviations, and that it attracted to the party "lumpen" elements or radicalized youth with little "political formation."

Nevertheless, despite these reservations and different interpretations, the interviews suggest that the strategy of popular rebellion had very strong support among Communist Party militants during its peak years in the mid-1980s, when the explosion of popular protests erupted against the military dictatorship. The main debate over the strategy, and the principal objections to it, did not revolve around the legitimacy or efficacy of taking up arms against the dictatorship; instead, disagreements centered on whether the strategy should have been modified when the political context changed in the late 1980s and whether any "military policy" was appropriate and viable in the midst of a democratic transition. Twelve Communist militants—all but one from middle-class or professional circles—criticized the party for failing to acknowledge the change in the political context or for delaying recognition of the "political moment" represented by the 1988 plebiscite campaign against Pinochet. Nevertheless, a majority of Communist militants, including all seven of the young pobladores interviewed, argued that the strategy of popular rebellion should remain intact, albeit adapted to the new set of political conditions prevailing under Chile's democratic regime. The interviews thus reflected the intense debate within the Communist Party during Chile's democratic transition regarding the validity of the party's "military policy" in a rapidly changing political environment; if there was a broad consensus in the party regarding the legitimacy of armed rebellion against the dictatorship, this consensus fractured as important sectors of the party demanded a strategic reorientation to facilitate incorporation within the democratization process.

The militants who supported a continuation of the strategy of popular rebellion did not believe it entailed taking up arms against the new democratic regime led by Patricio Aylwin. Instead, they saw it in general terms as a social rebellion against capitalism and injustice or as a process of popular organization to press for social reforms. Nevertheless, they insisted that the party should maintain a capacity to operate in the military terrain, not to threaten the Aylwin government, but to defend themselves and the new democratic regime from potential rightist enemies. As stated by one young poblador who had recently been elected to his neighborhood council or *junta de vecinos*: "We can't renounce popular rebellion, because we don't know how the armed forces and the bourgeoisie think, and we can't let them do what they did in the 1973 coup. We are a revolutionary party, we never compromised with the dictatorship. Popular rebellion is a right that the people exercise against oppression and injustice, so it is still valid. The political and military are always linked together, as we learned by suffering through painful experiences in these years." According to another young poblador, whereas popular rebellion against Pinochet "was to defend us from dictatorship, now it is to defend democracy from its enemies, from those who want to destroy it. We must have the people militarily prepared and educated . . . to defend and take care of democracy."

In short, many Communist militants—especially young pobladores, who had been the most active social force in the protest movement that rocked the dictatorship—were reluctant to dismantle the limited military capability that the Communist Party constructed in the 1980s, even though they did not envision its employment in any capacity against the new democratic regime.

Instead, they believed this military capacity should be held in reserve for whatever future contingency might emerge; whereas Socialist militants believed an alliance strategy was the most effective bulwark against future military intervention, many Communist militants believed a partisan military capability was the most viable form of defense. This clearly reflected the dominant patterns of experiential learning and political socialization within the party after the 1973 coup. These learning patterns had criticized the party's historic neglect of military affairs, emphasized the importance of tactical flexibility in order to operate in different terrains under changing circumstances, and identified the possession of a military capability as a sine qua non of a revolutionary party.

In contrast, only three members of the Socialist Party—all pobladores from the former Almeyda sector who were representative of the fundamentalist syndrome—argued that Left parties or popular forces should maintain a military capability after the regime transition. One of these militants, who had been to prison for his involvement with "subversive" organizations, was so perturbed by the Almeyda sector's shift toward electoral politics and its reunification with the Núñez branch that he was contemplating abandoning the party. Another, who had been the leader of the local nucleo of the Almeyda branch in her población, was the most openly aggressive subject interviewed from either party. This militant claimed to have been deeply affected by the authoritarian experience; in her words, sixteen years of dictatorship made her "more aggressive and more violent, because they repressed my own family members. . . . Before I was soft, more sentimental, but now I believe we must kill those from the CNI [the secret police under Pinochet]. I don't believe in reconciliation; those who killed should be tried and killed, not pardoned and forgotten." This militant argued that the Frente Patriótico Mañuel Rodríguez should be maintained to defend popular movements, and she criticized Allende and the Nicaraguan Sandinistas for being too "soft" toward opposition sectors.

Most Socialist militants, however, believed that the democratic transition had fundamentally altered the political climate, and they criticized the Communist Party for failing to adapt its strategic posture to changing circumstances. Nevertheless, a majority of Socialist militants, particularly those from the Almeyda branch of the party, expressed sympathy for the popular rebellion strategy so long as it was directed against the Pinochet dictatorship. According to one Socialist poblador, elected as the president of his neighborhood junta de vecinos, "Popular rebellion was necessary, because there was so much injustice, and it was necessary to wake up the people. It wasn't the Communist Party that started violence, it was the responsibility of the government. What the Communist Party did was raise its voice for all of us." Others manifested considerable respect for the Communist Party's commitment to struggle, including a middle-class militant who had worked in the electoral campaign of a Socialist congressional candidate in 1989: "The Communist Party is the one party on the Left that does what it says—it is a virtue of theirs. The Communist Party is in all the social organizations and all the electoral activities; they practice all forms of struggle, just like they say! The problem isn't with their violent line; that is a response to what we have all been through, and it is too easy to judge them now."

In contrast, most Socialists from the Núñez sector of the party believed that popular rebellion had always been a mistaken strategy. These militants argued that an armed strategy had been unrealistic and unviable under Chilean conditions, especially given the professionalism of the Chilean armed forces, or that it had been incongruent with the preferences of the Chilean people. According to one young militant,

There was so much radicalization that it detracted from our force. We didn't want anarchy, we needed unity. The armed forces are very professionalized and you can't confront them with force; you have to look for the weaknesses of your enemy and confront them with peaceful mobilization, not force, because force was to their advantage. . . . So popular rebellion was a great error of the Communist Party, since the people did not want it, they wanted peace, not war. And now the Communist Party is paying for it.

For another young militant from the former Almeyda sector,

We lived in a context of violence in the 1980s. Popular rebellion was understandable as part of that context, but you have to obtain the proper correlation of forces. Popular rebellion lacked the support of the masses, so it had the wrong correlation of forces, because the whole

Left didn't back it. The party of Almeyda had an insurrectionary discourse, but it didn't have the political practice or the political will to implement it. So I understand popular rebellion but I think it was wrong. The Almeyda party was wrong to live a political lie with its discourse; this only confused the bases of the party and created conflicts. It was all slogans, not practice, so it has created a lot of discontent now.

Finally, some members of the Núñez sector talked of how they had tried to promote a "culture of life" in the midst of a violent political context; in the words of one young militant from the highly combative, Communist-dominated población of La Victoria, "Everything symbolized death, like the rifle, while nothing symbolized life. So we tried to change that. We painted new kinds of murals, with a different Che Guevara, emphasizing his ideas and his life rather than his rifle, or murals of Martin Luther King, or Ghandi and John Lennon."

There were, then, significant differences between the Socialist and Communist militants in their patterns of experiential learning, with the Communist Party's emphasis on the role of force in the 1973 crisis carrying over to influence subsequent struggles against the Pinochet dictatorship and beyond. Although there was significant support for a strategy of armed rebellion in both parties during the mid-1980s, this support largely evaporated in the Socialist Party as Chile entered its democratic transition, and it began to erode in the Communist Party as well. The ambiguity of the Communist Party's role in the democratic transition was reflected in the divisions within the party militancy on the role of force in politics; although most militants wanted the party to be integrated within the democratic regime, many did not trust the new political institutions or the other actors in the political system and thus wanted their party to retain a capacity for military self-defense.

To what extent, then, did these differences within and between the two parties carry over to influence perspectives toward the Aylwin government and the participation of the Left in the democratic transition? As shown below, there was cautious support for the democratic coalition government in both parties and a widespread belief that the Left must work to help it succeed while promoting more profound institutional and socioeconomic reforms. There was also, however, strong support in both parties for the reconstruction of a more independent, unified political alternative of the Left.

Rethinking Political Roles and Strategies for a Democratic Era

Given the support in significant sectors of both parties for a strategy of popular insurrection in the mid-1980s, it is not surprising that there was considerable ambiguity in the perspectives of militants toward the new democratic government and the process of democratic transition in general. The interviews suggest that there was a virtually unanimous belief that the Left should participate in Chile's new democratic institutions and provide at least some measure of support for the government to fortify the regime against its rightist opposition. Only one Communist and two Socialist militants, representing especially hard-line fundamentalist positions, expressed the opinion that their party should reject the democratic process altogether or mobilize forces in opposition to the Aylwin government. One Communist youth called the new government "the other face of dictatorship," while an elderly worker from the Almeyda branch of the Socialist party said participation would only legitimize institutions inherited from the dictatorship. The vast majority of militants from both parties, however, thought their party should participate in the democratic process and support the Aylwin government. This support fell into two broad categories: those who thought their party should offer strong support to the new government and be part of its governing coalition, and those who thought their party should offer a more "critical" and independent form of support without assuming the responsibilities of governance.

In the Communist Party, a narrow majority of militants thought the party should support the democratic process while maintaining a critical and independent position toward the Aylwin government, largely conforming to the official party line of "constructive independence" during 1990. As one young poblador stated: "Our position toward the new government has to be one of constructive opposition. We are in the opposition because it isn't our government, we are not in charge of it. But our opposition has to be constructive, in the sense of not attacking the government, of supporting it with ideas and defending it from the possibility of any future coup. We have to reinforce the government, because our only hope now is democracy." A significant minority of Communist militants, however, believed their party should go beyond the official policy to work for a broader consensus with the governing Concertación coalition. Generally representative of a "renovationist" syndrome in the party, these militants favored more explicit cooperation with the political parties in the Concertación and a more complete and unambiguous incorporation of the party into the democratization process. According to one older poblador, "We have to work with everything we have for this democracy so that we won't return to what we had after 1973. We have to cooperate with the Christian Democrats and the government; all the parties have to cooperate now for democracy." And in the words of a university student and party dissident: "The policy of 'constructive independence' is insufficient and erroneous, and it doesn't have any real substance. What is there that is constructive, what are we supposed to be contributing? We have to contribute to the construction of democracy . . . but the current policy assumes that the new government will fail and allow the Communist Party to build a new alternative with the support of the Socialists. This is a false view of alliances, and it only helps the Right." In short, there was strong support among Communist militants for their party's incorporation into Chile's new democratic institutions, despite the initial reluctance of some militants to accept the shift to electoral participation in 1988 and a fear that the legalization of the party within the juridical norms bequeathed by the dictatorship would taint its principles. The ambiguous character of the party's incorporation, however, provoked sharp disagreements: whereas organizational loyalists were inclined to endorse the leadership's qualified support for democratization, dissident renovationists advocated a warmer embrace of the new regime.

In the Socialist Party, a majority of militants supported their party's role in the government and the Concertación. Many militants from the Núñez sector of the party expressed pragmatist positions; as stated by a former Mirista who had gravitated to the Núñez sector of the Socialist Party: "The program of the Concertación government is very good, and it encourages the participation of the people. So the objective of the Left now should be to fight for the complete implementation of the program of the government. The Right will oppose it, so the Left must defend this program in order to fulfill it. This program isn't just that of the Christian Democrats; it is also the program of the Left." A poblador from the Núñez sector added: "As Socialists our first commitment must be to democracy, to the Concertación and to the Aylwin government. The Socialist Party must never cease to be a party of the Left, but it can't be rigid and intransigent like in Eastern Europe. The party has to be flexible to keep the Center separate from the Right. That is what is good about the Concertación; it keeps the Center out of an alliance with the Right and it helps to prevent a new military intervention."

Yet a significant minority of Socialist militants objected to such pragmatist positions, arguing that it was necessary to support the democratization process while asserting a more independent stance to maintain the party's profile and transformative project. According to a young militant from the Almeyda sector, "The Socialist Party has to have a mission of the Left, and those who are in the government don't understand this, they don't understand the reality of the people at the base. It isn't wrong that they are in the government, but they are too individualistic; they should work more with the party and with the bases. The Socialist ministers are Aylwin's men, not the party's." Another young militant reiterated these complaints, arguing:

I don't like the anticommunism that is part of our alliance with the Christian Democrats. It is a renunciation of our traditions, of our past. We need a new political bloc that includes all the progressive forces, including the Communists. I agree with our having Socialist ministers in the cabinet, it is important to have a strong presence in the government. But the Christian Democrats are too close to the capitalists, and our presence in the government isn't doing enough to change things. The new government has strong support in public opinion, and it should use it to take the political offensive and be more forceful.

Despite these complaints, even most of those preferring a more independent position vis-à-vis the Christian Democrats accepted the party's participation in government and the Concertación coalition, believing this participation would help promote greater reform or provide administrative experience and credibility for future governing assignments. They also believed this participation was essential to help stabilize Chile's democratic transition and isolate the political Right. Indeed, only four Socialist militants representing more fundamentalist positions opposed their party's acceptance of cabinet posts in a governing partnership with the Christian Democrats, arguing that the party should not participate in a government that did not have an explicit socialist character.

Although there was strong support for participation in the democratization process, ambiguity and discontent were manifested in a variety of ways. Many militants from both parties volunteered that it had been difficult for them to accept a negotiated democratic transition or *salida política*; as stated by one Socialist woman who longed for the idealism and mystique of the Allende years: "This transition had to occur as it did, but it clearly isn't what I most wanted. I had old dreams of arriving at the Moneda [the presidential palace] in Jeeps and wearing olive green and unfurling a banner like the Sandinistas. It is a recurring image in my mind, but this transition doesn't have anything to do with that." Many of these militants questioned the democratic character of the new regime and chafed at the legal and institutional constraints that had been placed on the process of democratization by Pinochet's constitution. They were also disillusioned by the compromises inherent in the democratic transition and by the slow pace and tepid character of political and economic reforms. These militants sought a more complete break with Chile's authoritarian past and objected to the government's practice of negotiating reforms with the Right. In the Socialist Party, there was also considerable uneasiness, especially in the Almeyda sector, with the shift in alliance partners from the Communist Party to the Christian Democrats. More than half of the Socialist militants wanted to see some sort of reconstruction of the traditional alliance with the Communist Party; for these militants, the legacy of common struggles and the long-standing objective of constructing a united Left weighed heavily upon contemporary identities. As stated by one young poblador from the Almeyda sector: "There is only one Left in Chile. We all have the same objectives, even if the different parties believe they each know the correct path, or the truth, in order to arrive at that objective. We have to unite all the Left in order to have a strong foundation, including the Socialists, Communists, and the MIR. We're all one family, that of the Marxist Left, and I'm opposed to those who try to divide it." Typically, these militants thought that any alliance with the Christian Democrats should be of a short-term, tactical nature for the limited purpose of stabilizing the democratic transition, and they feared that any long-term alliance would threaten their party's political independence and traditional identities. In the words of another poblador from the Almeyda sector:

We're against an alliance with the Christian Democrats, because they supported the military coup and fascism in 1973. We can have a tactical alliance, an alliance of convenience, but nothing more. . . . Tactically, we can ally with anyone, but in a strategic alliance with the Christian Democrats we would cease to be a party of the Left. . . . So we don't need a long-term, strategic agreement with the Christian Democrats; our alliance with them is precisely for this current moment, for the transition to democracy, because they have their project and we have our own. If the Arratistas [the Núñez sector] think differently, it is because they aren't real Socialists.

Communist Party militants were clearly concerned about their party's growing political isolation, and all wanted the party to restore linkages to other democratic groups in Chilean society. According to one intellectual dissident from the "renovationist" camp with years of experience in the party before the 1973 coup, "I believe the great historical merit of the Communist Party was to be the axis of the Left. The Communist Party was always the key to the Left, it was always building alliances with others and working for a consensus within the Left and beyond. We knew that our party alone could not bring about fundamental change. But this capacity has been forgotten; the leadership of the party has carried us to total isolation, and today we lack allies for the future."

Although militants from both parties tended to support political alliances or forms of political accommodation to stabilize the new democratic regime, they differed on the desirability of social pacts between capital and labor. This was a controversial issue during the early months of Aylwin's administration, which strongly supported a negotiated pact between capital and labor to temper social conflict and enhance governability. A solid majority of Communist militants opposed such social pacts, generally arguing that capital would never make significant concessions, that power relationships were too unequal to enable labor to benefit, or that such agreements were negotiated at the elite level without adequate representation of workers. As one unemployed militant stated:

Labor can't achieve any advantages or benefits without a struggle. The social pact that was negotiated here was immoral, because the capitalist class has had exorbitant and immoral benefits for years, taking advantage of the dictatorship and its labor plan. Labor here is exploited to the maximum degree, with miserable salaries, and this pact doesn't provide any advantages. Do we really think that conversations with capitalists will make them more generous? Conversations never achieve anything, because the capitalists don't have a social conscience. Besides, this pact was negotiated over the heads of the labor organizations and citizens and those whom they have elected.

In contrast, a slim majority of Socialist militants supported efforts to negotiate agreements between capital and labor, generally viewing such pacts as important mechanisms to resolve conflict and help construct a political consensus favorable to democratic stability. In the words of one militant from the Núñez sector of the party: "We need mechanisms to resolve conflicts through agreements and negotiations. This doesn't mean that we can cover over conflicts, because conflict always exists. Labor is very weak now, but with greater organization it can have greater force and do better in these negotiations." Socialist militants were also more likely to oppose radical forms of social mobilization such as labor strikes and land seizures, arguing that they could be destabilizing to the new democratic order. According to one pragmatic poblador from the Núñez sector,

We can't ask for more than what the government can do. We've waited for sixteen years, but we have to be patient now, because there are many restrictions on this government. The Right, capital, and the big banks will take advantage of disorder if we demand too much; they'll try to make a new military coup with the armed forces. That is why the UDI [a pro-Pinochet party of the Right] is promoting land seizures in the *poblaciones*, to create disorder and help Pinochet's forces. We can't be irresponsible, we have to be cautious or there will be problems. Housing may be a right, but it is best to acquire it through organization and planning and dialogue.

Nevertheless, a majority of the militants in both parties argued that these more radical forms of popular mobilization were legitimate, either because they were an inalienable right or because popular mobilization and pressure were essential to deepen democracy and promote social reforms. As stated by one young Socialist poblador from the Almeyda sector: "Land seizures are a way in which the *pobladores* can recuperate what should be theirs. They are a legitimate form of recuperation, and strikes are an essential form of struggle. There are no gains without struggle; negotiations can't succeed, only struggle, because the rich won't give us anything."

In the aggregate, these responses suggest that base-level opinions on tactical issues were not as sharply divergent as might be assumed when looking at the contrasting roles performed by these two parties in Chile's democratic transition. Although Communist militants were more strongly wedded to an insurrectionary strategy against the dictatorship and were reluctant to renounce their party's military capacity, the overwhelming majority of militants from both parties supported the democratization process and favored their party's incorporation into the new institutions. There was strong support in both parties for a broad alliance strategy, and while Socialist militants were more favorable toward mechanisms of social concertation and more wary of destabilizing activities, militants from both parties were generally supportive of more confrontational forms of popular mobilization.

Given this partial convergence on tactical and strategic issues, it is logical to ask whether base-level opinions on fundamental ideological questions have converged or diverged. The following section addresses this issue by exploring how changes in the domestic and international political contexts have influenced traditional ideals and identities.

The Process of Ideological Change:
Rethinking Traditional Identities

There is little doubt that the Soviet perestroika posed significant ideological challenges to leftist militants in Chile, particularly in the Communist Party. The challenges were heightened after 1989, when the collapse of communism in Eastern Europe made it clear that perestroika would not merely lead to the democratization of socialism in the Soviet bloc—as the Communist Party had tentatively asserted—but rather to its eclipse and a restoration of capitalism. Nevertheless, militants from both the Socialist and Communist parties were overwhelmingly favorable toward perestroika at the time they were interviewed in 1990; none openly rejected Gorbachev's reforms, although a few argued that perestroika was not relevant to Chilean conditions or feared that it would lead to a restoration of capitalism. The vast majority of militants, however, admitted that Soviet communism was highly flawed on political and economic grounds, demonstrating the unviability of centralized, bureaucratic, and authoritarian models of socialism. They also claimed that the crisis in the Soviet bloc demonstrated the need for mechanisms of popular participation and democratic accountability under socialism.

By the time these interviews were conducted in 1990, the Soviet Union and Eastern Europe had all but disappeared as positive international referents for leftist militants in Chile. The same was not true, however, of Cuba, which remained an attractive referent, especially for the Communist Party. This demonstrated the enduring strength of traditional identities, as well as the contradictions that existed in international loyalties, since some militants embraced Cuba at the same time that they praised Gorbachev's reforms or criticized authoritarian models of socialism in Eastern Europe. The single most common external referent in the Communist Party, however, was not Cuba but the Nicaraguan Revolution, which was embraced by all of the young pobladores in the party, despite the Sandinista electoral defeat in early 1990. Clearly, the Nicaraguan Revolution was a powerful influence in the formative experience of the poblador youth who were the backbone of the popular rebellion strategy in the 1980s. Interestingly, however, more than one-third of the Communist militants insisted that their party should not identify with any particular nation or model of socialism, clearly reflecting the disillusionment and sense of betrayal that accompanied the decline and collapse of the Soviet model in Eastern Europe. As one young dissident—one of the best representatives of the "disoriented" syndrome[4]—bitterly expressed: "I've decided that I'm not going to defend Cuba anymore because I've never been there and I don't really know its reality. After all that's happened in Eastern Europe, what else can I do? For years I defended the socialist nations in Eastern Europe, believing the party line that they had built socialism, only to learn that the reality was very different. So now I don't know what to think about Cuba."

International referents for the Socialist Party were more sharply polarized. Those from the Núñez sector, where the renovationist and pragmatist tendencies predominated, were more inclined to mention Italy, Spain, France, or European social democracy as significant examples, referents that were not mentioned by any Communist militants. In contrast, militants from the Almeyda sector looked more closely to the example of the Nicaraguan Revolution.

The interviews not only suggested that identification with the Soviet model of socialism was considerably weakened but also that militants from both parties had largely ceased to conceive of socialism as a predetermined mode of economic production based on the collectivization of property and central planning. Indeed, statist and bureaucratic models of socialism had clearly fallen into disfavor, and in a patent reflection of the teleological crisis of the Left, socialism had come to be more commonly associated with abstract principles of social justice or equality rather than specific arrangements for production and distribution. Likewise, socialism was seen as inherently related to political democracy and its "deepening," themes that were central to the process of renovation in the Chilean Left. Many militants also associated socialism with ending exploitation, expanding public services to ensure basic needs, popular participation, and individual liberty. In the words of one young Socialist from the Almeyda sector: "Socialism for me is a dream, not a recipe. It is a world where there isn't as much suffering as we have here, a world where no one sleeps on the streets, where everyone has a bed and food to eat. Socialism means to have economic security, but it also means to have personal security, with the defense of human rights so that there is no torture and discrimination." And as stated by a young Communist poblador: "Socialism is where you don't have rich and poor, where people are equal. It is where the basic needs in education and health care are met and people earn what they deserve."

When militants were pressed to express their opinions on specific economic matters, they generally mentioned a mixed economy, social services, and more equitable wages as the changes they would advocate, rather than the nationalization of property or the introduction of central planning. A significant number stressed the limitations of state intervention in the economy. Emphasis was placed not on the elimination of private property or the market but on moderating their inegalitarian effects through the provision of basic public services.

These responses suggest that there was considerable eclecticism and pragmatism in the economic beliefs of most militants from both parties—so much, in fact, that the traditional vision of socialism as an alternative, predefined mode of production had largely faded from view. As a young Communist dissident stated:

I used to think I knew what socialism was, but now I'm not so sure. I believe it is where all people have a right to education and health care which would be provided by the state. These are the pillars of any society; the state should provide education in order to give opportunities to the people and then leave it up to the individual. I don't agree with Marxism-Leninism on the need for the state to control everything. I believe in a mixed economy, but the state must be responsible for health and education and cultural development, because the market can't do everything, and some things shouldn't be commercialized.

For these militants, the principles of economic justice and equality remained firmly intact, but they were not linked to a set of concrete, overarching structural changes such as the collectivization of property or the abolition of market relations. Most militants acknowledged an important developmental role for the market and private capital, but they strongly opposed the neoliberal economic model imposed by the military regime, which restructured society along market principles by privatizing state enterprises and public services. They preferred that the market and private capital be balanced by an active and democratically accountable state role through the provision of public services, the maintenance of a public productive sector, and the implementation of redistributive measures. In the words of another Communist militant:

My view of socialism has changed during these years. We used to think it would be easy to create a new man, that if we simply changed the structure of production we would change the consciousness of the people, but now we see that it is a much longer process. We also gave too much weight to the state, which was contrary to socialism and anti-Marxist. Marx said that under communism the state would disappear, but we dreamed of a statist model of socialism. Now we know the state can't play that role, and we recognize that private initiative has a role to play, we just can't let it be so exploitative.

But if these militants were inclined toward a reformist agenda, most were very reluctant to discard the revolutionary symbols and ideals that had long inspired the Chilean Left. A significant minority of Socialist militants, including those most clearly associated with the pragmatist syndrome, argued that a modern Left should have a postrevolutionary character. As stated by one member from the Núñez sector: "I'm in complete agreement with the idea that we must be a postrevolutionary Left. We have to leave behind the old ideas of confrontation and struggle; we've learned from our experiences that a party which speaks of revolution only frightens the people." Most of the Socialists and nearly all the Communists, however, argued that revolution was still a valid ideal and objective for the Left, at least as a principle of radical social transformation, if not necessarily as a violent conquest of state power. According to one young Communist, "Chile clearly is in a postrevolutionary situation, if you understand revolution as armed struggle. But I understand revolution as a profound change, and Chile needs a profound change, it needs a revolution in its culture and educational life. But the old mythical view of revolution has passed." The sentiments of those who were most strongly attached to the traditional revolutionary ideal were captured in the words of one Socialist militant, who argued that "the intellectuals who talk about a postrevolutionary era are well off, and they don't need a revolution. It's better to talk to those who are poor and marginalized, because this society has to change radically." For these militants, the ideal of revolution remained a fundamental principle, and it could not be abandoned, even in a political context dominated by piecemeal, gradual reform and various types of social and political *concertación*.

In short, revolution—at least as an ideal and a symbol—remained integral to the basic identities of most Socialist and virtually all Communist militants, even as their parties increasingly turned away from it as a political strategy. In fact, what appears to be taking place among many militants is a progressive fusion of the ideals of revolution, socialism, and democracy. In the eloquent words of a university activist from the Núñez sector of the Socialist Party who clearly embodied a renovationist position,

We have to reconceive revolution and give it another meaning, to conceive it as a process of change. Revolution is possible, but only as a progressive series of partial changes. Our utopia *does* still exist, we can still conceive of an alternative to capitalism . . . but now we don't have a *model* of this alternative, because our model before was too statist. Our only model today is democracy, and democracy must progressively create space for the people to participate and promote a gradual transformation.

Indeed, with revolution supported as a principle of social transformation and socialism equated with the deepening of democracy, the concept of democracy itself was infused with substantive components related to the values of popular participation and socioeconomic change. In both parties, democracy was more likely to be associated with the substantive issues of popular participation, individual liberties, and socioeconomic reform rather than with electoral procedures. Although militants in both parties were broadly supportive of elections and representative institutions, many saw them as inadequate forms of democratic accountability that needed to be supplemented with more participatory procedures. As stated by a young Socialist militant:

Electoral representation isn't enough; we need a participatory democracy, where the people decide things for themselves. We have to put an end to the paternalist state and have more local participation. Then we can move toward socialism, with greater justice and equality. That is the ideal of socialism for me, to deepen democracy and have the maximum possible extension of participation by the people in the decisions that affect their lives. People must be conscious of their role as social subjects, so that we can build what we used to call "popular power."

Others were more blunt in identifying the limitations of Chile's new political institutions, arguing that they fell considerably short of democratic norms or aspirations. According to one of the more fundamentalist militants from the Almeyda wing of the Socialist Party, "For me, democracy is socialism; they are the same thing. What we have today in Chile isn't democracy, it isn't what I want. It's just a legalistic model of democracy, and there is still torture in this country. If this is democracy, I don't want it."

The emphasis on participatory democracy was also prominent in the raging debates over "renovation" in both parties. Militants in both parties expressed a mixture of reverence and self-criticism toward their party organization, and most believed important changes were necessary. In the Communist Party, militants were most attracted to their party's tradition of uncompromising struggle and its identification with the popular sectors; in a phrase repeated like a mantra by organizational loyalists, their party was seen as el mas consequente, or the most committed and the most likely to live up to its word. The party's heroic, mythical self-image was only reinforced by the experience of armed insurrection in the 1980s, when the Communist Party viewed itself as the vanguard of a mass revolutionary movement that would eventually incorporate less committed or capable political actors. The Communist mystique was expressed in the following way by one young poblador, an organizational loyalist in the best sense of the term:

I joined the Communist Party because it was the most "consequential" party. I could have been in the Socialist Party or the Izquierda Cristiana, but the Communist Party was more consequential, the most disciplined party, despite all of our errors and our crisis today. It makes me mad that there are people who always criticize the party, dissidents who have never worked at the base with the people, because it is the Communist Party that really works with the people. One Communist is worth ten militants from any other party, because we always multiply, we know how to work. There is a campaign against us now, and its true that we are in a crisis today, but we'll never be destroyed, because we have force from below, in the bases, unlike all the other parties.

Socialist militants, in contrast, tended to have less heroic pretensions and at times were even apologetic about their presumed organizational deficiencies vis-à-vis the Communist Party. In part, this reflected the party's congenital factionalism and its historic failure to establish the Leninist organizational structures and disciplinary norms that prevailed in the Communist Party. Nevertheless, the organizational characteristics that traditionally distinguished the Socialist Party from the Communist Party were also the most frequently mentioned positive attributes of the party. In particular, Socialist militants stressed the attractiveness of their party's flexibility, its internal pluralism, and its nationalist and autonomous character. In the words of one middle-class militant from the Almeyda sector:

The Socialist Party was the only party that was big when it was born. It was a workers' party, a popular party, but it wasn't just for the proletariat, it included the middle class too. The Socialist Party always had to represent those sectors that weren't represented by the Communist Party. So we were born big and diverse, and we were never orthodox; we've always been unique. We're anti-imperialist and Latin Americanist, and we never accepted any international blocs, because we understood that our Marxism had to be rooted in the realities of Chile, not those of Europe. Our party has to have internal pluralism and democracy, where the base can express itself; if not, it would be like the Communist Party.

Despite the evident pride that existed in both parties, militants found ample reason to be critical. There was extensive criticism of elitist, vertical patterns of decision making in both parties; as stated by one Communist dissident, an economist by profession, "Our party lacks an organizational structure that would permit ideological debate and allow the whole party to know what is taking place. The leadership of the party rejects any views that aren't their own, and the party has a pyramidal structure so that opinions from the cells only make it as far as the local committees before they are swallowed up by the party structure. This organizational structure is now in crisis, because there is no longer a homogeneity of principles, which made it possible before." Similar sentiments were echoed by a young Socialist militant, who complained:

There is authoritarianism in the party, a lack of internal democracy, with a centralized leadership and a lot of machismo. There is prejudice and discrimination against women and youth, even among the leaders of the renovation; they discriminate too. A woman has to be ten times better than a man to get anywhere in the party, so our leaders have to go through a self-criticism for their paternalism. We have to question the internal *practice* of the party and its relationship to the people; we need a renovation in practice more than a renovation of ideology.

In the Socialist Party, criticisms of undemocratic and hierarchical decision making were coupled with the strong belief—especially in the former Almeyda sector—that party leaders were out of touch with their bases. Many militants perceived a sharp cleavage between themselves and their party's highly visible political and intellectual elites, both in their basic political orientations and socioeconomic or cultural backgrounds. In the concise summation of an older, disillusioned poblador with a fundamentalist orientation, "A socialist with a full belly can't think like a socialist." Indeed, some militants were openly hostile toward party leaders who had led the process of renovation, believing they were divorced from the party's popular bases. As one young poblador said: "In the Socialist Party the bases are much more combative, while the leadership of the party is always compromising. The leaders didn't live the reality of the protests and repression like we did; they lived a different reality. Some of them went into exile and didn't change, but some changed and became social democrats. Today they are more pacific, they aren't as combative." According to another militant who complained that returning exiles had lost touch with Chilean realities,

There are some people in the Socialist Party who look to Europe, and they aren't true socialists, they've lost their sense of what it means to be a socialist here. This "renovation" is a move toward social democracy; the leadership of the party is adapting to new winds, but they are becoming more distant from their bases and from their roots in Marxism. They are trying not to be left behind with the changes in the world, but the leaders are really opportunistic; they change with the times, but the times will change again, and things will be different tomorrow.

In the Communist Party, many militants were critical of their party's lingering Stalinist tendencies, although some pobladores also complained about the divisive activities of party dissidents. Another common criticism among middle-class militants was the poor political training provided for party cadres, generally a reference to young pobladores who were swept into the party during the heyday of the popular rebellion strategy. In the words of one long-time militant with a renovationist orientation who was concerned about the party's increasing social isolation and marginalization: "The problem with the Jota [the Communist youth organization] is that so many of the youth have little ideological formation. The party captured a lot of youth in the 1980s, but many joined just for the symbolism of the struggle, and they have problems with drugs and alcohol. It's good for the Jota to gain adherents, but it has to clean them up as well. There is a danger of us being a Communist Party for the communists and nobody else, a party without a national project that would be isolated from everyone else."

Not surprisingly, prescriptions for change and renovation largely coincided with these criticisms. Renovation in the Communist Party was overwhelmingly associated with organizational questions rather than ideological or strategic debates. In particular, militants expressed a strong desire for greater internal party democracy. Affiliated demands included greater base-level participation, more debate and discussion, more questioning of the party leadership, a greater flow of communication to the base level, and more internal pluralism to enable the party to reach out to new social sectors. As one longtime militant active in peasant organizational work stated: "Sixteen years of dictatorship have changed the party and its way of operating, due to the persecution we faced. This created certain deformations and problems for us; there was more centralism than democracy in the party, and when the leadership gave orders there was a lack of discussion due to the security problem, and new militants assumed positions of leadership with very little experience. So there is a need now for greater participation within the party." Likewise, a young poblador argued: "There is a lot that has to be changed in the Communist Party, especially the noxious Stalinist tendencies within the party. We need less verticalism and more participation and creativity. The older militants can't lead these changes within the party, because they are too tainted by Stalinism. So it is up to the youth; we were the force for rebellion in the 1980s, and today we are the force for renovation in the party. No other party has the political maturity to admit its errors like we do."

Interestingly, the desire for greater internal democracy cut across the cleavage between moderates and radicals in the Communist Party. Criticisms of the party leadership did not so much reflect a perception that it was out of touch with the bases—a common complaint in the Socialist Party—as much as a perception that it stifled grass-roots initiative. Even the young militants who were the backbone of popular rebellion were not beholden to a vertical, militaristic conception of party organization; indeed, they saw popular rebellion as a process of grass-roots participation, a new type of subjectivity, and thus as a form of renovation within the party. As expressed by a university dissident in the party youth organization, "All the dissidents in the Jota today supported popular rebellion before, and we all believed that the revolutionary line had to be a military line. But our criticisms today are over the internal conception of the party. There has been a radicalization of our ethic; we were the ones who fought the hardest, we were the most radical and committed, so we have developed a different ethic, and we don't accept the justifications of the past." This statement suggests that the experience of popular rebellion—or, perhaps, its imagery—was a two-edged sword that had a highly contradictory effect. Although it served to militarize the party apparatus and centralize power in an ever more secretive and enclosed party hierarchy, it also encouraged the formation of new popular subjects with new forms—and experiences—of political protagonism who were not inclined to follow blindly the directives issued from above.

In the Socialist Party, the most common prescriptions for change were for greater popular participation, followed by more internal democracy. While some called for the party to reassert its traditional leftist profile, others urged abandoning the attachment to violent revolution. Frequent demands for more work at the base level suggested discontent with the party's emphasis on governmental responsibilities; in the words of one labor activist from the Núñez sector: "We need less manipulation of the bases and regional organizations . . . so that all sectors of the party can take the initiative. This is an important part of the renovation process in the party. The leaders have to be elected by the bases; there have to be more electoral mechanisms, with direct voting, so that there will be a democratization of the party. And the leaders of the party have to work more at the base level."

Conclusion

Although the Socialist and Communist Parties diverged sharply under authoritarian rule, both the popular rebellion strategy of the Communist Party and the renovation process in the Socialist Party inculcated a strong participatory democratic ethos in grass-roots sectors of the parties. In both cases, however, this ethos clashed with internal party structures that were hierarchical and congenitally elitist. In the Communist Party, militants who had become political protagonists through manifold forms of grass-roots resistance chafed at the restrictions the party's hierarchical structure and disciplinary norms imposed on internal democratic expression. Although the more loosely structured Socialist Party provided greater latitude for internal debate, the professionalization of its political leadership created a deep cultural divide between party elites and grass-roots militants that compounded any ideological or strategic differences. This cleavage was indicative of a vital contradiction at the heart of the process of renovation in the Socialist Party: although its discourse encouraged a "revaluation" of democracy in all spheres of social relationships, it nevertheless reflected a secularization and intellectualization of political practice that increasingly divorced it from popular protagonism and was thus poorly suited to sustain grass-roots participation in the aftermath of a democratic transition.

It is hardly surprising, therefore, that there was widespread demobilization of grass-roots militants in both parties in the early 1990s. Whereas political initiative in the Communist Party is vested in a hierarchy that controls the organizational machinery, in the Socialist Party it is controlled by a technocratic elite that monopolizes intellectual discourse. In the Communist Party, this resulted in a progressive narrowing of the party base to a collection of organizational loyalists and fundamentalists who remained highly active in grass-roots social work but were largely content to follow directives issued from above. In contrast, the Socialist Party—in classic catch-all, electoralist fashion—has broadened its base but watered down the identities and transformative objectives that helped sustain high levels of participation in the past. Consequently, the monopolization of political space by an entrenched political class that one observes in contemporary Chile is not a mere artifact of institutional constraints that helped produce a conservative, pacted democratic transition; it is also a reflection of the internal characteristics and evolutionary dynamics of Chilean political parties. Their discourse aside, Chile's left-wing parties are contributors, not exceptions, to this general pattern. It is a pattern that will have to be broken if Chilean democracy is to be deepened beyond its current parameters.

The limitations of Chile's partisan Left, however, pale in comparison to those of the Left in contemporary Peru. In Chile, the Left retains a sizable electoral constituency and access to government through relatively secure democratic channels, important building blocks for future efforts at democratic reform. Indeed, midway through the second government of the Concertación, a Socialist leader—Ricardo Lagos—is the clear front-runner in the polls for the next presidential election. In Peru, by contrast, a once formidable electoral Left was undermined by economic crisis and political violence, then thoroughly eclipsed by the rise of an autocratic leader who wedded popular sectors to a project of neoliberal reform. Whereas the Chilean Left rose from the ashes of authoritarian repression to be reconstituted as a political force in the neoliberal era, the Peruvian Left floundered in its struggle to craft a popular alternative to Fujimori's neoliberal revolution. By the mid-1990s, it was on the brink of extinction as an independent political force. The collapse of the Peruvian Left stands in stark contrast to the Chilean experience, and it provides penetrating insight into the challenges confronted by the Latin American Left in a period of social dislocation and economic transformation. As such, it warrants a closer examination.

PART III

The Rise and Demise of the
Democratic Left in Peru

CHAPTER 7

Social Mobilization and the
Rise of the Left in Peru

IF Chile has been a qualified success for the democratic Left in Latin America, Peru has arguably been its most spectacular and unmitigated failure. In the late 1960s and 1970s, when military regimes in neighboring countries waged war on the partisan Left and deactivated popular movements in the name of "national security," Peru experienced the anomaly of a reformist military government that promoted social mobilization and tolerated the organizational efforts of leftist parties. After a transition to democratic rule, Peru boasted the strongest and most successful electoral Left in South America for most of the 1980s, with support concentrated among both the urban and rural lower classes. Peru thus seemed to offer one of the best-case scenarios for a deepening of democracy brought about by an alliance between leftist parties and diverse social movements. Late in the decade, as Peru's conservative and centrist parties were devastated by the burdens of governance in the midst of a spreading guerrilla insurgency and an ever-deepening economic crisis, the United Left (IU) coalition had an opportunity to elect Latin America's first Marxist government since Allende's ill-fated experiment in Chile.[1]

Riven by internal contradictions, however, the IU split before the decisive 1990 elections, and it was discredited politically as Peru's democratic regime unraveled in the early 1990s. The democratic Left was buried in the collapse of Peru's system of party representation, as voters rejected established parties and elected independent, "antipolitical" populists who appealed directly to an atomized electorate. The eclipse of the Left was so thorough that Alberto Fujimori successfully harnessed a lower-class constituency for a neoliberal project that had marked authoritarian features.

The sudden rise and precipitous decline of Peru's democratic Left are without parallel in the Latin American region, and they are highly instructive for an understanding of the conditions for the success or failure of strategies for the deepening of democracy. The explosive growth of the Peruvian Left in the 1970s was rooted in a broader process of social organization spanning the labor, peasant, student, and shantytown movements. In parallel fashion, the demise of the Left in the late 1980s and 1990s reflected a process of social decomposition induced by political violence and economic crisis. This crisis eroded the structural basis for class-based collective action by creating a more heterogeneous and informal workforce; it diminished the centrality and strength of organized labor; and it fragmented civil society by severing horizontal linkages and encouraging particularistic survival strategies.

The demise of the democratic Left in Peru, however, cannot be attributed to structural factors alone; failures of political agency also played a central role. A cohesive Left with a coherent political and economic project might have been able to counteract the process of social disintegration by coalescing diverse constituencies behind a common national project that responded to the nation's crisis. Instead, internecine struggles within the fractious Left produced a bewildering array of alternatives that merely contributed to the sense of fragmentation and decomposition. As the national crisis deepened, so did the incoherence of the Left: outside the IU, the Shining Path insurgency steadily increased in strength until its decapitation by security forces in 1992, while the IU itself became increasingly polarized between moderates who favored a national accord to salvage the democratic regime and radicals who wanted to mobilize forces for an alternative, "revolutionary" democratic order based on grass-roots forms of popular power. Neither a deepening nor a consolidating strategy was ever able to establish hegemony within the IU, yet each was strong enough to negate the other, preventing the Left from proposing a viable alternative to a neoliberal shock program.

The successive failures of conservative and centrist administrations to resolve Peru's crisis gave the IU a golden political opportunity in the late 1980s to construct a national governmental alternative of the Left. Its failure to do so had profound implications for the Peruvian political system. First, it undermined Peru's fragile democratic regime by encouraging individuals to look beyond existing institutions for a solution, whether it be the revolutionary messianism of the Shining Path or an outside "savior" like Alberto Fujimori. This, in turn, weakened the linkages between Peru's popular sectors and established representative institutions such as political parties and the Congress. Fujimori, in fact, fanned the flames of discontent with existing institutions, then received popular acclaim when he suspended the constitution, closed Congress, and purged the judiciary in a military-backed *autogolpe*, or presidential coup, in April 1992.[2] Second, the IU's failure made it increasingly likely that the economic crisis would be addressed through the imposition of a neoliberal structural adjustment. Indeed, the dramatic weakening of the Left and its affiliated social networks emasculated popular resistance to the neoliberal "shock" that Fujimori successfully imposed within weeks of assuming the presidency in 1990, in cavalier disregard of his campaign promises. The Peruvian experience thus reveals the numerous impediments confronted by radical democratic alternatives in an era of economic crisis and neoliberal reforms, and it helps explain why political resistance to neoliberalism has been so muted.

Historical Roots of the Peruvian Left

Distinctive features of the Peruvian Left shaped its role in the democratic system in the 1980s. First, in contrast to Chile, the Left has not been a powerful actor historically in Peru, and it did not develop a mass political constituency until a wave of social mobilizations in the 1960s and 1970s transformed the political landscape. Second, when the Left finally emerged as a significant political force in the late 1970s, it did so in a highly fractious manner, meaning that its diverse social constituencies did not have a unified political expression. Third, even as they entered the electoral arena in the 1980s, important sectors of the Left retained an explicitly revolutionary doctrine, creating significant contradictions between their ideological discourse and their political practices. To understand the recent failures of the Peruvian Left, it is necessary to explore these characteristics in greater depth.

Before the 1960s, the political space for the Peruvian Left was tightly constrained by the strength of APRA, one of the earliest and most influential populist parties in Latin American history.[3] APRA emerged during a period of student and labor mobilization in the 1920s that challenged Peru's oligarchic order. After its founding by youthful political activist Víctor Raúl Haya de la Torre during his exile in Mexico in 1924,[4] APRA successfully mobilized a popular, multiclass constituency behind a nationalist, anti-imperialist, and antioligarchic political program.[5] The party gradually backed away from its initial quasi-socialist orientation, but several early, aborted Aprista revolts left a legacy of conflict with the Peruvian armed forces that resulted in periodic political repression. Military and oligarchic hostility thus blocked the nation's largest political party from coming to power during Haya de la Torre's illustrious political career.[6] Despite political persecution, APRA organized and controlled the Confederación de Trabajadores Peruanos (CTP), which was Peru's largest labor federation until the Communist-affiliated Confederación General de Trabajadores del Peru (CGTP) overtook it in the 1970s.[7]

APRA's credentials as a popular, reformist party were weakened, however, when it gained reentry into the institutional political arena by agreeing to a pact of coexistence and power sharing with the oligarchic government of Mañuel Prado from 1956 to 1962. Subsequently, APRA joined congressional conservatives in blocking agrarian and other reforms proposed by the first government of Fernando Belaunde Terry between 1963 and 1968.[8] APRA's political opportunism and the abandonment of its earlier ideological trajectory caused the party to vacate political space to various leftist groups, while encouraging defections and factional schisms that swelled the ranks of the Left in the 1960s.

Historically, the most important of the leftist groups was the Peruvian Communist Party (PCP). Like APRA, the PCP grew out of the social ferment of the 1920s, and it was spawned by the organizational labor of the other great political and intellectual figure of that era, José Carlos Mariátegui, perhaps Latin America's most re-nowned and original Marxist thinker.[9] Initially linked to the work of Haya de la Torre and APRA, Mariátegui broke with Haya on doctrinal and organizational questions and founded the Peruvian Socialist Party (PSP) in 1928.[10] From its rather heterodox roots in the political thought and practice of Mariátegui, the PSP changed its name to the Peruvian Communist Party (PCP) following the early death of its founder in 1930. The PCP established an affiliation with the Third International and became a loyal adherent to Soviet ideological and organizational orthodoxy.[11]

Adhering to the Comintern's "class against class" line of the early 1930s, the PCP adopted a sectarian position that was overtly hostile to APRA and invited the political isolation of the party. Facing periodic political repression, the PCP lost ground to APRA in the labor movement and other popular organizations, and it never achieved the mass social and electoral support that the Communist Party attained in Chile. The growth of labor, peasant, and student activism in the 1950s and 1960s opened new political space for the party, however, and its strategic orientation moderated in accordance with Moscow's international objectives. The PCP supported democratic reforms under the Belaunde government in the 1960s, and its organizational work through the CGTP finally enabled the party to overtake APRA in the labor movement during the military-reformist government of General Juan Velasco Alvarado between 1968 and 1975, which the PCP openly embraced.[12]

Nevertheless, the social mobilization of the 1960s and 1970s was channeled less by the PCP than by a plethora of new Left groups that emerged to compete with both APRA and the Communist Party. At a time when APRA was tainted by its opportunistic shift to the Right and the PCP was marked by its reformism and doctrinal fealty to the Soviet Union, a variety of Maoist, Trotskyist, and Guevarist organizations outflanked the PCP to the Left, challenging the party's strategic moderation and its rigid international identities.

The Maoist movement in Peru developed into the strongest in all of Latin America. It emerged initially in the sector of the PCP that was most actively engaged in the party's work with peasant organizations, and it increased its profile as tensions built between the Soviet Union and China in the early 1960s. The Maoists rejected the Communist Party's faith in peaceful coexistence and democratic reform, and they raised the banner of a "prolonged popular war" as the path to socialism in Peru. The competing international identities and strategic differences culminated in a major rupture of the PCP[13] in 1964 and the founding of the pro-Chinese PCP-Bandera Roja, which assumed control over the PCP-led peasant federation, the Confederación Campesina de Peru (CCP). Later divisions of the PCP-Bandera Roja led to the creation of the PCP-Patria Roja in 1969, which came to control Peru's influential teachers' union, and the PCP-Sendero Luminoso in 1970, which was based at the National University of San Cristóbal of Huamanga in the department of Ayacucho. The decision of the PCP-Sendero Luminoso, or the Shining Path, to take up arms in 1980 would profoundly alter the nation's political dynamics.

Trotskyist organizations also surged during this period, developing a base in the labor movement as well as the peasant movement led by Hugo Blanco in the valley of La Convención near Cuzco in the early 1960s.[14] Like the Maoists, the Trotskyists condemned the strategic moderation of the Communist Party and proclaimed the necessity of violent revolution on the road to socialism. Also like the Maoists, the Trotskyists suffered from repeated divisions and factionalism.[15] Although Blanco's personal appeal gave the Trotskyists considerable weight in the Peruvian Left in the 1970s, they were unable to construct a viable party apparatus of their own. Initially marginalized from the IU electoral coalition, many Trotskyists, including Blanco, swelled the ranks of the newly founded Partido Unificado Mariateguista (PUM) in the mid-1980s.

Finally, the 1960s also witnessed the emergence of new, heterodox Left groups with diverse ideological and organizational origins. Heavily influenced by the Cuban Revolution and the guerrilla warfare theory of Che Guevara, several of these New Left groups were the direct organizational predecessors of the PUM, which ultimately became the most important party in the IU in the 1980s.[16] The first of these was the Movimiento de Izquierda Revolucionaria (MIR), a left-wing splinter of APRA founded by the lawyer Luis de la Puente Uceda in 1962. De la Puente and his followers were expelled from APRA in 1959 for criticizing the party's pact with the oligarchic government of Mañuel Prado. After a trip to Cuba in 1960, de la Puente evolved rapidly toward a Guevarist position and founded the MIR to become the *foco*, or focal point, of revolution in Peru. With little in the way of a party apparatus and few linkages to popular organizations, the MIR initiated guerrilla operations in 1965, believing the armed foco would be the catalyst for mass insurrection. But the MIR was quickly defeated and repressed; de la Puente was killed in action, and the group's military apparatus was dismantled.[17] Surviving cadres tried to reconstruct the movement following the 1965 defeat and shifted their focus from rural to urban guerrilla operations. The movement splintered in the early 1970s, as some factions stressed immediate preparations for guerrilla warfare, whereas others prioritized the construction of a political party with organizational linkages to popular movements as the precondition for successful revolutionary struggle.

A second group, known as the Ejercito de Liberación Nacional (ELN), was born in 1962 and also defeated militarily in 1965–66 when it began guerrilla operations. Led by the intellectual Hector Béjar, the ELN made a belated agreement with de la Puente to collaborate with the MIR in 1965, but the accord was too late to salvage either guerrilla movement. Following its military defeat, the ELN splintered and did not play a major role in the Peruvian Left thereafter.[18]

A third—and ultimately the most important—New Left group emerged in 1965, as the Peruvian Left felt the reverberations of the guerrilla movements in the Andean highlands. Known as Vanguardia Revolucionaria (VR), this group was initially led by Ricardo Napurí, Ricardo Letts, and Edmundo Murrugarra and had its roots in intellectual study circles and the university student movement. The VR was internally pluralistic, incorporating different ideological currents with a commitment to revolutionary struggle, including Maoism, Guevarism, and Trotskyism. Thus the VR was conceived as a nationalist partisan synthesis of the revolutionary Left, with the intention of superseding the "revisionist" reformism of the Communist Party as well as the international sectarianism of the exclusive Maoist and Trotskyist parties. Likewise, the VR sought to correct the errors of the MIR and the ELN by building a more substantial party organization and establishing links to popular movements to provide a sociopolitical foundation for guerrilla operations. Although the VR conducted a series of urban guerrilla activities in the late 1960s, it also developed political networks in the labor movement, particularly in the mining and fishing industries. In the early 1970s the VR engaged in extensive organizational work among the Andean peasantry, and by 1973 it had wrested control of the CCP peasant federation from the Maoist Bandera Roja.

The VR suffered a series of divisions after 1970, with the exodus of Trotskyist factions and other small groups that prioritized the construction of a military apparatus. Nevertheless, the core of the party expanded its organizational work in the student and peasant movements, as well as militant sectors of the labor movement that rejected the collaborative relationship established by the CGTP and the Communist Party with the Velasco regime. Despite its fragmentation in the mid-1970s, the VR was destined to become the principal organizational force within the PUM, which was founded in 1984 through the merger of diverse New Left groups, including the VR, the MIR, and a sector of the Partido Comunista Revolucionario (PCR), which had split off from the VR in 1974.[19]

In short, whereas the narrow left-wing political space in Peru was dominated by the PCP before 1960, with APRA existing as a powerful populist alternative, the 1960s and 1970s witnessed the explosive growth and proliferation of leftist alternatives. These alternatives broke down into four principal tendencies: the pro-Soviet PCP, the Maoist Communist parties, the Trotskyist organizations, and the diverse New Left groups that emerged from the MIR and the VR. Each of these alternatives, however, was highly fragmented; indeed, over three dozen leftist parties or movements existed in Peru in the 1970s, including seven that traced their roots to the PCP, thirteen to the VR, and eight to the MIR, in addition to seven Trotskyist organizations and several independent leftist groups.[20]

This fragmentation was all the more remarkable considering that it occurred almost entirely within the Marxist Left, since a non-Marxist, socialist Left had only a minimal expression in Peru during the 1960s and 1970s.[21] The Marxist groups shared common ideological roots and identified with the heritage of Mariátegui, and all but the Communist Party had a revolutionary orientation, with a Leninist ideological emphasis on the destruction of the "bourgeois" state and the revolutionary conquest of state power. The fragmentation of the Left, however, reflected the competing international loyalties and ideological currents in Peruvian Marxism, along with fierce tactical debates over the role of political parties, guerrilla movements, and social organizations in the revolutionary process.

Despite this extreme fragmentation, the political strength of the Left grew rapidly in the 1960s and 1970s as a result of an unusual and highly propitious set of social and political circumstances. Three principal factors joined together during this period to create new opportunities for the Left: the growing conservatism of APRA, the groundswell of social mobilization, and the existence of a military regime that deliberately stimulated popular organization to buttress redistributive socioeconomic reforms but failed to establish corporatist controls over the organizations it spawned. APRA's shift to the right prevented it from channeling or capitalizing politically on the new forms of social organization that emerged during this period, thus leaving a political vacuum that various leftist groups rushed to fill. Likewise, the failure of the military regime to incorporate newly organized groups into government-controlled channels of representation created opportunities for the Left to make inroads among popular sectors.[22] The context could hardly have been more ideal for an expansion of the radical Left: a surge of popular mobilization that was politically uncommitted and generally resistant to the entreaties of the Left's principal competitors, that is, government reformers and Aprista populism.

Social Mobilization and the Growth
of the Left in the 1960s and 1970s

The intense social mobilization of the 1960s and 1970s reflected structural and political conditions that were conducive to collective action among popular sectors. In particular, dense concentrations of subaltern groups were brought together in structural locations that encouraged collective identities and generated conflicts with the state or dominant economic groups. These conflicts provided unparalleled opportunities for the radical Left to develop contacts and cultivate support among new social groups by articulating their demands and linking them with others.

In the labor sphere, the 1960s through the mid-1970s was a period of rapid import-substitution industrialization in Peru, which increased the number of large industrial establishments and expanded the manufacturing labor force from 428,700 in 1961 to 643,900 in 1971.[23] This expansion of the industrial labor force was accompanied by two important changes in labor organization and industrial relations. First, levels of unionization increased dramatically: the number of industrial unions more than doubled during Velasco's tenure from 1968 to 1975, and the total number of unions increased sixfold between 1960 and 1975.[24] Second, the political orientation of the labor movement shifted to the left with the diffusion of militant organizational tactics. APRA's historic dominance of the labor movement had been rooted in vertical ties of patron-clientelism that linked the union rank and file to labor bosses and the owners of individual enterprises. This co-optive pattern of organization began to break down in the 1960s as workers in large industrial and mining establishments opted for class-based forms of organization characterized by horizontal ties, worker solidarity, union autonomy, and confrontation with the owners of capital over wages and union rights.[25]

Much of this new labor organizing was channeled into the Communist Party–led CGTP, which grew rapidly under the military regime and overtook the Aprista federation as the largest in the country. The Communist Party and the CGTP welcomed the efforts of the Velasco regime to organize labor, enhance employment security, and buttress the legal rights of unions. But many unions chafed at the corporatist restrictions associated with participation in profit-sharing "industrial communities" planned by the military reformers, and as the smaller parties of the radical Left increased their influence in the labor movement, more militant organizations emerged which rejected any form of collaboration with the government. When Velasco was replaced by General Francisco Morales Bermúdez in 1975, the military regime entered a second, more conservative phase in which social reforms were put on hold and austerity measures prescribed by the International Monetary Fund (IMF) were implemented to stabilize the economy. In response, the CGTP and the Communist Party joined the more radical unions and parties of the Left in organizing massive general strikes in 1977–78 that solidified the confrontational character of the new labor movement, along with its leadership position in opposition to the military regime.

Likewise, conditions were ripe for the mobilization of the largely indigenous highland peasantry in the 1960s and 1970s, when Peru developed one of the largest and most radical peasant movements in Latin America. Indigenous communities provided large aggregations of agricultural producers with deeply rooted ethnic and communal identities who were starved for land in Peru's highly concentrated agrarian structure. Agricultural commercialization in the postwar era helped spawn the peasant mobilizations that began in the late 1950s, accentuating conflicts over scarce land and loosening clientelistic dependence on landlord patrons.[26] The early 1960s brought a wave of land seizures as traditional haciendas were invaded by neighboring or residential peasant communities. Between 1960 and 1965, approximately 300,000 peasants from some 350 to 400 rural communities participated in organized invasions of hacienda lands.[27] Although Belaunde had promised agrarian reform in his presidential campaign, congressional opposition and governmental timidity ensured that the land redistributed would fall far short of the amount needed to pacify the Andean peasantry.

The land conflicts thus festered until Velasco and his cohorts deposed Belaunde and quickly proclaimed one of the most ambitious agrarian reforms in the history of Latin America. Both coastal plantations and highland haciendas were expropriated and transformed into agricultural cooperatives that were operated and managed (under the tutelage of the Agriculture Ministry) by their former workers and, in some cases, adjacent indigenous communities. But the elimination of large private landowners did not fully meet peasants' demands for land because temporary agricultural workers and many indigenous communities located outside the haciendas did not receive land or become members of the cooperatives. As Cynthia McClintock stated in her seminal study of the agrarian reform, "Although the Peruvian reform . . . hurt hacendados severely, it helped only some 10 or 15 percent of the nation's peasantry, namely those on the large coastal and highland haciendas. . . . The reform did virtually nothing for the poorest peasants, landless temporary workers."[28] The agrarian reform, therefore, swept away many traditional constraints on peasant organization that were rooted in coercive or clientelistic relationships in the countryside,[29] but it did not address the long-standing claims of many independent indigenous communities to recover lands that had been previously usurped by haciendas. The reform, therefore, only partially eliminated the land conflicts that provided incentives for mobilization, and in many regions it created new cleavages and conflicts.

These basic conflicts over land and property rights were tailor-made for the organizing strategies of Peru's militant Maoist, Trotskyist, and New Left parties. Their ability to capitalize on peasant mobilization was enhanced by the fact that APRA was very weak in the central and southern Andean highlands, given its historic concentration on rural workers from the sugar plantations along the northern coast of Peru. The partisan Left thus found political space to organize in an immense social sector that was politically uncommitted yet had radical demands leading to confrontational forms of collective action. Leftist parties organized local and regional peasant federations to press specific land claims and developed the CCP into a national association under the leadership of the VR and other militant groups.

Finally, the mushrooming shantytowns around Lima and other major cities provided fertile social terrain for the organizational efforts of the Left as well. The postwar era witnessed a massive, steady exodus of rural families to urban communities in search of job opportunities or other social and economic benefits. Many of these families had no choice but to locate in shantytown communities, or *pueblos jovenes*, that sprang up with the influx of new urban migrants. The population of Lima increased nearly tenfold from 645,172 to almost 6 million between 1940 and 1984, while the number of people living in Lima's pueblos jovenes rose from 119,886 in 1956 to more than 2 million in 1983, accounting for more than 36 percent of the capital's population.[30] These sprawling communities often lacked the most basic public services such as potable water, electricity, sewage disposal, and paved streets, and their residents typically did not have legal title to the land on which they lived.

The time-honored technique for acquiring land titles or public services in Peru was patron-clientelism—that is, the cultivation of personal or community ties to a government agency or political figure in a tacit exchange of political support for material benefits.[31] New political styles emerged, however, in response to the organizational efforts of the Velasco regime and the radical Left. The military government created a government agency, SINAMOS, to encourage the formation of community organizations and link them vertically to the state. Many grass-roots organizations, however, rejected rigid and intrusive government controls over resources, leadership selection, and the content and expression of demands, and they became politicized through their efforts to avoid co-optation and assert organizational autonomy.[32] In the process, new linkages were established to parties of the Left that denounced corporatist and clientelist controls over popular organizations. The radical Left encouraged popular organizations to maintain an autonomous stance and a confrontational posture vis-à-vis the government to maximize the impact of their demands.

By the second half of the 1970s, as the military regime entered its more conservative phase and an economic recession brought austerity and hardship, urban popular communities became bastions of opposition to the dictatorship. Vertical linkages to the government that segmented and controlled shantytown organizations began to fray, and new horizontal linkages were created. Local and regional federations of shantytown organizations blossomed to articulate economic demands and help coordinate protest activities. These federations joined with peasant associations, student groups, and other social organizations in the multisectoral regional fronts that were anchored by labor unions in an effort to provide broad popular support for the five national strikes that rocked the military regime during its last four years in power.[33]

Consequently, the period of military government from 1968 to 1980 witnessed rapid growth in the scope, density, militancy, and horizontal coordination of popular organizations. Clientelistic relationships that had predominated historically in agricultural, industrial, and urban popular settings began to break down, weakening the vertical ties between subaltern groups and well-placed patrons that had traditionally segmented popular sectors and sustained conservative and populist forms of political dominance. In their place, more horizontal class- and community-based forms of association emerged that resisted government co-optation and corporatist controls, while relying on confrontational forms of collective action to assert autonomous social and political demands. Organized labor played a leading role in this social mobilization, which peaked during the general strikes of 1977–78. The strike weapon—especially when centrally directed at the national level— gave labor a powerful form of political and economic leverage. With its organizing experience, national direction, and political ties, the labor movement served as a practical school for the diffusion of collective identities and organizational lessons. Labor activists frequently participated in community organizations and coordinated regional protest activities, helping to socialize and politicize broader urban popular sectors in the confrontational tactics of the *clasista* labor movement.[34] Social mobilization in Peru thus manifested the radial tendencies discussed in Chapter 3, whereby labor unions serve as the fulcrum or axis for broader forms of organization and protest.

The radical parties of the Left were both instigators and beneficiaries of these new forms of social mobilization, and they were inadvertently strengthened by reforms that were designed by the military regime to dampen class conflict and contain popular demands.[35] Since the Left had never been a significant electoral force in Peru—a left-wing coalition had obtained only 3 percent of the vote in the last national elections in 1963—it suffered little from the closure of electoral arenas of competition. Indeed, the Maoist, Trotskyist, and New Left parties had little but scorn for such "bourgeois" formalities, which had seemingly proved their futility when Belaunde failed to deliver on promised social reforms during his term in office. For these parties, democracy was associated with political marginalization and the maintenance of an oligarchic status quo, rather than a popular conquest leading to social or economic reform. The parties of the radical Left were classic vanguard groups that preferred to devote their energies to grass-roots organizational work in civil society, cultivating social networks that would eventually provide the foundation for a revolutionary assault on state power. The military regime was ideal for their organizational structures and goals because it closed formal political institutions that were relied on by the Left's competitors, but it was not so repressive as to damage the semiclandestine cadres of radical Left parties. Likewise, the regime consciously stimulated social mobilization but lacked the political or institutional capabilities to channel it into corporatist mechanisms of control, thus leaving fertile terrain for oppositional forms of organization.

This did not mean, however, that the bulk of the Left welcomed or supported the military regime. In fact, the Peruvian Left was unsure how to respond to the Velasco regime, which appropriated much of the Left's social agenda and represented a sui generis political phenomenon in the Latin American context—a military dictatorship that proclaimed a sweeping agrarian reform to break the back of oligarchic power, tried to transform private industries into profit-sharing industrial communities, incorporated leftist intellectuals as technical advisers, turned to the Soviet Union for military and economic assistance, expropriated U.S. multinational firms, and supported diverse forms of popular organization. After an initial period of hesitation, the Communist Party proclaimed its "total support" for the Velasco regime and capitalized on the military's desire to buttress the CGTP as an alternative to Aprista unionism. In contrast, the Maoist and Trotskyist groups declared that the military regime was "fascist" and committed themselves to frontal opposition. New Left groups like the VR were less decisive, condemning the regime's political makeup and corporatist tendencies, while recognizing that its social reforms, organizational efforts, and internal contradictions could be exploited by the Left.[36]

Tactical differences over whether and how to collaborate, oppose, or exploit the military regime accounted for much of the factionalism within the Peruvian Left in the 1970s, as the radical Left splintered into dozens of contending groups. Greater unity of purpose began to emerge in the late 1970s as the regime became more conservative, the economy entered into decline, and the level of social protest increased dramatically. Although the Communist Party insisted on the need to maintain the social reforms of the Velasco era, it joined the more radical parties in opposition to Morales Bermúdez, and the partisan Left helped organize local and regional networks or *frentes* that coordinated strike and protest activities. The political fragmentation of the partisan Left was clearly a limiting factor in its capacity to aggregate and centralize popular demands. Nevertheless, partisan cooperation in the social terrain was greater than in the arena of political organization, and it created momentum for the eventual construction of a leftist alliance following Peru's transition to democracy in 1980. The first step in this process was a gradual recomposition of the New Left groups, which began as they coordinated activities for the first national strike in July 1977. The fruit of this coordination was the creation of a coalition known as the Unidad Democrática Popular (UDP) by fourteen groups in December 1977, which launched the core political alliance that eventually culminated in the foundation of the PUM as the synthesis of New Left groups in 1984.

A democratic transition was the furthest thing from the minds of the UDP and other sectors of the radical Left, as they interpreted the explosion of popular protests and strikes as the emergence of a prerevolutionary situation that promised to build toward an insurrectionary rupture with the military regime and an uninterrupted process of socialist revolution.[37] For the military regime, however, the popular protests provided the impetus to initiate a gradual, controlled democratic transition that would allow the armed forces to return to the barracks, relinquish responsibility for managing Peru's deepening social and economic crisis, and bequeath the reins of government to trusted civilians. In particular, the military government entered into a collaborative relationship with APRA to plan a democratic transition, thus breaking the historic animosity between the armed forces and the party of Haya de la Torre. Still the largest party in Peru, APRA was now seen by the military as a conservative force and an effective bulwark to the advance of the radical Left and its affiliated social organizations. The regime thus called for the election of a constituent assembly in 1978 which would craft a new constitution to prepare for general congressional and presidential elections in 1980.[38]

The plans for a democratic transition radically transformed the strategic arena in Peru and created a critical juncture for the leftist parties and popular movements that had thrived during a decade of military rule. For the newer parties, this juncture represented the first time that they had been forced to define their political role under a democratic regime. Although it was initially more inadvertent than deliberate, it also marked the beginning of their efforts to deepen democracy in Peru.

Entering the System: Redemocratization and
the Dilemmas of Political Incorporation

Beyond the fact that the bulk of the Peruvian Left had little historical experience with democratic participation, their incorporation into the new democratic regime differed in important respects from that of the Left in Chile. First, whereas the Chilean Left and its affiliated social networks had been violently repressed and disarticulated under Pinochet, the social and political Left in Peru emerged much stronger from a period of military rule that was far less repressive and actually conducive to social mobilization. Second, the Peruvian generals placed far fewer institutional constraints on the process of democratization than Pinochet had, meaning that the Peruvian Left did not confront as many legal and institutional impediments to social reforms. Third, although the Peruvian military regime backed away from the radical reforms of Velasco during the latter half of the 1970s, it did not implement a neoliberal revolution like that of the Pinochet regime to curtail drastically the developmental role of the state and enhance the power of capital. In fact, the traditional agrarian oligarchy had been virtually eliminated by Velasco's reforms, and economic elites no longer thought of the military as a bulwark of the status quo or a safeguard against the radical demands of popular sectors. In contrast to Chile, the Peruvian Left did not have to face a capitalist class that was reflexively inclined to support authoritarianism to contain democratic pressures for social reform. In Peru, democracy had traditionally been elitist and conservative, and the most widespread social reforms had been associated with military rule.

These factors created a set of conditions that potentially made Peru one of the most likely cases for a deepening of democracy by the Left and its affiliated social networks in modern Latin America. It is ironic, then, that the Peruvian Left was one of the least inclined to tackle such an endeavor. The Left in Peru had never been a significant actor in a democratic context and had never earned more than 3 percent of the vote in a national election. It had often been excluded from participation in Peru's oligarchic democratic past, and the ideology of most leftist parties divorced democratic participation from the struggle for social justice. In contrast to the Left in Chile, the Peruvian Left had never had the experience of using democratic institutions to implement socioeconomic reforms, and it had never confronted severe repression as a result of the loss of democracy such as the Chilean Left suffered after 1973.

In short, the bulk of the Peruvian Left had little intention of building socialism through a deepening of democracy. They had never gone through the traumatic experiences that caused the Chilean Socialists to "revalue" democracy and reconceptualize it as an intrinsic component of the socialist project. Instead, they conceptualized democracy in essentially instrumental terms, as a new political arena for the accumulation of forces that would eventually put revolution on the political agenda. That is, democracy could be used to raise the profile of the Left, denounce the status quo, and mobilize popular support, but it was still seen as alien terrain by most parties of the Left because they did not envision coming to power or constructing socialism through formal democratic mechanisms. The Maoist, Trotskyist, and New Left parties all assumed that a rupture with democratic institutions was inevitable because in their conception of politics socialism was inextricably associated with a revolutionary conquest of state power.

The democratic transition thus placed these parties in an awkward predicament. Their organizational work in the social terrain had been designed to prepare for a revolutionary defeat of the military regime, but they had largely abandoned any serious effort to create an armed revolutionary apparatus, and they lacked the means to alter the military's plans to sponsor a preemptive democratic transition. As popular mobilization was diverted from street protests and general strikes to electoral participation, leftist parties were deprived of the levers by which they could modify or control the course of political events. These parties were thus forced to make a fundamental strategic choice. They could abstain from electoral politics, at the risk of isolation from the popular movements they had helped to build, or they could participate in elections as a new arena for political struggle, at the risk of compromising their revolutionary principles and contributing to the consolidation of a regime their ideology proclaimed to be transitory.

The Communist Party and the Revolutionary Socialist Party (PSR), a new organization formed by supporters of Velasco's reforms, reluctantly accepted the military's plans for a constituent assembly, hoping it would serve to institutionalize the social reforms implemented during the first phase of the military regime. The more radical parties were more hostile to the idea of a constituent assembly because they had emerged in the 1960s as revolutionary alternatives to the "reformist" opportunism of the Communist Party, and they had historically denied the validity or merit of "bourgeois" democracy. The MIR, for example, condemned the constituent assembly for its "reactionary essence" and claimed that the democratic transition was designed by the bourgeoisie and imperialism to "brake and deviate the combat of the people." For the MIR, redemocratization would enable traditional elites to "assume more directly the control of the state machinery" to mask the crisis of bourgeois domination.[39]

Nevertheless, the MIR said it was necessary to engage in "the political struggle for power at all moments and utilizing all forms of struggle," and it acknowledged that "the new electoral confrontation, in spite of its antidemocratic character, is an additional terrain for the advance of the popular movement."[40] Indeed, the bulk of Peru's New Left and Trotskyist groups opted to participate in the transition process; although two small splinters from the VR boycotted the constituent assembly elections, along with the Maoist Patria Roja and the clandestine Shining Path, the principal factions of VR participated through the UDP coalition along with the Revolutionary Communist Party and the diverse MIR factions.[41]

Five leftist organizations competed in the 1978 constituent assembly elections and jointly polled 29.5 percent of the vote[42] (see Table 7.1). This was nearly ten times the vote obtained by the Left

TABLE 7.1. *Peruvian Presidential and Municipal Election Results* (percent of valid vote)

Party	1962 Pres.	1978 C.A.[a]	1980 Pres.	1980 Mun.	1983 Mun.	1985 Pres.	1986 Mun.	1989 Mun.	1990 Pres.	1993 Mun.	1995 Pres.
Left											
IU				23.9	28.8	24.7	30.5	17.9	8.2	–	0.6
IS								2.3	4.8	3.9	
Multiple parties	3.5	29.5	13.9								
Center											
APRA	33.0	35.3	27.4	22.7	33.1	53.1	47.1	18.7	22.6	11.7	4.2
Right											
UNO	28.4	2.1									
AP	32.1	–	45.4	35.9	17.4	7.3	–	–	–	12.3	1.7
PPC		23.8	9.6	10.9	13.9	11.9	14.6			5.3	–
Fredemo								31.5	32.7	–	
Independents/Others											
Cambio 90[b]									29.1	–	63.7
Others	2.9	9.3	3.8	6.7	6.8	3.1	7.8	29.6	2.6	63.0	29.8[c]

[a]Constituent assembly elections.

[b]Cambio 90 is the electoral vehicle for Alberto Fujimori. In 1995 it ran in alliance with another pro-Fujimori group, Nueva Mayoría.

[c]Includes 22.4 percent obtained by the coalition backing the independent Javier Pérez de Cuellar.

ACRONYMS: IU—Izquierda Unida; IS—Izquierda Socialista; UNO—Unión Nacional Odrista; AP—Acción Popular; PPC—Partido Popular Cristiano; Fredemo—Frente Democrático.

SOURCES: For 1962–90, Richard Webb and Graciela Fernández Baca de Valdéz, eds., *Perú en Números 1991* (Lima: Cuánto S.A., 1991), pp. 1015–32. For 1993, Fernando Tuesta Soldevilla, *Perú político en cifras: Elite política y elecciones*, 2d ed. (Lima: Fundación Friedrich Ebert, 1994), pp. 35 and 135. Results for 1995 are taken from newspaper accounts of the election.

in the last national elections in 1963 and the highest vote ever obtained by a Marxist Left in Latin America outside of Chile, demonstrating the extent to which the Left had enhanced its power under the Peruvian military regime.[43] Trotskyist peasant organizer Hugo Blanco was the third highest vote-getter in the nation after APRA's Haya de la Torre and conservative leader Luis Bedoya Reyes. The Left thus placed a large bloc of representatives in the constituent assembly, although it remained a minority force and had few illusions about its capacity to shape the eventual design of Peru's new democratic institutions.

Most of the leftist groups saw the constituent assembly as a new forum in which to criticize the military regime, defend the rights and interests of popular sectors, and agitate on behalf of revolutionary alternatives. Their participation had both defensive and offensive objectives. Defensively, they hoped to block the imposition of an "antipopular" constitution by conservative forces, denounce human rights violations and the mass firing of strike leaders, and protect Velasco-era gains in employment security and the right to strike. Offensively, they hoped to reach out to new social sectors in electoral campaigns, establish a niche in new institutional arenas, and promote the creation of popular assemblies and other mechanisms of direct participatory democracy. By entering the arena of institutional politics, they hoped to plant the seeds of revolution in the heart of the bourgeois order.[44]

The political influence of the Left continued to be curtailed, however, by its congenital factionalism. The Trotskyist, New Left, and Maoist parties remained highly critical of the Communist Party and the PSR, claiming that they were braking the "revolutionary" mobilization of the popular movement, accepting the constitutional rules of the game, and contemplating an alliance with APRA. The moderate, "reformist" Left, they argued, sought to demonstrate its "responsibility" so it could obtain a place in the bourgeois political system.[45] As the constitutional process narrowed the range of political alternatives, however, and as the social protests waned—in part because of the reluctance of the Communist Party and the CGTP to support the strike proposals of more radical unions such as the Maoist teachers' federation—even most of the Maoist groups that had boycotted the constituent assembly opted to participate in the May 1980 presidential and legislative elections.[46] Initially, the Left coalesced into two political blocs in preparation for these elections, as the Trotskyists refused to work with the "bourgeois" and pro-Velasco PSR, which was allied to the Communist Party. The first bloc, known as the Unión de Izquierda, included the Communist Party, the PSR, and a much-reduced remnant of the Frente Obrero, Campesino, Estudiantil y Popular (FOCEP). The second bloc brought together the "revolutionary" forces of the New Left UDP, the Maoist front Unidad Nacional de Izquierda Revolucionaria (UNIR), and various Trotskyist parties in the Alianza Revolucionaria de Izquierda, which intended to support a presidential campaign by Hugo Blanco.

Both of these coalitions splintered, however, when they tried to negotiate common programs and distribute seats among the different parties on parliamentary electoral lists.[47] Distinct ideological identities and bitter competition between parties and personalities resulted in five separate tickets representing the Left in the general elections. A steep price was paid for this failure to construct a viable political alternative; the combined Left vote fell to 14 percent, and the elections returned Belaunde to the presidency after a twelve-year interregnum. The UDP and Blanco's Partido Revolucionario de Trabajadores both elected two senators and three deputies to the newly established congress; UNIR and the Communist Party/PSR alliance each elected two senators and two deputies, while FOCEP elected a single senator.

Chastened by their mediocre electoral showing and determined to collaborate so as to exercise greater leverage in the newly established democratic institutions, the different Left groups—minus Blanco and the Trotskyists—coalesced after the May 1980 elections in the Izquierda Unida (IU). Founded as an electoral alliance in September 1980, the IU represented the most serious left-wing political coalition in the history of Peru, bringing together the Communist Party, the PSR, the UDP, UNIR, the PCR, and FOCEP (see Table 7.2). The new alliance paid immediate dividends, as the IU received 23.9 percent of the vote nationwide in the November 1980 municipal elections and over 28 percent of the vote in Lima for its mayoral candidate, Alfonso Barrantes, an independent leftist who had been named as the first president of the IU.

TABLE 7.2. *Origins of the Peruvian Left*

Members of the United Left (IU)	Political Origins
Peruvian Communist Party (PCP)	Founded in 1930, origins in Mariátegui's Peruvian Socialist Party
Union of the Revolutionary Left (UNIR)	Maoist coalition founded in 1980, origins in the 1960's divisions of PCP; dominated by PCP-Patria Roja
Revolutionary Communist Party (PCR)	New Left party founded in 1974 through a rupture of Revolutionary Vanguard (VR)
Revolutionary Socialist Party (PSR)	Founded in 1976 by military and technocratic supporters of the Velasco regime
Workers, Peasants, Students and Popular Front (FOCEP)	Descendant of late 1970's Trotskyist coalition
Socialist Political Action (APS)	Founded in 1980 by newspaper editor Gustavo Mohme
Unified Mariateguista Party (PUM)	Founded in 1984 through a merger of New Left groups, primarily the VR, the Movement of the Revolutionary Left (MIR), and a faction of the PCR

Equally important, the Left assumed governmental responsibilities for the first time in Peruvian history, as the IU elected 13 of the nation's 188 district mayors, including 9 from the sprawling shantytown communities that encircled Lima.[48] While this success provided enticing evidence of the political opportunities associated with democratic participation, it also forced some of the contradictions of the Left out into the open. Moderate sectors in the IU perceived mayoral responsibilities as a golden opportunity to gain administrative experience, cultivate a reputation for probity and efficiency, experiment with new programs, mobilize popular sectors, and construct new channels for popular participation in the design and implementation of municipal services. In effect, they believed that municipal institutions could provide the basic building blocks for more direct, decentralized forms of democratic governance, allowing democracy to be deepened by opening its institutions to the political protagonism of grass-roots sectors. The assumption was that the deepening of democracy and the strengthening of the Left were cumulative and mutually reinforcing processes; as the Left grew stronger, new channels of participation would be established, which would redound to the political advantage of the Left in a cumulative process of social and political transformation.[49]

In contrast, radical sectors in the IU were wary of assuming governmental authority in the municipalities. To assume executive and administrative responsibilities, even at the local level, was different than the assumption of a parliamentary seat as part of a dissident minority that claimed to be agitating for revolution, like an insurrectionary Trojan Horse inserted in bourgeois institutions. By accepting mayorships, leftist parties were placed in the awkward situation of actually administering portions of a state apparatus most of them had pledged to overthrow. Not only was this patently incongruent with the formal doctrine of most of the Left, but it also clashed with their long-standing political practices and methods of grass-roots mobilization. For years, the Left had cultivated support among popular sectors with two basic strategic postulates—to maximize the demands placed on the government and to express those demands in a confrontational manner so as to maximize their visibility and political leverage. Such tactics may have garnered support for the Left when it was in opposition to a military dictatorship, but they could only enervate it when the Left itself had assumed governmental responsibilities for responding to popular demands. To govern municipalities, it was necessary to go beyond protests and denunciations by developing proposals for alternative political and economic programs. IU radicals were thus wary of entering the municipalities and facing widespread popular demands that the Left itself had fanned, especially when they would have limited power to address popular demands as a result of the centralization of political authority and the scarcity of resources at local administrative levels. The radicals believed that solutions to popular demands could not be found at the municipal level in a bourgeois state; to be held politically accountable for addressing such demands would not help the Left accumulate power and could actually reverse much of the progress that had been made in the 1970s.

These different conceptions of the value of municipal authority created internal conflicts that plagued many local IU govern-

ments. Ultimately, however, the IU had little choice but to embrace municipal-level opportunities for governance; where formal
democratic arenas exist to structure the distribution of political
rewards and penalties, the price of abstention is likely to be political marginalization.[50] The IU could hardly afford to abandon the
municipal terrain to populist or conservative competitors, especially when this decentralized terrain was the most accessible to
the population and provided unparalleled opportunities to forge political ties to diverse forms of grass-roots organization. Consequently, even the bulk of IU radicals came to accept municipal
governance as an opportunity to "accumulate forces"—that is, to
cultivate and empower community organizations that would be
the building blocks for the revolutionary political alternative of the
Left.[51]

Conditions remained propitious for an expansion of the Left
in the early 1980s, largely as a result of the political and economic
failures of the Belaunde government. After running on a modified populist platform in his 1980 campaign, Belaunde began to reverse the reforms of the military regime after taking office, and he
adopted a more orthodox development model that ran aground as
the debt crisis spread across Latin America. The Peruvian economy
contracted by nearly 12 percent in 1983, while the inflation rate
rose into the triple digits. Belaunde also stood by as the Shining
Path insurgency spread across Ayacucho and neighboring depart-
ments of the southern highlands between 1980 and 1982, relying
on an overmatched police force to contain the secretive guerrilla
movement. He then declared a state of emergency in large parts of
the highlands at the end of 1982, yielding political authority to
military commanders in emergency zones and turning a blind eye
to the scorched-earth counterinsurgency campaign that followed.[52]

These political and economic failures weakened the position of
Belaunde's Popular Action party, and the IU was quick to capitalize
politically. In the 1983 municipal elections the IU established itself
as the second largest political force in the country after APRA,
winning 28.8 percent of the national vote and 33 mayorships, including a sweep of 15 of the 16 districts in Lima with the highest
concentration of pueblos jovenes.[53] This success was crowned by
the election of Barrantes to the mayorship of metropolitan Lima,

arguably the second most important political post in the country. Barrantes had come to the IU by way of the New Left coalition UDP, but he was not affiliated with any particular party. His status as a respected independent leftist had made him a consensus figure for the presidency of the IU because his leadership was not expected to give advantages to any single party within the coalition. Barrantes was also an effective communicator with a common touch that reflected his provincial origins. These attributes made him a natural on the campaign stump and thus a logical choice to be the showcase mayoral candidate of the IU.

Barrantes organized an impressive team of young intellectuals and technocrats under the leadership of the prominent sociologist Henry Pease to help manage the affairs of municipal Lima. Pease and his associates saw municipal government as a practical laboratory to develop new programs and, most important, cultivate new forms of grass-roots participation and local self-government in political and economic affairs. Their most important initiatives included the mobilization of over 100,000 women through 7,500 local committees to implement a new "glass of milk" campaign for children; promotion of a new municipal tax to decentralize government financial resources; the delivery of over 100,000 property titles to residents of pueblos jovenes; programs to legalize, regulate, and organize street vendors and other informal sector workers; enhanced regulation of urban transit and waste disposal; and the promotion of communal organizations to support soup kitchens, housing and public health projects, and infrastructural development.[54]

The extensive experience with municipal governance in the 1980s helped transform the concept of *autogestión*, or community self-management, into the centerpiece of the Left's political alternative for the deepening of democracy. Divisions continued to exist within the Left as to whether new mechanisms of participatory self-government represented a deepening of existing democratic institutions or the seeds of an alternative, revolutionary political order. Nevertheless, a broad consensus existed within the IU that local channels of participation provided the foundation for a cumulative process of social and political transformation. In a society where state institutions had little effective presence in large parts of the territory and were typically coercive and corrupt in much of the territory where they were present, the idea of autogestión provided an appealing vision of the absorption of governmental functions within an activist, decentralized, and self-administering civil society.

This vision was hardly unique to the Peruvian Left; what set Peru apart, and encouraged the Peruvian Left to place so much ideological emphasis on autogestión, was its rich practical experience in building participatory channels for community self-management. In urban areas, the showcase was Villa El Salvador, a sprawling popular community on the outskirts of Lima founded through a land invasion in 1972. The grass-roots organizing that led to the land invasion and evoked support from the Velasco government spawned a dense network of community groups that transformed Villa El Salvador into an internationally recognized model of participatory self-government at the municipal level. Neighborhood committees created a central representative body that worked with community groups to acquire land titles, provide infrastructure, develop health and education programs, create a credit union and cooperative enterprises, and even construct an industrial park to create new economic opportunities. New Left parties were deeply involved in this grass-roots organizational work, making Villa El Salvador a bastion of electoral support for the IU in the 1980s.[55]

In rural areas, the Left's model of autogestión heralded the example of the *rondas campesinas*, or peasant self-defense patrols. The rondas emerged in the northern highlands department of Cajamarca as a grass-roots initiative to protect peasant communities from cattle rustlers. As the rondas developed and proliferated, they assumed quasi-governmental security and juridical functions, often defending communities from predatory local police forces (who at times were the perpetrators of cattle rustling), punishing individuals who violated community norms, and practicing dispute resolution in cases of domestic or community conflicts.[56] Since the rondas were initially independent of government institutions, they were seen by the Left as an archetypal method of grass-roots protagonism and popular empowerment; rondas seemed to demonstrate that participatory, self-governing institutions could be spawned by an organized civil society as both an alternative and contender to the formal institutions of the bourgeois state. They also created community-based impediments to the spread of the Shining Path insurgency in the highlands because the rondas defended community autonomy against externally imposed political projects, and the Shining Path could not countenance autonomous forms of community organization in the areas where it operated.[57]

The Peruvian social landscape thus provided myriad opportunities for the Left to experiment with grass-roots participation and self-governing initiatives. The IU, however, was far from the ideal political agent to synthesize and channel the energies of Peru's diverse popular subjects. The IU was a loose electoral coalition of distinct political parties that continued to compete among each other. Each party contributed two members to the national coordinating committee of the IU,[58] but the IU had no real organizational structure or membership of its own, and it provided little centralized political direction for the Peruvian Left or its affiliated social networks. In short, the IU was merely an electoral front rather than a mass political organization, and efforts to develop a more institutionalized structure following the coalition's first national congress in 1989 were negated by political polarization.[59]

Furthermore, the parties that constituted the IU remained relatively small, exclusive organizations that were more likely to fragment popular subjects than unify them. The majority of the parties—the PSR, FOCEP, PCR, and APS—were little more than political vehicles for a prominent personality, while the PUM, PCP, and UNIR were classic vanguard parties with some presence in organized social constituencies. Although the VR, the main force in the PUM, had placed relatively greater emphasis on party building and mass political work, all the parties of the New Left had been shaped by the *foquismo* of the 1960s. The MIR was born as a classic guerrilla foco, and even the VR began with the idea of creating a minimal party apparatus to help initiate and sustain eventual guerrilla operations. Consequently, these parties were founded as small, secretive, and conspiratorial groups whose cadres were composed largely of intellectuals and labor or student activists. These characteristics were reinforced by the political constraints of a decade of military dictatorship, as they enabled the parties to penetrate and organize the student, labor, peasant, and shantytown movements while limiting the exposure of party militants to potential repression. They were further reinforced by a shared Leninist ideology that stressed democratic centralism and an eventual recourse to revolutionary violence, along with extraordinary levels of fragmentation and factionalism that exacerbated the parties' sectarian attributes.

There was thus a significant contradiction between the organizational structures of these parties and the political requisites for sustaining mass electoral support in a period of open democratic contestation. After years of semiclandestine struggle, most of the leaders of the Left were not widely recognized as public figures, and they did not have the organizational, financial, or human resources required to mobilize electoral support on a national scale. The organizational fragmentation and sectarianism of the partisan Left impeded the construction of a coherent and viable political alternative, while the parties' selective cadre structures made it difficult to mobilize electoral support beyond their organized core constituencies.

Consequently, after years of specializing in agitation and protest, while proposing socialist revolution as the utopian alternative to military dictatorship, the exigencies of democratic contestation created pressures for change in the partisan Left. Leftist parties had to develop a more pragmatic, short-range political and economic program with concrete tasks and realistic goals, even if the ultimate objectives and the teleological vision of socialist revolution remained intact. They also needed to develop more open and inclusive organizational structures to broaden their ranks and facilitate new forms of popular participation.

This latter objective was paramount in the founding of the PUM in May 1984. Believing that only a "grand party" could provide coherent political direction for popular movements, the diverse New Left groups that were linked together in the UDP began a gradual process of unification that culminated in the birth of the new party.[60] The PUM quickly established itself as the strongest party on the Peruvian Left, with the broadest base of electoral support and the greatest participation in grass-roots social work. The

PUM was the dominant force in the CCP peasant association and the powerful miners' federation and an influential force among militant sectors of the Communist Party–led CGTP. The PUM was strongest in areas with well-organized popular sectors, such as the mining region in the central highlands, urban lower-class districts like Villa El Salvador, and the southern department of Puno, where the party worked closely with church-backed peasant associations. In the 1985 national elections, PUM leaders Javier Diez Canseco and Augustín Haya de la Torre were the leading vote-getters on the Left in the races for the Senate and the Chamber of Deputies, respectively.

The founding of the PUM did not resolve the IU's problems with political fragmentation and dispersion, however, but ultimately compounded them. The PUM remained a minority force within the seven-party coalition, and for all the PUM's weight in social organizations, there was still no individual party on the Left that was strong enough to compete with APRA on its own. The PUM, in fact, retained many of the features of a vanguardist party as defined in Chapter 3, and it was more adept at organizing in the social terrain than competing in the electoral arena. The IU, therefore, remained heavily dependent on the populist appeal of Barrantes to garner electoral support beyond the organizational networks of the coalition's vanguard parties.

Perhaps more important, the PUM established itself as the anchor of the radical wing of the IU, and the alliance became increasingly polarized as Peru sank deeper into crisis over the latter half of the 1980s. Paradoxically, the party of the Left that was most successful at mobilizing support within democratic institutions was also the least committed to those institutions; in fact, the PUM openly proclaimed that its grass-roots organizing efforts were designed to plant the seeds of an alternative set of governing institutions, arrived at through revolutionary action, and not a mere deepening of the existing democratic regime. The PUM believed that popular assemblies and local councils should provide the framework for a more "integral" and participatory form of democratic governance, one founded on the hegemony of subaltern sectors and extending popular sovereignty to socioeconomic as well as political relations.[61]

Conclusion

Although few could have recognized it at the time, the 1983 election of Barrantes to the mayorship of Lima and the 1984 convergence of the New Left in the PUM represented the apex of the Left's political ascendance in Peru and the beginning of its swift downhill slide. The IU would subsequently expand its representation in both congressional and municipal arenas of power, but the political dynamics that ultimately produced its dissolution were already set in motion by the mid-1980s. Nevertheless, at this juncture the IU was still confident that it was riding the crest of a wave of historic social and political transformation, steadily accumulating forces for the future advancement of a socialist project. What it did not realize was that this project had a fork in the road, leading to divergent political strategies and outcomes. These divergent paths generated two competing tendencies within the IU; both aimed at acquiring political power for the Left, but they differed fundamentally on how to obtain it.

The first tendency, associated with Barrantes and his followers, aimed to gain access to state power within the framework of Peru's established representative institutions. It thus perceived electoral contestation to be the exclusive channel of access to state power. As Peru's crisis deepened in the late 1980s, this tendency prioritized the consolidation of the tottering democratic regime and saw opportunities for electoral advancement in the successive failures of conservative and centrist competitors to resolve the crisis. The strategy of this tendency was to use the personal appeal of Barrantes to mobilize support within the broader electorate beyond the organized core constituencies of the IU.

Alternatively, the PUM and its allies thought power had to be constructed from below and outside existing state institutions to found an alternative, revolutionary political order. This radical tendency interpreted the crisis as evidence of the "exhaustion" of the democratic regime and the emergence of a potential revolutionary situation. The PUM did not think the Left should buttress the existing regime or associate political power with the ephemeral electoral gains of a personalist figure like Barrantes. For the PUM, political power was a function of grass-roots organization, not electoral appeal, and the success of the Left was contingent on the development of party structures and organized social networks.

These competing tendencies were kept submerged in the early 1980s, when the Left was too weak to be a serious contender for national power and the strategic environment left little choice other than to enter the democratic arena while maintaining a strict opposition stance. The contradictions within the IU rose to the surface after the mid-1980s, however, when the rejuvenation of Aprista populism and the deepening economic and security crisis placed new strategic options into consideration. The crisis polarized the IU, producing parallel processes of moderation and radicalization within the coalition, while eroding the structural bases and social networks for a radical democratic project. Ultimately, the crisis devastated the IU along with the rest of the party system, leaving it up to two radically different authoritarian projects to determine the resolution of the Peruvian crisis: the revolutionary messianism of the Shining Path and the autocratic neoliberalism of Alberto Fujimori.

CHAPTER 8

Crisis, Polarization, and the Collapse
of the Democratic Left in Peru

THE collapse of Peru's democratic Left in the early 1990s was as precipitous as its rise had been more than a decade before. Just as the rise of the Left was attributable to an unusual set of fortuitous circumstances, so did its collapse reflect a combination of unfavorable conditions. But the collapse of the IU can hardly be attributed to external conditions or constraints alone; although structural changes in Peruvian society eroded the social foundations for the IU's radical democratic project, they do not tell the whole story. Indeed, a more politically capable and coherent Left might have been able to exploit Peru's deepening crisis to advance its cause. The failure of the IU to do so can be explained only through an integrative analysis of both structure and political agency—that is, an analysis that explains how structural changes shaped the strategic environment and the choices made by the Left and why these choices bore the political consequences they did.

For generations, leftists have viewed social and economic crises as opportunities for political advancement, assuming that capitalism's demise would be accelerated by the deepening of its contradictions. Likewise, for most of the 1980s the Peruvian Left believed that the crisis of state-led capitalist development would lead inexorably to a socialist alternative. The IU, in fact, claimed that Peru's economic crisis had created a "disposition to rebel" within popular sectors that could be cultivated politically by the Left.[1] Scholars have also speculated that the exacerbation of poverty and inequality during Latin America's prolonged economic crisis would rekindle social protest and thus reinvigorate the Left.[2] As stated by Castañeda, "The twin trends of crisis and democratization have given birth to a promising outlook for the Left," as Latin America has "tended to turn to the Left in times of severe economic and social crisis."[3]

In theory, the IU could have benefited politically in two principal ways from the nation's crisis. First, it could have been the beneficiary of anti-incumbent voting patterns, given the abysmal failure of both orthodox (Fernando Belaunde) and populist (Alan García) administrations to resolve the economic crisis of the 1980s. These failures seriously discredited Belaunde's Popular Action party and García's APRA as political alternatives; through a process of elimination, the IU could have gained from the demise of its principal conservative and centrist competitors. Second, the IU might have gained the support of policy-oriented voters who were attracted to a political program that prioritized the defense of popular living standards during a period of economic hardship.[4]

The Peruvian experience, however, defied such expectations. Far from exploiting the crisis for its political advantage, the IU met its demise along with the political order it sought to transform. Indeed, Peru's multifaceted crisis had several corrosive effects that undermined prospects for a radical democratic project. The Left did not fully recognize the political effects of the social dislocation wrought by the economic crisis, and it failed to craft a political formula to counteract the process of social fragmentation. In fact, the Left itself was polarized by the crisis, thus compounding the problem of social fragmentation. The crisis, therefore, led not to socialism but to the imposition of one of the most rigid neoliberal structural adjustments that the Latin American region has seen. Peru's neoliberal revolution provided the ultimate confirmation of the political eclipse of the Left; indeed, it was built on the rubble left behind by the collapse of the IU, whose lower-class constituency gave political support to a rising autocratic figure who ultimately adopted the neoliberal agenda. The Peruvian case thus illustrates many of the social and political problems that have made it so difficult to construct an alternative to neoliberal solutions to the crisis of state-led development models.

The Structural Dimension: Economic Crisis, Social Fragmentation, and the Political Project of the Left

The political ascendance of the Peruvian Left in the 1970s was rooted in the mobilization and strengthening of popular collective subjects in the labor, peasant, and shantytown sectors of Peruvian society. The political strategies of the IU were predicated on the assumption that this process of mobilization was cumulative and continuous and that it would lead to the progressive empowerment of the Left. This assumption was not altogether unreasonable: a cumulative process of mobilization could occur, for example, if initial patterns of mobilization yield concrete benefits, spawn new collective identities and solidaristic ties, diffuse organizational models and collective action techniques, or encourage the development of new organizational skills and resources, all of which would provide political incentives or resources to increase levels of mobilization.

Social mobilization is rarely a cumulative and continuous process, however. As explained in Chapter 3, it often follows a cyclical pattern, ebbing and flowing in accordance with the structure of opportunities and constraints found in the political environment. In the Peruvian case, the political opportunity structure was favorable for social mobilization in the late 1970s, when a weak and divided military regime provided a unifying target for protest activities. The authoritarian character of the regime channeled political activity into the sphere of social organizations, and it provided broad-based incentives to protest as a result of efforts to impose intrusive corporatist controls and adopt economic austerity measures. The protest movement tapered off during the process of democratization, however, because the political opportunity structure was modified in ways that were less favorable to mobilization, primarily by removing the unifying military target, channeling organizational energies into the electoral arena, and accentuating divisive partisan competition in the social domain.

The changing political opportunity structure was not the only factor in the waning of social mobilization, however, as Peru's deepening economic crisis created a "social opportunity structure" that turned highly unfavorable over the course of the 1980s. The economic crisis began in the mid-1970s, when structural imbalances led to the adoption of orthodox stabilization policies under Morales Bermúdez and an IMF austerity package in 1976. A temporary rebound at the end of the decade merely set the stage for the next round of the crisis, which hit during the global recession and regional debt trauma of the early 1980s. The Peruvian economy shrank by more than 12 percent in 1982–83, while inflation climbed into the triple digits (see Table 8.1). The economic crisis seriously weakened the second administration of Belaunde, who left his populist roots behind while shifting to the political Right and adopting orthodox economic policies.[5]

The electorate, however, swung to the Left in the 1985 national elections. Belaunde's Popular Action party fell to 7.3 percent of the presidential vote, turning the race into a contest between the IU's Barrantes and the charismatic young APRA leader Alan García, a protégé of Haya de la Torre who won an internal battle for party leadership in 1983 and quickly resurrected APRA's populist and reformist heritage.[6] García cultivated an enormous personal following and won a landslide victory in the first round of the elections to lead APRA to the presidency for the first time in the party's history. His support grew as he pledged to limit debt service payments and implemented a heterodox program of wage hikes, price controls, and tax breaks to stimulate aggregate demand and lift Peru out of recession, thus generating a short-lived economic boom in 1986–87.

Initially, García's heterodox program counted on substantial business as well as popular support. Foreign exchange constraints and government deficits led to renewed inflationary pressures by 1987, however, and a capricious decision by García to nationalize the banking system provoked a business backlash and a resurrection of the Right under the leadership of the conservative novelist Mario Vargas Llosa. With the onset of hyperinflation in 1988, a series of adjustment programs produced the most violent economic contraction in national history, wiping out a third of Peru's industrial production between 1988 and 1990[7] (see Table 8.1). Per capita gross domestic product shrank by nearly 30 percent over the course of the 1980s, falling back to the level of 1960.

The economic crisis had several effects that might have been expected to increase support for the Left.[8] The proportion of the population living below the poverty line swelled to over 50 percent, and wages covered only a fraction of basic needs. The crisis also exacerbated inequalities; while the share of profits in the distribution of national income rose from 42.1 percent in 1980 to 60.6 percent in 1989, the share of wages and salaries fell from 35.2 percent to 19.8 percent.[9] Workers bore the brunt of efforts to stabilize the economy, as real wages by 1991 had plunged to only 38.7 percent of their 1980 level (see Table 8.1), and the minimum wage to a meager 16.8 percent. Wage cuts in the public sector were even more dramatic, falling to a mere 9.9 percent of their 1979 level by 1991.[10] An astounding 87.3 percent of the economically active population was considered unemployed or underemployed (mostly by reason of low income) by 1993 (see Table 8.2).

Rather than benefiting the partisan Left, however, the economic crisis undermined the structural conditions for class-based collective action. First, deindustrialization and huge cuts in public sector employment produced a dramatic informalization of the workforce. Between 1981 and 1991, the percentage of the economically active population that was formally employed declined from 60.7 percent to 47.4 percent, while the informal sector grew from 32.8 percent to 47.6 percent (see Table 8.3). Layoffs were concentrated in the most heavily unionized sectors of the economy—industry and public services. The industrial workforce in Lima shrank from 744,000 in 1976 to 430,100 in 1989.[11] The mining sector, which was a bastion of labor militancy and political support for the PUM, saw employment shrink from 58,185 in 1985 to 35,095 in 1993.[12] Second, industrial restructuring led to a deconcentration of industry, with the decline of large, labor-intensive enterprises and the growth of smaller, specialized firms that are more capital intensive and less heavily unionized. Third, firms that survived the crisis came to rely more heavily on temporary contract labor as opposed to permanent employees, who were more unionized and better protected by labor laws. By the early 1990s,

TABLE 8.1. *Peruvian Economic Indicators, 1982–91*

	1982	1983	1984	1985	1986	1987	1988	1989	1990	1991
GDP	0.2	−12.6	4.8	2.3	9.2	8.5	−8.3	−11.7	−5.1	2.4
Manufacturing growth	−1.2	−18.1	5.7	4.5	15.6	12.8	−11.2	−15.7	−6.9	5.8
Inflation	64.4	111.2	111.5	158.3	62.9	114.5	1722.6	2776.6	7657.8	185.4
Index of real wages (1980=100)	110.2	93.4	87.2	77.6	97.5	101.3	76.1	41.3	42.7	38.7

SOURCES: *Perú: Compendio Estadístico, 1991–1992*, Vol. 2 (Lima: Dirección Técnica de Indicadores Económicos, 1992), p. 428; Comisión Económica para América Latina y el Caribe (CEPAL), *Balance preliminar de la economía de América Latina y el Caribe* (Santiago: United Nations, 1991).

TABLE 8.2. *Levels of Employment in Lima* (percent of the economically active population)

	1982	1983	1984	1985	1986	1987	1988	1989	1990	1991	1992	1993
Adequately employed	65.4	57.7	54.3	–	52.1	60.3	–	18.6	18.6	15.6	14.7	12.7
Underemployed	28.0	33.3	36.8	–	42.6	34.9	–	73.5	73.1	78.5	75.9	77.4
Unemployed	6.6	9.0	8.9	–	5.3	4.8	–	7.9	8.3	5.9	9.4	9.9

SOURCE: Ministerio de Trabajo y Promoción Social, from *Perú: Compendio Estadístico, 1993–1994*, Vol. I (Lima: Dirección Técnica de Indicadores Económicos, 1994), p. 430.

TABLE 8.3. *Labor Market Segmentation in Peru*

(percent of the economically active population)

	1981	1982	1984	1986	1987	1989	1990	1991[a]
Formal sector	60.7	60.3	54.5	52.1	54.1	52.9	49.2	47.4
Informal sector	32.8	33.3	37.9	41.8	40.9	42.2	45.7	47.6
In-home	6.5	6.4	7.6	6.1	5.0	4.9	5.1	5.0

SOURCE: MTPS-DGEFP, Survey of Households in Lima, cited in Eliana Chávez O'Brien, "El mercado de trabajo y las nuevas tendencias en la estructura del empleo en el Perú," *Socialismo y Participación* 60 (December 1992): 20.

[a]Preliminary figures.

one-half of salaried workers were engaged in such precarious and unprotected forms of temporary labor.[13]

The net effect of these structural changes was to fragment the workforce, with fewer large concentrations of workers, less stable working relations, and structural differentiation between permanent employees, temporary contract labor, and informal workers. While unions catered to the increasingly defensive and insulated interests of permanent workers, temporary and informal workers pursued more individualistic strategies for survival. According to José Matos Mar, informal responses to the economic crisis tended to "reinforce individualism and dissolve traditional communal ties."[14] The differentiation of interests complicated collective action and the construction of collective identities. Without a stable network of organizational ties and common struggles against capitalists to forge collective identities, the political orientation of the informal sectors proved to be volatile and undependable, as demonstrated by Henry Dietz and Maxwell Cameron;[15] although urban popular sectors voted heavily for the IU in 1983, many supported García in 1985, then turned en masse to independent candidates at the end of the decade.

The Left had difficulty relating to individualistic informal workers, who tended to be ambiguous in their class positions and identities, combining both proletarian and petit bourgeois characteristics. An ideological discourse and political tactics oriented toward class solidarity were increasingly incongruent with the personal experiences of these workers, whose social and economic relationships generally revolved around family or kinship networks rather than social class.[16] With weak partisan and ideological commitments, they tended to relate to politics on the basis of immediate needs, adopting a flexible, pragmatic, and instrumentalist orientation. Urban popular sectors thus were made up of a floating and largely centrist mass of voters who were available to support a broad range of political candidates, depending on conjunctural appeals and instrumental calculations.[17]

Therefore, the fragmentation of the workforce severely weakened organized labor, a critical social base of the Left and an integrative force in the popular mobilizations of the 1970s. One indicator of this emasculation was the decline in the level of unionization from 80 percent of wage earners in the late 1970s to 48 percent in 1990, with wage earners constituting a mere 30 percent of the workforce.[18] Whereas 18 percent of the total workforce was unionized in the mid-1980s, only 7 percent was unionized by 1994.[19] A second indicator was the decline in labor militancy from its peak in the late 1970s to its meek response to Fujimori's shock program. Although strikes in the public sector increased when García's short-lived economic boom deflated in 1988, they were generally decentralized, and efforts to coordinate general strikes had limited success, in contrast to the national strike waves of the late 1970s. Labor militancy fell off dramatically as the crisis deepened and Fujimori implemented his structural adjustment. Between 1988 and 1993, the number of strikes fell by more than 80 percent, while the number of workers involved and the man-hours lost declined nearly 95 percent (see Table 8.4). The CGTP and other federations declared three general strikes between 1990 and 1992 to protest government policies, but their militant tactics were poorly heeded by the labor rank and file, suggesting that national-level union leaders had lost their capacity to represent or articulate the interests of many ordinary workers.

Clearly, organized labor is less centrally located and less representative of Peru's fragmented and heterogeneous workforce in the 1990s than it was in the 1970s. Employment has declined in highly unionized sectors of the economy while rising in the informal and temporary contract sectors, which are notoriously difficult to organize. Militancy waned when strike tactics lost their effectiveness for extracting economic or political concessions as the government

TABLE 8.4. *Labor Militancy in Peru*

Year	Number of strikes	Man-hours lost (thousands)	Workers involved
1970	345	5,782	110,990
1971	377	10,882	161,415
1972	409	6,331	130,643
1973	788	15,688	416,251
1974	570	13,413	362,737
1975	779	20,269	617,120
1976	440	6,822	258,101
1977	234	6,543	406,461
1978	364	36,145	1,398,387
1979	653	13,411	841,144
1980	739	17,919	481,484
1981	871	19,974	856,915
1982	809	22,751	572,263
1983	643	20,300	785,545
1984	509	13,816	702,859
1985	579	12,228	237,695
1986	642	16,867	248,851
1987	720	9,068	309,407
1988	814	38,275	693,252
1989	667	15,223	224,430
1990	613	15,068	268,570
1991	315	8,881	180,728
1992	219	2,319	114,656
1993	140	2,127	39,451

SOURCES: For 1970–78, Evelyne Huber Stephens, "The Peruvian Military Government, Labor Mobilization, and the Political Strength of the Left," *Latin American Research Review* (1983): 62. For 1979–93, Ministerio de Trabajo y Promoción, from *Perú: Compendio Estadístico, 1993–1994*, Vol. 1 (Lima: Dirección Técnica de Indicadores Económicos, 1994), pp. 510–12.

ceased to defend labor security and the pool of surplus labor grew. Indeed, many workers did not fight layoffs, opting instead to resign and accept lump-sum payoffs that would allow them to operate as independent entrepreneurs in the informal sector.[20] New cleavages thus emerged between labor leaders, who remained wedded to the partisan Left and the confrontational tactics that bore fruit during the 1970s, and rank-and-file workers, who retreated from militant tactics or opted for economic independence. Cleavages also deepened between workers in unionized, large-scale formal enterprises who were protected by laws of labor stability and the growing number of unorganized temporary and informal workers who lacked such legal protection. Union efforts to defend job tenure guarantees helped protect relatively privileged sectors of the workforce but did nothing to alleviate the precarious position of the unorganized mass of workers, thus exacerbating the distinctions within Peru's highly segmented working classes.[21] In short, organized labor ceased to be the radial actor in broader forms of social mobilization in Peru, and it increasingly came to be seen as an interest group defending narrow and relatively privileged particular interests. To the extent that the IU aligned itself with organized labor, it also became tainted as a defender of privilege and was increasingly vulnerable to the charges that neoliberal reformers and antiestablishment politicians like Fujimori leveled against organized interest groups.

In addition to these economic changes, the weakening and fragmentation of organized labor were also undisguised objectives of government policies. Post-Velasco reforms, from Morales Bermúdez to Fujimori, enervated the labor movement by reestablishing the disciplinary mechanisms of employers and markets. Morales Bermúdez slashed Velasco-era labor protections, especially job security guarantees, in response to business complaints and recessionary pressures but also as a strategy to weaken unions in a period of intense government-labor conflict. Under Morales Bermúdez, the profit-sharing industrial communities erected by Velasco began to be dismantled; strikes were banned under a state of emergency declared in response to antigovernment protests; restrictions were placed on collective bargaining and union recognition; criteria for job dismissals were relaxed; the probationary period to qualify for job security was extended from three months to three years; and a legislative decree fired 5,000 labor activists in retaliation for the July 1977 national strike.[22] Fragmentation of the labor movement was pursued by Fujimori through legislative decrees that deregulated the labor market and made it more "flexible" so as to reduce business costs and enhance competitiveness. Fujimori's free market reforms eased dismissals, limited the right to strike, facilitated temporary contract labor, and encouraged competing unions in the same workplace.[23]

Although less dramatic, perhaps, than in the urban industrial sector, structural changes in the countryside also undermined collective action among the peasantry. In the post-Velasco era, the dominant tendencies have been toward the parcelization of land and the differentiation of the agricultural population, with a diversity of small and medium producers coexisting with landless laborers and *comuneros* from indigenous communities.[24] This process has dampened the intense confrontations over land that provided opportunities for leftist parties to organize in peasant communities in the 1960s and 1970s. With the declining salience of the land issue in most regions,[25] market and commercial interests have risen in prominence, concerning such issues as crop prices, input costs, and access to credit and rural public services. The heterogeneous demands arising from such issues are less conducive to radical forms of collective action and political mobilization than the classic conflicts over property ownership that spawned the land seizures of the recent past.

Given these structural and organizational changes in productive spheres, it was hardly possible for the Peruvian Left to construct a radical democratic project on the foundation of class-based collective actors. This dilemma is not a novel one, as Marxist and post-Marxist scholars have long recognized that the proletariat could not fulfill its theoretically preordained role as the central protagonist of socialist transformation.[26] What makes the Peruvian case especially instructive is the failure of the IU to compensate for the decline of class-based actors through an effective articulation of the interests of new social movements and community organizations, which had proliferated in the 1970s alongside labor and peasant associations.

Although the IU was well represented in territorially based associations in both urban and rural areas, it was unable to translate shantytown organizations and rondas campesinas into a secure foundation for a radical democratic project at the national level. As in other parts of Latin America, many popular organizations jealously guarded their autonomy, and the fear of manipulation made them resist instrumentalization by parties or IU-controlled municipal governments. Others continued clientelistic relationships with government authorities in hopes of securing selective benefits, thus eschewing the more confrontational tactics promoted by the partisan Left.[27] Still others looked to nongovernmental organizations (NGOs) to support their activities, as NGOs frequently had more financial resources than leftist parties and made fewer political demands. Many popular organizations that supported the Left did so for instrumental reasons rather than ideological commitment, and they turned away from the IU when it ceased to serve their interests. As Cameron convincingly demonstrates, the core, radicalized constituency of the IU was a minority among popular sectors;[28] in the aggregate, the popular sectors tended to be pragmatic, flexible, pluralistic, and instrumental in their political orientations. They supported the Left when militant tactics or IU political power seemed to offer concrete gains, but they abandoned it when the IU failed to deliver or when other political forces made more convincing appeals.

Although the discourse of the IU heralded base-level groups as organs of popular power, many retreated to defensive, locally oriented survival tactics in response to economic hardship. Local soup kitchens and glass-of-milk committees flourished during the crisis with support from the church, nongovernmental organizations, or the government, but broader, more integrated forms of community association often broke down under the burdens of acute resource constraints. Tendencies toward particularism and localism circumscribed the influence and limited the capacity for horizontal integration of popular organizations. Because they emphasized immediate needs, the concerns of such groups were often distant from the ideological discourse and political objectives of the IU, and their segmented collectivism did not lead to cumulative gains in the political power of the IU.[29] Indeed, many had a self-help orientation that reflected a justifiable skepticism about the efficacy of political institutions for addressing urgent economic needs. In general, then, while the crisis weakened the integrative capacity of large-scale secondary associations like labor unions and peasant federations that undergirded the political project of the Left, it encouraged a retreat to more segmented and insulated primary groups with more fluid political associations.[30]

In summary, economic crisis tore at the social fabric of Peru, producing multiple and overlapping tendencies toward social atomization and informalization. This social decomposition undermined class-based collective action by fracturing horizontal networks and spawning individualistic or segmented collectivist strategies for survival. It also frayed established channels of political representation and eroded the linkages by which parties mediated between civil society and state institutions. The challenge of aggregating such fragmented and heterogeneous popular sectors severely taxed the IU's capacity for political articulation. Far from responding with a coherent, cohesive, and viable political alternative, the always fractious IU was polarized by the national crisis in the late 1980s. Rather than countering Peru's disintegrative tendencies, the IU contributed to the crisis of representation and accelerated the process of social and political dissolution.

The Dimension of Political Agency: Crisis and Polarization in the Peruvian Left

As shown in Chapter 7, the narrowing of strategic options associated with Peru's regime transition helped promote a convergence of the Left in the early 1980s—with the notable exception of the Shining Path—around an oppositional stance within democratic institutions. The strategic and ideological cleavages in the Left returned to the forefront, however, as changes in the political context created new opportunities that modified this clearly defined oppositional role. The growing success of the Left in municipal election campaigns led to the assumption of significant governmental responsibilities, which posed novel challenges to the IU and forced it to consider the divisive possibility of gaining access to executive office at the national level within the institutional confines of the "bourgeois" state. Municipal governance proved to be a mixed blessing and a divisive experience for the IU. Although IU officials viewed municipal governance as a practical laboratory to gain administrative experience and develop grass-roots forms of participatory democracy, it often exposed the administrative deficiencies of the IU, along with the gaps between its participatory discourse and its daily practice. Elected municipal officials clashed with local committees of the IU over a range of issues, including the exploitation of public office for partisan interests, the instrumentalization of social organizations, and widespread *caudillista* and clientelistic practices.[31] Conflicts generated by such "traditional" practices were especially debilitating for an alliance that claimed to represent a new style of democratic politics.

Municipal governments led by the IU were riven by partisan rivalries within the Left and overburdened by popular demands they could not fulfill, given their lack of power and resources in a highly centralized and virtually bankrupt state apparatus that deprived municipalities of an independent tax base.[32] The IU's widespread loss of municipal seats in 1989 and the early 1990s demonstrated that local governance was not necessarily a cumulative process, much less a springboard to national political prominence, as the IU was unable to broaden its base of support through effective response to community needs, the founding of new social organizations, or the creation of new channels for popular participation.

Likewise, parliamentary representation created new dilemmas and contradictions for the IU. As a minority force, the IU could denounce corruption, human rights violations, and orthodox economic policies, but it was not in a position to implement an alternative policy agenda. More important, parliamentary politics reinforced party hierarchies and shifted the focus of organizational work from the social terrain to the electoral sphere. The individual parties in the IU generally revolved around the leadership of a dominant personality who could easily acquire a congressional seat by negotiating a high position on the coalition's parliamentary list.[33] Because their leaders and cadres were preoccupied with congressional tasks and electoral campaigns, the parties became increasingly disengaged from popular struggles in the social sphere. Therefore, the IU not only became tainted by the generalized societal disillusionment with parties and congress but also suffered a diminution of its capacity to convoke social mobilization; as stated by former IU senator Rolando Ames: "We were carried into Parliament by the people, but we did not know how to tie parliamentary struggle to daily struggle and to the economic-union struggle."[34]

These problems were exacerbated by the burgeoning conflict

between Barrantes and the radical wing of the IU, which was anchored by the PUM in alliance with UNIR and FOCEP. Initially, Barrantes's political independence enabled him to be a consensus figure within the IU, as it shielded the coalition's presidency from intramural partisan squabbles and prevented any single party from exercising hegemony within the coalition. But this relative autonomy led to conflicts with the coalition's party organizations and made the IU leadership prone to personalist and populist tendencies, whereby mass identities were oriented more toward personality than parties or popular organizations. On one side, Barrantes's supporters hailed his common touch and popular appeal, which enabled him to attract electoral support that far surpassed that of the organized constituencies of the IU parties. In particular, this populist appeal allowed the Left to compete for the vote of the floating, lower-class mass electorate that lacked any stable partisan or ideological identity and was generally decisive in Peruvian electoral contests.[35] The pro-Barrantes tendency thus feared that the radicalism and sectarianism of party vanguards would alienate these independent, largely centrist voters and prevent the IU from broadening its base of electoral support.

In contrast, the PUM and its allies believed the personalism and electoralism of Barrantes hindered the development of party institutions and social organizations as agents of change. Barrantes tended to be an aloof leader who was disengaged from the internal affairs of the IU coalition, and he preferred a direct, personal mandate from the electorate over party or organizational mediation. In the eyes of IU radicals, this leadership style favored vertical ties between voters and the candidate over horizontal linkages between popular sectors. It also gave priority to the individual voter over collective action and limited participation to the electoral arena. It was thus a direct challenge to their project of developing new organs of popular power at the grass roots; indeed, the radicals criticized Barrantes and the IU leadership for failing to transform the Left's stronghold in Lima's municipal government into an effective instrument for building grass-roots organizational support. Instead, the PUM argued, the municipal government had fallen prey to economistic solutions while becoming isolated from popular movements, thus relinquishing political terrain to a resurgent

APRA.[36] The radicals also criticized Barrantes for his failure to transform the municipality into a center of opposition to the national government. They accused the IU leadership of "temporizing with officialism" and adopting a conciliatory approach in an opportunistic effort to smooth the road to electoral victory.[37]

The IU's leadership conflict was also fueled by strategic disputes over alliance questions. The rejuvenation of APRA in the mid-1980s posed a strategic dilemma for the Left, as García resurrected the party's reformist and anti-imperialist discourse and, for the first time in a generation, enabled it to compete effectively on the social and ideological terrain of the Left. Historically, the Left had held a special animus toward APRA, owing to the legacy of bitter competition for popular sector support and to the Left's perception of APRA's ideological deviation, political opportunism, and organizational sectarianism.[38] So long as APRA was in collusion with the Right, there was no question as to the Left's adoption of an adversarial posture, but as APRA swung back toward the Left under García and reappropriated part of the IU's discourse and agenda, the relationship became less clear. Moderates within the IU were tempted by the possibility of constructing a broad political bloc with APRA to isolate the Right and establish a clear popular political majority capable of dominating Peru's democratic institutions. Barrantes—himself a former Aprista—recognized points of programmatic coincidence between the IU and APRA and expressed a willingness to collaborate with APRA both when it was in opposition to Belaunde and when it was in power under García after 1985. Barrantes, in fact, called on the IU to recognize APRA as part of Peru's popular sector and to cast aside the Left's traditional anti-Aprismo. After García's election, Barrantes strongly advocated a "national accord" to buttress Peru's fledgling democratic regime against the "terrorist" threat of the Shining Path and manifested a willingness to collaborate with APRA and the armed forces. Barrantes also held frequent personal meetings with García and went so far as to enter negotiations with APRA leaders for joint IU-APRA candidacies in the 1986 municipal elections. As Barrantes stated, "United Left and APRA can reach agreement—as they have done in the past—on some issues which are necessary to insure constitutional government in Peru. APRA and United Left have differences in ideology and method, but this does not prevent us from reaching a consensus that could prevent Peru from returning to dictatorship."[39]

This flirtation with APRA infuriated the IU's radical wing, which saw APRA as the embodiment of a top-down, clientelistic program of populist reform that was incompatible with grass-roots empowerment for revolutionary change. The PUM, for example, condemned any alliance with APRA as an abandonment of revolutionary objectives,[40] arguing that such an alliance would not enable the Left to accumulate forces, but rather drag it into a repressive counterinsurgency war and vacate opposition space to the Shining Path.[41] Convinced that García was continuing the militarization of Peru and clearly fearing that his populist appeal would encroach on the social agenda and political base of the Left, the PUM became an advocate of frontal opposition to the APRA government.

The central cleavage in the IU deepened in the late 1980s, when the contending camps chose polarized responses to the burgeoning national crisis. A series of labor strikes in May 1987 signaled the end of García's honeymoon, and the mercurial president tried to rally popular support in July with his surprise announcement to nationalize Peru's largest private banks, provoking a backlash from the political Right and the business community. As hyperinflation hit four digits in 1988—where it would remain during García's final three years in office—the APRA administration tried a variety of unsuccessful economic adjustments and finally implemented a shock program in September which brought about the virtual collapse of productive activities and real wages. The economic crisis provoked rumors of a military coup and a possible resignation by García, and it provided fertile terrain for an upsurge of guerrilla activities by the Shining Path and a second, smaller revolutionary movement, the Movimiento Revolucionario Túpac Amaru. The spiral of violence was compounded by a sharp increase in human rights violations and the emergence of Peru's first right-wing death squads, with links to the armed forces and APRA's long-standing paramilitary groups.[42]

IU moderates feared that the economic crisis and the spreading insurgency would threaten the democratic regime by leading to a military coup or a Shining Path victory. Either of these denouements would reverse the hard-earned gains made by the IU in Peru's institutional order and eliminate the possibility of an electoral ascension to power. The moderates thus made regime consolidation a first-order priority, and a national accord—envisioned as a pact between political parties, the military, business, and labor—became the preferred instrument for political and economic stabilization, as well as the centerpiece of Barrantes's campaign for the presidency in 1990. As stated by Barrantes, "In periods as difficult and hard as that which [the country] has lived, politics has to be an instrument that looks inevitably for consensus."[43] In a context of profound crisis, Peru needed a "socialist option that, for its realism, viability, and democratic sentiment, expresses the common interests of workers, peasants, middle sectors and national business."[44]

For these moderates, the crisis was a source of tantalizing political opportunities as well as manifest dangers. Having earlier punished Belaunde's Popular Action party, the crisis suddenly promised to eliminate APRA as a viable competitor, and it thrust Barrantes to the top of the list of potential presidential candidates in public opinion polls. But the IU could fill this political void only if it reached beyond its customary quarter to a third of the electorate to attract centrist and independent voters who were alienated from APRA. The moderates believed this constituency expansion would be possible only if the IU softened its image and clearly committed itself to resolve the national crisis within the constitutional order. A national accord was central to this strategy because it would demonstrate the IU's commitment to the regime and its willingness to compromise by setting aside objectives for radical change in the interests of political and economic stability. Barrantes thus proclaimed his support for both domestic and international private capital and argued that the costs of a neoliberal shock could be avoided if a nonpartisan team of economists could devise an economic stabilization plan on which workers and capitalists could agree to hold the line on wages and prices.[45]

Barrantes and his supporters viewed the PUM and UNIR as patent obstacles to this strategy. As Barrantes stated, "The United Left has very rapidly become the country's second most powerful force. Yet some people still do not act with the level of responsibility appropriate to that position."[46] IU moderates disdained the "vanguardist-militarist" parties of the Left, accusing them of a "mental fossilization" that held rigidly to doctrinaire Leninism and resisted ideological renovation.[47] In the words of Barrantes, "I cannot respect them because they speak of armed struggle while they continue in the parliament or remain in the university lecture halls filling them with smoke and discussions, but they are not capable of making a concrete proposal to resolve the problems of the country."[48] Barrantes feared that the radical parties would drive away centrist and independent voters and seriously disrupt the policymaking process if they were included in an IU government. The Allende experience in Chile, he argued, demonstrated the unviability of a governing coalition with multiple parties and a narrow leftist base.[49] Claiming that the radical Left lacked a commitment to democracy and was unprepared for governmental responsibilities,[50] moderates sought to marginalize the most powerful parties in the IU,[51] trusting that a campaign which emphasized food relief for the poor and Barrantes's charisma could attract a mass of voters beyond the traditional partisan constituencies of the IU.[52] As Barrantes succinctly put it, "Neither in France nor in Peru do the people read the programs [of political parties], the people vote for persons of flesh and bones in whom they have confidence."[53]

The PUM and UNIR responded very differently to Peru's deepening crisis. A national accord, they argued, was an opportunistic attempt to gain votes and access to government by capitulating to economic elites and liquidating the Left's commitment to radical change. IU radicals thus pledged to resist "any attempt to look for a compromise with the forces responsible for the crisis."[54] Moreover, they feared that an electoral victory by Barrantes would bring the Left into office without providing the institutional power to manage the national crisis or transform social and economic relations. Far from accumulating forces for revolutionary change, it would likely elicit a violent reaction from the Right that could destroy the Left and its political project. According to PUM senator Javier Diez Canseco:

A major difference that we have with Barrantes is that he takes the present state of affairs, the existing institutions, as given. We base our program on a counter-state, rooted in popular organizations. . . . The

Left should not even be contemplating trying to be the government if it lacks a power base. . . . Just getting there could do a disservice to the Left. It would be political suicide. One does not get to the government in order to fail. One goes there with a strategy for victory, which means with the intention and the means to transform the country.[55]

Indeed, the PUM believed the crisis had seriously weakened the democratic regime, creating a potential revolutionary situation. Rather than a defensive strategy or a national accord to stabilize the regime, the PUM wanted to take the political offensive, accelerating the attrition of the APRA government through a national strike of workers and peasants. It also promoted the Asamblea Nacional Popular, a representative body of social organizations, as the core of an alternative set of potential governing institutions. According to the PUM, "the only way to enter the revolutionary situation with the possibility of victory is to develop the mass struggle in an insurrectionary sense, preparing the conditions for the development of the war of all the people."[56] As such, the PUM defended the right of peasant communities and popular organizations to arm themselves for self-defense, in a context in which they confronted both state repression and the violent threats of the Shining Path.

For all their talk of building alternative institutions, however, the radicals had little choice but to participate within established channels, where they lost considerable ground at the end of the decade. The radicals had very little political space in which to maneuver: ideologically committed to a revolutionary alternative, they could not fully embrace Peru's embattled "bourgeois" regime, but neither could they exit to a revolutionary terrain that was already occupied by the violent and sectarian Shining Path. But if the crisis had a moderating effect on Barrantes's supporters, it reinforced radical tendencies in sectors of the PUM and UNIR. The PUM interpreted the crisis as evidence that the democratic regime was "exhausted" and incapable of responding to the challenges it faced. Convinced that the regime was a transitory arrangement corresponding to a preliminary stage in the revolutionary confrontation of forces, the PUM saw no reason to prop it up through social or political compromise. Indeed, the PUM feared—correctly, as it turned out—that the decay of the regime eroded the legitimacy and strength of all the political forces it incorporated. It also feared that participation in institutional politics had distanced the IU from social movements by encouraging the "professionalization" and moderation of leftist leaders.[57] Rather than make a full commitment to the democratic regime and risk being destroyed in its wake, the PUM sought to mobilize forces for a more popular alternative.

IU radicals' insistence on working for a revolutionary alternative made it impossible for Barrantes to make the compromises and build the coalitions that were integral to his electoral strategy. Likewise, the radical project was sure to elicit virulent opposition from the armed forces, thus jeopardizing any potential IU government. Indeed, the moderate and radical agendas were mutually negating: the electoralism of Barrantes marginalized and diffused the grass-roots organs of popular power that were integral to the PUM's strategy, while its radical demands polarized the political arena in ways that made it impossible for Barrantes to perform an integrative role. The polarization of the IU itself undermined the coalition's political coherence and attractiveness: with neither the moderates nor the radicals able to establish a hegemonic position within the Left, the IU could neither buttress nor deepen the democratic regime, much less build an alternative locus of power outside established institutions.

Ultimately, the implications of a schism were poorly understood by both sides. Barrantes grossly underestimated the political costs he would incur by causing a rupture in the IU, and he overestimated his personal hold on the loyalties of leftist voters by assuming they would back him after he had broken with the IU to woo centrists and independents. Likewise, the PUM miscalculated its grass-roots strength and underestimated the impact of the economic crisis on the Left's organized social constituencies. Perhaps most fundamental, the PUM overestimated its capacity to reconstitute the Left under its leadership following the exodus of Barrantes.[58] The only ones who seemed to recognize the potential costs of a schism were in the "neutral" bloc of the IU, consisting primarily of the Communist Party and independent Left Christians led by Senators Henry Pease and Rolando Ames, but they were perceived as organizationally weak and ultimately dispensable by the moderate and radical poles. For Barrantes to marginalize the PUM and UNIR, it was essential for him to garner the support of this neutral bloc. But while the Communist Party and the Left Christians preferred Barrantes's presidential candidacy and generally supported his moderate positions, they were unwilling to break with the IU's radical wing, which had a stronger organizational base in social movements.[59] Insisting that the unity of the Left was paramount, the neutral bloc refused to support Barrantes unless he renewed his commitment to the IU,[60] accepted the resolutions of the coalition's 1989 congress, and legitimized his presidential candidacy through primary elections.[61]

Barrantes, however, refused to submit his candidacy to such a test in the face of organized partisan opposition, saying that a candidacy backed by a broad majority could not be held captive to the will of a small number of party militants.[62] Subsequently, Barrantes and his supporters—grouped together in the Acuerdo Socialista (AS)[63]—made a definitive break with the IU in September 1989 by deciding to sponsor separate tickets in upcoming municipal and presidential elections. The AS received a rude awakening when Enrique Bernales received only 2.2 percent of the vote for the mayorship of Lima and Barrantes a dismal 4.8 percent to finish in fifth place in the April 1990 presidential race. As in 1980, voters rejected a divided Left and were especially harsh in their judgment of moderate leaders who broke with the leftist coalition. Barrantes's showing most likely suffered as well from the long-standing ambivalence in his relationship to the IU, a lackluster campaign, and his general detachment from the political process after resigning as the IU president in 1987, which did little to engender an image of decisive or engaged leadership.

Yet, if Barrantes's gambit ended in failure, the neutral bloc and the radicals who remained in the IU fared little better. In the November 1989 municipal elections the IU sponsored an experienced ticket of Henry Pease and the former mayor of Villa El Salvador, Michel Azcueta, for the mayorship of Lima. But the well-known duo finished with only 11.5 percent of the vote, a far cry from the 33.2 percent the IU had averaged in municipal races in Lima in 1980, 1983, and 1986. In rejecting the IU, popular sectors threw their support to an independent newcomer to the political arena, television personality Ricardo Belmont, who ran a pragmatic campaign that emphasized his apolitical character and commitment to public works. Pease subsequently led the IU presidential ticket for the April 1990 national elections, running a campaign that pledged to resolve the economic crisis with a thorough tax reform, wage indexation, support for small industrial and agricultural producers, and administrative decentralization.[64] Pease finished just ahead of Barrantes, however, with only 8.2 percent of the vote. Combining the IU and its pro-Barrantes splinter, now known as the Izquierda Socialista, the Left's congressional representation was slashed to 9 senators and 20 deputies, down from 15 senators and 48 deputies. The IU was reduced to a hollow shell shortly after the election when the PUM decided to withdraw from the coalition's national directorate and chart a more independent course after the directorate voted to allow individual members of the IU to serve in the cabinet of President-elect Alberto Fujimori.

In summary, it is evident that the Peruvian social and political Left confronted severe problems of political agency and social coordination which impeded its efforts to deepen democracy. Diverse forms of collective action in civil society temporarily converged in the late 1970s in a common struggle against a military dictatorship, with horizontal networks growing up around union and party organizational efforts. These networks gradually unraveled over the course of the 1980s, however, as unions lost their capacity for radial organizing, the partisan Left polarized into competing political and ideological camps, and grass-roots actors retreated to localized, crisis-induced survival and self-help strategies. The parties of the Left that were most deeply inserted in civil society were classic vanguard organizations that thrived under the dictatorship but were too radical, narrow, and sectarian to undergird a successful electoral project. Electoral success thus hinged on the broad personalist appeal of a populist figure, but Barrantes was too aloof as a leader and too inclined toward elite-level accommodation to complement grass-roots empowerment. Once divorced from the organized constituencies of the Left, his populist appeal rapidly dissipated. Ultimately, as Barrantes's supporters liked to say, the competing projects of IU moderates and radicals were "like oil and water":[65] unable to converge on a coherent political alternative, they compounded the fragmentation of Peru's popular sectors rather than welding them together in their diversity.

The result was not only a devastating political defeat but the virtual dissolution of the democratic Left following the election of Fujimori in 1990. The eclipse of the democratic Left stood in stark contrast to the relentless advance of the Shining Path and the sudden rise of a novel variant of popular-based, autocratic neoliberalism under Fujimori. Indeed, as shown below, both of these authoritarian alternatives developed in the popular political void that the IU was unable to occupy, and they were thus nourished by the demise of the democratic Left. Whereas the IU's efforts to deepen democracy were contingent on the strength of an organized civil society, the political projects of the Shining Path and Fujimori thrived in a context of social disintegration and atomization. The collapse of the IU and the fragmentation of its social networks thus cleared the way for a direct confrontation between competing authoritarian projects that had similar sociological breeding grounds but radically different political trajectories.

Social Fragmentation and the
Impact of the Shining Path

The process of social fragmentation and the polarization of the democratic Left cannot be understood in isolation from the impact of the Shining Path insurgency. The Shining Path shared common ideological roots with much of the legal Left in Peru, and it emerged in the same intellectual milieu, although the Shining Path was unique in its provincial, southern Andean origins.[66] The Shining Path diverged from its cohorts in the late 1970s, when it intensified underground preparations for guerrilla warfare as the rest of the Left reluctantly entered the terrain of electoral contestation. The eruption of the Shining Path insurgency created serious dilemmas for the legal Left because there was no disguising the fact that this obscure provincial offshoot had put into practice the armed struggle that all of Peru's Maoist, Trotskyist, and Guevarist movements had preached, even if it did so in a highly sectarian and militaristic manner.

Consequently, much of the legal Left adopted an ambiguous response to the Shining Path insurgency, especially during the early 1980s. On one hand, they considered the Shining Path to be part of the "popular camp" in Peru, and they admired the commitment of its militants and the boldness of its practical adherence to a revolutionary doctrine. On the other hand, they rejected the Shining Path's sectarian style of political operation, its isolation from broader patterns of social and political organization, and the "militaristic deviations" that were manifested in its employment of terrorist tactics. This ambiguity can be seen, for example, in a 1983 speech by then VR leader Javier Diez Canseco when he recognized "with discrepancies and with differences, but in a united effort and within a common revolutionary project, the struggle, the dedication, the sacrifice of life that combatants are offering today in the country, with whom we disagree but respect."[67] Among the more radical sectors of the IU, it was sometimes believed that the Shining Path insurgency was useful for breaking the state's monopoly of military force and creating alternative, "popular" military forces that could eventually be "rectified" and incorporated within a broader revolutionary project.[68]

As the insurgency spread during the 1980s, however, it became increasingly clear for most of the democratic Left that the projects of the IU and the Shining Path were mutually exclusive and very much in competition with each other. After Belaunde sent the army into Ayacucho and other southern Andean provinces at the end of 1982, the Shining Path responded to military repression by escalating its own violence against civilian targets and fanning out into new regions of the country. As it did so, it inevitably came into conflict with legal Left parties and their organized social constituencies. This conflict emerged because the IU and the Shining Path were in direct competition for the political loyalties of Peru's working and lower classes, and they represented very different logics of collective action as a response to the national political and economic crisis. The IU was strongest where popular organizations in civil society were the most highly developed; in contrast, the Shining Path penetrated more easily where popular organizations were weak and social relations were more atomized,[69] although it eventually found ways to penetrate the pueblos jovenes that were bastions of left-wing grass-roots organizing as the crisis deepened in the late 1980s.[70] Given its ideological dogmatism, sectarian organizational structure, and ultra-vanguardist conception of politics, the Shining Path was highly intolerant of political pluralism and autonomous forms of grass-roots organization. Rather than work with autonomous or preexisting groups, it sought to recruit individuals into a collective revolutionary project that exerted strict hierarchical control over "generated organisms," or Shining Path–sponsored associations for workers, students, professionals, the urban poor, and other groups.[71] Social organizations that were politically independent or linked to the IU were seen as "revisionist" competitors that alleviated the suffering of the masses, created illusions of peaceful reform, and buttressed the established order by diverting revolutionary energies toward institutionalized forms of political participation. Viewed as political enemies, these popular organizations became targets of the Shining Path's military aggression and political intimidation.

Consequently, the expansion of the Shining Path insurgency in the 1980s was both a cause and a consequence of the failure of the IU to integrate and empower popular sectors within Peru's democratic institutions. Indeed, the Shining Path contributed both to the social fragmentation that eroded the foundations for a radical democratic project and to the political polarization that undermined the integrative capacity of the IU. The disintegrative effects of economic crisis were seriously compounded by escalating political violence. Trade unions and popular organizations faced not only economic hardship and periodic repression from state security forces but also systematic efforts by the Shining Path to penetrate, divide, capture, or decapitate them. The Shining Path created parallel, competing social organizations or infiltrated existing ones to advocate more militant tactics, demonstrate the failure of "reformist" strategies, and then divide or capture the movement. It also spread rumors of corruption to discredit grass-roots leaders and carried out selective assassinations of community organizers who refused to be intimidated. According to Jo-Marie Burt, "Over 100 community leaders were killed in Lima's shantytowns between 1989 and 1992, including female leaders of the milk program and community soup kitchens. Hundreds of other leaders quit their positions, and some fled into exile."[72] Community activists with links to the IU were specifically targeted to create a political vacuum and eliminate grass-roots competition.[73]

The Shining Path correctly viewed an organized civil society as the most effective bulwark against the advance of its insurgency, and its violent tactics were brutally efficient at undermining autonomous forms of organization, fragmenting civil society, and eliminating democratic and reformist alternatives that occupied the political space between its revolutionary project and the Peruvian armed forces. By the early 1990s, with popular organizations in retreat and the IU in disarray, the guerrilla movement had even succeeded in penetrating Villa El Salvador—the crown jewel of the IU's urban political strategy—and neutralizing the grass-roots organizations that had nurtured that community's innovative experiment in political and economic self-management. The Shining Path infiltrated and acquired influence in Villa's centralized neighborhood association, the small business federation, and the women's federation, and it used violence to silence its opponents, including the brutal 1992 assassination of community leader and IU vice-mayor María Elena Moyano, who had organized resistance to the Shining Path's advance.[74] With over 27,000 persons killed by the Shining Path and state security forces (see Table 8.5), and another 600,000 in internal exile, numerous communities were disrupted, popular organizations lost valuable leadership experience, and countless individuals were intimidated into silence or inactivity.

If the Shining Path exacerbated social fragmentation, it also contributed to the polarization of the IU. The existence of such a violent, sectarian insurgency had a moderating effect on much of the legal Left and pushed it toward the political mainstream. In part, this moderation was a defensive mechanism designed to differentiate the legal Left from the Shining Path and shield it from the repressive fallout of the counterinsurgency campaign. It also reflected efforts to buttress a democratic regime that, for all its defects, provided organizational space and institutional access for legal Left

TABLE 8.5. *Deaths Attributed to Political Violence in Peru*

Year	Political killings
1980	3
1981	4
1982	170
1983	2,807
1984	4,319
1985	1,359
1986	1,268
1987	697
1988	1,986
1989	3,198
1990	3,452
1991	3,180
1992	3,101
1993	1,692
	Total: 27,236

SOURCES: For 1980–91, Comisión Especial de Investigación y Estudio sobre la Violencia y Alternativas de Pacificación, *Violencia y pacificación en 1991* (Lima: Senado de la República, 1992), p. 84. For 1992–93, Washington Office on Latin America, *After the Autogolpe: Human Rights in Peru and the U.S. Response* (Washington, D.C.: Washington Office on Latin America, 1994), p. 8.

parties that would be closed in the eventuality of a military coup or a Shining Path victory. Moderate leaders of the IU quickly accommodated themselves to political democracy in the 1980s, as they developed a new appreciation for the opportunities it provided and encouraged an ideological "renovation" that reassessed the complementarity between socialist and democratic values.[75] As in other parts of Latin America, this ideological renovation was reinforced by international intellectual trends and the impact of the crisis in the Soviet bloc, which discredited traditional socialist political and economic models. Indeed, the Shining Path provided an unparalleled example of the authoritarian defects that plagued revolutionary models of socialism when taken to their logical extreme.

While the relentless advance of the Shining Path encouraged moderation in the electoralist, pro-Barrantes sector of the Left, it created intense competition at the grass-roots level for vanguardist parties like the PUM, which were more deeply inserted in popular organizations. For all its deviations, the Shining Path demonstrated the potential viability of a revolutionary project as a response to the Peruvian crisis; indeed, the Shining Path was the only force on the Left that consistently gained strength over the course of the 1980s. In so doing, it exposed the repressive character of the Peruvian state and the incapacity of its democratic institutions to respond to popular demands or resolve the social and economic crisis. The advance of the Shining Path convinced the PUM that Peru's democratic institutions were "exhausted" and that the country was entering a potential revolutionary crisis. As PUM secretary general Eduardo Cáceres in 1990 asserted:

We believe these institutions are purely formal, and they don't serve for anything. It is an illusion to think they can be fortified, or to think that with two or three cabinet ministers anything is going to change. We have to forge new institutions, with an autonomous space for popular associations and self-defense fronts. The prevailing institutions have collapsed and become a trap. There is no democracy here; we have to liquidate this "democracy," because it is a regime that is completely separated from society.[76]

Given this interpretation of the crisis, the PUM had little interest in expanding the electoral constituency of the IU toward the center. It was more concerned about the danger of losing popular bases to the Shining Path, and the intense competition with the guerrilla movement at the grass-roots discouraged any process of moderation that could leave a political void to be filled by the insurgents. As stated by Cáceres, "At the base level, especially in the countryside in regions like Puno, our only real competitor is Sendero [the Shining Path]. The other groups often don't exist. It is just the PUM against Sendero."[77] The PUM was torn apart by these conflicting pressures: moderate leaders abandoned the party in 1988 as a result of its militant stance and its refusal to support Barrantes,[78] while much of the party's radicalized peasant base in the Puno region left in 1993.[79] Violent competition with the Shining Path at the grass roots left the IU confused and demoralized; IU leaders, many of whom came out of student movements in the 1960s and 1970s, were especially concerned that their parties had ceased to attract Peruvian youth, who made up the bulk of Shining

Path recruits. Public opinion polls verified these concerns. In 1991, one poll found that only 2 percent of youth between the ages of 15 and 24 were affiliated with political parties, and 13 percent were sympathizers. In contrast, 25 percent justified participation in armed insurgent movements, up from 9 percent three years before.[80]

The guerrilla insurgency thus drove IU moderates toward the political center at the same time that it reinforced the radicals' search for an alternative revolutionary project in civil society. Neither the revolutionary vision of the PUM nor the electoral project of Barrantes proved to be viable in the context of Peru's national crisis and the international crisis of the Left. The radicals tried to shrug off the crisis in the Soviet bloc, arguing that bureaucratic and authoritarian models of socialism had nothing to do with their own vision of direct, participatory democracy exercised by autonomous collective subjects in civil society.[81] Nevertheless, they were clearly tainted by the collapse of the Soviet bloc,[82] and they were unable to sketch a compelling portrait of a socialist economic alternative in a context of hyperinflation and a bankrupt, discredited state. Indeed, their radical democratic project did not pose a direct solution to Peru's economic crisis, and it clashed with the hierarchical and vanguardist tendencies within the parties themselves. Barrantes, in contrast, was hard-pressed to differentiate his more moderate project from the ill-fated populism of Alan García. Unable to achieve consensus within the Left, it was a weak foundation for a national accord in the society at large.

The failure of the legal Left to reconstitute the social fabric and propose a compelling response to the national crisis played into the hands of the Shining Path. Since the insurrection developed on the margins of, and in opposition to, the organizational networks in civil society that the IU relied on, it did not suffer as a result of the crisis-induced dissolution of these networks. To the contrary, the Shining Path fed off this crisis and thrived in a context of social fragmentation and despair that led many individuals to lose hope in nonviolent methods of collective action.

Likewise, the autocratic populism of Fujimori was tailor-made for an atomized electorate that had rejected Peru's political establishment. IU moderates rightly believed that the 1990 election would be decided by a huge bloc of unattached voters; what they failed to see was that these voters would opt for an independent newcomer to the political arena rather than the traditional standard-bearer of the Left. In effect, Fujimori won the 1990 election using Barrantes's game plan: a personalist campaign that avoided partisan obligations and ideological definition, an appeal to lower-class and independent voters, and an emphasis on political accommodation rather than a neoliberal shock as the solution to the national crisis. But whereas Barrantes's message was discredited by the internecine battles of the IU, Fujimori cultivated the image of an untainted outsider who was above the fray of partisan politics, one who was capable of representing the interests of common people against the sectarianism and self-interested machinations of conventional politicians. The resonance of Fujimori's message provided ample evidence of the IU's failure as an agent of political representation and of the erosion of its capacity to channel the democratic aspirations of Peru's popular majority.

Conclusion: Fujimorismo and the Demise of the Left

The collapse of the IU in Peru provides instructive lessons for social movements and the political Left in Latin America, and it helps to explain why the demise of state-led capitalist development in the 1980s led to neoliberalism rather than a swing to the Left. Although the Peruvian Left was exceptionally strong in both electoral and social arenas when Peru returned to democratic rule, it was unable to capitalize on the failures of its competitors or to render more than token resistance when neoliberal reforms were adopted in response to economic crisis. The IU experience demonstrates that political gains are not necessarily cumulative, despite the discourse about "accumulating forces." While enhancing its parliamentary visibility, the Left lost much of its capacity to convoke and direct social mobilization; by acquiring municipal authority, the IU too often demonstrated how little its practices differed from those of traditional parties; and after helping to build base-level social organizations, the Left learned how hard it can be to empower them politically or incorporate them in a national-level political movement.

Indeed, the base-level social units of the Left's radical demo-cratic project proved to be highly contingent and subject to erosion by social, political, and economic forces. The Peruvian case thus confirms the tendency for social mobilization to ebb and flow in accordance with changes in political opportunities and constraints. Militant forms of social mobilization were facilitated, albeit inad-vertently, by state efforts to organize popular sectors under Velasco. Mobilization waned, however, as state policies shifted to weaken and fragment the labor movement and as the IU became an in-creasingly fractious agent of political representation.

The Peruvian case suggests, however, that opportunity struc-tures for social movements are not only political or institutional but also economic. Social mobilization declined as a prolonged eco-nomic crisis undermined class-based identities, fragmented collec-tive action, severed horizontal linkages, and weakened the partisan Left's organizational ties to civil society. The IU was far too polar-ized internally to overcome this social fragmentation through ef-fective political agency; Peru's pragmatic popular sectors aban-doned a nonviable political force and turned to personality rather than partisanship or ideology as the basis for political aggregation. Ultimately, then, informalization in the political and economic spheres was a parallel and mutually reinforcing process; the decline of the formal, salaried workforce was reflected in the emascula-tion of formal representative institutions such as parties and labor unions and the emergence of antiestablishment personalist leaders from outside traditional political arenas.

This experience lends credence to Castañeda's contention that socioeconomic crises erode the organized constituencies of reform-ist democratic projects. Likewise, the advance of the Shining Path before its decapitation in 1992 buttresses his assertion that more radical forces are likely to flourish as economic crises expand the ranks of the urban poor.[83] But the dominant response of Peru's ur-ban poor to the economic crisis was neither social democratic re-form nor Maoist revolution; it was, instead, economic informal-ization and political attachment to a new variant of autocratic populism that proved to be remarkably congruent with the require-ments of neoliberal restructuring. Like traditional Latin American populism, this new variant mobilized a heterogeneous, multiclass electoral constituency in support of a personalistic authority figure who eschewed ideological definition while challenging established elites. Unlike traditional populism, however, it rejected statist and redistributive policies in order to follow neoliberal prescriptions for economic austerity and market discipline.[84] This neoliberal variant of populism was predicated on the deinstitutionalization of intermediary organizations in civil and political society, while its direct, unmediated relationship between individual voters and Fujimori became the political correlate to the market individualism of neoliberalism.

The rejection of partisan representation was one of the most notable features of this new form of populism, as it arose in the political void created by the fragmentation of the IU and the debacle of Aprismo.[85] As such, it captured the sociopolitical constituency of the Peruvian Left, while harnessing it to a radically different project for society. As Cameron demonstrates, class distinctions continued to shape voting behavior in 1990, but partisan appeals made on the basis of class had lost their capacity to galvanize the electorate.[86] Indeed, the IU's class-based discourse and political ties to organized labor positioned the Left as the defender of the narrow corporate interests of an increasingly marginalized social and political actor. Fujimori, by contrast, pitched his appeal to the far more numerous but much less organized informal sectors; once elected to office, he portrayed organized labor as yet another privileged, self-interested bastion of the political establishment, and he easily bypassed its demands while implementing a neoliberal program that further emasculated the labor movement. An economic model predicated on the technocratic insulation of policymaking from organized popular interests thus found refuge in a political model that likewise bypassed institutional mediations in favor of direct ties between a caudillo and an atomized mass electorate.[87]

Ironically, Fujimori proclaimed this new political project to be an exercise in direct democracy. It is, however, far removed from the vision of direct democracy that inspired the project of the Peruvian Left, with its emphasis on the creative participation of organized collective subjects in the process of governance. Direct democracy, for Fujimori, provides no role for such collective subjects, and it restricts popular participation to the individual act of casting a ballot for an autocratic leader who is insulated from institution-alized mechanisms of democratic accountability. This "delegative" variant of democracy, is, in fact, the antithesis of direct democracy as it has been understood traditionally in democratic theory.[88] Nevertheless, it has proven to be a potent political force in the context of Peru's crisis of representation. Fujimori blamed Peru's *partidocracia* for the nation's ills, then swept away representative institutions in the April 1992 autogolpe while concentrating political authority in the executive branch. Regional governments were dissolved, congress and the judiciary were restructured to ensure executive dominance, and the office of the presidency claimed a near monopoly over public works projects. If Fujimori's rise to power signaled the exhaustion of Peru's traditional representative institutions, his landslide reelection in 1995 was a testament to his success at blocking the emergence of new ones.

To say that Fujimori's success leaves the Peruvian Left in disarray in an understatement. By the mid-1990s a once formidable Left had essentially disappeared as a national political force, reduced to a handful of prominent personalities who had lost any capacity to mobilize popular support. Former IU moderates led by Henry Pease constructed a new party, the Movement of the Democratic Left (MDI), which gained four seats in the 80-member constituent assembly elected at the end of 1992. With its skilled and experienced leadership, the MDI played a significant role in the debates surrounding the drafting of a new constitution in 1993, but it was unable to galvanize much popular support for the failed venture of former UN secretary general Javier Pérez de Cuellar in the 1995 presidential election. The PUM and other sectors of the radical Left abstained from the constituent assembly elections, then tried to regroup to sponsor an IU ticket in the 1995 elections, which gained barely one-half of 1 percent of the vote. At the municipal level, the Left's stronghold in the 1980s, the MDI and the IU combined for a mere 3.9 percent of the nationwide vote in 1993, when independent candidates and political fronts swept 64.7 percent of the vote.[89] The fact that leftist parties supported some of these independent candidacies was little solace, as it verified the Left's collapse as an organized, national political force.

The rise of Fujimori clearly signified the passing of an era of partisan-based political representation in Peru. Fujimorismo may well prove to be a transitory political phenomenon; by the middle of his second term in office, the contradictions inherent in the marriage of populism and neoliberalism were increasingly apparent,[90] and the president's lofty approval ratings fell sharply amid spreading discontent with his economic policies and authoritarian political practices. In contrast to classic populists like Peron, Cárdenas, and Haya de la Torre, Fujimori has done little to build a party institution or mass organizations to buttress his rule, and he has been unable to transfer his own popularity to municipal candidates of his choosing. His principal base of institutional support thus continues to be the armed forces command. Nevertheless, opposition to Fujimori has been very slow to develop institutionalized forms of political expression, leaving serial autocracy as the most likely scenario for Peruvian politics if and when Fujimori abandons the scene. One of the few certainties on the political landscape is that as the Left attempts to regroup and renovate itself for the neoliberal era, it confronts a social order that has been thoroughly transformed from that which spawned its political power and its vision of radical participatory democracy in the not so distant past.

CHAPTER 9

Conclusion: Comparative Perspectives
on the Left in an Era of Neoliberalism

IN most respects, Chile and Peru represent opposite poles of the Latin American development experience. They embody radically different political traditions, party systems, and patterns of social and economic development. Nevertheless, in recent years striking similarities have arisen across the two cases in three basic areas: both nations have experienced an autocratic imposition of a neoliberal social and economic model, both have developed restricted democratic institutions as the political correlate to this new model of society, and both have witnessed the disintegration of mass social and political movements that advocated radical democratic alternatives to neoliberalism. These similarities are highly instructive for understanding the current predicament of the social and political Left in Latin America, and they shed light on the impediments faced by strategies for the deepening of democracy in the region.

Several conclusions can be derived from the comparative analysis of these two cases. First, the formidable sweep of the neoliberal revolution in Latin America should not be attributed simply to the theoretical persuasiveness of its prescriptions or the empirical success of its policies, both of which remain subject to considerable doubt.[1] Likewise, the breadth of this revolution is not a mere reflection of the dearth of alternative propositions; although traditional socialist and populist models retain little credibility, there have been numerous efforts to sketch the outlines of viable alternatives to neoliberalism that would maintain a more active developmental role for the state and a political commitment to equity and social justice.[2] Rather, the sweep of the market revolution reflects the remarkable capacity of neoliberalism to neutralize and dissolve its opposition or countervailing forces. This stands in diametrical opposition to Marx's understanding of industrial capitalism, which was presumed to create, aggregate, and strengthen its antithesis and eventual gravedigger, the proletariat, to the extent that it expanded its own range of operations.[3] The globalized, neoliberal variant of capitalism, by contrast, is both a product and an accelerator of the fragmentation and weakening of popular collective subjects, the labor movement in particular. In the Chilean case, neoliberalism was the economic correlate of an authoritarian political project designed to emasculate the partisan Left and its organized social constituencies. In the Peruvian case, neoliberalism was adopted in response to an economic crisis that had already produced severe social dislocations, thus eroding the capacity of popular sectors to resist implementation of market reforms or give political sustenance to an alternative project. Once implemented, neoliberalism accelerated the decomposition of the labor movement through a combination of structural changes in the workforce and legal reforms that sacrificed organizational rights and employment stability to the exigencies of a more flexible labor market. The anomaly, then, is that leaders like Pinochet and Fujimori are able to implement policies that directly threaten the interests of large sectors of society but simultaneously undercut these sectors' capacity for collective response.

The atomized social landscape of the neoliberal era wreaks havoc with Marx's teleological vision of socialism as the ultimate product of the political agency of a class-conscious proletariat. The partisan Left in Latin America, however, has yet to craft a compelling political response to the dispersion of Marx's class subject. One response has been to continue to ground the project of the Left in the collective action of organized popular constituencies but to expand the scope of such constituencies to encompass the new social movements that transcend traditional class categories. This was the strategy attempted by the PUM in Peru and the Communist Party in Chile, but both of these vanguardist parties ended up thoroughly marginalized from the political process in the 1990s. In both cases, the party leadership sought to combine a revolutionary discourse and objectives with incorporation into a democratic arena; neither party, however, developed an adequate theoretical rationale for the deepening of democracy, and their political roles were ultimately more polarizing than integrative. Likewise, in their interaction with social movements, both parties manifested severe contradictions between a discourse that called for autonomous, participatory grass-roots protagonism and an organizational structure that was centralized, hierarchical, and intolerant of pluralism.

Consequently, both parties had organized pockets of strength in civil society, corresponding to popular sectors they had "captured" and incorporated within their ranks, or at least sectors whose political and economic claims the parties had taken up. Neither party, however, was able to build these pockets into broader networks of social and political support, the way the more "organic" and heterogeneous Workers' Party (PT) has done in Brazil. Both the PUM and the Communist Party remained insulated organizations of activist and ideological minorities, and they articulated the interests of affiliated subaltern groups that were progressively fragmented, isolated, and put on the defensive by political and economic changes. These vanguardist parties thrived under authoritarian conditions, when the closure of formal representative institutions placed a premium on organizational work in civil society. They found it difficult, however, to translate their strength in civil society into sustainable electoral success, and as their political contexts changed, both ultimately lost considerable force in civil society as well.

In contrast, the pro-Barrantes sector of the Peruvian Left and the Socialist/PPD bloc in Chile produced eloquent theoretical rationales for a reconceptualization of socialism as the deepening of democracy brought about by organized popular subjects. Nevertheless, these sectors of the Left adopted electoralist orientations that were targeted more at the mass of heterogeneous individual voters than at organized class or sectoral constituencies. This orientation entailed an emphasis on the consolidation of formal electoral institutions, a proclivity for elite-level social and political pacts to ensure institutional stability, and a retreat from ideological expressions and mobilizational strategies that might engender political conflict or alienate moderate voters. As catch-all electoral forces that aimed to appeal to national constituencies, the Socialists and Barrantistas did not want to be too closely affiliated with a distinctive ideological position or a particular social category. They trumpeted their pragmatism and moderation as signs of political maturity and responsibleness, and they sought to expand their electoral appeal toward three principal blocs of voters: those without fixed partisan identities, those located in the political Center, and those drawn from the middle class.

In many respects, the electoralist orientation conforms to the more atomized, individualistic social landscape of the neoliberal era, with its concomitant decline of large-scale class-based collective actors who can serve as a captive electoral constituency. Not surprisingly, it has met with greater political success during democratic periods in these two countries than the vanguardist orientations of the PUM and the Chilean Communist Party. In Peru, the populist variant of the electoralist orientation had short-term success under Barrantes, but it was an abysmal failure in the long term because it was unable to achieve hegemony within the Left, and it produced a bifurcation of the United Left coalition. The populist model was ideally suited for an independent outsider like Fujimori, however, who rode it to power and then adapted its message and content for an authoritarian neoliberal project.

In Chile, the electoralist orientation found expression in two closely related catch-all parties, the Socialist Party and the PPD, which gradually expanded their electoral bases and their political leverage in the governing coalition following the regime transition. Although the organizational weakness and factionalization of the Socialist Party made it a subordinate actor in the protest movement against Pinochet, its open, pluralistic character and pragmatic orientation allowed the party to attract diverse individual voters once electoral competition was restored. Yet both the Socialist Party and the PPD were top-heavy parties that were dominated by prominent personalities, with relatively weak grass-roots structures and tenuous linkages to organized popular constituencies. In the PPD, this reflected the party's genesis as an elite-created vehicle to circumvent authoritarian restrictions on electoral participation; in the Socialist Party, it was attributable to the successful alliance-building and electoral strategies of the Núñez faction, which had been cut off from the party's social constituencies inside Chile after the 1979 division of the party in exile. Taken together, the Peruvian and Chilean cases suggest two basic paradoxes. First, the sectors of the Left with the most clearly elaborated and theoretically refined vision of a deepening of democracy are not necessarily those with the grass-roots organizational networks needed to pull it off. In these two cases, the leftist parties with the best organized social constituencies retained more traditional vanguardist and revolutionary conceptions of political empowerment, whereas their more "renovated" competitors were frequently divorced from grass-roots collective action. Hence the logic of deepening democracy has been far more present as an intellectual discourse than as a guide to political practice. Second, the parties with the strongest base in civil society are not necessarily those that will be the strongest in electoral competition. This can be seen clearly in Chile, where the Núñez Socialists—the faction with the most shallow roots in organized popular constituencies— emerged as the strategic leader and the dominant electoral force on the Left during Chile's regime transition. This demonstrates that leftist electoral success can easily be divorced from base-level organizational strength under the atomized conditions of the neoliberal era.

In Chile, the strategic choices made by the Núñez Socialists enabled the party to play a vital role in the consolidation of the country's new democratic regime. These same choices, however, combined with the party's weak grass-roots networks to limit the prospects for a deepening of democracy, which the Núñez Socialists had themselves taken the lead in theorizing. With the decline of extraelectoral social mobilization after the defeat of the protest movement in the mid-1980s, the political arena came to be dominated by Chile's powerful caste of professional politicians, and little leverage remained to negotiate away the political and economic constraints on democracy bequeathed by the military dictatorship.

Chile's rapid and frequently lauded reconstruction of democratic stability must be understood in the context of these constraints, for the leadership of the Concertación has surely traded deeper reforms for short-term gains in political stability. This returns our analysis full circle to the query raised in the introduction—namely, whether the historically unique durability of Latin America's contemporary democracies may primarily be an artifact of the diminished capacity of popular sectors to challenge elite interests, rather than the strength of democratic institutions themselves. The historical record, and that of Chile in particular, clearly suggests that elite tolerance of democracy varies inversely with the level of the perceived threats posed by popular sovereignty. If Chilean democracy seems more stable today than it did in the early 1970s, it is largely because there is little chance that popular sectors or the political parties that claim to represent them will use democratic institutions to alter radically the social hierarchy.

In the terms of Dahl's well-known formulation, the prospects for polyarchy have brightened as the costs of tolerance have diminished.[4] The authoritarian enclaves left in place by Pinochet were designed to place durable constraints on the exercise of popular sovereignty, and they have forced the new democratic government to negotiate—from a position of weakness—any reforms for the deepening of democracy. Ultimately, however, the structural constraints created by Pinochet's neoliberal revolution may prove to be more permanent, as they have dissolved much of the social foundation for an alternative political and economic project and created an imbalance of socioeconomic and political power that seriously narrows the maneuvering space of the governing parties. The result is very much along the lines of what O'Donnell foresaw before the recent wave of democratic transitions began: an attempt to restore narrowly defined citizenship rights in the political domain, while simultaneously suppressing substantive demands expressed by class and popular subjects. If O'Donnell thought it would be a "miracle" to restore democratic citizenship rights while maintaining the "exclusion of the popular sector," it was only because he did not foresee the social dislocations and power reconfigurations that would be engendered by Latin America's economic crisis and subsequent neoliberal revolutions.[5]

Given the depth of these structural changes in both of the countries considered here and the ways in which they have reshaped political dynamics, it is appropriate to ask whether the onset of the neoliberal era represents a new "critical juncture" in the historical development of Latin American societies. As Ruth Berins Collier and David Collier have argued, regime dynamics in Latin America for most of the twentieth century were heavily influenced by the political incorporation of labor movements and the reactions of elite sectors to the challenges posed by the emergence of labor-backed parties.[6] Although it is clearly too early to identify the long-term legacies of neoliberal critical junctures, it seems increasingly evident that the political dynamics set in motion by the process of labor incorporation have been fundamentally altered during the neoliberal era. The political and economic centrality of organized labor has sharply diminished, and it no longer provides a viable social foundation for anti–status quo political projects, whether of the populist or socialist variety. In contrast to the early twentieth century, the new social and political landscape provides neither an ascendant mobilizing ideology nor a strategically located popular collective subject to undergird radical challenges to the dominance of capital. The heterogeneity and dispersion of popular sectors impede the organization of an effective counterweight to capital, which has the advantage of being less reliant on collective action to defend its interests.

In the Peruvian case, the complete collapse of APRA and the IU in the early 1990s is indicative of the eclipse of an ancien regime that revolved around the conflict between popular-based political parties and traditional elites. What remains is a highly personalistic political system that is virtually devoid of representative institutions and thus is uniquely propitious for a neoliberal restructuring of society according to the principles of market individualism. Although the dearth of representative institutions makes it difficult to project the autocratic Fujimori regime into the future, the new forms of state and social domination that it reflects are likely to be enduring, given the extreme levels of social dislocation in Peru.

In Chile, at first glance there seems to be remarkable continuity between the pre- and post-Pinochet periods in political parties and the basic "three-thirds" alignment of voting loyalties.[7] This apparent continuity can be deceiving, however, as the Chilean party system and the broader polity have undergone fundamental transformations as a result of the authoritarian experience and economic restructuring. Until 1973, in the Colliers' terms, the Chilean party system was highly polarized and confrontational, with centrifugal competitive dynamics that were driven by radically divergent development projects.

What emerged in the 1990s was an "integrative" party system that incorporated popular sectors in a nonconfrontational manner, with a high level of consensus on the core features of the development model and a centripetal competitive dynamic that pulled the partisan Left toward the Center. These changes are not mere artifacts of the transitional conjuncture but a basic shift in the political matrix that is rooted in the structural dislocation of a historic, labor-backed democratic socialist project. Indeed, far from a polarized polity, Chile today seems to be consolidating a new form of capitalist hegemony, as manifested by the acceptance of the neoliberal restructuring by its erstwhile opponents in the Concertación and the political marginalization of antisystem forces that revolve around the Communist Party.

Where, then, does this leave the project of the Left as Latin America prepares to enter the twenty-first century? It is more than a little ironic that variants of social democracy have been frequently proposed in recent years by scholars who are searching for an alternative to neoliberalism.[8] Historically, social democracy has been grounded in conditions that are not present in contemporary Latin America and are highly unlikely to develop under an increasingly transnational neoliberal model of capitalist development—namely, centralized and densely organized labor movements that have close political ties to mass socialist parties, ample fiscal resources to sustain universal norms of social citizenship, and domestic power balances that spawn institutionalized forms of class compromise in which democratic checks are placed on the privileges and functioning of capital.[9] At a time when the bastions of European social democracy have been hard-pressed to sustain historic achievements under the constraints of evolving social structures and the competitive pressures of a transnational economic order,[10] it seems clear that such a model remains a distant hope for more economically dependent and less well endowed Latin American nations. Were any to attempt such a model, they would invariably have to contend with the limited density of organized labor, the diffuse demands of more heterogeneous sociopolitical constituencies, and resource constraints that mandate targeted rather than universal social benefits. Likewise, social democratic experiments would have to find means to limit the "exit options" of capitalists who operate in a new global market and are thus less constrained by domestic-level power balances or efforts to extend democratic controls over market activities.[11] Whatever emerges from such experiments would undoubtedly differ markedly from social democracy as it has traditionally been conceived in Western Europe.

More likely than a model of social democracy, with its tradition of centralized social and political organization and top-down, state-led reform, would be a process of decentralized, bottom-up reform that could, potentially, build from municipal to national levels of power. In recent years the Left has accumulated considerable experience in municipal governance in Latin America, and this experience has been more favorable in countries like Uruguay, Brazil, and Venezuela than in the Peruvian case analyzed above.[12] In these nations, municipal governments of the Left have had varying levels of success in improving the efficiency of public services, creating new social programs, enhancing the transparency and accountability of democratic decision making, and crafting new channels for popular participation. In so doing, they have created opportunities for the strengthening of the Left at the level of national politics as well, although the Peruvian experience provides a sobering reminder that a process of cumulative empowerment is far from automatic.

Equally important, these municipal experiments are indicative of conscious efforts to find political mechanisms that build bridges between diverse social movements and community organizations. In the Brazilian case, the organic character of the PT's relationship to the leading labor confederation, the United Workers' Central (CUT), along with community-based organizations, has provided a common political space that links popular social and political struggles while respecting their relative autonomy.[13] Indeed, the CUT itself has performed a vital role in the articulation of diverse interests, not only by taking the lead in the founding of the PT but also by reaching out beyond its initial urban industrial constituency to encourage rural unionization and establish ties to Christian base communities and other grass-roots organizations among the urban poor.[14] In contrast to the tendencies among organized labor in Peru and Chile, which were put on the defensive by political and economic changes and became increasingly insulated from other forms of popular struggle as they defended particularistic interests, the CUT has tried to develop a "radial" character that places it at the axis of diverse popular struggles. It thus stands as a crucial exception to the regional pattern of diminished labor strength, and although this is at least partially attributable to the absence of a wrenching period of deindustrialization in Brazil's adaptation to the neoliberal era, it is also a testament to the effectiveness of the CUT's articulation strategies. The combination of effective political articulation and an organic party-society relationship has enabled the Brazilian Left to avoid the radical disjuncture between social movement and electoral strength that one finds in the Left in Peru and Chile, where vanguardist and electoralist orientations have predominated.

Proponents of radical democratic projects have long recognized the importance of the political articulation of pluralistic collective actors in the absence of a cohesive, hegemonic class subject.[15] This has led to a new emphasis on the role of diverse social and cultural subjects in the struggle for change. Recognition of the vital role of women's organizations, community associations, ethnic groups, and other nonclass actors, however, should not obscure the importance of groups based on material interests or economic and productive activities. If the neoliberal era has foreclosed the possibility of a radical democratic alternative founded on the strength of the traditional organized labor movement, it has also generated new social contradictions that may yet spawn novel forms of collective resistance, along with diverse class fractions that could be incorporated in a project to deepen democracy and regulate the market through creative articulation strategies.[16] The challenge that lies before labor organizations and leftist parties is not so much to defend traditional particularistic rights as to discover new spaces, of encounter with rural workers and *campesinos*, temporary contract workers, and the informal and microenterprise sectors.

It is obvious that both interests and identities will vary widely across these sectors; only creative political agency can find areas of convergence and common purpose in the midst of such social heterogeneity and thus build bridges between subaltern sectors that are otherwise isolated or in competition with each other. In the absence of horizontal articulation, localized or particularistic forms of collective action will do little to challenge concentrations of private economic power or a logic of capital accumulation that is increasingly transnational in scope. The market revolution in Latin America has generated new inequalities, a multitude of unmet needs, and a host of insecurities that are amenable to political response; as yet, however, there is an enormous gap between the segmented and decentralized forms of resistance spawned by this revolution and the national and transnational power structures that sustain it. Stronger forms of horizontal articulation—including transnational linkages—will be imperative if collective democratic controls are to be asserted over the global logic of capital.

The electoral future of the Left in Latin America may not hinge on such forms of articulation between political parties and organized grass-roots constituencies. As Kitschelt demonstrates in his study of European social democracy, the electoral prospects of leftist parties are not necessarily doomed by the social transformations and policy constraints associated with the challenge of market efficiency in a more global economy. When party leaders are relatively autonomous from party bases and organized social constituencies, they generally have greater strategic flexibility to appeal to new electoral constituencies, adjust a party's alliance positions, and alter its programmatic orientation in accordance with the exigencies of a new sociopolitical environment.[17] This has been the course followed by the Chilean Socialist Party and the PPD, which found avenues for electoral expansion by buttressing the autonomy of party leaders, appealing to a broad range of individual voters, and flexibly adapting to a market-based restructuring of economic relations. The Chilean case suggests, however, that electoral success based on such a strategy will pose few challenges to the new forms of social domination enshrined in the neoliberal model and will not generate the forms of popular participation required to deepen democracy beyond the minimum levels attained in Latin America today. To deepen democracy requires that party leaders be more, rather than less, accountable to their constituencies. Likewise, it requires that organized social constituencies be actively engaged at various stages of the policymaking process, not passive observers of a political scene controlled by a technocratic elite.

Can Latin America's new democratic regimes be deepened in such a manner without jeopardizing the contingent bases of consent on which their stability rests? The answer remains uncertain, as their elasticity has yet to be seriously tested. With the regional wave of democratization now two decades old, it seems clear that democratic regimes are less difficult to establish and sustain (if not necessarily to consolidate) than was previously thought. It no longer seems plausible for scholars to argue that low levels of development, Iberian political cultures, or acute class inequalities foreclose the prospects for political democracy; the old debates regarding the "preconditions" for democracy have been rendered less urgent, as authoritarian alternatives have lost their viability, and a pro-democratic international environment can at least partially compensate for unfavorable domestic conditions for the creation of democratic regimes. The crucial question for Latin America today is not what leads to democracy but what limits it, as the structural factors that used to be seen as precluding democracy may still wield influence as significant constraints on popular sovereignty.

According to Huber, Rueschemeyer, and Stephens, the domestic structural factors that are most conducive to the emergence of democracy—a strong working class to balance the interests of elite sectors and a densely organized civil society to balance the power of the state—are the same as those that facilitate its deepening.[18] In contemporary Latin America, the balance of these structural forces may allow for democracy, but they have clearly been unfavorable to its deepening or extension. In a context of rigid class inequalities, the new democratic regimes have tried to maintain their stability by demobilizing social actors, restraining popular demands, and buttressing the social hierarchy, thus reassuring elite sectors that democracy is not an intrinsic threat to their interests. The trade-offs between deepening and consolidating democracy, however, are not necessarily permanent; as O'Donnell and Schmitter state, "Conditions that are conducive in the short run to an orderly and continuous democratic transition, such as the drafting of interim pacts, may subsequently impede democratic consolidation if their restrictive rules and guarantees produce substantive disenchantment and procedural deadlock."[19] The Venezuelan case provides ample evidence of the long-term destabilizing consequences of elitist, consensual arrangements that try to consolidate democracy by avoiding political conflict, evading difficult choices, and containing popular demands.[20] Over the long term, democracy is not served by self-containment; it thrives on deep social roots, a broad base of support, and a capacity to adapt to changing circumstances and newly emerging social pressures, all of which require a participatory civil society. Democratic regimes that short-circuit such participation may be deceptively calm on the surface, but they often contain deep seismic rifts that periodically shake their foundations and threaten their institutional edifice. This is especially the case where democratic citizenship operates in awkward coexistence with deeply entrenched social inequalities. If the Latin American Left has learned hard lessons regarding the limitations on the scope and pace of social reform under political democracy, it must also be cognizant of the often hidden dangers of democratic self-containment or emasculation. Only then, perhaps, will it test the possibilities for a deepening of democracy.

Reference Matter

Glossary of Spanish Terms and Acronyms

AP Acción Popular (Popular Action). Peruvian party of the center-right founded in 1956. For most of its history, the AP was led by former president Fernando Belaunde Terry.

APRA technically known as the Partido Aprista Peruano (PAP), APRA is the Peruvian populist party founded by Victor Raúl Haya de la Torre in 1924.

APS Acción Política Socialista (Socialist Political Action). A Peruvian Socialist party founded in 1980 by Gustavo Mohme. The APS was a member of the IU before joining the MDI in 1992.

AS Acuerdo Socialista (Socialist Accord). The AS was an alliance of moderate socialists in Peru who broke with the IU in 1989.

Asamblea Nacional Popular (ANP)—the National Popular Assembly, a representative body of social organizations in Peru during the mid-1980s.

autogestión a term referring to community self-government or self-management.

autogolpe a "self-coup" in which an incumbent president adopts unconstitutional measures to close or suppress other institutions of government.

campesinos term generally used for the peasantry in Latin America.

caudillo a forceful, personalistic political leader, generally with authoritarian tendencies.

CCP Confederación Campesina de Perú (Peasant Confederation of Peru). The CCP is the largest peasant confederation in Peru, with close historic ties to the PCP-Bandera Roja, the VR, and the PUM.

CGTP Confederación General de Trabajadores del Perú (General

Workers' Confederation of Peru). The CGTP has been Peru's largest labor federation since the 1970s. It is closely affiliated with the PCP.

clasista   a term referring to labor movements that promote class solidarity and generally favor militant organizational tactics.

CNI   Central Nacional de Informaciones (National Information Center). The CNI operated as the national intelligence service and secret police under the Pinochet dictatorship after 1977, when it replaced the notorious secret police force known as the DINA.

Concertación   a multiparty, center-left alliance that led the campaign to defeat the Pinochet regime in Chile's 1988 plebiscite and subsequently formed the new democratic government. It was formally known as the Concertación de Partidos por el NO (Concertation of Parties for NO), then as the Concertación de Partidos por la Democracia (Concertation of Parties for Democracy).

CORFO   Corporación de Fomento de la Producción (Corporation for the Promotion of Production). CORFO was a state development corporation that played a leading role in the industrialization of Chile from the 1930s until 1973.

CPC   Confederación de la Producción y Comercio (Confederation of Production and Commerce). The CPC is the leading association for business interests in Chile.

CTP   Confederación de Trabajadores Peruanos (Peruvian Workers' Confederation). Labor federation affiliated historically with APRA.

CUP   Congreso Unitario de Pobladores (Unitary Congress of Pobladores). The CUP was a representative body that sought to coordinate grass-roots mobilization in the poblaciones against the Pinochet regime in the mid-1980s.

CUT   Central Unica de Trabajadores (United Workers' Central). The CUT is Chile's largest labor confederation, with historic ties to the Communist Party, the Socialist Party, and the Christian Democratic Party. In Brazil, the CUT refers to Central Unica dos Trabalhadores, the labor confederation linked to the PT.

el mas consequente   a term used by Communist militants in Chile to refer to their party as the most "consequential" or committed.

ELN   Ejercito de Liberación Nacional (Army of National Liberation). The ELN was a Peruvian guerrilla movement that took up arms briefly in 1965.

FLACSO   Facultad Latinoamericano de Ciencias Sociales (Latin American Faculty of Social Sciences). FLACSO is a Chilean think tank that became a center of intellectual dissent and a leader in the process of socialist renovation under the military regime of General Augusto Pinochet.

FMLN Frente Farabundo Martí para Liberación Nacional (Farabundo Martí Front for National Liberation). The FMLN was a front of five Salvadoran guerrilla movements founded in 1980. It was transformed into a political party following El Salvador's 1992 peace accords.

FOCEP Frente Obrero, Campesino, Estudiantil y Popular (Workers, Peasants, Students and Popular Front). A coalition of Peruvian Trotskyist groups founded in 1977. The front split apart after 1978 and became a small party under the leadership of Genaro Ledesma. FOCEP helped found the IU in 1980.

FOSIS Fondo de Solidaridad e Inversión Social (Fund for Solidarity and Social Investment). FOSIS is a fund established by the government of Patricio Aylwin in Chile to support poverty relief and social investment projects.

FPMR Frente Patriótico Mañuel Rodríguez (Mañuel Rodíguez Patriotic Front). The FPMR was an armed movement founded in 1983 with close ties to the Chilean Communist Party.

FREDEMO Frente Democrático (Democratic Front). A conservative electoral front formed in Peru in 1988 by the AP, the PPC, and the Movimiento Libertad of the novelist Mario Vargas Llosa. FREDEMO sponsored the presidential campaign of Vargas Llosa in 1990, then dissolved following his defeat.

hacienda a large, traditional landed estate.

IC Izquierda Cristiana (Christian Left). The IC was a leftist faction that broke with Chile's Christian Democratic Party in 1971 to support the Popular Unity government of Salvador Allende.

IS Izquierda Socialista (Socialist Left). The IS was an alliance of leftist groups that supported Alfonso Barrantes's campaign for the presidency of Peru in 1990.

IU Izquierda Unida (United Left). The IU was an electoral alliance of six Peruvian leftist parties during the 1980s. The alliance broke apart in 1989–90 but survived in a reduced form thereafter.

Jota the Communist youth organization in Chile.

junta de vecinos neighborhood councils in Chile.

la democracia de los acuerdos the democracy of agreements.

MAPU Movimiento de Acción Popular Unitaria (United Popular Action Movement). MAPU was a leftist faction that broke with Chile's Christian Democratic Party in 1969 and subsequently joined the Popular Unity coalition of Salvador Allende.

MAPU-OC Movimiento de Acción Unitaria-Obrero Campesino (United Popular Action Movement-Worker Peasant). The MAPU-OC emerged from a division within MAPU and was also a member of Allende's Popular Unity coalition.

MDI   Movimiento Democrático de Izquierda (Movement of the Democratic Left). Peruvian leftist movement founded in 1992 by moderate leaders who broke with the IU. The principal leader of the MDI is Henry Pease.

MIDA   Movimiento de Izquierda Democrática Allendista (Movement of the Democratic Allendista Left). MIDA is a Communist Party–led alliance formed in the aftermath of Chile's democratic transition.

MDP   Movimiento Democrático Popular (Popular Democratic Movement). The MDP was an alliance of Chilean leftist parties founded in 1983, with leadership from the Communist Party and the Almeyda sector of the Socialist Party.

milicias Rodriguistas   militia groups, generally organized among poblador youth, who supported protest activities in Chile against the Pinochet dictatorship and supported the armed activities of the FPMR.

MIR   Movimiento de la Izquierda Revolucionaria (Movement of the Revolutionary Left). Militant parties with this name appeared in both Chile and Peru during the 1960s.

Movimiento Revolucionario Túpac Amaru (MRTA)   the Túpac Amaru Revolutionary Movement in Peru.

NGOs   nongovernmental organizations.

OEPs   Organizaciones económicas populares (popular economic organizations). OEPs refer to small-scale, grass-roots organizations engaged in collective production or consumption activities. They are often organized on a community basis.

PAIS   Partido Amplio de Izquierda Socialista (Broad Party of the Socialist Left). PAIS was a short-lived "instrumental" party founded by the Communist Party, the Almeyda Socialists, and other leftist parties in Chile to evade legal restrictions on their participation in the 1989 elections.

PCP   Partido Comunista Peruano (Peruvian Communist Party). The PCP was founded by Marxist intellectual José Carlos Mariátegui under the name of the Peruvian Socialist Party in 1928. It changed its name in 1930 and became the principal Moscow-line communist party in Peru.

PCP-Bandera Roja   Partido Comunista Peruano-Bandera Roja (Peruvian Communist Party–Red Flag). Maoist splinter from the PCP in 1964.

PCP-Patria Roja   Partido Comunista Peruano-Patria Roja (Peruvian Communist Party–Red Fatherland). The PCP-Patria Roja was a Maoist splinter from the PCP-Bandera Roja which became the leading force in UNIR after 1980.

PCR Partido Comunista Revolucionario (Revolutionary Communist Party). The PCR was a Maoist splinter of the VR founded in 1974. Part of the party joined the PUM in 1984, while a sector led by Mañuel Dammert remained an independent member of the IU and eventually broke with the front in 1989 to support the presidential aspirations of Alfonso Barrantes.

PDI Participación Democrática Izquierda (Democratic Left Participation). The PDI was a movement founded by dissidents who broke with the Chilean Communist Party in 1990 and entered into an electoral alliance with the Socialist/PPD bloc in the Concertación.

población a Chilean term for shantytowns or other lower-class communities.

pobladores a Chilean term for the residents of shantytowns and other lower-class communities.

POS Partido Obrero Socialista (Workers' Socialist Party). The POS was the predecessor to the Chilean Communist Party, founded in 1912 by Luis Emilio Recabarren.

PPC Partido Popular Cristiano (Popular Christian Party). Peruvian conservative party founded in 1967.

PPD Partido por la Democracia (Party for Democracy). The PPD was founded by Ricardo Lagos and other member of the Núñez branch of the Socialist Party in 1987. The PPD separated ranks from the Socialist Party in 1992 but remained in an electoral federation with the Socialists within the broader Concertación alliance.

profundizando la democracia the deepening of democracy, generally implying greater levels of popular participation or empowerment.

PRD Partido de la Revolución Democrática (Party of the Democratic Revolution). Mexican leftist party led by Cuauhtémoc Cárdenas.

PSP Partido Socialista Peruano (Peruvian Socialist Party). The PSP was founded by José Carlos Mariátegui in 1928 and changed its name to the Peruvian Communist Party in 1930.

PSR Partido Socialista Revolucionaro (Revolutionary Socialist Party). The PSR was a Peruvian socialist party founded by prominent leaders from the reformist military government of General Juan Velasco Alvarado (1968–75). The PSR was a founding member of the IU but broke with the front in 1989 to support the presidential aspirations of Alfonso Barrantes.

PT Partido dos Trabalhadores (Workers' Party). Brazilian socialist party founded by labor leaders in 1979, led by Luís Inácio Lula da Silva.

pueblos jovenes a Peruvian term that means "young towns," generally used for shantytown settlements and lower-class communities that developed from land seizures.

PUM   Partido Unificado Mariateguista (Unified Mariateguista Party).
A Peruvian New Left party founded by sectors of the VR, the MIR,
and the PCR in 1984. Under the leadership of Javier Diez Canseco,
the PUM anchored the radical wing of the IU after its founding.

renovación   a term used to refer to a set of interconnected ideological
and strategic changes within the political Left. The term generally
implies a departure from Leninist principles and a strong emphasis
on the democratic character of the socialist tradition.

RN   Renovación Nacional (National Renovation). The RN is the largest party of the Chilean Right under the new democratic regime
and generally an ally of the UDI in opposition to the government
of the Concertación.

rondas campesinas   a term referring to community-based peasant patrols in Peru.

salida política   a term used to refer to a negotiated, peaceful transition from authoritarian rule in Chile.

Sendero Luminoso   the Shining Path guerrilla movement in Peru, formally known as the PCP-Sendero Luminoso (Peruvian Communist Party–Shining Path).

SINAMOS   Sistema Nacional de Mobilización Social (National System for the Support of Social Mobilization). SINAMOS was a government agency established by the Peruvian military government
of General Juan Velasco Alvarado (1968–75) to support grass-
roots mobilization and incorporate popular organizations into
government-sponsored social programs.

UDI   Unión Democrática Independiente (Independent Democratic
Union). The UDI is a pro-Pinochet party committed to the defense
of the military regime's political and economic legacy in Chile.

UDP   Unidad Democrática Popular (Popular Democratic Union). A
coalition of New Left groups founded in Peru in 1977. The bulk of
the parties in the UDP eventually helped found the PUM in 1984.

UNIR   Unidad Nacional de Izquierda Revolucionaria (Union of the
Revolutionary Left). A front of Peruvian Maoist parties founded in
1980. Led by the PCP-Patria Roja, the UNIR was a founding member of the IU in 1980.

vacío histórico   a term used in the Chilean Communist Party to refer
to its historic neglect of military factors.

vía armada   the armed or revolutionary road to socialism.

vía pacífica   the "peaceful" or democratic road to socialism.

VR   Vanguardia Revolucionaria (Revolutionary Vanguard). Peruvian
New Left party founded in 1965. After a series of divisions, the
core of the VR founded the UDP in 1977 and the PUM in 1984.

Notes

CHAPTER 1 *Introduction*

1. The breadth and durability of the new democratic regimes are discussed in Remmer 1992–93.

2. For a perceptive analysis of these efforts to qualify the democratic concept, see Collier and Levitsky 1997.

3. Stahler-Shock 1994.

4. O'Donnell (1994b: 166) argues that "low-intensity citizenship" is characteristic of "schizophrenic democracies" that combine authoritarian and democratic traits.

5. Loveman 1994.

6. Remmer 1986.

7. O'Donnell 1994a.

8. For an overview of these challenges to democratic governance, see Domínguez and Lowenthal 1996 or Conaghan 1996.

9. The key works include O'Donnell, Schmitter, and Whitehead 1986; Malloy and Seligson 1987; Diamond, Linz, and Lipset 1989; Huntington 1991; and Diamond and Plattner 1993.

10. See, for example, Mainwaring, O'Donnell, and Valenzuela 1992; Tulchin 1995; and Linz and Stepan 1996.

11. This can be seen most clearly in the consistent pattern whereby electorates select presidential candidates who promise gradualist, "security-oriented" alternatives to the free market "shocks" of neoliberal programs, only to have those candidates implement neoliberal reforms themselves after taking office. See Stokes 1995b.

12. Black 1993: 545.

13. For a representative view of democracy as a popular conquest, see Pease García 1981.

14. On the exclusionary character of many military regimes in Latin America, see O'Donnell's classic studies of bureaucratic authoritarianism (1973 and 1979).

15. General treatments of the Left's reincorporation into democratic politics can be found in Castañeda 1993; Carr and Ellner 1993; and Angell 1996.

16. For a prominent statement of socialism conceived as the deepening and extension of democracy, see Garretón 1989b: 19.

17. See Castañeda 1993, chap. 12.

18. The concept of a master frame is developed in Tarrow 1994: 131.

19. For examples of the early optimism see *América Latina 80*, or the essays in Slater 1985. More cautious reflections can be found in Escobar and Alvarez 1992. Some of the more pessimistic accounts include Adrianzén and Ballón 1992 and Pásara et al. 1991.

20. See Huber, Rueschemeyer, and Stephens 1997.

21. This theme is developed most cogently in Calderón 1995.

22. See, for example, Castañeda 1993; Rodríguez Elizondo 1990; Haris 1992; or *Proyectos de cambio* 1988.

23. O'Donnell and Schmitter 1986: 4–5.

24. For a seminal analysis of these different conceptions of democracy, see Barros 1986.

25. Castañeda 1993, chap. 11.

26. See Remmer 1992–93: 17–18, or Huber, Rueschemeyer, and Stephens 1997: 331–32.

27. Rueschemeyer, Stephens, and Stephens 1992: 41.

28. See O'Donnell 1994b, esp. pp. 162–63.

29. Latin America's neoliberal revolution is analyzed in Williamson 1994 and Edwards 1995.

30. The often tense relationships between democracy and neoliberalism are analyzed in Smith, Acuña, and Gamarra 1994; Nelson 1994; Haggard and Kaufman 1995; Haggard and Webb 1994; and Conaghan and Malloy 1994.

31. For analyses that link neoliberalism to authoritarian politics, see Garretón 1989a or Foxley 1983.

32. The impact of neoliberalism on poverty and inequality is analyzed in Bulmer-Thomas 1996. For insightful analyses of the social dislocations and realignments engendered by neoliberalism, see Smith and Korzeniewicz 1997.

CHAPTER 2 *Transformation of the Left in Latin America*

1. See the chapter "De la revolución a la democracia" in Lechner 1988. See also Carr and Ellner 1993.

2. For an overview and critique of the Left's approach to democracy in Latin America, see Moulian 1981 or Petkoff 1981: chap. 1.

3. Salvador Allende and his followers, though not the leadership of his political party, represent a notable exception to this generalization, as will be discussed in Chapter 4.

4. A penetrating analysis of these traditional perspectives can be found in Barros 1986. See also Rodríguez Elizondo 1990.

5. Garretón 1989b: 20.

6. Changes in political beliefs in Chile are discussed in Valdés 1986. For a regionwide perspective, see the essay "El Surgimiento de una nueva ideología democrática en América Latina" in Flisfisch 1987.

7. See Schmitter and Karl 1993: 39.

8. See Rénique 1995: 178.

9. Aricó 1989: 118–21.

10. Flisfisch 1987: 157.

11. These alternative responses are analyzed in Barros 1986.

12. See Bernstein 1961 or Gay 1952. For an explicit appeal to Bernstein's vision by an influential Brazilian intellectual, see Weffort 1993: 90–91.

13. See Weffort 1989: 36–39.

14. Garretón 1989b: 26.

15. See *América Latina 80* 1981.

16. This new vision contained a critique of traditional party-society linkages in which social organizations were controlled or manipulated by vanguard parties. The emphasis on the autonomy of civil society can be seen in Garretón 1985.

17. On the penetration of Gramscian influences in the Latin American Left, see Aricó 1988 or Martín del Campo 1985.

18. See Ottone 1986.

19. For a discussion of the questions that arise from the ambiguity of democracy's basic meaning, see Dahl 1989: 3–5.

20. This is different from the scale of the democratic polity, which concerns the territorial range and the size of the population incorporated within the reach of democratic practices. The scope or operative domain refers here to the range of societal institutions and the social spheres or issues to which democratic norms are applied.

21. See Held 1987: chap. 1. See also Dahl 1989: chap. 1 or Sartori 1987: chap. 10.

22. A leading analysis of participatory mechanisms in modern polities is Barber 1984. The most influential theoretical treatment of participatory democrary is Pateman 1970.

23. For suggestions in the Latin American context, see Castañeda 1993: chap. 12.

24. A pathbreaking treatment of democracy as a narrowly defined political regime is Schumpeter 1943. The idea of a procedural minimum is discussed in Dahl 1982, which provides a listing of seven procedural criteria for political democracy (pp. 10–11). For a slightly expanded set of procedural criteria, see Schmitter and Karl 1993: 45–46.

25. According to Lowenthal and Domínguez (1996: 7–8), one of the problems with a dichotomous conception of democracy is that it leads to a narrow focus on holding elections and avoiding or reversing coups, to the general neglect of the broader and more permanent practices of democratic governance.

26. Huntington 1991: 11–12.

27. Schmitter and Karl 1993: 47.

28. For an explicit conceptualization of democracy as a continuous variable, see Cunningham 1987, esp. chap. 3. O'Donnell and Schmitter (1986: 9) also recognize that democratization "admits of gradations," although they claim it would be difficult to specify "what rules and procedures would be more or less democratic."

29. Dahl 1971: chap. 1.

30. Bollen 1991.

31. O'Donnell and Schmitter 1986: 11–13.

32. The distinction between procedural methods and substantive outcomes is discussed in Sartori 1987: 11. According to Peruvian scholar Carlos Franco, this distinction is an outgrowth of the Western experience that is highly problematic in developing contexts, where it may invite individuals to associate substantive justice with nondemocratic procedures. See Franco 1990: 125–26.

33. See the classic analysis of social citizenship in Marshall 1965.

34. See, for example, Vilas 1997.

35. A good discussion of the issues and problems associated with an extension of the democratic domain can be found in Beetham 1992.

36. On the domain issue, see Held 1987: chap. 9.

37. See Macpherson 1973: chap. 3 or Markovic 1994.

38. For a thorough assessment of the rationale for the extension of democratic principles to business enterprises and economic relationships, see Dahl 1985. See also Bowles and Gintis 1986, esp. chap. 3.

39. A concise argument against the inclusion of "substantive" outcomes such as social equity in the conception of democracy can be found in Karl 1990: 2.

40. These two dimensions find parallels in Carl Cohen's discussion of the "depth" and "range" of democracy; see Cohen 1971: chap. 3. Cohen adds a third dimension, democratic breadth, to refer to the proportion of the political community that is incorporated in the decision-making process. For my analytical purposes, however, this third dimension can be considered an aspect of the deepening process which relates to the intensity of popular sovereignty. Cohen's three-dimensional conceptualization has been applied to Latin America in Booth 1989: 12–13.

41. The challenges confronted by social democracy are analyzed in Kitschelt 1994.

42. See, for example, the prescriptions in Barber 1984, esp. chap. 10.

43. For a theoretical sketch, see Markovic 1982.

44. See, for example, Moulian 1983 or Rodríguez Elizondo 1990.

45. Examples include Brunner 1990 or Flisfisch 1991.

46. For examples of work on market socialism outside the Latin American context, see Roemer 1994 or Bardhan and Roemer 1993.

47. This neglect has been pointed out in Barros 1986: 68.

48. For a most insightful analysis of politics as warfare, see Moulian 1989. See also Flisfisch 1987: 236–37.

49. On the character of these new models of authoritarian capitalism, see O'Donnell 1973 or Garretón 1989a.

50. Held 1987: chap. 2.

51. Barros 1986: 49.

52. For an understanding of democracy as the outcome of a stalemate between competing political projects, none of which is powerful enough to impose its own project over the will of others, see the influential argument in Rustow 1970.

53. For this reason, it is a dilemma for democratic theory when societies that are segmented along ethnic or cultural lines produce permanent majorities and minorities. Consociational adaptations to such problems are discussed in Lijphart 1977.

54. Schmitter and Karl 1993: 46–47.

55. Przeworski 1991: chap. 1.

56. For a conception of democracy as the institutionalization of uncertainty, see Przeworski 1986: 58.

57. Higley and Gunther 1992.

58. See Karl 1986 or Hagopian 1990.

59. O'Donnell and Schmitter 1986: 38.

60. Przeworski 1991: 90.

61. O'Donnell and Schmitter 1986: 69.

62. The Venezuelan case is instructive; see McCoy et al. 1995.

63. The characteristics of integrative party systems are discussed in Collier and Collier 1991: 502–5.

64. On the characteristics of polarizing party systems, see Sartori 1976.

65. The integrative role of the Socialist Party in Spain's process of democratization is analyzed in Maravall 1982: Part 3 and Share 1989.

66. For an analysis of political learning in Chilean parties under the dictatorship, see Garretón 1989c.

67. See Walker 1990 and Puryear 1994.

68. The literature on democratization sees such moderation as a common response to authoritarian experiences; see Bermeo 1992 or Higley and Gunther 1992. For an insightful analysis of the differential impact of political experiences on individual-level political identities, see Hite 1996.

69. Mauceri 1996: 31.

70. Kitschelt 1994: chap. 5.

71. Panebianco 1988: chap. 4.

72. As the Soviet experience suggests, a leadership succession might place reformers in charge of the hierarchical controls of such a party, with considerable leverage to initiate change. Normally, however, organizational screening devices prohibit radical reformers from reaching the pinnacle of such a centralized and self-reproducing party hierarchy, and bureaucratic inertia is likely to frustrate innovative change, as Gorbachev learned.

73. See March and Olsen 1989, esp. chap. 2.

74. Kitschelt 1994: 208.

75. Panebianco 1988: chap. 4. Likewise, North (1990: chap. 9) argues that decentralization enhances adaptive efficiency in institutions by facilitating learning through trial and error.

76. Kitschelt 1994: chap. 5. See also Levitsky 1995 and Schlesinger 1965: 777.

77. Deutsch 1963: 92.

78. Ideological and discursive constraints on strategic flexibility are discussed in Kitschelt 1994: chap. 6.

79. See Duetsch 1963: 92.

80. The role of intellectuals in the process of change is discussed in Puryear 1994.

81. Kitschelt 1994: chap. 5.

82. On the influence of European perspectives, see Arrate 1985: chap. 5.

83. Castañeda 1993: chap. 8.

CHAPTER 3 *Social Structures and Collective Action*

1. In Latin American scholarship, a broad variety of social organizations and grass-roots community associations are typically lumped

together under the rubric of "social movements" or "popular organizations." I abide by this convention and use these generic terms interchangeably. Following Alvarez and Escobar (1992: 321), I conceive social movements as "organized collective actors who engage in sustained political or cultural contestation through recourse to institutional and extrainstitutional forms of action."

2. Pease García 1981: 13.

3. This shift is discussed in the introduction to Escobar and Alvarez 1992. Prime examples of the more pessimistic assessments include Adrianzén and Ballón 1992 and Pásara et al. 1991.

4. Calderón and Jelin 1987: 25.

5. This concept has previously been used by Calderón and Jelin 1987: 36 and by Pásara and Zarzar 1991: 199.

6. On the manipulation of labor movements by parties and states, see Collier and Collier 1991. On tensions between the partisan Left and women's movements, see Jaquette 1994.

7. See Laclau 1985 or Hellman 1992.

8. Calderón, Piscitelli, and Reyna 1992: 23.

9. On the political culture and collective identities of new social movements, see Oxhorn 1995: chap. 4 or Mainwaring and Viola 1984. A more skeptical assessment of the distinctive political culture of social movements can be found in Pásara and Zarzar 1991.

10. See Przeworski and Wallerstein 1988 or Lindblom 1977: chap. 13.

11. On the exercise of exit options, see Hirschman 1970.

12. The importance of organization for the learning process that leads to the construction of lower-class identities is emphasized in Rueschemeyer, Stephens, and Stephens 1992: 54. On the social construction of popular movements more broadly, see Klandermans 1992.

13. Przeworski 1985: 20–21.

14. See Stokes 1995a on the process of cultural change in new social movements.

15. Similarly, Wickham-Crowley (1992: 138–51) argues that peasant support for revolutionary movements is generated through social networks rather than individual ideological conversions.

16. See Olson 1965.

17. See the compelling critique of the rational choice formulation of collective action problems in Ferree 1992. For constructive efforts to assess rationality in its broader social contexts, see Anderson 1994 or Taylor 1988.

18. These revisions of Olson's model are introduced by Moe 1980: chap. 2. See also Lichbach 1995 for numerous "solutions" to Olson's collective action problem.

19. See Mueller 1992.

20. On the limited range of applicability of rational choice theories, see Almond 1991: 48–49.

21. See the discussion of social transaction costs in Tarrow 1994: 16–23.

22. Tarrow (1994) concedes the significance of social structure in premodern settings, when collective action grew out of local, particularistic grievances and aimed at immediate targets. With socioeconomic modernization, however, came a broader repertoire of collective actions that could be flexibly adopted in a range of settings by a diversity of actors, thus facilitating larger-scale social movements and, presumably, enhancing their relative autonomy from structural determination. See especially chapter 3.

23. On the group-binding functions of social conflict, see Coser 1956: chap. 2.

24. Marx 1978: 179.

25. For an analysis of how party systems take root in underlying social cleavages, see Lipset and Rokkan 1967.

26. Marx 1963: 123.

27. See, for example, the study of Chilean nitrate workers in Bergquist 1986: chap. 2, or the analysis in Lipset 1960: 104.

28. See Tarrow 1994: 93–94.

29. See, for example, Dietz 1980; Stokes 1995; or Gay 1994.

30. Przeworski 1985: chap. 1.

31. Kitschelt 1994: 55.

32. Dix 1989: 23–37.

33. The radial concept is used, with reference to authority in political regimes, in Remmer 1989.

34. See the account of the protest movements in Tovar Samanez 1982.

35. Stokes 1995: chaps. 5 and 6 or Mauceri 1996: 100.

36. For an overview of socioeconomic restructuring and its political effects in Latin America, see Smith and Korzeniewicz 1997, or Chalmers et al., 1997.

37. For an overview, see Collier and Collier 1991.

38. Pontusson 1995.

39. See, for example, the analysis of the Peruvian case in Balbi 1997.

40. Sulmont Samain 1994: 11.

41. For the Chilean case, see Díaz 1993, esp. pp. 23–24.

42. See Balbi 1991, especially pp. 128–31.

43. O'Donnell 1994b: 170.

44. See, for example, Laclau and Mouffe 1985; Slater 1985; or Calderón, Piscitelli, and Reyna 1992.

45. Identity approaches are analyzed in Cohen 1985.

46. See, for example, Mainwaring and Viola 1984; Evers 1985; and Alvarez and Escobar 1992: 325–28.

47. A good example is Fals-Borda 1992.

48. For an excellent overview of the impediments posed by patron-clientelism to reformist projects, see Weyland 1996a.

49. For example, it has been estimated that 220,000 persons participated in a variety of grass-roots organizations in lower-class districts or *poblaciones* in Santiago in 1985 at the height of popular mobilization against the military regime. This constituted 16 percent of the population living in *poblaciones* in Santiago. See Valdes 1987: 307. For a comparative empirical analysis that demonstrates the relatively low levels of participation in urban popular organizations, see Portes and Itzigsohn 1997.

50. Castañeda 1993: 172.

51. The emergence of personalist leaders in the context of socio-economic crises has been discussed, among others, by O'Donnell 1994a; Tironi Barrios 1986; and Zermeño 1989. On the populist proclivities of the urban poor, see Franco 1991.

52. The counterintuitive affinities between populism and neoliberalism are explored in Weyland 1996b and Roberts 1995.

53. Barros 1986: 65.

54. Tarrow 1994: 149.

55. This problem is discussed in Oxhorn 1995, esp. pp. 20–21.

56. This point has also been made in analyses of new social movements in Europe; see Offe 1990: 234–35. In the Latin American context, see Mainwaring and Viola 1984: 41.

57. See Tarrow 1994: chap. 2. Tarrow's argument about the flexible, "modular" character of collective action remains valid, but the progression toward more integrated forms of collective action has been reversed in Latin America.

58. Friedman and McAdam 1992: 164.

59. Laclau 1985: 34.

60. See Fals Borda 1992: 308.

61. See Vilas 1997: 32–33.

62. One of the best examples of this was the decision of the São Paulo workers movement led by Lula to found the PT in 1980; see Keck 1992, Chapter 4, or Sader and Silverstein 1991, chapter 3.

63. See Slater 1985: 8 or Fals Borda 1992: 305–6.

64. See, for example, Oxhorn 1994 or Canel 1992.

65. A good overview of the concept of political entrepreneurship can be found in Moe 1980: chap. 3.

66. See Schneider 1995: chap. 1.

67. See ibid.: 10 on the importance of such structural definitions of social problems. The role of issue framing is analyzed in Tarrow 1994: chap. 7.

68. In the case of the Brazilian Workers' Party, see Keck 1992: chap. 8.

69. On catch-all parties, see Kirchheimer 1966. In the terminology of Panebianco (1988: chap. 14), these parties are known as "electoral-professional" parties.

70. Panebianco 1988: 262.

71. Early risers are discussed in Tarrow 1994: chap. 9.

72. On the significance of Vazquez's charismatic leadership for the Broad Front in Uruguay, see Winn and Ferro-Clérico 1997: 450–51.

73. The tendency for populism to undercut autonomous organizational efforts in civil society is analyzed in Mouzelis 1985.

74. This may, however, be changing in Europe as well. As Kitschelt (1994) has shown, socialist parties in recent times have often been weakened electorally by organic ties to traditional labor movements, which have denied party leaderships the autonomy and strategic flexibility required to appeal to new constituencies.

CHAPTER 4 *Authoritarian Rule and the Left*

1. For an insider's perspective on the process of consensus building written by a prominent Socialist intellectual and government strategist, see Flisfisch 1994. See also the essays in Tulchin and Varas 1991 or Drake and Jaksic 1995.

2. O'Donnell 1994a: 64, 68.

3. Munck 1994: 1.

4. The impact of economic crises on anti-incumbent voting patterns is analyzed in Remmer 1991b.

5. At the level of political elites, see Valdés 1986. At the level of mass public opinion, see Huneeus 1987.

6. See Scully 1992: 199–202.

7. In contrast to its centrist predecessor, the Radical Party, the Christian Democratic Party eschewed political alliances in the 1960s in favor of a go-it-alone strategy of governance, undermining the capacity of the Center to broker agreements with Chile's powerful and polarized Left and Right tendencies. See ibid.: chap. 4 or Valenzuela 1978. An excellent history of the Christian Democratic Party can be found in Fleet 1985.

8. See Collier and Collier 1991, esp. chap. 7.

9. One of the few works to give an overview of both parties after 1973 is Bascuñán Edwards 1990.

10. See, for example, Oxhorn 1994 or Canel 1992.

11. For historical analyses of the Chilean labor movement, see Angell 1972; DeShazo 1983; and Bergquist 1986: chap. 2.

12. An official history of the early years of the Communist Party can be found in Ramírez-Necochea 1965. See also Furci 1984: chap. 2.

13. As noted by Caballero (1986: 123–27), the Chilean Communist Party was never granted a prominent role in the Latin American Secretariat of the Comintern, despite the fact that it was more successful than its regional cohorts in mobilizing a mass working-class base of support.

14. See Soledad Gómez 1988.

15. The heterogeneous makeup of the Socialist Party is analyzed in Drake 1978, which emphasizes the party's early populist tendencies; see especially chapter 5. See also Jobet 1987: 89–90.

16. Furci 1984: 48.

17. An overview of the Left during the Popular Front period and its aftermath can be found in Faúndez 1988: chap. 4.

18. Were it not for the independent candidacy of a leftist, defrocked Catholic priest who obtained 3.3 percent of the presidential vote, Allende might have won the election in 1958.

19. See Scully 1992: 156.

20. Frei was the father of the current president of the same name.

21. Scully 1992: 156–57.

22. Ibid.: 143.

23. The permanent tensions between these currents are analyzed in Pollack and Rosenkranz 1986.

24. An overview of the radicalization of the Socialist Party in the 1960s can be found in Walker 1990: 136–46.

25. See the resolutions from the Socialist Party's 22d Congress in Chillán, reprinted in Jobet 1987: 313.

26. The literature on Allende's reforms is voluminous; among the best accounts are Bitar 1980 and Stallings 1978. Good analyses of the Popular Unity period can also be found in Valenzuela and Valenzuela 1976 and Gil, Lagos, and Landesberger 1979.

27. The electoral coalition incorporated the much-reduced Radical Party and several other small groups, including the Movimiento de Acción Popular Unitaria (MAPU), a left-wing splinter from the Christian Democratic Party. A second splinter from the Christian Democrats, the Izquierda Cristiana (IC), joined the coalition in 1971, while a split in MAPU led to the addition of MAPU Obrero-Campesino (MAPU-OC). MAPU and the IC often sided with the Socialists in internal disputes, while the Radical Party and MAPU-OC generally supported the more moderate positions of the Communist Party.

28. The dynamics within the Left are analyzed in Faúndez 1988, Part III.

29. Allende's reforms frequently engendered new forms of political mobilization and class identity among popular sectors. For a classic account of political change in the labor movement, see Winn 1986.

30. Among the leading accounts of this political polarization are Valenzuela 1978 and Garretón and Moulian 1983.

31. For overviews of the military regime and its repressive character, see Remmer 1991a, chap. 5; Constable and Valenzuela 1991; Garretón 1989a; Arriagada 1985; and Spooner 1994.

32. Remmer 1980: 282.

33. Roberts-Hite 1991: 4.

34. According to the Socialist Party secretary general at the time of the coup, Carlos Altamirano, the party maintained a military force of between 1,000 and 1,500 members before the overthrow of Allende. This force, however, melted away with the commencement of the coup and was not even able to provide protection for the party leadership, much less challenge the military takeover. See the extensive interview with Altamirano in Politzer 1989: 33.

35. See the listing of Central Committee members in Walker 1986: 80.

36. In an interview with the author in Santiago on July 10, 1990, party leader Luis Urtubia said that he was one of only ten members of the Central Committee to remain inside Chile while avoiding detention during the first six months following the coup. All of these leaders, however, were subsequently detained and disappeared or forced into exile, leading to a complete restructuring of the party's internal leadership in the mid-1970s.

37. Yocelevsky 1986: 120–21.

38. For example, the June 1990 discovery of mass graves near a former prison camp in Pisagua provided graphic evidence of the execution of the entire regional directorate of the Socialist Party from the northern city of Iquique following the coup.

39. Ricardo Solari, who eventually became the subsecretary general of the presidency under Patricio Aylwin, asserted that he and three other youth leaders went to a park outside Santiago in January 1976 to plan the reorganization of the party's clandestine hierarchy. Personal interview, August 16, 1990.

40. Ricardo Núñez, an ally of Altamirano on the External Secretariat and an eventual secretary general of the party, justified this support for both leadership factions inside Chile, claiming that the repeated decapitations of the Internal Directorate undermined its effectiveness and legitimacy. Consequently, the external leadership was willing to

support *any* Socialist faction inside the country that was capable of political action. Personal interview, Santiago, July 11, 1994. Another Altamirano ally on the External Secretariat and future secretary general, Jorge Arrate, said the Secretariat thought "we had to try to integrate all sectors of the party, and therefore we maintained a relation with the Coordinadora [the CNR] and with other groups that existed in the country, and we hoped they would be integrated into the party directorate." Personal interview, Santiago, July 15, 1991.

41. See "La Revolución Chilena," a report delivered by Secretary General Luis Corvalán to the first plenary meeting of the Central Committee in exile in August 1977.

42. Interview with Mañuel Cantero, a member of the Political Commission of the Communist Party who joined Marín in the reconstruction of the internal directorate, Santiago, July 25, 1990.

43. "A la democracia con todo," p. 17.

44. In an interview with the author in San Bernardo, Chile on August 17, 1993, former secretary general Luis Corvalán said cells were broken down into three member subgroups, with meetings restricted to no more than three members.

45. Under conditions of severe repression, there is a tendency for grass-roots activists to redirect their energies from partisan political work to the social arena; see Oxhorn 1995: chap. 1.

46. The gap between the party's formal Leninist structure and its actual practices is discussed in Almeyda 1991.

47. This can be seen in the party's first clandestine declaration after the coup, entitled "A los trabajadores de Chile," p. 8. Also see the party declaration "Ultraizquierdismo, caballo de troya del imperialismo."

48. Untitled clandestine document produced by the Communist Party in March 1974, p. 8.

49. See, for example, the manifesto "Llamamiento al Pueblo de Chile a Formar un Frente Antifascista."

50. The leaders of the Christian Democratic Party believed that the Leninist doctrine of the Communist Party was inherently incompatible with democracy, no matter what political practices the party actually followed; see Arriagada Herrera and Orrego Vicuña 1976.

51. See the manifesto "Al partido y al pueblo de Chile."

52. See the manifesto "Patriotas: Solo unidos derrotaremos al fascismo," p. 5.

53. One of the first signs of this shift in emphasis was an article written by the party literary figure and exile leader Volodia Teitelboim (1977).

54. See "La Revolución Chilena."

55. See Teitelboim 1977: 32–33.

56. For example, an early, authoritative Soviet source said the Chilean coup demonstrated the "tremendous importance of being prepared to promptly change forms of struggle," as well as the need to develop the "ability to repel the counter-revolutionary violence of the bourgeoisie with revolutionary violence." See Ponomaryov 1974: 10.

57. This was the case, at least, within the political leadership of the party. Leading exiled intellectuals who became strong proponents of an insurrectionary strategy harbored broader criticisms of the party's organizational structure, political culture, and ideological identities, but these did not circulate widely in the leadership's narrowly circumscribed strategic debates during this time period. Personal interviews with Mañuel Fernando Contreras and Alvaro Palacios, two of the leading theoreticians of the party's insurrectionary strategy, Santiago, August 22, 1990, and August 11, 1993, respectively.

58. According to Augusto Samaniego, a party theoretician who became a member of the Central Committee and a prominent dissident in 1990, intellectuals who stressed the party's "military policy" presented their arguments through direct personal contacts with exiled members of the political leadership, rather than within official party forums or assemblies. For many traditional political leaders, the new emphasis was difficult to grasp because "it was not only a change in our line but of our conception of the party and of its relationship to the masses." Personal interview, Santiago, June 25, 1990.

59. Distinctions between "simple" and "complex" patterns of political learning are noted in Deutsch 1963: 92.

60. "Documento del Comité Central del Partido Socialista de Chile," p. 43, better known as the "March Document."

61. Ibid., p. 12.

62. For example, Jorge Arrate, an exile leader who became a political architect of the "renovation" process, complained that the "March Document" of the Internal Directorate claimed "that the Socialist Party bore primary responsibility for the failure of the Popular Unity for not having been sufficiently Leninist." Personal interview, Santiago, July 15, 1991.

63. See Altamirano 1977, esp. chap. 4, for the Socialist leader's initial assessment of the Allende experiment. As will be seen below, Altamirano's political line changed considerably by the end of the 1970s.

64. An analysis of the CNR's positions can be found in Trevor 1989.

65. On the role of intellectuals in the process of ideological change, see Puryear 1994, esp. chap. 3.

66. See, for example, Silva Solar 1977 or Bitar 1980.

67. Garretón and Moulian 1983: 18.

68. The first explicit effort to incorporate Gramscian insights into the analysis of the Chilean experience was Viera-Gallo 1976–77.

69. For a collection of influential essays posing these theoretical critiques, see Moulian 1983. See also Tironi Barrios 1984.

70. Garretón 1987: 32–33.

71. González was an influential intellectual figure and the principal author of the party's landmark statement of political principles in 1947, entitled "Directivas fundamentales del programa de 1947," reprinted in Jobet 1987: 379–86. A good synopsis of González's conception of democratic socialism is González 1972.

72. See Flisfisch 1987: 216–25.

73. Politzer 1989: 150.

74. According to Jorge Arrate, it was only natural that the critical theoretical reflections which characterized the renovation process should be more extensive in exile, where there was a more fluid "interchange of ideas" and greater exposure to diverse experiences and models of socialism. In contrast, "in the interior the people did not have time to read, only to survive," and the pressures of authoritarianism encouraged them to defend their existing identities and "consolidate the ideas they had" at the time of the coup. Personal interview, Santiago, July 15, 1991.

75. See the document "Salida de Carlos Altamirano Orrego," issued by the Internal Directorate, p. 3. According to German Correa, a leader of the Internal Directorate who eventually became party secretary general and the interior minister after Chile's democratic transition, ideological changes in the exterior exacerbated tensions within the party but were overshadowed by more basic conflicts over whether ultimate political authority should be vested in the internal or external party apparatus. Personal interview, Santiago, August 18, 1993.

76. See the interviews with Carlos Altamirano and Jorge Arrate in "La crísis en el socialismo chileno," 1979: 119–29.

77. "Resoluciones del Tercer Pleno Nacional Extraordinario," p. 50.

78. According to Jaime Perez del Arce, then a student leader in Chile who became party vice-president after the democratic transition, party militants were very confused about the political conflicts that engendered the 1979 division. Since Altamirano had long been associated with the party's radical wing, his evolution toward a social democratic orientation was poorly understood within the ranks of the party inside Chile. Personal interview, Santiago, July 18, 1990.

79. In an interview with the author in Santiago on July 19, 1994, Núñez, now a senator, acknowledged that he returned to Chile without any organized support in the interior. His principal collaborator in the early process of party building was another future senator, Hernán Vodánovic, who was one of a small number of isolated militants inside the country to support the leadership of Altamirano over that of the Internal Directorate.

80. In formal terms, the Communist Party did not implement popular rebellion as an alternative to the antifascist front line, as it viewed rebellion as a strategy to cultivate broader support; interview with Political Commission member Jorge Insunza, Santiago, August 1, 1991. In practice, however, the new insurrectionary strategy clearly displaced the earlier emphasis on the construction of a political front.

81. For an example of this interpretation, see Darién 1985. The Communist Party generally equated the Chilean situation to that of Nicaragua because of the reality of personalist dictatorship, largely ignoring the profound differences in socioeconomic contexts, party systems, political traditions, and the strength of state and military institutions.

82. Interview with Augusto Samaniego, an intellectual architect of the popular rebellion strategy, Santiago, June 25, 1990.

83. Interview with Volodia Teitelboim, Santiago, July 7, 1994. Interestingly, political leaders of the Communist Party interviewed by the author such as Teitelboim, Jorge Insunza, and Mañuel Cantero emphasized the institutionalization project of Pinochet as the primary motivation for the party's strategic shift. In contrast, intellectual theoreticians of the popular rebellion strategy such as Mañuel Fernando Contreras, Augusto Samaniego, and Alvaro Palacios were more inclined to stress the failure of the antifascist front line and the need to develop new forms of struggle to invigorate popular resistance.

84. This is discussed in Moulián and Torres D. 1988.

85. The Leipzig Group was established by the exiled leaders of the party shortly after the coup and incorporated intellectuals from diverse academic fields. By the late 1970s these intellectuals were convinced that the strategy of seeking a political alliance with the Christian Democrats was doomed to failure and that it had little hope of activating popular resistance to the dictatorship. They believed popular mobilization would flourish only if the Communist Party took the political offensive and performed a vanguard role in the promotion of diverse forms of rebellion. Interview with Mañuel Fernando Contreras, a prominent figure in the Leipzig Group, Santiago, August 22, 1990.

86. For example, former Central Committee member Luis Guastavino claimed that he had not been privy to the debates surrounding the party's strategic shift. Personal interview, Santiago, August 14, 1990. The party later acknowledged that the strategic shift was made "without having been discussed with the interior [party organization] and without being measured by means of a democratic debate in the party." See the party document "A la democracia con todo," p. 18.

87. In 1990 the author conducted interviews with 28 base-level party militants; although 11 of these were critical of the party leader-

ship for retaining the popular rebellion strategy in the midst of Chile's democratic transition, only one claimed to have opposed it when it was implemented against the dictatorship in the early 1980s. See Chapter 6 for further detail. According to Fanny Pollarolo, a prominent human rights activist and later an influential party dissident, she and other militants embraced popular rebellion as a logical extension of their social resistance and did not view it as a radical shift in the party's strategic orientation. Personal interview, Santiago, August 21, 1991.

88. Among the few who openly opposed the new line were a group of dissident leaders from the party youth organization who had developed sympathies for Eurocommunism while in exile. Upon their return to Chile, however, the party's clandestine apparatus blocked these dissidents from airing their grievances in party forums, and they subsequently abandoned the party. Interview with former youth leader Hugo Rivas, Santiago, August 19, 1991.

89. On the revolutionary character of the social and economic changes wrought by the military regime, see Martínez and Díaz 1996.

90. Stallings 1978: 46–47.

91. The neoliberal revolution is dissected in Foxley 1983. See also Remmer 1991a: chap. 6.

92. Barrera and Valenzuela, 1986: 234.

93. Ibid., pp. 235–36.

94. Díaz 1989: 29.

95. Figures are calculated from data in Foxley 1986: 17 and Vergara 1993: 239.

96. Díaz 1993: 12.

97. By 1979, 28 percent of the land in the reform sector had been returned to previous owners, 20 percent had been sold, and 52 percent had been distributed in land grants to peasants. See Silva 1988: 447.

98. These changes are analyzed in ibid.

99. For an analysis of the new labor code, see Barrera and Valenzuela 1986: 253–58.

100. Ibid., p. 258.

101. Data are taken from Scully 1992: 156, and the Statistical Appendix in *Economía y trabajo en Chile: Informe anual, 1993–1994*.

102. Echenique 1990: 146.

CHAPTER 5   *The Struggle to Deepen Democracy*

1. For a recent discussion of these issues see Munck and Skalnik Leff 1997.

2. See Karl 1990. Karl is less sanguine about the long-term prospects for political adaptation in pacted democracies, as is Hagopian 1990.

3. For an overview of the democratization process in Chile, see Drake and Jaksic 1995.

4. For an analysis of how the economic crisis changed the "political opportunity structure" for social movements in Chile, see Schneider 1992.

5. The role of the Communist Party in the protest movement of *pobladores* is stressed in Schneider 1995.

6. Oxhorn 1995: chap. 5.

7. For a discussion of the shift from functional to territorial forms of popular organization, see ibid., pp. 7–8.

8. The reticence of the Communist Party's labor bases to participate in the more militant aspects of the popular rebellion strategy was acknowledged to the author in an interview with Political Commission member Jorge Insunza, Santiago, August 1, 1995.

9. The FPMR was named for an early nineteenth-century patriot and hero of Chile's independence struggle, Mañuel Rodríguez, in a manifest attempt to evoke nationalist symbols that transcended the Communist Party's more narrow partisan loyalties.

10. For a study of insurrectionary activities against the dictatorship, see Fruhling and Waiser 1992.

11. In a letter released by the Central Committee of the Communist Party in September 1984 with the title "A los presidentes y secretarios generales de los partidos de oposición al régimen militar," the party declared that the FPMR was not its armed wing, although "it counts with all our sympathy and appreciation, because it helps achieve the erosion of the regime and because its members possess a high combative morale, convinced that the cause of liberty imposes risks and sacrifices." Conflicts between the party and the armed movement led to a division of the FPMR and the appearance of an "autonomous" faction in 1987.

12. Interview with Augusto Samaniego, Santiago, August 22, 1990.

13. See "Llamamiento a la unidad y al combate," a joint declaration of leaders from the Communist Party, the Almeyda Socialists, and six other leftist parties.

14. See Pérez 1981.

15. According to Secretary General Clodomiro Almeyda, "We never thought . . . that our own military force was going to play a central role. We thought the party had to play the role of an agent of mobilization of the masses, to be an organizer of the masses and the protests. . . . The Communist Party, at least those within the FPMR, were thinking of a military confrontation, but we never thought of that." Personal interview, Santiago, July 4, 1990.

16. The Comandantes were led by Eduardo Gutiérrez, one of the

more radical members of the youthful leadership that reconstituted the Internal Directorate after 1976. This faction was politically marginalized following its exodus from the Almeyda branch of the party. According to Gutiérrez, factionalism within the Almeyda party increased considerably as the economic crisis and social protests plunged the regime into crisis and posed new strategic choices over alliance options and forms of struggle. Personal interview, Santiago, August 23, 1991.

17. For general overviews of the perspectives of this branch of the Socialist Party, see Almeyda 1986 or 1987.

18. For useful collections of writings on the socialist renovation, see Núñez 1991 or *La Renovación socialista: Balance y perspectivas*, 1987. See also Arrate 1983 and 1985 and Lagos 1987.

19. An influential summary of these concerns can be found in a letter written by Ricardo Núñez entitled "Carta abierta a los dirigentes y militantes de la izquierda chilena," December 17, 1986.

20. The evolving alliance strategy of the Christian Democratic Party is analyzed in Ortega Frei 1992, esp. chaps. 4 and 5.

21. The recent literature on democratization has often emphasized the importance of internal divisions within an authoritarian regime for the initiation of democratic transitions; see O'Donnell and Schmitter 1986: chap. 3, or Przeworski 1991: chap. 2.

22. This corresponds to O'Donnell's (1979) analysis of the need for bureaucratic-authoritarian regimes to reestablish at least partial "mediating" institutions between the state and civil society.

23. Many of Pinochet's supporters, along with other members of the military junta, spoke in favor of a civilian candidate who would be sympathetic to the "project" of the regime but less polarizing in a plebiscite campaign. In the end, however, Pinochet's dominance of the junta guaranteed his own nomination.

24. The diminishing role of middle-class sectors in the protest movement is discussed in Garretón 1989d: 269, and Salazar 1990: 381–82.

25. An early, influential argument along these lines can be found in a document for internal party discussion written by José Joaquín Brunner, "Notas para la discusión."

26. Initially, many people were reluctant to register, believing it would be futile to vote in a context that was so prone to fraud and coercion, and they did not want to legitimize an undemocratic exercise. As the plebiscite date approached, however, the Constitutional Tribunal took steps to ensure an impartial electoral process, and it became clear that the regime itself—confident in its own polls that predicted a Pinochet victory—wanted a "clean" process (though not a large turnout) to maximize its legitimating effect.

27. See "Propuesta del PC es aporte al acuerdo, sin exclusiones," *El Siglo*, March 16–31, 1987, p. 5.

28. Moderate leaders of the Almeyda Socialists inside Chile had from the outset maintained ties to the Núñez sector and supported the early process of "convergence," but their hands were tied by the opposition of the Comandantes and other radical tendencies. The exodus of the Comandantes allowed these moderate leaders, such as German Correa, Ricardo Solari, and Jaime Pérez del Arce, to establish some distance from the Communist Party and work for a rapprochement with the Núñez Socialists. Interview with Socialist Party president German Correa, August 18, 1993.

29. Ibid.

30. The 1989 elections are discussed in Caviedes 1991: chap. 4.

31. Within five months of its reunification the party had registered nearly 25,000 members, approximately 19,000 of which came from the Núñez branch, whose ranks had swelled as a result of a membership drive and the organization of a party congress in 1989. The Almeyda branch, in contrast, had better disciplined and organized cadres after its experience with clandestine resistance, but it lacked mass affiliation at this stage of the transition. Personal interview with Nestor Ortíz, director of the Socialist Party membership campaign, Santiago, May 29, 1990. As the party consolidated its organization in the early 1990s and held internal elections for the party leadership, it became clear that this initial balance of forces was misleading and that the former Almeyda branch retained greater influence at the base level than the Núñez sector.

32. Escalona had been the leader of a military contingent that was formed within the Almeyda branch of the party in the mid-1980s, but this contingent, known as the Destacamento 5 de Abril, did not have the full support of the party hierarchy and never developed the force of the FPMR. Many of Escalona's followers resisted the process of unification with the Núñez branch, but ultimately Escalona acknowledged that if Socialists wanted to prevent the Christian Democrats "from exercising hegemony over the plurality of democratic forces," it was necessary "to have the weight of a unified Socialist Party." Personal interview, Santiago, January 10, 1990. On the other side, some moderates from the Núñez sector thought their party should have delayed reunification until their predominance over the *Almeydistas* was assured, since they were confident their party was in ascendance.

33. On the factional tendencies and internal politics within the Socialist Party, see Lucy Davila, "Partido Socialista: De nuevo al rincón," *Hoy*, November 13–19, 1995.

34. This alliance included the Almeyda Socialists, who ran candi-

dates on the Concertación slate as well as that of the Communist-led pact.

35. The Communist Party was able to get the more than 55,000 signatures required for legalization in 1990, but most of these were sympathizers rather than members. In 1991 the party claimed a membership of some 20,000 individuals who were organized into 2,000 active cells that met weekly and paid regular dues. Increasingly, cells had a territorial basis, reflecting the party's organizational work in *poblaciones* and the relative demise of workplace cells. Interview with Victor Contreras, member of the party's task force on computation and membership, Santiago, August 19, 1991.

36. See, for example, "USSR: Renovación a fondo," *El Siglo*, April 1–15, 1987, p. 14.

37. As stated by Gladys Marín, "we look with greater sympathy and closeness to what occurs in Latin America. Frankly, for us, what occurs in Cuba interprets our situation much better, because it is Latin American." Interview in *APSI*, August 15–21, 1990, p. 15.

38. The critical perspectives of the party's moderate wing are captured in Guastavino 1990.

39. Former Central Committee member Fanny Pollarolo said she was shocked by the personal attacks of the party hierarchy against the former congressman and dissident Luis Guastavino at the party's national congress in May 1989. When the hierarchy sanctioned Guastavino for taking his criticisms public the following year, Pollarolo resigned from the Central Committee and helped lead a large exodus from the party, claiming that it was an "antidemocratic machine" that was "absolutely closed" to debate about the changes taking place in Chile and the world. Personal interview, Santiago, August 21, 1991.

40. Another prominent dissident, Patricio Hales, who had served as the party's public spokesperson during the early 1980s, said the apparatus blocked him from expressing his criticisms within regular party channels and told his cell he could not serve as a delegate to its local committee before the 1989 party congress. Personal interview, Santiago, August 17, 1993.

41. During its first year, the PDI attracted some 600 "adherents" and another 1,200 "episodic" participants, about 90 percent of whom came from the Communist Party. Interview with Carlos Fuchslocher, member of the National Council of Organization of the PDI, Santiago, August 21, 1991.

42. The binomial system created electoral districts with two representatives; a party or electoral pact could gain both seats in a district by doubling the percentage of the vote received by the next largest party or pact. Besides creating strong incentives to form electoral alliances, the

practical effect of this system in Chile's "three-thirds" polity was a highly disproportional pattern of representation that gave the minority Rightist coalition almost as many seats as the majoritarian Concertación, while completely excluding the Communist Party and its allies, who obtained 15 to 20 percent of the vote in several districts but could not achieve representation because of the narrowness of their electoral coalition. For an analysis of the skewed and potentially volatile patterns of representation that result from this system, see Siavelis and Valenzuela 1996.

43. Opinion polls showed widespread antipathy for the more violent and confrontational forms of protest, and less than 50 percent of the population supported even nonviolent forms of protest such as strikes, marches, demonstrations, and the banging of pots. See Huneeus 1987: 173.

44. See ibid., esp. chap. 6.

45. Indeed, the process of socialist renovation included proposals for organizational as well as ideological and strategic change to break definitively with Leninist norms and make the Socialist Party more open, pluralistic, and inclusive; see Garretón 1985.

46. The new vision of the PPD is spelled out in *¿Qué es el PPD?*, 1989. There is as yet no major study of the PPD in English; for an insightful overview, see Plumb 1995.

47. In 1992 municipal elections, the Socialist-PPD subpact within the Concertación garnered 17 percent of the vote nationwide, of which slightly more than half was accounted for by the PPD. In 1993 congressional elections the subpact increased to 24 percent of the vote, with the Socialists accounting for slightly more than half the total. The two parties claimed 22.9 percent of the vote in the 1996 municipal elections, with the PPD winning 11.8 percent and the Socialists 11.1 percent.

48. The rationale for greater organizational flexibility and a reconceptualization of party membership is spelled out in Almeyda 1991: 35–36. See also Arrate 1994: chap. 6.

49. For an analysis of this effort to control and demobilize the CUP, see Oxhorn 1994: 59–60.

50. Even the more radical sectors of the Almeyda party recognized the tactical successes of the Núñez branch. Congressional deputy Camilo Escalona, for example, said the Almeyda Socialists committed a "grave error" in not having founded an instrumental party like the PPD earlier; this error created new organizational space for the Núñez branch and allowed it to "gain in the social and political struggle" at a time when it "did not have the same dimensions that we did." Personal interview, Santiago, January 10, 1990.

51. The elaborate efforts of the Pinochet regime to tie the hands of the new democratic government are dissected in Loveman 1991. See also Ensalaco 1995.

52. As stated by Socialist senator Hernan Vodánovic: "You cannot be in the government and agitate social demands; it is one or the other. . . . When you are leaving a dictatorship, the maximum value is not economic but political. And the maximum value of the first democratic government is not to do the most it possibly can but to deliver power to a second democratic government in a free election. . . . The government of Aylwin will be successful if in 1993 there are new elections and the winner is someone who is not from the Right." Personal interview, Santiago, January 25, 1990.

53. The concept of reserve domains is analyzed in Valenzuela 1992: 64–66.

54. As argued by Linz and Stepan (1996: chap. 13), the Chilean military regime was unusually successful in implanting constitutional constraints on the incoming democratic government, thus ensuring relatively high levels of continuity with the authoritarian project.

55. Munck and Skalnik Leff 1997: 346.

56. See Cardoso 1986.

57. Following a purge of the Air Force command in 1978, Pinochet wielded extraordinary personal control over the armed forces and the governing military junta; see Remmer 1989 or Arriagada 1985. The staunch support of Chilean capitalists for the military regime and its neoliberal model is analyzed in Silva 1996; Frieden 1991: chap. 5; and Campero 1995.

58. The Chilean case closely conforms to the influential model of democratic transitions outlined by Rustow (1970), who argued that democratization is most likely to occur in response to a deadlock between contending forces, none of which is capable of imposing its preferred political order against the interests of other actors.

59. These constitutional reforms are analyzed in Ensalaco 1994. For an overview of the limitations of the 1980 constitution, see Maira 1988.

60. These restrictions are further detailed in Loveman 1991.

61. Military prerogatives are discussed in Stepan 1988.

62. See the interview with German Correa published in *Hoy*, June 21–27, 1993, p. 23.

63. This report, generally known as the "Rettig Report" after the chair of the commission, identified 1,158 persons killed and another 957 missing during the period of authoritarian rule. See *Síntesis del informe de la Comisión Nacional de Verdad y Reconciliación*, p. 92.

64. For a revealing analysis of the judiciary's abdication of respon-

sibility for defending human rights under the dictatorship, see Constable and Valenzuela 1991: chap. 5. Following the regime transition, several military officials were prosecuted for human rights violations that were exempted from the amnesty law. In the most prominent case, the Supreme Court ruled in May 1995 that the two top officials of Pinochet's secret police force, Retired General Marcelo Contreras and Brigadier General Pedro Espinoza, were guilty of plotting the assassination of Allende's former foreign minister, Orlando Letelier, who was killed in a car bomb in Washington, D.C., in 1976. Contreras and Espinoza were sentenced to seven and six years in prison, respectively. After resisting arrest with tacit military support, Espinoza was detained and began serving his sentence in June 1995 in a special prison facility built for military officials convicted of human rights violations. Contreras resisted arrest by taking refuge in a military hospital, thus posing a flagrant challenge to the constitutional authority of Chile's civilian government. He finally began serving his term in the special prison facilities in October 1995.

65. For a leading critique by a prominent Christian Democratic economist and the future minister of finance under Aylwin, see Foxley 1983. For a Socialist perspective, see Lagos 1987 or Guardia Basso 1986.

66. See the 1983 essay reprinted as Lagos 1991: 187–88.

67. See the data in Vergara 1994: 239.

68. See CEPAL 1991: 110–11.

69. Marcel and Solimano 1994: 219.

70. See Flisfisch 1991.

71. Speech by Ricardo Núñez before the Social Union of Christian Managers and Executives, Santiago, July 17, 1986.

72. For a general overview of the new government's economic strategy, see Ominami 1991.

73. The politics of this tax reform are explained in Boylan 1996. A new round of negotiations in 1993 led to an agreement to maintain the value-added tax at 18 percent through 1995, then to reduce it back to 16 percent. The Frei government, however, invoked its right to maintain the higher rate into 1996. See *El Mercurio Internacional*, August 3–9, 1995, p. 1.

74. The redistributive policies of the Aylwin government are detailed in Weyland 1997.

75. Data are taken from the statistical annex in *Economía y trabajo en Chile, 1993–1994*, pp. 212, 214, and 218.

76. Calculated from ibid., pp. 221 and 224.

77. *El Mercurio Internacional*, August 10–16, 1995, p. 5.

78. Mañuel Silva G., "Distribución del ingreso en Chile: Una torta difícil de repartir," *El Mercurio*, November 30, 1996, p. D1.

79. See *From Plan to Market*, 1996, pp. 196–97.

80. Hardy 1997: 121.

81. Early efforts at "social concertation" are analyzed in Fortunatti 1991.

82. The acceptance of a market economy reflected the ideological moderation that had taken place within the ranks of the labor movement under the dictatorship, as well as its limited political leverage following the economic reforms and social transformations of the military regime. For an analysis of these changes and how they shaped the role of the labor movement in Chile's regime transition, see Drake 1996: chap. 6.

83. See Rojas Miño 1991 and Herrera 1992.

84. Hardy 1997: 130.

85. See Rafael Otano's report on CPC leader José Antonio Guzman, "El Gendarme del modelo," *APSI*, April 3–16, 1996, pp. 22–25. Guzman's predecessor, Mañuel Feliú, was considered to be more amenable to social concertation.

86. See Frías Fernández 1993.

87. The discontents of organized labor are expressed in an interview with then CUT president and Christian Democratic labor leader Mañuel Bustos, who insisted on characterizing the government of the Concertación as being of the "center-right"; see *Hoy*, July 11–17, 1994, pp. 24–28.

88. On the importance of centralized representative organizations for social bargaining, see Weyland 1997: 52–59.

89. For a general overview of corporatist arrangements in Western Europe, see Lehmbruch and Schmitter 1982.

90. The contributions of encompassing organizations to the provision of collective goods are discussed in Olson 1986.

91. See Frías Fernández 1993.

92. Francisco Dagnino, "Subiendose a la vereda: Los avances del PC," *Hoy*, April 12–18, 1996, p. 7.

93. Guardia Basso 1993: 40.

94. Díaz 1993: 5.

95. Personal interview with Alvaro Díaz, a leading Socialist economist and the executive director of the Program on Technological Innovation and Development at Chile's Ministry of the Economy, Santiago, August 13, 1993.

96. See *Propuesta programática de los Socialistas*, 1992.

97. Statistical Annex, *Economía y trabajo en Chile, 1993–1994*, p. 214.

98. Ibid., p. 218.   99. Díaz 1993: 23.

100. Márquez Belloni 1994: 135.   101. Echenique 1990: 153.

102. Venegas 1993: 62.
103. See Díaz 1990.
104. Echenique 1990: 146.
105. Statistical annex in *Economía y trabajo en Chile, 1993–1994*, p. 230.
106. Campero 1994: 257.
107. The housing policies of the new government are analyzed in Urmeneta 1994.
108. Del Pino 1993: 229.
109. For a compelling analysis of the transformation of collective action in urban popular sectors, see Fitzsimmons 1995.
110. For an analysis of the challenges faced by OEPs, see Petras, Leiva, and Veltmeyer 1994: 125–128.
111. Del Pino 1994.
112. For a discussion of the low levels of participation, see Moulian 1997.
113. The enduring constraints to popular collective action are analyzed in Garretón 1997.
114. These changes in Chile are discussed in Baño 1994: 129–32.
115. Calculated from data provided in *El Mercurio*, October 29, 1996, p. A1.
116. The Concertación could more easily double the vote of the Right in many districts and thus capture both congressional seats at stake if it could add the votes of the Communist Party—presuming, of course, that the governing alliance did not lose more votes to the Right than it picked up to the Left. As Lowden points out (1995: 43), the Christian Democrats have apparently calculated that this trade-off would not pay net electoral dividends.
117. Personal interview with Communist Party secretary general Volodia Teitelboim, Santiago, July 7, 1994.
118. Personal interview with Ricardo Lagos, Santiago, August 16, 1993.
119. Fox 1993.
120. An especially insightful analysis of this "genetic code" can be found in Moulian 1994.

CHAPTER 6 *Party Militants and Political Change*

1. For a revealing portrait of change and continuity in the political identities of leftist political elites in Chile, see Hite 1996.
2. For a critical analysis of fundamentalist tendencies in the Latin American Left, see Rodríguez Elizondo 1990.
3. On the issue of value change within the Left, see the essay "Los ideales y la izquierda: La racionalidad del cambio," in Flisfisch 1987.

4. This particular militant, who came from a family with deep roots in the Communist Party, eventually withdrew from the party and ceased active participation in politics. He later told the author, only partly in jest, that his disillusionment and abandonment of the party had provoked such a personal identity crisis that he had even gone to talk to a Catholic priest about his problems—a difficult admission for someone with his background.

CHAPTER 7 *Social Mobilization and the Rise of the Left*

1. As Peru's crisis deepened in the late 1980s, Alfonso Barrantes—the former IU mayor of Lima—led public opinion polls for the 1990 presidential race until the division of the leftist coalition undermined his prospects. For example, in a March 1988 poll, Barrantes was preferred by 36 percent of the electorate, followed by Mario Vargas Llosa of the rightist coalition FREDEMO with 25 percent and Aprista candidate Luis Alva Castro with 22 percent. See *Debate* 10 (March–April 1988): 10.

2. Fujimori's public approval rating jumped from 59 percent to 82 percent during the week of this *autogolpe;* see Apoyo S. A. 1992: 8. Analyses of this support can be found in Balbi 1992 and Conaghan 1995.

3. Peru has one of the strongest populist traditions in Latin America; for a leading study of *Aprismo* and other expressions of populism in Peru, see Stein 1980.

4. Technically, the Alianza Popular Revolucionaria Americana (APRA) was founded by Haya de la Torre in 1924 as a continent-wide, Latin American revolutionary and anti-imperialist alliance. Its Peruvian branch, the Partido Aprista Peruano (PAP), was founded in 1928 and goes by the name of APRA in Peru.

5. For insight into the early principles of Haya de la Torre and APRA, see Haya de la Torre 1986.

6. In particular, the hostility of the armed forces was provoked by a 1932 uprising in the northern coastal city of Trujillo, an *Aprista* stronghold, and by the involvement of APRA youth in a 1948 naval rebellion in the port of Callao. Both of these incidents resulted in prolonged periods of political repression and clandestinity.

7. For a history of Peru's labor organizations, see Sulmont 1980.

8. See Cotler 1978: chaps. 6 and 7.

9. Mariátegui (1971) is widely recognized as a classic Marxist analysis of class and ethnicity in Latin America.

10. In particular, Mariátegui emphasized the class character of the socialist project in Peru, and he challenged Haya de la Torre's faith in the progressive and nationalist character of the middle classes and the

bourgeoisie, thus anticipating by some 40 years the dependency theory critiques of orthodox Marxism. Additionally, he criticized Haya de la Torre's personalistic or *caudillista* style of leadership and his 1928 decision to construct an Aprista party rather than maintain a broader national and anti-imperialist front. See Franco 1981: chap. 3.

11. On the origins and development of the PCP, see Bernales 1987: Part 1.

12. The Velasco regime encouraged the strengthening of the CGTP as a counterpart to the APRA-controlled CTP federation, reflecting the military's congenital antipathy for APRA.

13. Following this division, the pro-Soviet party came to be known as the PCP-Unidad (PCP-U).

14. The powerful peasant movement in La Convención is discussed in Paige 1975: chap. 3.

15. For a fictional account of the Peruvian Trotskyist movement that provides a searing indictment of its factionalism and sectarianism, see Vargas Llosa 1986. For a factual account, see Alexander 1973: chap. 8.

16. See Guevara 1961.

17. For an overview of the MIR's guerrilla experience, see Gott 1978: Part 4. The MIR's faith in the capacity of an armed vanguard to create the subjective conditions for popular insurrection can be seen in de la Puente Uceda 1965.

18. Béjar subsequently worked for the Velasco regime after spending time in prison and eventually became the editor of the highly regarded journal *Socialismo y Participación*. For a perceptive and self-critical account of the ELN's guerrilla experience, see Béjar Rivera 1969.

19. The PCR was led by Mañuel Dammert, Santiago Pedraglio, and Augustín Haya de la Torre and had its roots in the radicalized Catholic youth movement. Dammert's group published the influential magazine *Crítica Marxista-Leninista*, and after a brief period of participation in the MIR it joined the VR in 1972, only to leave the party two years later to establish an independent organization.

20. For a detailed, though highly partisan, overview of this process of fragmentation written by a leader of the VR, see Letts 1981, esp. chaps. 2–5.

21. A group known as Acción Popular Socialista (APS) broke off from President Belaunde's Acción Popular party in 1968 and subsequently supported the reforms of the Velasco regime. Another party known as the Partido Socialista Revolucionario (PSR) was created in 1976 by a group of intellectuals and military officials who had participated in the Velasco regime. Both of these small parties eventually became members of the IU coalition in the 1980s, with the APS par-

ticipating under the name of Acción Política Socialista. These groups were minor actors within the IU, however, and wielded influence largely through the activities of prominent leaders (the senators Enrique Bernales of the PSR and Gustavo Mohme of the APS) rather than through the strength of their party organizations or mass constituencies, which were minimal.

22. The military government led by Velasco came to power in October 1968 in a coup that toppled the elected government of Belaunde, and it was motivated in part by frustration with the slow pace of promised reforms under the democratic regime. In marked contrast to the conservative national security dictatorships across Latin America during this time period, the Velasco regime supported popular mobilization and redistributive socioeconomic reforms. Analyses of the Velasco regime can be found in Stepan 1978; Lowenthal 1975; McClintock and Lowenthal 1983; and Gorman 1982.

23. Balbi 1989: 44.

24. Stephens 1983: 61, 67. The growth of the labor movement is also analyzed in Scurrah and Esteves 1982.

25. See Balbi 1989: chaps. 1 and 2, or Parodi 1986: chaps. 2 and 3.

26. See Paige 1975: chap. 3.

27. McClintock 1982: 136.

28. McClintock 1981: 62–63.

29. The removal of these constraints was advantageous to the organizing efforts of the Shining Path in the province of Ayacucho; see McClintock 1989: 73–74.

30. Matos Mar 1984: 72.

31. For the peasantry, see McClintock 1981: chap. 3. For the labor movement, see Balbi 1989: chap. 1. For urban popular sectors, see Collier 1976; Dietz 1980; or Leeds and Leeds 1974.

32. See Dietz 1980: chaps. 7 and 8, or Stokes 1995a: chap. 3.

33. See Tovar Samanez 1982a or Hayworth 1985.

34. On the broader political impact of labor activists on urban popular movements, see Stokes 1995a: chap. 5, or Tovar Samanez 1982b: 33.

35. See Stephens 1983.

36. For overviews of some of the internal debates over how to relate to the military regime, see the SINAMOS publications *Vanguardia Revolucionaria* (1976) and *MIR: Movimiento de Izquierda Revolucionaria* (undated).

37. See, for example, the document of the PCR entitled *II Conferencia Nacional: Linea básica de la Revolución Peruana*, pp. 10–13. For an overview, see Pease García 1988: chap. 3.

38. Haya de la Torre capped his political career by being elected to the presidency of the new constituent assembly in 1978, but he died

before the 1980 general elections could provide him with the opportunity to fulfill his lifelong dream of winning the national presidency.

39. See the MIR document *Unidad Para la Revolución*, p. 1.

40. Ibid.

41. The faction Vanguardia Revolucionaria-El Proletario led by Javier Diez Canseco and Edmundo Murrugarra was a leading force in the UDP and later in the foundation of the PUM. The Partido Vanguardia Revolucionaria led by Ricardo Letts was also an early member of the UDP, although its tactical disputes with VR-El Proletario helped delay the New Left's unification for several more years.

42. The five organizations were the Frente Obrero, Campesino y Popular (FOCEP), a predominantly Trotskyist coalition which obtained 12.3 percent of the total vote behind the strong support for Hugo Blanco; the pro-Velasco Revolutionary Socialist Party, which obtained 6.6 percent of the vote; the Moscow-line Communist Party, which received 5.9 percent of the vote; the New Left UDP coalition, which obtained 4.6 percent; and the Frente Nacional de Trabajadores y Campesinos, which obtained 3.9 percent of the vote. Electoral data are taken from Tuesta Soldevilla 1987: 231.

43. A coalition of leftist parties including the Communist Party obtained 14 percent of the vote in a 1967 complementary election in Lima, but the Peruvian Left had never obtained more than 3 percent of the vote in a national election before 1978.

44. For an analysis of the role of the Left in the constituent assembly, see Nieto 1983: chap. 4.

45. See, for example, "Adonde Vá la 'Izquierda Responsable'?" *Amauta*, October 4, 1979, p. 2.

46. The PCP-Patria Roja was the principal force behind the creation of the Maoist front Unidad Nacional de Izquierda Revolucionaria (UNIR) in order to participate in the 1980 elections. In contrast, the Shining Path shifted from clandestine opposition to guerrilla warfare, symbolically launching its first armed operation in the department of Ayacucho by burning ballot boxes on election day in May 1980.

47. For an overview of the internal debates and divisions within the Left during this period, see the various articles in *Realidad* 2 (January 1980), or Tuesta Soldevilla 1979.

48. The strength of the IU in the poorest urban districts is analyzed in Tuesta Soldevilla 1989.

49. For an analysis of the opportunities provided by municipal governance, see Pease García 1989.

50. See Przeworski 1985: 10.

51. For a sketch of this revolutionary conception of municipal governance, see Delgado S. 1980.

52. See Americas Watch 1984. The tensions between political democracy and counterinsurgency are analyzed in Cornell and Roberts 1990.

53. Tovar S. 1986: 81.

54. See Pease García 1989, esp. chaps. 3 and 5, or Pease García 1986.

55. The experience of Villa El Salvador is analyzed in Mauceri 1996: chap. 6, and Burt and Espejo 1995.

56. For an overview of the *rondas*, see Starn 1992. The faith placed in the *rondas* by the Peruvian Left can be seen in Lopez 1986.

57. Under the administrations of Alan García and, more successfully, Alberto Fujimori, the government came to recognize the utility of *rondas* in the counterinsurgency campaign against the Shining Path. The political autonomy of many *rondas* began to erode as the government encouraged the military to coordinate their activities and provide them with weapons. On the militarization of the *rondas*, see Starn 1991.

58. The coordinating committee also included two independent, nonpartisan representatives. A major problem with this leadership model was that very small parties had equal representation on the coordinating committee with larger parties like the PUM and UNIR.

59. This national congress and the internal conflicts that disrupted the institutionalization of the IU are analyzed in Salcedo 1989.

60. The principal founders of the PUM were various factions of Vanguardia Revolucionaria, the MIR, and the Revolutionary Communist Party, which split in this process of organizational convergence. The PUM eventually incorporated significant Trotskyist sectors, including the legendary peasant organizer Hugo Blanco, who told the author he joined the party so as to belong to a larger and more influential organization. Personal interview, Lima, September 7, 1990.

61. A good outline of the PUM's positions can be found in the party document *Informe político: Crear, Forjar, y conquistar poder popular,* 1988.

CHAPTER 8 *Crisis, Polarization, and Collapse*

1. See the document *I Congreso Nacional de Izquierda Unida: Documentos y resoluciones,* p. 171.

2. See, for example, Ellner 1993: 17. Empirical work on Mexico suggests that economic hardship can be associated with leftist voting; see Brophy-Baermann 1994.

3. Castañeda 1990: 485.

4. On policy-oriented voting, see Kiewiet 1981. Remmer (1991b) has demonstrated that economic crises produced anti-incumbent voting

patterns throughout Latin America in the 1980s, but that it generally did not lead to policy-oriented voting on behalf of the Left.

5. The twists and turns of Peruvian economic policymaking in the midst of the deepening crisis are detailed in Conaghan and Malloy 1994.

6. On the rise of García and the rejuvenation of Aprista populism, see Sanborn 1991: chap. 8.

7. The collapse of García's heterodox program is analyzed in Pastor and Wise 1992.

8. For a good overview of the multifaceted character of the Peruvian crisis, see Stein and Monge 1988.

9. Degregori 1991b: 87.

10. *Perú: Compendio estadístico, 1991–92,* Vol. 1 (Lima: Dirección Técnica de Indicadores Económicos, 1992), p. 584.

11. Wilkie and Contreras 1992: 373.

12. *Perú: Compendio estadístico, 1993–1994,* Vol. 1 (Lima: Dirección Técnica de Indicadores Económicos, 1994), p. 458.

13. See Chávez O'Brien 1992: 20.

14. Matos Mar 1984: 63.

15. See Dietz 1985 and 1986–87, or Cameron 1994: chap. 2.

16. See Lobo 1982.

17. See Cameron 1994: chaps. 2 and 3; Franco 1991; and Tovar S. 1986.

18. The weakening of labor unions and changes in the labor market are discussed in Balbi 1997.

19. U.S. Department of State, 1995: 495.

20. See Parodi 1986: chap. 5, and Balbi 1989: chap. 4.

21. See Balbi 1997.

22. Balbi 1989: 111–22.

23. See Balbi 1997.

24. On changes in the countryside, see Hunefeldt 1997.

25. There are exceptions, most notably in the southern department of Puno, where peasant federations repeatedly clashed with cooperatives over land rights in the 1980s; see Rénique 1990.

26. See, for example, Przeworski 1985, or Laclau and Mouffe 1985.

27. Clientelistic practices continued through the 1980s alongside more radical, confrontational practices, even in lower-class communities that were bastions of leftist electoral support; see Stokes 1995a: chaps. 4 and 5.

28. See the spatial model of political identities in Cameron 1994: chap. 6.

29. This social fragmentation and segmented collectivism are analyzed in Pásara et al. 1991. See also Tovar S. 1986 and Ballón 1992.

30. See Tironi Barrios 1986: 14.

31. The case of the Lima lower-class district San Martin de Porres is instructive. The IU won the mayorship in 1980, but its first administration was plagued by conflicts between the mayor, a member of UNIR, and grass-roots organizations that were linked to the New Left predecessors of the PUM. Subsequent administrations were led by a mayor from the PUM, but he clashed with local PUM militants who accused him of manipulating social organizations to build a personal political base. By the end of the decade the mayor followed Barrantes in leaving the IU, social organizations had been widely deactivated, and the IU lost the municipality to the rightist coalition FREDEMO. See Calderón and Valdeavellano 1991: chap. 2.

32. These problems are discussed in Stokes 1995a: chap. 4.

33. These dominant personalities included the senators Javier Diez Canseco of the PUM, Jorge del Prado of the Communist Party, Enrique Bernales of the PSR, Gustavo Mohme of the APS, and Genaro Ledesma of FOCEP, along with congressional deputy Mañuel Dammert of the PCR. The top slots on the IU's parliamentary list were reserved for these party leaders, although open list voting allowed some reshuffling of candidates to take place. In reality, the "parties" of Bernales, Mohme, Ledesma, and Dammert were little more than personal vehicles for their respective leaders, with only the shell of an organization and no mass constituency.

34. Cited in *Resúmen Semanal*, March 2–8, 1990, p. 4.

35. See Cameron 1994: chap. 3.

36. The PUM's critical assessment of Barrantes's municipal administration was outlined in the party document "Los resultados del 14 de Abril y el reajuste de la táctica," pp. 8–17.

37. Ibid., pp. 11–12.

38. The latter was perhaps best captured in APRA's historic political slogan that "Solo el APRA salvará Peru" ("Only APRA will save Peru").

39. See the interview with Barrantes in *NACLA Report on the Americas* 20 (September–December 1986): 60.

40. See the PUM document "Afianzar las conquistas democráticas del pueblo," p. 13.

41. These arguments are made in Wiener 1987: chaps. 4 and 5.

42. Studies of political violence during this period include Instituto de Defensa Legal, *Perú 1989: En la espíral de violencia*, and Comisión Especial del Senado Sobre las Causas de la Violencia y Alternativas de Pacificación en el Perú, *Violencia y pacificación*.

43. *La República*, March 12, 1990, p. 4.

44. *Resúmen Semanal*, January 25–February 23, 1990, p. 8.

45. See, for example, *Resúmen Semanal*, November 11–17, 1988, p. 3, and January 12–18, 1990, p. 2.

46. *NACLA Report on the Americas*, 20 (September–December 1986): 59.

47. Personal interview with IU senator and PSR leader Enrique Bernales, Lima, September 18, 1990.

48. *La República*, March 8, 1989, p. 11.

49. Ibid.

50. See Mendoza F. and Velásquez Savatti 1988.

51. The PUM and UNIR dominated the IU's congressional delegation and together with the Communist Party led Peru's major labor, peasant, and shantytown organizations. In contrast, the two small IU parties that unequivocally backed Barrantes—the PSR and the PCR—had little presence in social organizations.

52. Barrantes, in fact, called on the PUM and UNIR to leave the IU if they believed in insurrection, saying that a coalition government which incorporated such political forces could never establish the necessary "unity of criteria." *Resúmen Semanal*, January 27–February 17, 1989, pp. 3–4.

53. *La República*, March 8, 1989, p. 10.

54. Declaration of the PUM, UNIR, and FOCEP, published in *La República*, November 4, 1988, p. 10.

55. *Peru Report* 3 (May 1989): B3–4.

56. See the PUM document *Perú 1989: Crísis y salida política*, p. 28.

57. Personal interview, Javier Diez Canseco, Lima, April 10, 1990.

58. In a candid admission, former PUM secretary general Eduardo Cáceres acknowledged that the party miscalculated its strength when it withdrew from the IU national directorate following the 1990 elections to chart an independent course. In particular, he thought the PUM failed to recognize how its organized social constituencies had evaporated under the impact of the crisis. Personal interview, Lima, June 29, 1994.

59. For example, in a personal interview in Lima on September 19, 1990, former senator Rolando Ames, a leader of the Christian Left, asserted that the PUM represented a "different political project." Ames, however, said it was imperative to retain the participation of the radical parties and their social bases for any democratic Left project to be successful; acknowledging the weakness of the moderate Left at the base level, Ames saw the PUM as a bulwark against the penetration of the Shining Path within popular movements, and expressed fear that alienated youth from the popular sectors would turn to the Shining Path if IU radicals were marginalized from the democratic process.

60. The internal conflicts had led to Barrantes's resignation as the IU

president in 1987 and his subsequent marginalization from the practical affairs of the alliance.

61. An instructive game-theoretic analysis of these factional positions and the eventual division of the IU can be found in Cameron 1994: chap. 5.

62. Barrantes was quick to point out that only 15,000 militants voted in the IU primary, compared to some 1.5 million that voted for him in the 1983 mayoral race; see *Resúmen Semanal*, September 22–28, 1989, p. 1.

63. The *Acuerdo Socialista* included the PSR, the PCR, and independent leftists backing Barrantes.

64. The IU's economic program is detailed in *Plan de gobierno de Izquierda Unida, 1990–1995*.

65. Personal interview with Senator Enrique Bernales, Lima, September 18, 1990.

66. These origins at the National University of San Cristóbal of Huamanga in Ayacucho are analyzed in Degregori 1990. Other insightful interpretations of the Shining Path phenomenon include Palmer 1994 and Gorriti Ellenbogen 1990.

67. See the closing speech of Diez Canseco at the VR's Third National Congress, published in *Tercer Congreso Nacional de Vanguardia Revolucionaria*, p. 8.

68. As stated by former PUM congressional deputy Ricardo Letts, although the "minority" leadership of the Shining Path was lost to dogmatism and intransigence, "a majority of those who are organized around this group can still be rescued"; see *Pagina Libre*, May 15, 1990, p. 13. For a broader analysis of the legal Left's ambiguity toward the issues of democracy and revolution, see Pásara 1990.

69. See Palmer 1994: 267.

70. See Burt 1997 for a fascinating and disturbing analysis of the Shining Path's penetration of Villa El Salvador. The Shining Path's urban strategy is also detailed in Degregori 1991a.

71. These "support organizations" are discussed in Tarazona-Sevillano 1994.

72. Burt 1997: 286.

73. The political motives behind the Shining Path's violence are analyzed in Marks 1994.

74. The tactics that allowed the Shining Path to build a base of support in Villa are described in Burt 1997.

75. This ideological moderation is discussed in Rochabrún Silva 1988 and Rospigliosi 1988.

76. Personal interview, Lima, September 12, 1990.

77. Ibid.

78. The dissident leaders declared that "we disagree with those that underestimate the struggle to form a government while privileging confrontation and the fortification of the [party] apparatuses." See *Resúmen Semanal*, September 30–October 6, 1988, p. 2. According to Siniezo Lopez, a prominent intellectual who broke with the PUM during this period, the moderate tendency was especially pronounced among intellectuals who entered the PUM by way of the old MIR, only to clash with the more radical dominant tendency in the party that came from Vanguardia Revolucionaria. The moderates not only thought the PUM should back Barrantes but also advocated a fundamental renovation of the party's ideological and organizational principles. Personal interview, Lima, September 12, 1990. For an influential statement of the political positions of these intellectual dissidents, see "Izquierda: Una Revolución Copérnica," 1985.

79. This latter schism reflected opposition to moderating tendencies that had emerged in the party leadership, as well as regional resentment of the political controls exercised by the national party apparatus. Personal interview with Eduardo Cáceres, Lima, June 29, 1994.

80. See the public opinion survey in Luis Fernán Cisneros C., "Entre la ira y la paz," *Debate* 15 (September–October 1992): 36.

81. Personal interview with Javier Diez Canseco, Lima, April 10, 1990.

82. The crisis in the Soviet bloc exploded shortly before the 1990 elections, undermining public confidence in all sectors of the Peruvian Left. As a loyal defender of Soviet communism, the Peruvian Communist Party was the most directly affected; it was weakened in its efforts to mediate between the PUM and Barrantes and was able to elect only one senator and no deputies in the 1990 elections, compared to two senators and eight deputies in 1985.

83. Castañeda 1993: 172.

84. For analyses of this new variant of populism and its unconventional association with neoliberalism, see Roberts 1995; Weyland 1997; or Panfichi and Sanborn 1996. For analyses of more traditional forms of populism, see Conniff 1982.

85. On the generalized erosion of the Peruvian party system, see Cotler 1993 and 1995.

86. Cameron 1994: chap. 6.

87. For a broad overview of the Fujimori regime and its logic of governance, see Tuesta Soldevilla 1996.

88. The concept of delegative democracy was introduced in O'Donnell 1994a.

89. Tuesta Soldevilla 1994: 36.

90. These contradictions are discussed in Roberts 1995: 114–15.

CHAPTER 9 *Conclusion*

1. For an analysis of neoliberalism's theoretical and empirical limitations, see Przeworski 1993.
2. See, for example, Bresser Pereira, Maravall, and Przeworski 1993; Sunkel 1993; Castañeda 1993: chaps. 13–14; and Vellinga 1993.
3. In the words of Marx and Engels, "But not only has the bourgeoisie forged the weapons that bring death to itself; it has also called into existence the men who are to wield those weapons—the modern working class—the proletarians. . . . In the proportion as the bourgeoisie, i.e., capital, is developed, in the same proportion is the proletariat, the modern working class, developed." See "Manifesto of the Communist Party," reprinted in Tucker 1978: 478–79.
4. Dahl 1971: 15–16.
5. O'Donnell 1979: 314.
6. See Collier and Collier 1991.
7. See Scully 1995 or Siavelis and Valenzuela 1996 for analyses of the underlying continuities in the Chilean party system.
8. Variants of social democratic proposals for Latin America can be found in the works cited in note 2 above.
9. See, for example, Przeworski 1985; Przeworski and Sprague 1986; or Korpi 1983.
10. The challenges posed to social democracy by global economic integration are discussed in Scharpf 1991 and Wilde 1994.
11. The domestic-level policy constraints that arise from global financial markets are analyzed in Goodman and Pauly 1993.
12. See the special issue on the Left and municipal governance in *NACLA Report on the Americas* 29 (July–August 1995). See also Nylen 1997 and Winn and Ferro-Clérico 1997.
13. For an overview of the historical development of the PT and its linkages to the "new unionism" in Brazil, see Keck 1992.
14. By the early 1990s, in fact, one-third of the CUT's membership was drawn from rural unions; see Rodrigues 1994 for an analysis of the CUT and its articulatory practices.
15. Laclau and Mouffe 1985.
16. The eventual emergence of new collective responses to the self-regulating market is an underlying theme in Smith and Korzeniewicz 1997.
17. Kitschelt 1994.
18. See Huber, Rueschemeyer, and Stephens 1997.
19. O'Donnell and Schmitter 1986: 65–66.
20. On the crisis of Venezuela's pacted democracy, see McCoy et al. 1995.

Works Cited

Party Documents

Chile

SOCIALIST PARTY

"Carta abierta a los dirigentes y militantes de la izquierda chilena."
December 1986 (from Ricardo Núñez).
"Documento del Comité Central del Partido Socialista de Chile."
March 1974.
"Notas para la discusión." September 1986. Unpublished internal
party document written by José Joaquín Brunner.
"Propuesta programática de los Socialistas para el Segundo Gobierno
de la Concertación de Partidos por la Democracia." September 1992.
"Resoluciones del Tercer Pleno Nacional Extraordinario (Resolutivo)
del Partido Socialista de Chile." April 1979.
"Salida de Carlos Altamirano Orrego: Las razones de su relevo y expul-
sión." May 8, 1979. Political Commission of the Partido Socialista de
Chile.

COMMUNIST PARTY

"A la Democracia con todo." May 1989. Report from the Central Com-
mittee to the Fifteenth National Congress.
"A los presidentes y secretarios generales de los partidos de oposición
al régimen militar." September 1984.
"A los trabajadores de chile." September 1973.
"Al partido y al pueblo de Chile." December 1974.

"Llamamiento a la unidad y al combate." May 1982. Declaration of the Communist Party and seven allied groups.

"Llamamiento al pueblo de Chile a formar un Frente Antifascista para derrotar a la dictadura." May 1974.

"Patriotas: Solo unidos derrotaremos el fascismo." September 1986.

"La Revolución Chilena, la dictadura fascista y la lucha por derribarla y crear una nueva democracia." August 1977. Report to the Plenary Meeting of the Central Committee.

"Ultraizquierdismo, caballo de troya del imperialismo." September 1975.

Peru

"Afianzar las conquistas democráticas del pueblo." March 1987. Second Plenary Session of the Central Committee, Partido Unificado Mariateguista.

"Informe político: Crear, forjar y conquistar poder popular." June 1988. Second National Congress of the Partido Unificado Mariateguista.

I Congreso Nacional de Izquierda Unida: Documentos y resoluciones. Lima: Izquierda Unida, 1989.

"Perú 1989: Crísis y salida política." January 1989. Partido Unificado Mariateguista.

Plan de gobierno de Izquierda Unida, 1990–1995. Lima: Izquierda Unida, 1990.

"Los resultados de 14 de Abril y el reajuste de la táctica." May 1985. Second Plenary Session of the Central Committee of the Partido Unificado Mariateguista.

"Tercer Congreso Nacional de Vanguardia Revolucionaria." January 1983. Vanguardia Revolucionaria.

"II Conferencia Nacional: Línea básica de la revolución peruana." March 1979. Partido Comunista Revolucionario.

"Unidad para la revolución." October 1979. Movimiento de Izquierda Revolucionario.

Books, Articles, and Papers

Adrianzén, Alberto, and Eduardo Ballón. 1992. *Lo Popular en América Latina: ¿Una visión en crísis?* Lima: DESCO.

Alexander, Robert. 1973. *Trotskyism in Latin America.* Stanford: Hoover Institution Press.

Almeyda, Clodomiro. 1986. *Pensando en Chile.* Santiago: Terranova Editores.

———. 1987. *Reencuentro con mi vida.* Santiago: Las Ediciones del Ornitorrinco.

———. 1991. "Cambiar también la organización partidaria." *Convergencia* 19–20 (February–March): 32–37.
Almond, Gabriel A. 1991. "Rational Choice Theory and the Social Sciences." In *The Economic Approach to Politics: A Critical Reassessment of the Theory of Rational Action*, edited by Kristen Renwick Monroe. New York: Harper Collins.
Altamirano, Carlos. 1977. *Dialéctica de una derrota*. Mexico City: Siglo Veintiuno Editores.
Alvarez, Sonia E., and Arturo Escobar. 1992. "Conclusion: Theoretical and Political Horizons of Change in Contemporary Latin American Social Movements." In *The Making of Social Movements in Latin America: Identity, Strategy, and Democracy*, edited by Arturo Escobar and Sonia E. Alvarez. Boulder: Westview Press.
América Latina 80: Democracia y movimiento popular. 1981. Lima: DESCO.
Americas Watch. 1984. *Abdicating Democratic Authority: Human Rights in Peru*. New York: Americas Watch.
Anderson, Leslie. 1994. *The Political Ecology of the Modern Peasant: Calculation and Community*. Baltimore: Johns Hopkins University Press.
Angell, Alan. 1972. *Politics and the Labor Movement in Chile*. London: Oxford University Press.
———. 1996. "Incorporating the Left into Democratic Politics." In *Constructing Democratic Governance: Latin America and the Caribbean in the 1990s—Themes and Issues*, edited by Jorge I. Domínguez and Abraham F. Lowenthal. Baltimore: Johns Hopkins University Press.
Apoyo, S. A. 1992. *Informe de opinión*. September.
Aricó, José. 1988. *La Cola del diablo: Itinerario de Gramsci en América Latina*. Caracas: Editorial Nueva Sociedad.
———. 1989. "El Marxismo en América Latina: Ideas para abordar de otro modo una vieja cuestión." In *Socialismo, Autoritarismo, y Democracia*, edited by Fernando Calderón. Lima and Buenos Aires: Instituto de Estudios Peruanos and CLACSO.
Arrate, Jorge. 1983. *El socialismo chileno: Rescate y renovación*. Barcelona and Rotterdam: Instituto del Nuevo Chile.
———. 1985. *La Fuerza democrática de la idea socialista*. Barcelona and Santiago: Ediciones Documentas and Las Ediciones del Ornitorrinco.
———. 1994. *La Postrenovación: Nuevos desafíos del socialismo*. Santiago: Las Producciones del Ornitorrinco.
Arriagada, Genaro H. 1985. *La Política militar de Pinochet*. Santiago: Salesianos.
Arriagada Herrera, Genaro, and Claudio Orrego Vicuña. 1976. "La Teo-

ría: El concepto Leninista de la revolución." In *Leninismo y Democracia*, edited by Genaro Arriagada Herrera and Claudio Orrego Vicuña. Santiago: Ediciones Aconcagua.

Balbi, Cármen Rosa. 1989. *Identidad clasista en el sindicalismo*. Lima: DESCO.

——. 1991a. "Una inquietante encuesta de opinión." *Quehacer* 72 (July–August): 40–45.

——. 1991b. "Modernidad y progreso en el mundo informal." *Pretextos* 2 (February): 121–35.

——. 1992. "Del Golpe de 5 de Abril al CCD: Los Problemas de la transición a la democracia." *Pretextos* 3–4 (December): 41–61.

——. 1997. "Politics and Trade Unions." In *The Peruvian Labyrinth*, edited by Philip Mauceri and Maxwell A. Cameron. University Park: Pennsylvania State University Press.

Ballón, Eduardo. 1992. "Actores sociales y populares: Orientaciones y cambios." In *Lo Popular en América Latina: ¿Una visión en crísis?*, edited by Alberto Adrianzén and Eduardo Ballón. Lima: DESCO.

Baño, Rodrigo. 1994. "La Transformación económico-social de Chile contemporaneo." *Proposiciones* 24 (August): 129–32.

Barber, Benjamin. 1984. *Strong Democracy: Participatory Politics for a New Age*. Berkeley: University of California Press.

Bardhan, Pranab K., and John E. Roemer, eds. 1993. *Market Socialism: The Current Debate*. New York: Oxford University Press.

Barrera, Mañuel, and J. Samuel Valenzuela. 1986. "The Development of Labor Movement Opposition to the Military Regime." In *Military Rule in Chile: Dictatorship and Oppositions*, edited by J. Samuel Valenzuela and Arturo Valenzuela. Baltimore: Johns Hopkins University Press.

Barros, Robert. 1986. "The Left and Democracy: Recent Debates in Latin America." *Telos* 68 (Summer): 49–70.

Bascuñán Edwards, Carlos. 1990. *La Izquierda sin Allende*. Santiago: Grupo Editorial Planeta.

Basso, Alexis Guardia. 1986. "Del Fracaso neoliberal a los desafíos de la economía mixta." In *Siete ensayos sobre democracia y socialismo en Chile*. Santiago: Ediciones Documentas, 1986.

Beetham, David. 1992. "Liberal Democracy and the Limits of Democratization." *Political Studies* 40 (Special Issue): 40–53.

Béjar Rivera, Hector. 1969. *Perú 1965: Notes on a Guerrilla Experience*. New York: Monthly Review Press.

Bergquist, Charles. 1986. *Labor in Latin America: Comparative Essays on Chile, Argentina, Venezuela and Colombia*. Stanford: Stanford University Press.

Bermeo, Nancy. 1992. "Democracy and the Lessons of Dictatorship." *Comparative Politics* 24 (April): 273–91.

Bernales, Enrique. 1987. *Socialismo y nación*. Lima: Mesa Redonda Editores.

Bernstein, Edward. 1961. *Evolutionary Socialism: A Criticism and an Affirmation*, 4th ed. New York: Schocken Books.

Bitar, Sergio. 1980. *Transición, socialismo y democracia: La Experiencia chilena*. Mexico City: Siglo Veintiuno Editores.

Black, Jan Knippers. 1993. "Elections and Other Trivial Pursuits: Latin America and the New World Order." *Third World Quarterly* 14: 545–54.

Blanchard, Peter. 1982. *The Origins of the Peruvian Labor Movement, 1883–1919*. Pittsburgh: University of Pittsburgh Press.

Bollen, Kenneth A. 1991. "Political Democracy: Conceptual and Measurement Traps." In *On Measuring Democracy: Its Consequences and Concomitants*, edited by Alex Inkeles. New Brunswick, N.J.: Transaction Books.

Booth, John A. 1989. "Elections and Democracy in Central America: A Framework for Analysis." In *Elections and Democracy in Central America*, edited by John A. Booth and Mitchell A. Seligson. Chapel Hill: University of North Carolina Press.

Bowles, Samuel, and Herbert Gintis. 1986. *Democracy and Capitalism: Property, Community, and the Contradictions of Modern Social Thought*. New York: Basic Books.

Boylan, Delia M. 1996. "Taxation and Transition: The Politics of the 1990 Chilean Tax Reform." *Latin American Research Review* 31: 7–31.

Bresser Pereira, Luiz Carlos, José María Maravall, and Adam Przeworski. 1993. *Economic Reforms in New Democracies: A Social Democratic Approach*. New York: Cambridge University Press.

Brophy-Baermann, Michelle. 1994. "Economics and Elections: The Mexican Case." *Social Science Quarterly* 75 (March): 125–35.

Brunner, José Joaquín. 1990. "El Socialismo, los funcionarios y el mercado." *Crítica Social* 1 (May): 1–6.

Bulmer-Thomas, Victor, ed. 1996. *The New Economic Model in Latin America and Its Impact on Income Distribution and Poverty*. London: Institute of Latin American Studies.

Burt, Jo-Marie. 1997. "Political Violence and the Grassroots in Lima, Peru." In *The New Politics of Inequality in Latin America: Rethinking Participation and Representation*, edited by Douglas Chalmers, Carlos Vilas, Katherine Roberts Hite, Scott B. Martin, Kerianne Piester, and Monique Segarra. New York: Oxford University Press.

Burt, Jo-Marie, and Cesar Espejo. 1995. "The Struggles of a Self-Built Community." *NACLA Report on the Americas* 28 (January–February): 19–25.

Caballero, Mañuel. 1986. *Latin America and the Comintern.* Cambridge: Cambridge University Press.

Calderón, Fernando. 1995. *Movimientos sociales y política: La Década ochenta en Latinoamerica.* Mexico City: Siglo Veintiuno Editores.

Calderón, Fernando, and Elizabeth Jelin. 1987. *Clases y movimientos sociales en América Latina: Perspectivas y realidades.* Buenos Aires: CEDES.

Calderón, Fernando, Alejandro Piscitelli, and José Luis Reyna. 1992. "Social Movements: Actors, Theories, Expectations." In *The Making of Social Movements in Latin America: Identity, Strategy, and Democracy,* edited by Arturo Escobar and Sonia E. Alvarez. Boulder: Westview Press.

Calderón, Julio, and Rocío Valdeavellano. 1991. *Izquierda y democracia: Entre la utopia y la realidad.* Lima: Instituto de Desarrollo Urbano.

Cameron, Maxwell. 1994. *Democracy and Authoritarianism in Peru: Political Coalitions and Social Change.* New York: St. Martin's Press.

Campero, Guillermo. 1994. "Asalariado moderno y movimiento sindical: Hacia un nuevo modelo de acción?" *Proposiciones* 24 (August): 55–58.

———. 1995. "Entrepreneurs Under the Military Regime." In *The Struggle for Democracy in Chile,* edited by Paul W. Drake and Iván Jaksic. Lincoln: University of Nebraska Press.

Canel, Eduardo. 1992. "Democratization and the Decline of Urban Social Movements in Uruguay: A Political-Institutional Account." In *The Making of Social Movements in Latin America: Identity, Strategy, and Democracy,* edited by Arturo Escobar and Sonia E. Alvarez. Boulder: Westview Press.

Cardoso, Fernando Henrique. 1986. "Entrepreneurs and the Transition Process: The Brazilian Case." In *Transitions from Authoritarian Rule: Comparative Perspectives,* edited by Guillermo O'Donnell, Philippe C. Schmitter, and Laurence Whitehead. Baltimore: Johns Hopkins University Press.

Cardoso, Fernando Henrique, and Enzo Faletto. 1979. *Dependency and Development in Latin America.* Berkeley: University of California Press.

Carnoy, Martin. 1984. *The State and Political Theory.* Princeton: Princeton University Press.

Carr, Barry, and Steve Ellner, eds. 1993. *The Latin American Left: From the Fall of Allende to Perestroika.* Boulder: Westview Press.

Carvajal, Juan. 1981. "Acerca de la perspectiva insurreccional." *Cuadernos de Orientación Socialista* 9 (November): 39-56.

Castañeda, Jorge. 1990. "Latin America and the End of the Cold War." *World Policy Journal* 7 (Summer): 469-92.

———. 1993. *Utopia Unarmed: The Latin American Left After the Cold War.* New York: Random House.

Cavarozzi, Marcelo, and Mañuel Antonio Garretón, eds. 1989. *Muerte y resurrección: Los partidos políticos en el autoritarismo y las transiciones del Cono Sur.* Santiago: FLACSO.

Caviedes, César N. 1991. *Elections in Chile: The Road Toward Redemocratization.* Boulder: Lynne Rienner, 1991.

CEPAL. 1991. "Una estimación de la magnitud de la pobreza en Chile, 1987." *Colección Estudios CIEPLAN* 31 (March): 107-29.

Chalmers, Douglas A., Carlos M. Vilas, Katherine Hite, Scott B. Martin, Kerianne Piester, and Monique Segarra, eds. 1997. *The New Politics of Inequality in Latin America: Rethinking Participation and Representation.* New York: Oxford University Press.

Chang-Rodríguez, Eugenio. 1987. *Opciones políticas peruanas.* 2d ed. Trujillo, Peru: Editorial Normas Legales.

Chávez O'Brien, Eliana. 1992. "El mercado de trabajo y las nuevas tendencias en la estructura del empleo en el Peru." *Socialismo y Participación* 60 (December): 15-20.

Cohen, Carl. 1971. *Democracy.* Athens: University of Georgia Press.

Cohen, Jean. 1985. "Strategy or Identity: New Theoretical Paradigms and Contemporary Social Movements." *Social Research* 52 (Winter): 663-717.

Collier, David. 1976. *Squatters and Oligarchs: Authoritarian Rule and Policy Change in Peru.* Baltimore: Johns Hopkins University Press.

———, ed. 1979. *The New Authoritarianism in Latin America.* Princeton: Princeton University Press.

Collier, David, and Steven Levitsky. 1997. "Democracy with Adjectives: Conceptual Innovation in Comparative Research." *World Politics* 49 (April): 430-51.

Collier, Ruth Berins, and David Collier. 1991. *Shaping the Political Arena: Critical Junctures, the Labor Movement, and Regime Dynamics in Latin America.* Princeton: Princeton University Press.

Comisión Especial del Senado Sobre las Causas de la Violencia y Alternativas de Pacificación en el Péru. 1989. *Violencia y pacificación.* Lima: DESCO and La Comisión Andina de Juristas.

Conaghan, Catherine M. 1995. "Polls, Political Discourse, and the

Public Sphere: The Spin on Peru's Fuji-golpe." In *Latin America in Comparative Perspective: New Approaches to Methods and Analysis*, edited by Peter H. Smith. Boulder: Westview Press.

——. 1996. "A Deficit of Democratic Authenticity: Political Linkage and the Public in Andean Politics." *Studies in Comparative International Development* 31 (Fall): 32–55.

Conaghan, Catherine M., and James Malloy. 1994. *Unsettling Statecraft: Democracy and Neoliberalism in the Central Andes*. Pittsburgh: University of Pittsburgh Press.

Conniff, Michael L., ed. 1982. *Latin American Populism in Comparative Perspective*. Albuquerque: University of New Mexico Press.

Constable, Pamela, and Arturo Valenzuela. 1991. *A Nation of Enemies: Chile Under Pinochet*. New York: Norton.

Cornell, Angela, and Kenneth Roberts. 1990. "Democracy, Counterinsurgency, and Human Rights: The Case of Peru." *Human Rights Quarterly* 12 (November): 529–53.

Coser, Lewis. 1956. *The Functions of Social Conflict*. New York: Free Press.

Cotler, Julio. 1978. *Clases, Estado y nación en el Perú*. Lima: Instituto de Estudios Peruanos.

——. 1993. "Descomposición política y autoritarismo en el Perú." Documento de Trabajo 51. Lima: Instituto de Estudios Peruanos.

——. 1995. "Political Parties and the Problems of Democratic Consolidation in Peru." In *Building Democratic Institutions: Party Systems in Latin America*, edited by Scott Mainwaring and Timothy R. Scully. Stanford: Stanford University Press.

"La Crísis en el socialismo chileno." 1979. *Chile-America* 54–55 (June–July): 81–137.

Cunningham, Frank. 1987. *Democratic Theory and Socialism*. Cambridge: Cambridge University Press.

Dahl, Robert. 1971. *Polyarchy: Participation and Opposition*. New Haven: Yale University Press.

——. 1982. *Dilemmas of Pluralist Democracy*. New Haven: Yale University Press.

——. 1985. *Preface to Economic Democracy*. Berkeley: University of California Press.

——. 1989. *Democracy and Its Critics*. New Haven: Yale University Press.

Daire T., Alonso. 1988. "La Política del Partido Comunista desde la post-guerra a la Unidad Popular." In *El Partido Comunista en Chile*, edited by Augusto Varas. Santiago: CESOC-FLACSO.

Darién, Graco. 1985. "Enseñanzas teóricas de la revolución nicaraguense." *Araucaria de Chile* 31: 59–72.

De la Puente Uceda, Luis. 1965. "The Peruvian Revolution: Concepts and Perspectives." *Monthly Review* 17 (November): 12–25.

Debray, Regis. 1967. *Revolution in the Revolution?* New York: Monthly Review Press.

Degregori, Carlos Iván. 1990. *El Surgimiento de Sendero Luminoso: Ayacucho 1969–1979.* Lima: Instituto de Estudios Peruanos.

———. 1991a. "Al Filo de la Navaja: La estrategia urbana de Sendero." *Quehacer* 73 (September–October): 26–29.

———. 1991b. "El Aprendiz de Brujo y el Curandero Chino: Etnicidad, modernidad, y ciudadanía." In Carlos Ivan Degregori and Romeo Grompone, *Elecciones 1990: Demonios y redentores en el Nuevo Peru.* Lima: Instituto de Estudios Peruanos.

Del Campo, Julio Labastida Martín, ed. 1985. *Hegemonía y alternativas políticas en América Latina.* Mexico City: Siglo Veintiuno Editores.

Del Pino, Jaime. 1993. "Análysis de las organizaciones económicas populares, 1989–91." In *Economía y trabajo en Chile: Informe anual 1992–1993.* Santiago: Programa Economía y Trabajo.

———. 1994. "Organización popular y participación." In *Economía y trabajo en Chile: Informe anual 1993–1994.* Santiago: Programa Economía y Trabajo.

Delgado, Angel S. 1980. "Los Comunistas en las municipalidades." *Crítica Marxista-Leninista* 13 (December): 91–104.

DeShazo, Peter. 1983. *Urban Workers and Labor Unions in Chile, 1902–1927.* Madison: University of Wisconsin Press.

Deutsch, Karl. 1963. *The Nerves of Government: Models of Political Communication and Control.* London: Free Press of Glencoe.

Diamond, Larry, Juan J. Linz, and Seymour Martin Lipset, eds. 1989. *Democracy in Developing Countries: Latin America.* Boulder: Lynne Rienner.

Diamond, Larry, and Marc F. Plattner, eds. 1993. *The Global Resurgence of Democracy.* Baltimore: Johns Hopkins University Press.

Díaz, Alvaro. 1989. "La Reestructuración industrial autoritaria en Chile." *Proposiciones* 17: 14–35.

———. 1990. "Modernización autoritaria y régimen de empresa en Chile." *Proposiciones* 18: 54–69.

———. 1993. "Restructuring and the New Working Classes in Chile." Discussion Paper 47. Geneva: United Nations Research Institute.

Dietz, Henry A. 1980. *Poverty and Problem-Solving Under Military Rule: The Urban Poor in Lima, Peru.* Austin: University of Texas Press.

———. 1985. "Political Participation in the Barriadas: An Extension and Reexamination." *Comparative Political Studies* 18 (October): 323–55.

———. 1986–87. "Electoral Politics in Peru, 1978–1986." *Journal of Inter-American Studies and World Affairs* 28 (Winter): 139–63.

Dix, Robert. 1989. "Cleavage Structures and Party Systems in Latin America." *Comparative Politics* 22 (October): 23–37.

Domínguez, Jorge I., and Abraham F. Lowenthal, eds. 1996. *Constructing Democratic Governance: Latin America and the Caribbean in the 1990s*. Baltimore: Johns Hopkins University Press.

Drake, Paul W. 1978. *Socialism and Populism in Chile, 1932–1952*. Urbana: University of Illinois Press.

———. 1996. *Labor Movements and Dictatorships: The Southern Cone in Comparative Perspective*. Baltimore: Johns Hopkins University Press.

Drake, Paul, and Iván Jaksic, eds. 1995. *The Struggle for Democracy in Chile*. 2d ed. Lincoln: University of Nebraska Press.

Echenique, Jorge. 1990. "Las Dos Caras de la agricultura y las políticas posibles." *Proposiciones* 18 (January): 145–58.

Eckstein, Susan. 1989. *Power and Popular Protest: Latin American Social Movements*. Berkeley: University of California Press.

Economía y trabajo en Chile: Informe anual, 1993–1994. 1994. Santiago: Programa de Economía y Trabajo.

Edwards, Sebastian. 1995. *Crisis and Reform in Latin America: From Despair to Hope*. Oxford: Oxford University Press.

Ellner, Steve. 1993. "Introduction: The Changing Status of the Latin American Left in the Recent Past." In *The Latin American Left: From the Fall of Allende to Perestroika*, edited by Barry Carr and Steve Ellner. Boulder: Westview Press.

Ensalaco, Mark. 1994. "In with the New, Out with the Old: The Democratizing Impact of Constitutional Reform in Chile." *Journal of Latin American Studies* 26 (May): 409–29.

———. 1995. "Military Prerogatives and the Stalemate of Chilean Civil-Military Relations." *Armed Forces and Society* 21 (Winter): 255–70.

Escobar, Arturo, and Sonia E. Alvarez, eds. 1992. *The Making of Social Movements in Latin America: Identity, Strategy and Democracy*. Boulder: Westview Press.

Evers, Tilman. 1985. "Identity: The Hidden Side of Social Movements in Latin America." In *New Social Movements and the State in Latin America*, edited by David Slater. Amsterdam. CEDLA.

Fals-Borda, Orlando. 1992. "Social Movements and Political Power in Latin America." In *The Making of Social Movements in Latin America: Identity, Strategy and Democracy*, edited by Arturo Escobar and Sonia E. Alvarez. Boulder: Westview Press.

Faúndez, Julio. 1988. *Marxism and Democracy in Chile: From 1932 to the Fall of Allende*. New Haven: Yale University Press.

Ferree, Myra Marx. 1992. "The Political Context of Rationality: Rational Choice Theory and Resource Mobilization." In *Frontiers in Social Movement Theory*, edited by Aldon D. Morris and Carol Mc-Clurg Mueller. New Haven: Yale University Press.

Fitzsimmons, Tracy. 1995. "Paradoxes of Participation: Organizations and Democratization in Latin America." Ph.D. dissertation, Stanford University.

Fleet, Michael. 1985. *The Rise and Fall of Chilean Christian Democracy*. Princeton: Princeton University Press.

Flisfisch, Angel. 1987. *La Política como compromiso democrático*. Santiago: FLACSO.

———. 1991. "Estatismo, economía y democracia en la crísis actual del socialismo." In *Capitalismo, democracia y reformas*, edited by Norbert Lechner. Santiago: FLACSO.

———. 1994. "La Gestión estratégica de un proceso de transición y consolidación: El caso chileno." *Proposiciones* 25 (October): 20–33.

Fortunatti, Rodolfo. 1991. "Concertación social, una opportunidad histórica." In *Economía y trabajo en Chile: Informe anual 1990–1991*. Santiago: Programa de Economía y Trabajo.

Foweraker, Joe, and Ann L. Craig, eds. 1990. *Popular Movements and Political Change in Mexico*. Boulder: Lynne Rienner.

Fox, Jonathan. 1993. *The Politics of Food in Mexico: State Power and Social Mobilization*. Ithaca, N.Y.: Cornell University Press.

Foxley, Alejandro. 1983. *Latin American Experiments in Neoconservative Economics*. Berkeley: University of California Press.

———. 1986. "The Neoconservative Economic Experiment in Chile." In *Military Rule in Chile: Dictatorships and Oppositions*, edited by J. Samuel Valenzuela and Arturo Valenzuela. Baltimore: Johns Hopkins University Press.

Frías, Patricio. 1993. "Perspectivas de redefinicíon de la acción sindical." In *Economía y trabajo en Chile: Informe anual 1992–1993*. Santiago: Programa de Economía y Trabajo.

Franco, Carlos. 1981. *Del Marxismo Eurocéntrico al Marxismo Latinoamericano*. Lima: Centro de Estudios Para el Desarrollo y la Participación.

———. 1990. "Para la construcción de un régimen político democrático-participativo." In *Estratégias para el desarrollo de la democracia en Perú y América Latina*, edited by Julio Cotler. Lima: Instituto de Estudios Peruanos.

———. 1991. *Imagenes de la sociedad peruana: La otra modernidad*. Lima: Centro de Estudios para el Desarrollo y la Participación.

French-Davis, Ricardo. 1991. "Desarrollo económico y equidad en Chile: Herencias y desafios en el retorno a la democracia." *Colección Estudios CIEPLAN* 31 (March): 31–51.

Frieden, Jeffry A. 1991. *Debt, Development, and Democracy: Mod-

ern Political Economy and Latin America, 1965–1985. Princeton: Princeton University Press.

Friedman, Debra, and Doug McAdam. 1992. "Collective Identity and Activism: Networks, Choices, and the Life of a Social Movement." In *Frontiers of Social Movement Theory,* edited by Aldon D. Morris and Carol McClurg Mueller. New Haven: Yale University Press.

Fruhling, Hugo, and Myriam Waiser. 1992. *La Violencia contra el estado en Chile, 1976–1991.* Santiago: Centro de Estudios del Desarrollo.

Furci, Carmelo. 1984. *The Chilean Communist Party and the Road to Socialism.* London: ZED Books.

Gamero, Julio. 1990. "Sueldos y salarios: Caída en picada." *Quehacer* 66 (September–October): 11–13.

Garretón, Mañuel Antonio. 1985. "Partido y sociedad en un proyecto socialista." *Opciones* 7 (September–December): 182–90.

———. 1987. "En qué consistió la renovación socialista? Síntesis y evaluación de sus contenidos." In *La Renovación socialista: Balance y perspectivas de un proceso vigente.* Santiago: Ediciones Valentín Letelier.

———. 1989a. *The Chilean Political Process.* Boston: Unwin Hyman.

———. 1989b. "The Ideas of Socialist Renovation In Chile." *Rethinking Marxism* 2 (Summer): 8–39.

———. 1989c. "La Oposición política partidaria en el régimen militar chileno: Un proceso de aprendizaje para la transición." In *Muerte y resurrección: Los Partidos políticos en el autoritarismo y las transiciones del Cono Sur,* edited by Marcelo Cavarozzi and Mañuel Antonio Garretón. Santiago: FLACSO.

———. 1989d. "Popular Mobilization and the Military Regime in Chile: The Complexities of the Invisible Transition." In *Power and Popular Protest: Latin American Social Movements,* edited by Susan Eckstein. Berkeley: University of California Press.

———. 1997. "Los Desafíos de la profundización democrática." In *Chile 96: Análisis y opiniones.* Santiago: FLACSO.

Garretón, Mañuel Antonio, and Tomás Moulian. 1983. *La Unidad popular y el conflicto politico en Chile.* Santiago: Ediciones Minga.

Gay, Peter. 1952. *The Dilemma of Democratic Socialism: Edward Bernstein's Challenge to Marx.* New York: Columbia University Press.

Gay, Robert. 1994. *Popular Organization and Democracy in Rio de Janeiro.* Philadelphia: Temple University Press.

Gil, Federico G., Ricardo Lagos E., and Henry A. Landesberger, eds. 1979. *Chile at the Turning Point.* Philadelphia: Institute for the Study of Human Issues.

González, Eugenio. 1972. "Fundamentación teórica del programa del Partido Socialista." In *Pensamiento teórico y político del Partido Socialista de Chile*, edited by Julio César Jobet and Alejandro Chelén R. Santiago: Editora Quimantu.

Goodman, John B., and Louis W. Pauly. 1993. "The Obsolescence of Capital Controls? Economic Management in an Age of Global Markets." *World Politics* 46 (October): 50–82.

Gorman, Stephen M. 1982. *Post-Revolutionary Peru: The Politics of Transformation*. Boulder: Westview Press.

Gorriti Ellenbogen, Gustavo. 1990. *Sendero: Historia de la guerra milenaria en el Perú*. Lima: Editorial APOYO.

Gott, Richard. 1978. *Guerrilla Movements in Latin America*. London: Thomas Nelson.

Guardia Basso, Alexis. 1986. "Del fracaso neoliberal a los desafíos de la economía mixta." In *Siete ensayos sobre democracia y socialismo en Chile*. Santiago: Vector and Ediciones Documentas.

———. 1993. "Herencia económica y reconversión." In *Como cambiar al estado? Los casos de Chile y Peru*. Lima: Grupo Propuesta.

Guastavino, Luis. 1990. *Caen las catedrales*. Santiago: Editorial Hachette.

Guevara, Ernesto. 1961. *Guerrilla Warfare*. New York: Monthly Review Press.

Haggard, Stephan, and Robert R. Kaufman. 1995. *The Political Economy of Democratic Transitions*. Princeton: Princeton University Press.

Haggard, Stephan, and Steven B. Webb. 1994. *Voting for Reform: Democracy, Political Liberalization, and Economic Adjustment*. Oxford: Oxford University Press.

Hagopian, Francis. 1990. "Democracy by Undemocratic Means? Elites, Political Pacts and Regime Transition in Brazil." *Comparative Political Studies* 23 (July): 147–70.

Hardy, Clarisa. 1997. "Las Políticas sociales en Chile." In *Chile 96: Análisis y opiniones*. Santiago: FLACSO.

Harris, Richard L. 1992. *Marxism, Socialism, and Democracy in Latin America*. Boulder: Westview Press.

Haya de la Torre, Victor Raúl. 1986. *El Antiimperialismo y el APRA*. Lima: Ediciones LYDEA.

Hayworth, Nigel. 1985. "Political Transition and the Peruvian Labor Movement, 1968–1985." In *Labor Autonomy and the State in Latin America*, edited by Edward Epstein. Boston: Unwin Hyman.

Held, David. 1987. *Models of Democracy*. Stanford: Stanford University Press.

Hellman, Judith Adler. 1992. "The Study of New Social Movements in

Latin America and the Question of Autonomy." In *The Making of Social Movements in Latin America: Identity, Strategy, and Democracy,* edited by Arturo Escobar and Sonia E. Alvarez. Boulder: Westview Press.

Herrera, Gonzalo. 1992. "La Negociación colectiva: Eje de la acción sindical." *Economía y trabajo en Chile: Informe anual 1990–1991.* Santiago: Programa Economía y Trabajo.

Higley, John, and Richard Gunther, eds. 1992. *Elites and Democratic Consolidation in Latin America and Southern Europe.* Cambridge: Cambridge University Press.

Hirschman, Albert O. 1970. *Exit, Voice, and Loyalty.* Cambridge, Mass.: Harvard University Press.

Hite, Katherine. 1996. "The Formation and Transformation of Political Identity: Leaders of the Chilean Left, 1968–1990." *Journal of Latin American Studies* 28: 299–328.

Huber, Evelyne, Dietrich Rueschemeyer, and John D. Stephens. 1997. "The Paradoxes of Contemporary Democracy: Formal, Participatory, and Social Dimensions." *Comparative Politics* 29 (April): 323–42.

Huneeus, Carlos. 1987. *Los Chilenos y la política: Cambio y continuidad en el autoritarismo.* Santiago: Centro de Estudios de la Realidad Contemporanea and Instituto Chileno de Estudios Humanísticos.

Hunefeldt, Christine. 1997. "The Agrarian Landscape: Enterprises, Producers, and Peasant Communities." In *The Peruvian Labyrinth,* edited by Philip Mauceri and Maxwell A. Cameron. University Park: Pennsylvania State University Press.

Huntington, Samuel P. 1991. *The Third Wave: Democratization in the Late 20th Century.* Norman: University of Oklahoma Press.

"Izquierda: Una revolución copérnica." 1985. *El Zorro de Abajo* 3 (November–December): 3–9.

Jaquette, Jane, ed. 1994. *The Women's Movement in Latin America: Participation and Democracy,* 2d ed. Boulder: Westview Press.

Jobet, Julio César. 1987. *Historia del Partido Socialista de Chile.* 2d ed. Santiago: Ediciones Documentas.

Jobet, Julio César, and Alejandro Chelén R., eds. 1972. *Pensamiento teórico y político del Partido Socialista de Chile.* Santiago: Editora Nacional Quimantu.

Karl, Terry Lynn. 1986. "Petroleum and Political Pacts: The Transition to Democracy in Venezuela." In *Transitions from Authoritarian Rule: Latin America,* edited by Guillermo O'Donnell, Philippe C. Schmitter, and Laurence Whitehead. Baltimore: Johns Hopkins University Press.

———. 1990. "Dilemmas of Democratization in Latin America." *Comparative Politics* 23 (October): 1–22.

Keck, Margaret. 1992. *The Workers' Party and Democratization in Brazil*. New Haven: Yale University Press.

Kiewiet, D. Roderick. 1981. "Policy-Oriented Voting in Response to Economic Issues." *American Political Science Review* 75 (June): 448–59.

Kirchheimer, Otto. 1966. "The Transformation of the Western European Party Systems." In *Political Parties and Political Development*, edited by Joseph LaPolombara and Myron Weiner. Princeton: Princeton University Press.

Kitschelt, Herbert. 1994. *The Transformation of European Social Democracy*. Cambridge: Cambridge University Press.

Klandermans, Bert. 1992. "The Social Construction of Protest and Multiorganizational Fields." In *Frontiers of Social Movement Theory*, edited by Aldon D. Morris and Carol McClurg Mueller. New Haven: Yale University Press.

Korpi, Walter. 1983. *The Democratic Class Struggle*. London: Routledge & Kegan Paul.

La Renovacíon socialista: Balance y perspectivas de un proceso vigente. 1987. Santiago: Ediciones Valentín Letelier.

Laclau, Ernesto. 1985. "New Social Movements and the Plurality of the Social." In *New Social Movements and the State in Latin America*, edited by David Slater. Amsterdam: CEDLA.

Laclau, Ernesto, and Chantel Mouffe. 1985. *Hegemony and Socialist Strategy*. London: Verso.

Lagos, Ricardo. 1985. *Democracia para Chile: Proposiciones de un socialista*. Santiago: Pehuen Editores.

——. 1987. *Hacia la democracia*. Santiago: Ediciones Documentas.

——. 1991. "Chile: Los grandes temas y tareas de la reconstrucción." In *Socialismo: 10 Años de Renovación*, Vol. 2, edited by Ricardo Núñez. Santiago: Las Ediciones del Ornitorrinco.

Lechner, Norbert. 1982. *Qué significa hacer política?* Lima: DESCO.

——. 1988. *Los Patios interiores de la democracia*. Santiago: FLACSO.

Leeds, Anthony, and Elizabeth Leeds. 1974. "Accounting for Behavioral Differences: Three Political Systems and the Responses of Squatters in Brazil, Peru, and Chile." In *The City in Comparative Perspective*, edited by John Walton and Louis H. Masotti. New York: Sage.

Lehmbruch, Gerhard, and Philippe Schmitter, eds. 1982. *Patterns of Corporatist Policymaking*. Beverly Hills: Sage.

Letts, Ricardo. 1981. *La Izquierda peruana: Organizaciones y tendencias*. Lima: Mosca Azul Editores.

Levitsky, Steven. 1995. "Populism Is Dead! Long Live the Populist Party! Party Adaptation Through Coalitional Realignment in Peronist Argentina." Paper presented at the Nineteenth International

Congress of the Latin American Studies Association, Washington, D.C., September 28–30.

Lichbach, Mark Irving. 1995. *The Rebel's Dilemma*. Ann Arbor: University of Michigan Press.

Lijphart, Arend. 1977. *Democracy in Plural Societies: A Comparative Exploration*. New Haven: Yale University Press.

Lindblom, Charles. 1977. *Politics and Markets*. New York: Free Press.

Linz, Juan J., and Alfred Stepan. 1996. *Problems of Democratic Transition and Consolidation: Southern Europe, South America, and Post-Communist Europe*. Baltimore: Johns Hopkins University Press.

Lipset, Seymour Martin. 1960. *Political Man: The Social Bases of Politics*. New York: Doubleday.

Lipset, Seymour Martin, and Stein Rokkan. 1967. "Cleavage Structures, Party Systems, and Voter Alignments: An Introduction." In *Party Systems and Voter Alignments: Cross-National Perspectives*, edited by Seymour Martin Lipset and Stein Rokkan. New York: Free Press.

Lobo, Susan. 1982. *A House of My Own: Social Organization in the Squatter Settlements of Lima, Peru*. Tucson: University of Arizona Press.

Lopez, Siniezo. 1986. "La Revolución de los machetes." *El Zorro de Abajo* 4 (March): 19–21.

Loveman, Brian. 1991. "Misión Cumplida? Civil Military Relations and the Chilean Political Transition." *Journal of Interamerican Studies and World Affairs* 33 (Fall): 35–74.

———. 1994. "Protected Democracies and Military Guardianship: Political Transitions in Latin America, 1979–1993." *Journal of Interamerican Studies and World Affairs* 36 (Summer): 105–89.

Lowden, Pamela. 1995. "What Is Left of the Left in Chile?" In *Neoliberalism with a Human Face? The Politics and Economics of the Chilean Model*, edited by David E. Hojman. Liverpool: Institute of Latin American Studies, University of Liverpool.

Lowenthal, Abraham F., ed. 1975. *The Peruvian Experiment: Continuity and Change Under Military Rule*. Princeton: Princeton University Press.

Lowenthal, Abraham F., and Jorge I. Domínguez. 1996. "Introduction: Constructing Democratic Governance." In *Constructing Democratic Governance: Latin America and the Caribbean in the 1990s—Themes and Issues*, edited by Jorge I. Domínguez and Abraham F. Lowenthal. Baltimore: Johns Hopkins University Press.

Macpherson, C. B. 1973. *Democratic Theory: Essays in Retrieval*. Oxford: Clarendon Press.

Mainwaring, Scott, Guillermo O'Donnell, and J. Samuel Valenzuela, eds. 1992. *Issues in Democratic Consolidation: The New South American Democracies in Comparative Perspective.* Notre Dame: University of Notre Dame Press.

Mainwaring, Scott, and Timothy R. Scully, eds. 1995. *Building Democratic Institutions: Party Systems in Latin America.* Stanford: Stanford University Press.

Mainwaring, Scott, and Eduardo Viola. 1984. "New Social Movements, Political Culture, and Democracy: Brazil and Argentina in the 1980s." *Telos* 61 (Fall): 17–52.

Maira, Luis. 1988. *La Constitución de 1980 y la ruptura democrática.* Santiago: Editorial Emisión.

Malloy, James M., and Mitchell A. Seligson, eds. 1987. *Authoritarians and Democrats: Regime Transition in Latin America.* Pittsburgh: University of Pittsburgh Press.

Maravall, José María. 1982. *The Transition to Democracy in Spain.* London: Croom Helm.

Marcel, Mario, and Andrés Solimano. 1994. "The Distribution of Income and Economic Adjustment." In *The Chilean Economy: Policy Lessons and Challenges,* edited by Barry P. Bosworth, Rudiger Dornbusch, and Raúl Labán. Washington, D.C.: Brookings Institution.

March, James G., and Johan P. Olsen. 1989. *Rediscovering Institutions: The Organizational Basis of Politics.* New York: Free Press.

Markovic, Mihailo. 1982. *Democratic Socialism: Theory and Practice.* New York: St. Martin's Press.

———. 1994. "Radical Democracy." In *Critical Perspectives on Democracy,* edited by Lyman H. Legters, John P. Burke, and Arthur DiQuattro. Lanham, Md.: Rowman and Littlefield.

Marks, Tom. 1994. "Making Revolution with Shining Path." In *Shining Path of Peru,* edited by David Scott Palmer. New York: St. Martin's Press.

Mariátegui, José Carlos. 1971. *Seven Interpretative Essays on Peruvian Reality.* Austin: University of Texas Press.

Márquez Belloni, Francisco. 1994. "La Inserción precaria en el trabajo." *Proposiciones* 25 (October 1994): 132–43.

Marshall, T. H. 1965. *Class, Citizenship, and Social Development.* Garden City, N.Y.: Anchor Books.

Martín del Campo, Julio Labastida, ed. 1985. *Hegemonía y alternativas políticas en América Latina.* Mexico City: Siglo Veintiuno Editores.

Martínez, Javier, and Alvaro Díaz. 1996. *Chile: The Great Transformation.* Washington, D.C., and Geneva, Switzerland: Brookings Institution and the United Nations Research Institute for Social Development.

Marx, Karl. 1963. *The Eighteenth Brumaire of Louis Bonaparte*. New York: International Publishers.

——. 1978. "The German Ideology: Part I." In *The Marx-Engels Reader*, 2d ed., edited by Robert C. Tucker. New York: Norton.

Matos Mar, José. 1984. *Desborde popular y crísis del estado: El nuevo rostro del Peru en la década de 1980*. Lima: Instituto de Estudios Peruanos.

Mauceri, Philip. 1996. *State Under Siege: Development and Policy Making in Peru*. Boulder: Westview Press.

Mauceri, Philip, and Maxwell A. Cameron, eds. 1997. *The Peruvian Labyrinth*. University Park: Pennsylvania State University Press.

McClintock, Cynthia. 1981. *Peasant Cooperatives and Political Change in Peru*. Princeton: Princeton University Press.

——. 1982. "Post-Revolutionary Agrarian Politics in Peru." In *Post-Revolutionary Peru: The Politics of Transformation*, edited by Stephen Gorman. Boulder: Westview Press.

——. 1989. "Peru's Sendero Luminoso Rebellion: Origins and Trajectories." In *Power and Popular Protest: Latin American Social Movements*, edited by Susan Eckstein. Berkeley: University of California Press.

McClintock, Cynthia, and Abraham F. Lowenthal, eds. 1983. *The Peruvian Experiment Reconsidered*. Princeton: Princeton University Press.

McCoy, Jennifer, Andrés Serbin, William C. Smith, and Andrés Stambouli, eds. 1995. *Venezuelan Democracy Under Stress*. Miami: University of Miami North-South Center.

Mendoza F., Sebastián, and José Luis Velásquez Savatti. 1988. *La Capitulación del PUM*. Lima: Convergencia Socialista.

MIR: Movimiento de izquierda revolucionaria. N.d. Lima: SINAMOS.

Moe, Terry M. 1980. *The Organization of Interests*. Chicago: University of Chicago Press.

Morris, Aldon D., and Carol McClurg Mueller. 1992. *Frontiers of Social Movement Theory*. New Haven: Yale University Press.

Moulian, Tomás. 1981. "Crítica a la crítica Marxista de las democracias burguesas." In *América Latina 80: Democracia y movimiento popular*. Lima: DESCO, 1981.

——. 1983. *Democracia y socialismo en Chile*. Santiago: FLACSO.

——. 1989. "El Languaje sobre la democracia: Mercado y guerra." *Opciones* 16 (May–August): 45–51.

——. 1994. "Limitaciones de la transición a la democracia en Chile." *Proposiciones* 25 (October): 34–45.

——. 1997. "El Chile actual y su secreto." In *Chile 96: Análisis y opiniones*. Santiago: FLACSO.

Moulian, Tomás, and Isabel Torres D. 1988. "Continuidad o cambio en la línea política del Partido Comunista de Chile." In *El Partido Comunista en Chile*, edited by Augusto Varas. Santiago: CESOC-FLACSO.

Mouzelis, Nicos. 1985. "On the Concept of Populism: Populist and Clientelist Modes of Incorporation in Semi-Peripheral Polities." *Politics and Society* 14: 329–48.

Mueller, Carol McClurg. 1992. "Building Social Movement Theory." In *Frontiers of Social Movement Theory*, edited by Aldon Morris and Carol McClurg Mueller. New Haven: Yale University Press.

Munck, Gerardo L. 1994. "Democratic Stability and Its Limits: An Analysis of Chile's 1993 Elections." *Journal of Interamerican Studies and World Affairs* 36 (Summer): 1–38.

Munck, Gerardo L., and Carol Skalnik Leff. 1997. "Modes of Transition and Democratization: South America and Eastern Europe." *Comparative Politics* 29 (April): 343–62.

Nelson, Joan M., ed. 1994. *A Precarious Balance: Democracy and Economic Reforms in Latin America*. Vol. 2. San Francisco: Institute for Contemporary Studies Press.

Nieto, Jorge. 1983. *Izquierda y democracia en el Peru, 1975–1980*. Lima: DESCO.

North, Douglas. 1990. *Institutions, Institutional Change and Economic Performance*. Cambridge: Cambridge University Press.

Núñez, Ricardo, ed. 1991. *Socialismo: 10 años de renovación*. Vols. 1 and 2. Santiago: Las Ediciones del Ornitorrinco.

Nylen, William. 1997. "Reconstructing the Workers' Party (PT): Lessons from North-Eastern Brazil." In *The New Politics of Inequality in Latin America: Rethinking Participation and Representation*, edited by Douglas A. Chalmers, Carlos M. Vilas, Katherine Hite, Scott B. Martin, Kerianne Piester, and Monique Segarra. New York: Oxford University Press.

O'Donnell, Guillermo. 1973. *Modernization and Bureaucratic-Authoritarianism: Studies in South American Politics*. Berkeley: Institute of International Studies.

———. 1979. "Tensions in the Bureaucratic-Authoritarian State and the Question of Democracy." In *The New Authoritarianism in Latin America*, edited by David Collier. Princeton: Princeton University Press.

———. 1994a. "Delegative Democracy." *Journal of Democracy* 5 (January): 55–69.

———. 1994b. "The State, Democratization, and Some Conceptual Problems: A Latin American View with Glances at Some Post-Communist Countries." In *Latin American Political Economy in* the Age of Neoliberal Reform: Theoretical and Comparative Perspectives for the 1990s, edited by William C. Smith, Carlos Acuña, and Eduardo Gamarra. Miami: University of Miami North-South Center.

O'Donnell, Guillermo, and Philippe C. Schmitter. 1986. *Transitions from Authoritarian Rule: Tentative Conclusions About Uncertain Democracies*. Baltimore: Johns Hopkins University Press.

O'Donnell, Guillermo, Philippe C. Schmitter, and Laurence Whitehead, eds. 1986. *Transitions from Authoritarian Rule: Prospects for Democracy*. Baltimore: Johns Hopkins University Press.

Offe, Claus. 1990. "Reflections on the Institutional Self-Transformation of Movement Politics: A Tentative Stage Model." In *Challenging the Political Order: New Social and Political Movements in Western Democracies*, edited by Russell J. Dalton and Manfred Kuechler. New York: Oxford University Press.

Olson, Mancur. 1965. *The Logic of Collective Action: Public Goods and the Theory of Groups*. Cambridge, Mass.: Harvard University Press.

———. 1986. "A Theory of the Incentives Facing Political Organizations." *International Political Science Review* 7 (April): 165–89.

Ominami, Carlos. 1991. "Promoting Economic Growth and Stability." In *From Dictatorship to Democracy: Rebuilding Political Consensus in Chile*, edited by Joseph S. Tulchin and Augusto Varas. Boulder: Lynne Rienner.

Ortega Frei, Eugenio. 1992. *Historia de una alianza: El Partido Socialista de Chile y el Partido Demócrata Cristiano*. Santiago: CED-CESOC.

Ottone, Ernesto. 1986. "Democratización y nueva hegemonía en Chile." In *Siete ensayos sobre democracia y socialismo en Chile*. Santiago: Vector and Ediciones Documentas.

Oxhorn, Philip. 1994. "Where Did All the Protesters Go? Popular Mobilization and the Transition to Democracy in Chile." *Latin American Perspectives* 21 (Summer): 49–68.

———. 1995. *Organizing Civil Society: The Popular Sectors and the Struggle for Democracy in Chile*. University Park: Pennsylvania State University Press.

Paige, Jeffrey. 1975. *Agrarian Revolution*. New York: Free Press.

Palmer, David Scott. 1994. "Conclusion: The View from the Windows." In *Shining Path of Peru*, 2d ed., edited by David Scott Palmer. New York: St. Martin's Press.

Panebianco, Angelo. 1988. *Political Parties: Organization and Power*. Cambridge: Cambridge University Press.

Panfichi, Aldo, and Cynthia Sanborn. 1996. "Fujimori y las raíces del neopopulismo." In *Los Enigmas del poder: Fujimori 1990–1996*, edited by Fernando Tuesta Soldevilla. Lima: Fundación Friedrich Ebert.

Parodi, Jorge. 1986. *Ser obrero es algo relativo*. Lima: Instituto de Estudios Peruanos.

Pásara, Luis. 1990. "El doble sendero de la izquierda legal peruana." *Nueva Sociedad* 106 (March–April): 58–72.

Pásara, Luis, and Alonzo Zarzar. 1991. "Ambiguedades, contradicciones e incertidumbres." In Luis Pásara, Nena Delpino, Rocío Valdeavellano, and Alonzo Zarzar, *La Otra cara de la luna: Nuevos actores sociales en el Perú*. Buenos Aires: Centro de Estudios de Democracia y Sociedad.

Pásara, Luis, Nena Delpino, Rocío Valdeavellano, and Alonzo Zarzar. 1991. *La Otra cara de la luna: Nuevos actores sociales en el Perú*. Buenos Aires: Centro de Estudios de Democracia y Sociedad.

Pastor, Mañuel, Jr., and Carol Wise. 1992. "Peruvian Economic Policy in the 1980's: From Orthodoxy to Heterodoxy and Back." *Latin American Research Review* 27: 83–118.

Pateman, Carole. 1970. *Participation and Democratic Theory*. Cambridge: Cambridge University Press.

Pease García, Henry. 1981. "La Democracia como proceso de autodeterminación de los pueblos latinoamericanos." In *América Latina 80: Democracia y movimiento Popular*. Lima: DESCO.

———. 1986. "Elecciones municipales: Valió la pena." *Quehacer* 43 (October–November): 6–14.

———. 1988. *Democracia y precariedad bajo el populismo aprista*. Lima: DESCO.

———. 1989. *Democracia local: Reflexiones y experiencias*. Lima: DESCO.

Pérez, Robinson. 1981. "Tendencias de la lucha política en Chile." *Cuadernos de Orientación Socialista* 9 (November): 25–39.

Perú 1989: En la espíral de violencia. 1990. Lima: Instituto de Defensa Legal.

Perú: Compendio estadístico 1991–1992. 1992. Vol. 1. Lima: Dirección Técnica de Indicadores Económicos.

Perú: Compendio estadístico 1993–1994. 1994. Vol. 1. Lima: Dirección Técnica de Indicadores Económicos.

Petkoff, Teodoro. 1976. *Proceso a la izquierda*. Bogotá: Editorial Oveja Negro.

———. 1981. *Democracia para el socialismo*. Caracas: Ediciones Sorocaima.

Petras, James, Fernando Ignacio Leiva, and Henry Veltmeyer. 1994. *Democracy and Poverty in Chile: The Limits to Electoral Politics*. Boulder: Westview Press.

Plumb, David. 1995. "El Partido por la Democracia: Redefining Leftist Politics in Chile." Senior thesis, Princeton University.

Politzer, Patricia. 1989. *Altamirano*. Buenos Aires: Grupo Editorial Zeta.

Pollack, Benny, and Hernan Rosenkranz. 1986. *Revolutionary Social Democracy: The Chilean Socialist Party*. London: Pinter.

Ponomaryov, Boris. 1974. "The World Situation and the Revolutionary Process." *World Marxist Review* 17 (June): 3–15.

Pontusson, Jonas. 1995. "Explaining the Decline of European Social Democracy: The Role of Structural Economic Change." *World Politics* 47 (July): 494–533.

Portes, Alejandro, and José Itzigsohn. 1997. "The Party or the Grassroots: A Comparative Analysis of Political Participation in the Caribbean Basin." In *Politics, Social Change, and Economic Restructuring in Latin America*, edited by William C. Smith and Roberto Patricio Korzeniewicz. Miami: University of Miami North-South Center.

Proyectos de cambio: La izquierda democrática en América Latina. 1988. Carácas: Editorial Nueva Sociedad.

Przeworski, Adam. 1985. *Capitalism and Social Democracy*. Cambridge: Cambridge University Press.

———. 1986. "Some Problems in the Study of the Transition to Democracy." In *Transitions from Authoritarian Rule: Comparative Perspectives*, edited by Guillermo O'Donnell, Philippe C. Schmitter, and Laurence Whitehead. Baltimore: Johns Hopkins University Press.

———. 1991. *Democracy and the Market: Political and Economic Reforms in Eastern Europe and Latin America*. Cambridge: Cambridge University Press.

———. 1993. "The Neoliberal Fallacy." In *Capitalism, Socialism, and Democracy Revisited*, edited by Larry Diamond and Marc F. Plattner. Baltimore: Johns Hopkins University Press.

Przeworski, Adam, and John Sprague. 1986. *Paper Stones: A History of Electoral Socialism*. Chicago: University of Chicago Press.

Przeworski, Adam, and Michael Wallerstein. 1988. "Structural Dependence of the State on Capital." *American Political Science Review* 82 (March): 11–29.

Puryear, Jeffrey M. 1994. *Thinking Politics: Intellectuals and Democracy in Chile, 1973–1988*. Baltimore: Johns Hopkins University Press.

Qué es el PPD? 1989. Santiago: Ediciones Atanor.

Ramírez-Necochea, Hernan. 1965. *Orígen y formación del Partido Comunista de Chile*. Santiago: Editorial Austral.

Remmer, Karen L. 1980. "Political Demobilization in Chile, 1973–1978." *Comparative Politics* 12 (April): 275–301.

———. 1986. "Exclusionary Democracy." *Studies in Comparative International Development* 20: 64–83.

———. 1989. "Neopatrimonialism: The Politics of Military Rule in Chile, 1973–1987," *Comparative Politics* 21 (January): 149–70.

———. 1991a. *Military Rule in Latin America.* Boulder: Westview Press.

———. 1991b. "The Political Impact of Economic Crisis in Latin America in the 1980's." *American Political Science Review* 85 (September): 777–800.

———. 1992–93. "The Process of Democratization in Latin America." *Studies in Comparative International Development* 27 (Winter): 2–24.

Rénique, José Luis. 1990. "La Batalla por Puno: Violencia política en la sierra del Perú." Columbia/NYU Consortium Conference Paper 36.

———. 1995. "The Latin American Left: Epitaph or New Beginning?" *Latin American Research Review* 30: 177–94.

Roberts, Kenneth M. 1995. "Neoliberalism and the Transformation of Populism in Latin America: The Peruvian Case." *World Politics* 48 (October): 82–116.

———. 1996. "Economic Crisis and the Demise of the Legal Left in Peru." *Comparative Politics* 29 (October): 69–92.

Roberts-Hite, Katherine. 1991. "Chile: A Rough Road Home." *NACLA Report on the Americas* 24 (February): 4–7.

Rochabrun Silva, Guillermo. 1988. "Crisis, Democracy, and the Left in Peru." *Latin American Perspectives* 15 (Summer): 77–96.

Rodrigues, Iram Jacome. 1994. "The CUT: New Unionism at a Crossroads." *NACLA Report on the Americas* 28 (May–June): 30–34.

Rodríguez Elizondo, José. 1990. *La Crisis de las izquierdas en América Latina.* Madrid and Carácas: Instituto de Cooperación and Editorial Nueva Sociedad.

Roemer, John E. 1994. *A Future for Socialism.* Cambridge, Mass.: Harvard University Press.

Rojas Miño, Irene. 1991. "Las Reformas laborales." In *Economía y trabajo en Chile: Informe anual 1990–1991.* Santiago: Programa Economía y trabajo.

Rospigliosi, Fernando. 1988. *Juventud obrera y partidos de izquierda.* Lima: Instituto de Estudios Peruanos.

Rueschemeyer, Dietrich, Evelyne Huber Stephens, and John D. Stephens. 1992. *Capitalist Development and Democracy.* Chicago: University of Chicago Press.

Rustow, Dankwart. 1970. "Transitions to Democracy: Towards a Dynamic Model." *Comparative Politics* 2 (April): 337–63.

Sader, Emir, and Ken Silverstein. 1991. *Without Fear of Being Happy: Lula, the Workers Party and Brazil.* London: Verso.

Salazar, Gabriel. 1990. *Violencia política popular en las "Grandes Alamedas."* Santiago: Ediciones Sur.

Salcedo, José María. 1989. "IU: El drama recién empieza?" *Quehacer* 57 (January–February): 26–40.

Sanborn, Cynthia. 1991. *The Democratic Left and the Persistence of Populism in Peru, 1975–1990.* Ph.D. dissertation, Harvard University.

Sartori, Giovanni. 1976. *Parties and Party Systems: A Framework for Analysis.* Cambridge: Cambridge University Press.

———. 1987. *The Theory of Democracy Revisited.* Chatham, N.J.: Chatham House.

Scharpf, Fritz W. 1991. *Crisis and Choice in European Social Democracy.* Ithaca: Cornell University Press.

Schlesinger, James A. 1965. "Political Party Organization." In *Handbook of Organizations*, edited by James G. March. Chicago: Rand McNally.

Schmitter, Philippe C., and Terry Lynn Karl. 1993. "What Democracy Is . . . And Is Not." In *The Global Resurgence of Democracy*, edited by Larry Diamond and Marc F. Plattner. Baltimore: Johns Hopkins University Press.

Schneider, Cathy Lisa. 1992. "Radical Opposition Parties and Squatters Movements in Pinochet's Chile." In *The Making of Social Movements in Latin America: Identity, Strategy, and Democracy*, edited by Arturo Escobar and Sonia E. Alvarez. Boulder: Westview Press.

———. 1995. *Shantytown Protests in Pinochet's Chile.* Philadelphia: Temple University Press.

Schumpeter, Joseph. 1943. *Capitalism, Socialism and Democracy.* London: Allen and Unwin.

Scully, Timothy R. 1992. *Rethinking the Center: Party Politics in Nineteenth- and Twentieth-Century Chile.* Stanford: Stanford University Press.

———. 1995. "Reconstituting Party Politics in Chile." In *Building Democratic Institutions: Party Systems in Latin America*, edited by Scott Mainwaring and Timothy R. Scully. Stanford: Stanford University Press.

Scurrah, Martin J., and Guadalupe Esteves. 1982. "The Condition of Organized Labor." In *Post-Revolutionary Peru: The Politics of Transformation*, edited by Stephen M. Gorman. Boulder: Westview Press.

Share, Donald. 1989. *Dilemmas of Social Democracy: The Spanish Socialist Workers Party in the 1980s.* New York: Greenwood Press.

Siavelis, Peter, and Arturo Valenzuela. 1996. "Electoral Engineering and Democratic Stability: The Legacy of Authoritarian Rule in Chile." In *Institutional Design in New Democracies: Eastern Europe and Latin America*, edited by Arend Lijphart and Carlos H. Waisman. Boulder: Westview Press.

Silva, Eduardo. 1993. "Capitalist Coalitions, the State, and Neoliberal Economic Restructuring: Chile, 1973–1988." *World Politics* 45 (July): 526–59.

——. 1996. *The State and Capital in Chile: Business Elites, Technocrats, and Market Economics.* Boulder: Westview Press.

Silva, Patricio. 1988. "The State, Politics, and Peasant Unions in Chile." *Journal of Latin American Studies* 20 (November): 433–52.

Silva Solar, Julio. 1977. "Reflexiones sobre las contradiciones internas de la Vía Chilena." *Chile-América* 37–38 (November–December): 122–26.

Síntesis del informe de la Comisión Nacional de Verdad y Reconciliación. 1991. Santiago: Comisión Chilena de Derechos Humanos and Centro Ideas.

Slater, David, ed. 1985. *New Social Movements and the State in Latin America.* Amsterdam: CEDLA.

Smith, William C., Carlos H. Acuña, and Eduardo A. Gamarra, eds. 1994. *Latin American Political Economy in the Age of Neoliberal Reform.* Miami: University of Miami North-South Center.

Smith, William C., and Roberto Patricio Korzeniewicz. 1997. *Politics, Social Change, and Economic Restructuring in Latin America.* Miami: University of Miami North-South Center.

Soledad Gómez, María. 1988. "Factores nacionales e internacionales de la política interna del Partido Comunista de Chile (1922–1952)." In *El Partido Comunista en Chile*, edited by Augusto Varas. Santiago: CESOC-FLACSO.

Spooner, Mary Helen. 1994. *Soldiers in a Narrow Land: The Pinochet Regime in Chile.* Berkeley: University of California Press.

Stahler-Shock, Richard. 1994. "El Salvador's Negotiated Transition: From Low-Intensity Conflict to Low-Intensity Democracy." *Journal of Interamerican Studies and World Affairs* 36 (Winter): 1–59.

Stallings, Barbara. 1978. *Class Conflict and Economic Development in Chile, 1958–1973.* Stanford: Stanford University Press.

Starn, Orin. 1991. "Sendero, soldados, y ronderos en el Mantaro." *Quehacer* 74 (November–December): 60–68.

——. 1992. "I Dreamt of Foxes and Hawks: The Peasant Rondas in Northern Peru." In *The Making of Social Movements in Latin America: Identity, Strategy, and Democracy*, edited by Arturo Escobar and Sonia E. Alvarez. Boulder: Westview Press.

Stein, Steve. 1980. *Populism in Peru: The Emergence of the Masses and the Politics of Social Control.* Madison: University of Wisconsin Press.

Stein, Steve, and Carlos Monge. 1988. *La Crísis del estado patrimonial en el Perú.* Lima: Instituto de Estudios Peruanos.

Stepan, Alfred. 1978. *The State and Society: Peru in Comparative Perspective.* Princeton: Princeton University Press.

——. 1988. *Rethinking Military Politics: Brazil and the Southern Cone.* Princeton: Princeton University Press.

Stephens, Evelyne Huber. 1983. "The Peruvian Military Government, Labor Mobilization and the Political Strength of the Left." *Latin American Research Review* 43: 57–93.

Stokes, Susan C. 1995a. *Cultures in Conflict: Social Movements and the State in Peru.* Berkeley: University of California Press.

——. 1995b. "Democracy and the Limits of Popular Sovereignty in South America." In *The Consolidation of Democracy in Latin America,* edited by Joseph S. Tulchin and Bernice Romero. Boulder: Lynne Rienner.

Sulmont, Denis. 1980. *El Movimiento obrero peruano (1890–1980).* Lima: Tarea.

——. 1994. "El Trabajo en el Perú de hoy: Ajuste sin reestructuración." *Cuadernos Laborales* 100 (May): 8–12.

Sunkel, Osvaldo, ed. 1993. *Development from Within: Toward a Neostructuralist Approach for Latin America.* Boulder: Lynne Rienner.

Taranzona-Sevillano, Gabriela. 1994. "The Organization of Shining Path." In *Shining Path of Peru,* edited by David Scott Palmer. New York: St. Martin's Press.

Tarrow, Sidney. 1994. *Power in Movement: Social Movements, Collective Action, and Politics.* Cambridge: Cambridge University Press.

Taylor, Michael. 1988. "Rationality and Revolutionary Collective Action." In *Rationality and Revolution,* edited by Michael Taylor. Cambridge: Cambridge University Press.

Teitelboim, Volodia. 1977. "Reflexiones sobre los 1000 días de gobierno de la Unidad Popular." *Revista Internacional,* 32–37.

Therborn, Goran. 1977. "The Rule of Capital and the Rise of Democracy." *New Left Review* 103 (May–June): 3–41.

Tironi Barrios, Eugenio. 1984. *La Torre de Babel: Ensayos de crítica y renovación política.* Santiago: Ediciones Sur.

——. 1986. "Para una sociología de la decadencia: El concepto de disolución social." *Proposiciones* 12 (October–December): 12–16.

Tovar Samanez, Teresa. 1982a. *Movimiento barrial: Organización y unidad (1978–81).* Lima: DESCO.

——. 1982b. *Movimiento popular y paros nacionales.* Lima: DESCO.

———. 1986. "Barrios, ciudad, democracia y política." In *Movimientos sociales y democracia: La fundación de un nuevo orden*, edited by Eduardo Ballón E. Lima: DESCO.

Trevor, Robert. 1989. "Ideologías y discursos políticos del Partido Comunista y del Partido Socialista de Chile, bajo el régimen militar (1973–1987)." M.A. thesis, FLACSO-Chile.

Tucker, Robert C., ed. 1978. *The Marx-Engels Reader*, 2d ed. New York: Norton.

Tuesta Soldevilla, Fernando. 1979. "Análisis del proceso electoral a la Asamblea Constituyente: El caso de la UDP y el FOCEP." M.A. thesis, Pontífica Universidad Católica de Lima.

———. 1987 and 1994. *Perú político en cifras: Elite política y elecciones*, Vols. 1 and 2. Lima: Fundación Friedrich Ebert.

———. 1989. *Pobreza urbana y cambios electorales en Lima*. Lima: DESCO.

———, ed. 1996. *Los enigmas del poder: Fujimori, 1990–1996*. Lima: Fundación Friedrich Ebert.

Tulchin, Joseph S., with Bernice Romero, eds. 1995. *The Consolidation of Democracy in Latin America*. Boulder: Lynne Rienner.

Tulchin, Joseph S., and Augusto Varas. 1991. *From Dictatorship to Democracy: Rebuilding Political Consensus in Chile*. Boulder: Lynne Rienner.

Urmeneta, Roberto. 1994. "Políticas habitacionales: Pobladores, allegados y pobreza." In *Economía y trabajo en Chile: Informe anual 1993–1994*. Santiago: Programa de Economía y Trabajo.

U.S. Department of State. 1995. *Country Reports on Human Rights Practices for 1994*. Washington, D.C.: U.S. Government Printing Office.

Valdés, Juan Gabriel. 1986. "Cultura y democracia: Una mirada desde la clase política." In *Democracia en Chile: Doce Conferencias*, edited by Ignacio Walker. Santiago: CIEPLAN.

Valdés, Teresa. 1987. "El movimiento de pobladores, 1973–1985: La Recomposición de las solidaridades sociales." In Jordi Borja, Teresa Valdés, Hernán Pozo, and Eduardo Morales, *Descentralización del estado: Movimiento social y gestión local*. Santiago: FLACSO.

Valenzuela, Arturo. 1978. *The Breakdown of Democratic Regimes: Chile*. Baltimore: Johns Hopkins University Press.

Valenzuela, Arturo, and J. Samuel Valenzuela. 1986. "Party Oppositions Under the Chilean Authoritarian Regime." In *Military Rule in Chile: Dictatorship and Oppositions*, edited by Juan Samuel Valenzuela and Arturo Valenzuela. Baltimore: Johns Hopkins University Press.

———, eds. 1976. *Chile: Politics and Society*. New Brunswick, N.J.: Transaction Books.

Valenzuela, Eduardo. 1984. *La Rebellión de los jovenes.* Santiago: Ediciones Sur.

Valenzuela, J. Samuel. 1992. "Democratic Consolidation in Post-Transitional Settings: Notion, Process, and Facilitating Conditions." In *Issues in Democratic Consolidation: The New South American Democracies in Comparative Perspective*, edited by Scott Mainwaring, Guillermo O'Donnell, and J. Samuel Valenzuela. Notre Dame: University of Notre Dame Press.

Valenzuela, J. Samuel, and Arturo Valenzuela, eds. 1986. *Military Rule in Chile: Dictatorship and Oppositions.* Baltimore: Johns Hopkins University Press.

Vanguardia Revolucionaria. 1976. Lima: SINAMOS.

Varas, Augusto, ed. 1988. *El Partido Comunista en Chile.* Santiago: CESOC-FLACSO.

Vargas Llosa, Mario. 1986. *The Real Life of Alejandro Mayta.* New York: Farrar, Strauss and Giroux.

Vellinga, Menno, ed. 1993. *Social Democracy in Latin America: Prospects for Change.* Boulder: Westview Press.

Venegas, Sylvia. 1993. "Programas de apoyo a temporeros y temporeras en Chile." In *Los Pobres del campo: El trabajador eventual*, edited by Sergio Gómez and Emilio Klein. Santiago: FLACSO and PREALC.

Vergara, Pilar. 1994. "Market Economy, Social Welfare, and Democratic Consolidation in Chile." In *Democracy, Markets and Structural Reform in Latin America: Argentina, Bolivia, Brazil, and Chile*, edited by William C. Smith, Carlos H. Acuña, and Eduardo A. Gamarra. Miami: University of Miami North-South Center.

Viera-Gallo, José Antonio. 1976–77. "Reflexiones para la Formulación de un Proyecto Democrático Para Chile." *Chile-América* 25–27 (November–January): 50–65.

Vilas, Carlos M. 1997. "Participation, Inequality, and the Whereabouts of Democracy." In *The New Politics of Inequality in Latin America: Rethinking Participation and Representation*, edited by Douglas A. Chalmers, Carlos M. Vilas, Katherine Hite, Scott B. Martin, Kerianne Piester, and Monique Segarra. New York: Oxford University Press.

Violencia y pacificación. 1989. Lima: DESCO and La Comisión Andina de Juristas.

Walker, Ignacio. 1986. "Del Populismo al Leninismo y la 'Inevitabilidad del Conflicto': El Partido Socialista de Chile (1933–1973)." Notas Técnicas 91. Santiago: CIEPLAN.

———. 1990. *Socialismo y democracia: Chile y Europa en perspectiva comparada.* Santiago: CIEPLAN-Hachette.

Weffort, Francisco. 1989. "La Muy diferente revolución posible." *Convergencia* 16 (October–December): 36–39.

——. 1993. "The Future of Socialism." In *Capitalism, Socialism and Democracy Revisited*, edited by Larry Diamond and Marc F. Plattner. Baltimore: Johns Hopkins University Press.

Weyland, Kurt. 1996a. *Democracy Without Equity: Failures of Reform in Brazil*. Pittsburgh: University of Pittsburgh Press.

——. 1996b. "'Growth with Equity' in Chile's New Democracy." *Latin American Research Review* 32: 37–67.

——. 1997. "Neopopulism and Neoliberalism in Latin America: Unexpected Affinities." *Studies in Comparative International Development* 32 (Fall): 3–31.

Wickham-Crowley, Timothy. 1992. *Guerrillas and Revolution in Latin America: A Comparative Study of Insurgents and Regimes Since 1956*. Princeton: Princeton University Press.

Wiener, Raúl. 1987. *(El Antizorro): El Debate sobre el "Acuerdo Nacional."* Lima: Ediciones Debate Mariateguista.

Wilde, Lawrence. 1994. *Modern European Socialism*. Aldershot, England: Dartmouth.

Wilkie, James W., and Carlos Alberto Contreras, eds. 1992. *Statistical Abstract of Latin America*. Vol. 29. Los Angeles: UCLA Latin American Center.

Williamson, John, ed. 1994. *The Political Economy of Policy Reform*. Washington, D.C.: Institute for International Economics.

Winn, Peter. 1986. *Weavers of Revolution: The Yarur Workers and Chile's Road to Socialism*. New York: Oxford University Press.

Winn, Peter, and Lilia Ferro-Clérico. 1997. "Can a Leftist Government Make a Difference? The Frente Amplio Administration of Montevideo, 1990–1994." In *The New Politics of Inequality in Latin America: Rethinking Participation and Representation*, edited by Douglas A. Chalmers, Carlos M. Vilas, Katherine Hite, Scott B. Martin, Kerianne Piester, and Monique Segarra. New York: Oxford University Press.

World Bank. 1996. *From Plan to Market: World Development Report, 1996*. Washington, D.C.: World Bank.

Yocelevsky, Ricardo A. 1986. "El Partido Socialista de Chile bajo la dictadura militar." *Foro Internacional* 27 (July–September): 102–31.

Yopo, Boris. 1988. "Las Relaciones internacionales del Partido Comunista." In *El Partido Comunista en Chile*, edited by Augusto Varas. Santiago: CESOC-FLACSO.

Zermeño, Sergio. 1989. "El Regreso del líder: Crísis, neoliberalismo, y desorden." *Revista Mexicana de Sociología* 51 (October–December): 115–50.

Index

In this index an "f" after a number indicates a separate reference on the next page, and an "ff" indicates separate references on the next two pages. A continuous discussion over two or more pages is indicated by a span of page numbers, e.g., "57–59." *Passim* is used for a cluster of references in close but not consecutive sequence.

240, 256; and peasants, 202, 212, 229, 235, 244f, 262; and popular sectors, 9, 43, 196, 201–3, 209–35 *passim*, 240–59 *passim*, 264, 271–72, 278; and revolution, 44f, 201–8 *passim*, 216–21 *passim*, 225–33 *passim*, 250, 257–58, 262f, 271, 273; rise of, 202–9, 221, 231–35 *passim*; and shanty-towns, 202, 212, 229, 235; and students, 202, 229, 262–63. *See also* IU; New Left
Leipzig Group, 110, 306
Leninism, 20f, 46, 50f, 75, 86, 92, 102–9 *passim*, 134, 167, 187, 191, 303; in Peru, 209, 229, 252
Letts, Ricardo, 207, 320, 325
"Lula," 77, 299

Mañuel Rodríguez Patriotic Front, *see* FPMR
Maoist organizations, 205–08, 212–23 *passim*, 258, 265. *See also* PCP-Bandera Roja; PCP-Patria Roja; PCP-Sendero Luminoso; PCR; UNIR; VR
MAPU, 103, 125, 132, 301
MAPU-Obrero Campesino, 103, 125, 132, 301
MAPU-OC, 103, 125, 132, 301
Mariátegui, José Carlos, 205, 208. *See also* PCP
Marín, Gladys, 96, 116, 135, 139, 311
Marshall, T. H., 28
Marx, Karl, 34, 60–67 *passim*, 188, 270, 327
Marxism, 3, 20, 22, 34, 68, 94, 221, 244, 270; and Chile, 8, 51, 84, 87, 103–7 *passim*, 130, 143, 167, 182, 187–92 *passim*; and Peru, 201, 205–9 *passim*
Matos Mar, José, 240
McAdam, Doug, 72
McClintock, Cynthia, 212

MDI, 267. *See also* Pease, Henry
MDP, 126f
Mexico, *see* Cárdenas; PRD
MIDA, 133, 159
milicias Rodriguistas, 124
military dictatorship, *see* authoritarian rule
MIR (Chile), 91–95 *passim*, 100, 103, 159, 180, 182
MIR (Peru), 206, 208, 219, 223, 228, 321
Mohme, Gustavo, 223, 319, 323
Morales, Francisco Bermúdez, 210, 236, 243
Movement of the Democratic Allendista Left (MIDA), 133, 159
Movement of the Democratic Left (MDI), 267
Movement of the Revolutionary Left (Chile), *see* MIR (Chile)
Movement of the Revolutionary Left (Peru), *see* MIR (Peru)
Movimiento de Acción Popular Unitaria, 103, 125, 132, 301
Movimiento de Acción Unitaria-Obrero Campesino, 103, 125, 132, 301
Movimiento de Izquierda Revolucionaria (Chile), *see* MIR (Chile)
Movimiento de Izquierda Revolucionaria (Peru), *see* MIR (Peru)
Movimiento Revolucionario Túpac Amaru (MRTA), 250
Moyano, María Elena, 260
MRTA, 250
Munck, Gerardo, 82, 142
Murrugarra, Edmundo, 207, 320

Napurí, Ricardo, 207
National Coordinator of Regions, 95f, 103, 106
National Information Center (CNI), 175
National Renovation, 145, 148, 150
neoliberalism, 5, 12, 17, 21, 54,

Library of Congress Cataloging-in-Publication Data

Roberts, Kenneth M.

Deepening democracy? : the modern left and social
movements in Chile and Peru / Kenneth M. Roberts.

p. cm.

Includes bibliographical references and index.

ISBN 0-8047-3193-4 (cloth). — ISBN 0-8047-3194-2 (pbk.)

1. Chile—Politics and government—1973– 2. Peru—
Politics and government—1980– 3. Democracy—Chile.
4. Democracy—Peru. 5. Social movements—Chile.
6. Social movements—Peru. 7. Right and left (Political
science) I. Title.

JL2631.R6 1999

320.983′09′049—dc21   98-16557

⊚ This book is printed on acid-free recycled paper.

Original printing 1998

Last figure below indicates year of this printing:

06 05 04 03 02 01 00 99 98